EX LIBRIS

VINTAGE CLASSICS

LEN HOWARD

Len Howard (1894–1973) was a British naturalist and musician best known for her studies of birds, published as *Birds as Individuals* (1952) and *Living with Birds* (1956).

In her early life, Howard pursued a career in music in London, giving music lessons, organising concerts for the children of the poor and playing the viola professionally in an orchestra under Malcolm Sargent. In 1938, she purchased a plot of land outside the village of Ditchling, Sussex, and built the house she called Bird Cottage. There she developed an intimate and unusual relationship with the wild birds in the area, providing food (including her own war rations), chasing away predators, tending to damaged nests, and allowing the birds to fly and roost throughout her home. Her musical training gave her a unique insight into the diverse character of birdsong. Howard died at Bird Cottage in 1973.

LEN HOWARD

BIRD LIFE

Birds as Individuals
and
Living with Birds

WITH AN INTRODUCTION TO *BIRDS AS INDIVIDUALS* BY
Stephen Moss

VINTAGE CLASSICS

1 3 5 7 9 10 8 6 4 2

Vintage Classics is part of the Penguin Random House group of companies

Vintage, Penguin Random House UK,
One Embassy Gardens, 8 Viaduct Gardens, London SW11 7BW

penguin.co.uk/vintage-classics
global.penguinrandomhouse.com

This edition published in Vintage Classics in 2026
Birds as Individuals first published in Great Britain by Collins in 1952
Living with Birds first published in Great Britain by Collins in 1956

Copyright © Len Howard 1952, 1956
Introduction to *Birds as Individuals* copyright © Stephen Moss 2024

The moral right of the author has been asserted

Penguin Random House values and supports copyright. Copyright fuels creativity, encourages diverse voices, promotes freedom of expression and supports a vibrant culture. Thank you for purchasing an authorised edition of this book and for respecting intellectual property laws by not reproducing, scanning or distributing any part of it by any means without permission. You are supporting authors and enabling Penguin Random House to continue to publish books for everyone. No part of this book may be used or reproduced in any manner for the purpose of training artificial intelligence technologies or systems. In accordance with Article 4(3) of the DSM Directive 2019/790, Penguin Random House expressly reserves this work from the text and data mining exception.

Printed and bound in Great Britain by Clays Ltd, Elcograf S.p.A.

The authorised representative in the EEA is Penguin Random House Ireland,
Morrison Chambers, 32 Nassau Street, Dublin D02 YH68

A CIP catalogue record for this book is available from the British Library

ISBN 9781784879365

Penguin Random House is committed to a sustainable future
for our business, our readers and our planet. This book is made
from Forest Stewardship Council® certified paper.

BIRDS AS INDIVIDUALS

AUTHOR'S NOTE

Thanks are due to the editors of *Countrygoer* and *Out of Doors* for permission to reprint some sections of the Bird Biographies, etc. Also I wish to express my sincere thanks to Dr Julian Huxley for writing a foreword and for the interest he has shown.

The majority of the photographs were especially taken for this book at Bird Cottage and I am much indebted to Eric Hosking for making two visits to my cottage to photograph the birds.

Contents

Introduction by Stephen Moss	xi
Foreword by Dr Julian Huxley	xvii

PART ONE
BIRD BEHAVIOUR

I.	Preliminary: Confidence, Sense and Intelligent Behaviour	3
II.	Bird Biography: Great Tits	11
III.	Bird Biography: Blackbirds	54
IV.	Autumn Robin Notes	63
V.	Recognition, Friendship and Games	74
VI.	Roosts, Food, and Nesting-Boxes	86
VII.	Finches and Others	97
VIII.	The Mind of a Bird	109
	Emotions	109
	Fear	109
	General	112
	Memory and Recognition	116
	Intelligence	117
	Flight Performances	126

PART TWO
BIRD SONG

IX.	Atmosphere and Song	131
X.	Analysis of Technique in Bird Song	136
	Types of Rhythm and Technical Analysis of Species	138
XI.	Songs of Warblers and Thrush Tribes	146
	Chiffchaff	146
	Willow-Warbler	147
	Blackbird	148
	Song-Thrush	154
	Mistle-Thrush	155

	Nightingale	156
	Robin	157
	Blackcap	159
	Garden-Warbler	160
	Whitethroats	160
	Wood-Warbler	161
	Reed-Warbler	162
	Sedge-Warbler	163
XII.	Songs of Tits, Finches, Pipits, etc.	164
	Blue Tit	164
	Great Tit	164
	Marsh-Tit and Coal-Tit	167
	Cuckoo	168
	Bullfinch	169
	Linnet	170
	Sparrows	172
	Goldfinch	172
	Greenfinch	174
	Corn-Bunting	175
	Yellowhammer	176
	Curlew, Redshank, etc.	176
	Tree-Pipit	177
	Sky-Lark	178

Introduction

When I first heard about *Birds as Individuals*, written by Len Howard, I made the careless assumption that the author was a man. I later discovered that 'Len' was simply a shortened version of Gwendolen, her given name. But I do wonder if, like the nineteenth-century novelist George Eliot (born Mary Ann Evans), Howard deliberately chose a more masculine moniker. Perhaps it was her way of circumventing the ubiquitous climate of sexism towards women writers, which lasted throughout her lifetime and beyond.

Another contemporary naturalist and writer, S. Vere Benson, also never used her first name (Stephana), and likewise, was often assumed to be male. Vere Benson's best-known work, *The Observer's Book of Birds*, was first published in 1937, and became one of the bestselling bird books of the twentieth century – and for me, and many others of my generation, our first bird guide.

Yet Len Howard did not achieve such worldly success or fame. Her two published works (this 1952 book *Birds as Individuals* was followed, four years later, by *Living with Birds*), achieved modest sales, and received little notice in the press. One notable exception was from an anonymous reviewer in *Spectator* magazine, who wrote that 'Miss Howard's book of bird observation is the most remarkable I have ever read.'

Author Keggie Carew featured Howard's life and work in her 2023 book *Beastly: The Epic 40,000-Year Story of Animals and Us*. Carew believes that her intimate and detailed long-term studies were never really given the credit they deserve, despite their astonishing findings and the originality of her approach:

> One of her great tits lived for nine years, debunking the belief that they might have three years if they were lucky. Her musician's ear was the perfect tool for picking up their slightest inflections and she was so attentive to every nuanced behaviour.

Perhaps there is another reason why Howard's books did not become bestsellers. Unlike today, when bookshop tables are heaving with the latest crop of 'new nature-writing' volumes, the post-war period – and indeed most of the second half of the last century – was hardly a golden age for writing about the natural world.

There were plenty of scientific studies – including the celebrated New Naturalist series, also from Howard's publisher Collins, which was hugely popular amongst a post-war public eager to learn more about nature. This period also saw the first true 'field guides', including the 'birdwatcher's bible', *A Field Guide to the Birds of Britain and Europe* (also from Collins). But works of what we would now call 'creative non-fiction' – narratives with the author placed at the centre of the work – were few and far between.

For example, although written in the 1940s, *The Living Mountain*, by Howard's near-contemporary Nan Shepherd, was not published until 1977, shortly before the author's death. This demonstrates how Len Howard truly was ahead of her time.

Not until the early years of the current century did women nature-writers finally attain their long-deserved equal status with men. Having been excluded for so long, they soon began to dominate the genre: works such as *H is for Hawk* by Helen Macdonald, *The Outrun* by Amy Liptrot, and *Wilding* by Isabella Tree topping the bestseller lists as well as winning literary awards.

Birds as Individuals is certainly very different from today's nature writing. It reads like a cross between a diary and a textbook: the prose is unadorned, the tone brisk and the approach matter-of-fact. Indeed at times it feels as if the reader is being lectured by a rather strict (but deeply knowledgeable) schoolteacher.

And although Howard does give us an insight into her domestic life (notably the messy chaos resulting from allowing wild creatures inside her home), this is always subservient to the birds themselves, which are right at the heart of her writing. She clearly gained a great deal of pleasure from her relationship with them; yet her focus is never on her own innermost thoughts and feelings, but always on the life and behaviour of each individual bird.

This is just one of several aspects that make her work so interesting and valuable today, more than seventy years after it was first written and published.

*

Born in Wallington, Surrey in 1894, towards the end of Queen Victoria's long reign, Len Howard was raised in a family steeped in literature and culture: her father, (Henry) Newman Howard, was a published poet and dramatist. From an early age she showed a gift for music, and after leaving school she gave music lessons, played the viola in an orchestra and organised concerts for children from poor and deprived backgrounds.

In 1938, a year before the start of the Second World War, Howard purchased a plot of land just outside the Sussex village of Ditchling, on the South Downs north of Brighton. Here, she built a small house, which she named Bird Cottage, where she lived for the remaining three decades of her life.

Yet until she moved to Sussex – by then in her mid-forties – she had not shown much interest in the specific details of bird behaviour, as she herself confessed:

> When I first came to Bird Cottage I had not before been able to study bird behaviour for myself, although in London the libraries had supplied me with much bird literature. I was not expecting much intelligence to be shown . . .

But one spring morning, just three months after she had settled in, a single incident changed the course of Len Howard's life. As she was busily going about her household tasks, a blue tit entered through the open door:

> She hovered agitatedly close in front of me, her eyes fixed on mine, crying as I had never heard a Blue Tit cry before; it was at once obvious something was wrong and she was asking for my help.

Howard went outside to investigate and discovered that the birds' nest – complete with a dozen tiny eggs – had been pulled out of their nestbox, presumably by a local cat. With no time to waste, she gathered up the nesting material and eggs and carefully placed them back into the box. To her surprise, ten days later the whole clutch hatched, and the brood ultimately fledged successfully.

Her conclusion was that the distressed bird had quite deliberately sought her out for help – something she herself admitted was shamelessly anthropomorphic, in that she clearly attributed human emotions to its unusual behaviour. Going one step further, she also gave her birds names, enabling her to recall individuals. And she broke down the barriers between herself and the natural world by effectively creating an 'open house' for the birds, as Keggie Carew notes:

> When the great tits wanted to peck at her butter dish, normally forbidden, they looked at the butter, then up at her face, then at the butter. If she said 'Come on', coaxingly, they helped themselves, if she said 'No', firmly, they kept away. An angrier 'No!' could make them fly to the window.

Anyone who has ever owned a dog will be familiar with this kind of human–animal dynamic, yet like the Austrian zoologist Konrad Lorenz, Howard managed to achieve it with wild – or more accurately habituated – birds.

However, then, as they might still be now, scientists were highly suspicious of her informal and apparently haphazard approach. As Julian Huxley, at the time one of Britain's leading evolutionary biologists, noted in his conclusion to the book's foreword:

> Miss Howard will not expect professional biologists to accept all her conclusions. But they will be grateful for her facts; and I, personally, can testify to the enjoyment and interest her book has provided.

Despite this hint of scepticism, Huxley went on to praise Howard for her extraordinarily detailed observations. He also noted that by gaining the confidence of her garden birds, and losing their innate fear, she was able 'to be let into the secrets of their lives, and discover the degree of their intelligence'.

That she even gave up some of her meagre supplies of food – both during and after the war (food rationing continued until the early 1950s) – is a testimony to Howard's dedication to her feathered friends. And it worked: the birds soon lost their fear of humans – or more accurately they lost their fear of *her* – which allowed her to gain a deep insight into their lives, that few others have ever managed to achieve.

To maintain their trust, she became something of a recluse, rarely allowing visitors to enter her home. She even put up a typically blunt warning sign to deter any casual passers-by:

> NO VISITORS
> NESTING BIRDS
> MUST KEEP COTTAGE QUIET
> NO CALLERS

Yet when she reluctantly allowed someone to enter the hallowed portal, usually for purely practical reasons, she – and they – were richly rewarded, as she recounts in the opening chapter of her book:

> I always remember the words of an electrician who once called to attend to fittings in my Sussex cottage. He stopped in amazement before my doorway, watching countless birds flying down from the trees to perch on me . . . Then his whole countenance seemed to alter, his face glowed, his eyes shone and he kept murmuring: 'How wonderful!'

As her relationship with the birds deepened, Howard began to develop her theory that their behaviour was not governed solely by instinct, but was also shaped by their individual intelligence.

She was not alone in suggesting this: two very eminent ornithologists, Alexander Skutch and Bernd Heinrich, both concluded that birds are not mere automatons, and are far more intelligent than we usually give them credit for. Each of them published well-received books – Skutch's *The Minds of Birds* (1996) and Heinrich's *Mind of the Raven* (1999) – which contain many examples of complex behavioural traits that seem to go way beyond our usual perception of birds being, well, 'bird-brained'.

Yet for me, the fascinating questions about birds' intelligence raised by Len Howard's writing are trumped by something far simpler and yet more urgent: the population declines of so many once-common species since she first made her observations, back in the 1950s.

My own passion for birds began a decade or so later, as a young child. So I am fascinated by the changes in status of the bird visitors to her Sussex garden and its surroundings, which have happened in a mere two generations since she made her observations.

Several species that Howard considered commonplace are now either very scarce or have virtually disappeared from Sussex, and from much of the rest of southeast England. She writes of a pair of spotted flycatchers nesting just outside her window; of flocks of not just house sparrows but also tree sparrows; of corn buntings and house martins – all of whose numbers have fallen dramatically. And birds that were once so common that they are deeply ingrained in our nation's folklore, culture and literature – notably the cuckoo and the nightingale – have also vanished from much of our lowland countryside.

We don't need to be told the reasons for this. The dramatic declines in insects are primarily the result of modern industrial farming, as revealed in the work of Professor Dave Goulson, just down the road from Ditchling at the University of Sussex. These have combined with more unpredictable weather patterns as a result of the climate crisis, including a higher frequency of droughts, floods and other extreme weather events.

Together, these are reducing populations of birds we once took for granted to a mere remnant of what Len Howard would have known and enjoyed. The record she set down of the ordinary birds in a single garden in the middle of the twentieth century vividly highlights their decline. The stark comparison between then and now is perhaps the greatest legacy of her diaries and observations and one which, of course, she could never have imagined.

Gwendolen Howard died at Bird Cottage on 5 January 1973, in her eightieth year. For almost half a century afterwards she was more or less forgotten. But during the past decade or so her books and articles have been rediscovered and celebrated by a new generation of nature writers.

And now, thanks to this Vintage Classics edition, Len Howard's work can be read and enjoyed again by a new generation of naturalists and writers, who will surely enjoy reading her extraordinary accounts, observations and comments about our familiar – yet always fascinating – garden birds.

Stephen Moss, 2024

Foreword

Miss Howard has given us an unusual book. It is unusual because there are very few people in existence who love birds as much as she does, who have given so much time to watching them at such close quarters, and have taken the trouble to make notes of what they have seen and produce a book out of them.

Her title indicates one of the main points of interest that she brings out. When one watches birds day by day, year in and year out, one gets to know them individually, and finds that the behaviour of individuals differs much more than most people would suppose. I commend Miss Howard's observations on this point to my professional biological colleagues as well as to the general public.

A second point of interest is the way in which fear inhibits normality of behaviour. Only when birds have come to lose their fear, can a human observer really begin to be let into the secrets of their lives, and discover the degree of their intelligence. This point too is one to be taken to heart by professional biologists.

Finally, Miss Howard has paid a great deal of attention to the songs of her birds, and since she is a professional musician, her observations and conclusions are of more than ordinary interest and value. I was particularly struck by her account of the cock Blackbird who composed (the word is Miss Howard's, and seems appropriate) a phrase almost identical with the opening phrase of the Rondo in Beethoven's Violin Concerto. At any rate, he gradually worked it up from a simple beginning.

Miss Howard has a stimulating and entertaining chapter on play in birds, and gives us a number of incidental observations of considerable interest, such as the relaxation of territorial rivalry and aggressiveness during a period of drought.

Miss Howard will not expect professional biologists to accept all her conclusions. But they will be grateful for her facts; and I, personally, can testify to the enjoyment and interest her book has provided.

Julian Huxley

Part One
BIRD BEHAVIOUR

CHAPTER I

Preliminary: Confidence, Sense and Intelligent Behaviour

A great many people have shown interest in my tame-wild birds. Often strangers see me with them perched on my hand down the road and stop to ask how it is these birds have got so tame. In this 'better world' now being planned for future generations will it still be so rare to see the beautiful wild birds perching fearlessly on human hands? I always remember the words of an electrician who once called to attend to fittings in my Sussex cottage. He stopped in amazement before my doorway, watching countless birds flying down from the trees to perch on me. He had looked an ordinary man with a work-a-day expression until he saw these birds, then his whole countenance seemed to alter, his face glowed, his eyes shone and he kept murmuring: 'How wonderful!' Then he said: 'But why shouldn't it be like that? It ought to be like that.'

There are, of course, great difficulties in living as I do, in continual company of numbers of birds. The practical ones are many, such as cleaning up, having things spoilt, the rooms always looking as if prepared for the sweep with newspapers spread over furniture and books covered with cloths: then the disturbance of sleep, for they hammer furiously on the panes if I shut the windows at dawn to keep them outside when the nights are short, and they do all they can to prevent my concentrating upon anything except themselves. But there are even worse problems. Living with birds, it is impossible not to get fond of each individual. But their lives are short and there are many tragedies. There is the havoc wrought by cats unless I am continually on the watch. Bird Cottage is not in an isolated position; it is built in a strip of old farm orchard at one end of a fairly large village in Sussex. This farm was converted into several private properties so these houses are around mine, besides others that have sprung up over the way. But the garden is well secluded by trees and tall hedges, and I leave much of it to grow half-wild in its own graceful way, with briars, may-trees, wild plum and elder seeding themselves, and thick ivy clambering up the tall stumps of old apple and pear trees. These provide food and cover for the birds, the ivy berries especially useful as they ripen at a time when other food is often scarce through frost. Around my boundaries I let the grass grow high during the nesting season. This gives cats more trouble to find entrance when it is wet with dew or rain; but nothing that I do will keep them away.

Then there are the Jackdaws and Magpies that steal young birds. Magpies have become far too plentiful and have practically wiped out the Marsh- and Coal-Tits in this neighbourhood. My birds rely upon me to keep away all these plunderers. Most mornings recently I have been awakened at five o'clock by a Great Tit making agitated flights to and fro from my bed to the window while uttering loud alarm cries. He is telling me to come out quickly, the Magpie is endangering his young, so I leap from bed and chase off this enemy with a stick. I return to bed, but soon there is more trouble, the Blackbird calls me up by agitated 'tchinks' close to my window, and again I go out to frighten away the cat by flinging a jug of water at it with a big splash. It slinks off through the bushes, of course avoiding getting wet. In spite of all my efforts some birds fall victims to the cats and Magpies. If I go on a holiday so many disasters occur that I very rarely go away, although wanting to watch other kinds of birds farther afield.

There are often injured ones among my many birds, dependent upon me for their recovery. In one way and another my birds demand attention from dawn until dusk. They do all they can to hinder any concentrated work, – while I am trying to write this page some are perching on the typewriter, some pulling at my hair, others flying to my hands and falling off as I start to tap the keys. There is one other person who knows from experience how demanding my Great Tits can be. This is a man named 'Old Harry,' who, like me, loves all the wild creatures. He lives in his own little hut in a spinney about ten minutes walk from my cottage. One of my Great Tits this year was crowded out of my garden and she nested in his spinney. Until her young were hatched she used to fly back to me every morning and evening, urgently demanding a good feed. Then this kind old man, who feeds the birds, became the victim of her imperious ways. 'Proper tart, she is,' said Old Harry; 'she calls me up at dawn by tugging at the blankets and pecking at my face. You can't stop her and you've got to give her all she wants, and quickly too.' I knew at once from his description which bird it was, for this was exactly how the little tart had always treated me.

Perhaps it is because of my intense love for birds that they come to me quickly and I have not found any difficulty in gaining their confidence. Directly I moved into Bird Cottage I put up a bird-table and bath close to the french window, and a Robin, Blue Tit and Blackbird came at once, many more species, including the Great Tit, soon following. I have always talked to my birds in a normal speaking voice, for they soon learn to understand something of speech by its tone. Very quickly this great intimacy developed and the numbers rapidly increased. Besides loving their company, I find immense interest in studying their individual characters and through this close intercourse I can reach a better understanding of their minds.

When I first came to Bird Cottage I had not before been able to study bird behaviour for myself, although in London the libraries had supplied me with much bird literature. I was not expecting much intelligence to be shown in their behaviour and was very surprised when the following incident occurred. It was a spring morning, three months after my little cottage had been built, and I was busy within, near an open door, when a Blue Tit came fluttering up with cries of distress. She hovered agitatedly close in front of me, her eyes fixed on mine, crying as I had never heard a Blue Tit cry before; it was at once obvious something was wrong and she was asking for my help. Her mate was with her but perched just outside, watching me intently. Directly I went out she stopped crying and they led me to her nesting-box, flying on in front and at suitable perches on the way, turning round to see that I followed. The whole of her nest had been pulled in fragments from the nesting-box and her twelve eggs lay scattered over the hard wooden floor of the box. The lid was shut, so it appeared a cat had clawed out the nest in pieces through the entrance hole. (From this experience I learnt that nest-boxes should be deeper than five inches.)

Both Tits waited close by, silently watching while I quickly gathered the fragments of nest from the ground, removed the eggs and re-formed the nest in the box as well as I could, then replaced the eggs on the right side of the box, thinking she would like it as near as possible the same as before. Directly I had finished the mother bird flew in, and after removing her eggs to the other side of the rather large box, brooded her clutch again. Ten days later the eggs hatched, and she brought off her brood in spite of the calamity because she had sensibly thought of appealing to me for help. What else except thought could have made her act thus? It is not a bird's instinct to seek man but avoid him over anything in connection with nesting affairs. I had not then been long in my cottage and no other bird had been helped over nesting difficulties or anything else. I had merely fed the birds and watched unseen while they built their nests. But many birds had grown very tame and they trusted me.

It had been interesting to watch this Blue Tit and her mate during nest-building. He had at first tried to interest her in a tree-stump hole, but she refused to pay much attention to this, the large nesting-box attached to another tree having taken her fancy. She spent much time popping in and out of this while he stood on the ledge outside, peering cautiously through the entrance hole or examining the lid and sides of the box. Then he started going inside with her and much eager-sounding twittering went on between them, with playfulness in their manner when he chased her out and around the trees, she again flying back to her chosen nesting-box. This went on for over a month before the first material was brought to the nest, not the usual moss or wool but packing-case shavings for foundation. She flew with the shavings into the nesting-box, he flying after her and watching through the entrance hole until she flew for more. Afterwards came moss and, finally, white horses' hair and feathers, the latter continuing to be added occasionally after the twelve eggs were laid. Her mate gave no practical help over the building, which took a month, but his enthusiasm for accompanying and watching her was equal to her evident pleasure in this work and his presence.

All Blue Tits do not show the same attachment for each other. It varies in degree and more often their behaviour, once nesting has started, is extremely quiet and secretive. I think this applies to the older, experienced birds, who have found it wiser, for this ecstatic couple afterwards adopted a comparatively quiet and sober caution directly nesting began.

Later that year two nestling Robins, before they were fledged, fell from their insecure nest in a shallow tree-hole. The remaining two were in danger of falling and the parents showed much concern. I put the four babies into a coconut shell, where they snuggled down contentedly, then I tied this improvised nest to the seat of a chair placed underneath the tree, surrounding the chair-seat with leafy twigs and covering it with sacking, only leaving a small hole for the parent Robins' entrance. They were meanwhile occupied on the nearby hedge, flitting about and 'tic-ticing' at my neighbour's cat. They appeared not to notice my interference, but Robins often turn their backs and look unconcerned when really interested. I retired, wondering if they would find their nestlings, especially through so small an opening, but they soon left the hedge and flew straight to the coconut nest although the babies were silent. The parents did not once return to their old nest, yet I had taken two babies from it. The young never attempted to leave their coconut nest until a week later when they were ready to fly.

I have no doubt the Blue Tits and Robins would not have behaved intelligently if they had feared my presence. Often bird behaviour is judged when the bird is panicked with fear of the watcher. But many humans would prefer not to have an intelligence test when they or their young are in probable danger of immediate death. I find the normal thing is for birds, especially Tits, to act intelligently in unusual circumstances unless they get flustered through fear.

I once half-raised the lid of a Blue Tit's nesting-box but, finding she was sitting, very quickly closed it again. She was alarmed, not having seen the lid opened before, and flew from the entrance hole straight to her mate who was at the other side of my cottage, and could not possibly have seen what had happened. They returned quickly together to the nest, she to continue brooding her eggs and he to behave exactly as if he knew the cause of her fright. First he examined the lid carefully, then looked at her through the entrance hole and after another inspection of the box, settled down on a narrow ledge outside the entrance hole, apparently to keep guard or give her confidence. Occasionally he put his head inside the nesting-box to look at her. He had never before behaved like this while she brooded. After about half an hour she came off to feed; he never again stayed outside while she was sitting – this would be against their natural behaviour for it would attract notice to the nest.

It seems evident that birds can communicate with each other by slight inflections of voice and of movement, because I find those that know me well understand much by their sensitive interpretation of my voice or least movement. For example, when Great Tits want to peck at my butter dish, which they know is usually forbidden, they perch a little way off and look first at the butter, then at my face, hesitating although longing to help themselves, for they have a passion for butter. If I say 'come on' coaxingly, they confidently step up and eat it. If I say 'no' just a little sternly they remain where they are, but continue to look pleadingly at me and then at the butter. A shade crosser 'no' sends them hopping farther off; an angry 'no' makes them fly to the open window, but if I quickly call out, 'Here, come on,' in a very coaxing tone, they at once return and if I keep quiet, inch by inch they hop along the table towards the butter, still eyeing me for further signs of objection. Once on their guard by 'no' in the first place, they will not step up with the airy confidence shown when I encourage them by saying 'come on' at first. They interpret correctly any sign of objection in voice or movement, but without the encouraging tone of voice they will not touch butter while I am looking because I have once or twice forbidden them by an angry 'no.' Their extreme sensitiveness makes them learn extraordinarily quickly. I have to know the bird before communicating satisfactorily by voice inflection; strangers are naturally uncertain through nervousness, but Great Tits generally learn my meaning very soon.

Some Blackbirds, and a few other individuals to a lesser degree, I have found sensitive in the same way. A Blackbird from next door (called Thief and referred to in Chapter 3) once got the better of me in his characteristic manner after he had been obeying nicely like the Tits in the above butter dish example. Bread and potatoes had been the only food allowed him for all the obedience and intelligence he had shown, while on my knee was a plate containing meat – my lunch and about half the week's ration! Suddenly Thief threw all discretion to the winds and flew up under my very nose, snatched the whole slice of meat from the plate in my lap and was over the hedge with a chuckle-note before I had time to object or realise what had happened. Among Blackbirds, only Thief with his pick-pocket action would dare, and accomplish successfully, such theft from under my nose.

Great Tits sometimes commit similar thefts when they see I am thinking of something else. As well as interpreting voice inflections and movements, they appear to know a great deal by watching eyes and facial expressions, for I notice when looking at them with thoughts absorbed elsewhere they act as if my back is turned and then commit sins they never dare when I am looking consciously at them, watching and thinking of them.

Watching birds closely and intimately, there are continual actions that cannot be accounted for by instinct and automatic reaction, but intelligence varies much with the individual as well as the species, and of the birds with which I am intimately acquainted, Great Tits reach the highest level of intelligence, consequently also of individuality within the species.

Some people are under the delusion that Great Tits are cruel to other birds because of the late Viscount Grey of Fallodon's story of the Great Tit who ate the Sparrow's brains when both were trapped in a cage. During ten years of constant observation of the Great Tit I have not seen one act of cruelty committed by this species. Sparrows frequently bully other birds, Great Tits included, and the Great Tit does not even hit back. He merely spreads his wings in a display of protest and then flies off, for he is a good-tempered bird and normally does not fight other species. It is unfair to judge a bird when frenzied by captivity and starvation. Great Tits have tremendous vitality and the Tit may have outlived the Sparrow in the cage and had the sense to save himself from starvation by a meal off the dead bird's brain. If he did kill the Sparrow probably the latter, as is his custom, began the fight and the Great Tit, being in captivity, could not retreat as he does when free. Blue Tits are more pugnacious with other species than Great Tits. It is amusing to watch a Blue Tit attacking a Great Tit, who usually only displays in return, showing remarkable tolerance for his small relation. I have seen a Blue Tit attack a Blackbird who pecked at the Tit's suet which had fallen from its usual suspended position. The Blackbird retorted by lifting the Blue Tit on his beak and tossing him a couple of feet away, as if the Tit was no more than a leaf. The Blackbird then continued to eat the suet with his back turned to the sprawling Blue Tit who soon picked himself up and flew away.

During autumn and winter for the last three years there has been a daily episode at dusk in my cottage. A Blue Tit flutters through the sitting-room, hesitatingly because of the dim light, and flies to the sliding doors that separate my two rooms. They have been left open for her, and she wants to slip through a very narrow crevice between the runner of the doors and the beam. She flutters her wings while trying to gain a foothold, but often fails on her first attempt. She retires to a chair-back for a moment, then tries again, her wings beat vigorously as she steadies herself and slowly squeezes her small body through the slit into a recess above the beam – a spacious bedroom for a Blue Tit. If the doors are closed at her bedtime she flies up to me with a whimpering cry, and I open them for her; when she is inside the recess they can be pulled across; she taps on the beam to be let out if they are shut when she awakens at dawn. Sometimes she oversleeps, the doors are open and I am drawing back the window curtains before she is up, then she quickly slips from her roost – getting out being easy – and flies to the window, still sleepy-looking and flying as if half-awake. Once out in the open, she is all life and energy in her movements and starts her day by a vigorous preen on the trees near my window. She has taken such a fancy to this roost that she was not put off even when last year she took a wrong turning from bed one morning and fell over the back end of the door, getting trapped in unknown dark regions, this necessitating my fetching a builder to release her. She was unperturbed and returned the next night as usual. This autumn her mate flutters behind her to the sliding doors at dusk; he is at present a beginner at manœuvring the crevice, and has many failures before he gains a roost near her on the inside beam.

CHAPTER 2

Bird Biography: Great Tits

I

Watching the nesting affairs of birds in my garden has shown much variety of behaviour within the species, especially among Great Tits. It is consistent with their greater intelligence that their behaviour should differ more. Although I have found that they mate for life, some seem indifferent to each other's company except during the nesting season, other couples keep together always, and if they lose sight of their mate for a few minutes an alert expression and fixed posture is maintained until the mate reappears. If one mate of these devoted couples dies the successor is regarded comparatively with indifference, sometimes even during nesting season. In these cases I have seen of special devotion, they have been young birds, not previously mated. The same applies to other species.

There are various ways by which I recognise my Great Tits individually. They are easier to distinguish than most species. Having such close contact with them, I get to know their different facial expressions and characteristic mannerisms and poses. Also, there are considerable variations in their frontal attire and sometimes in the shape of their white facial markings, or there may be slight differences in the tone-colourings of their plumage. But the birds that figure prominently in the following biographies I was able to recognise even if their plumage was darkened and disordered by being wet after their bath, and therefore bereft of any distinguishing marks. Their whole bearing and personality was too individual for confusion to arise when I had them at close quarters. Generally, the same markings of plumage are kept after the moult, except, of course, the fledgling moult and change to adult plumage. But when the young are in moult I am able to follow day by day the changes that occur, for those with whom I am intimate are so frequently on my hand or lap, as also are their parents.

One female Great Tit was under my close observation for six years.

She was reared in my neighbour's orchard and mated a bird of the same age from my garden. They reared two broods each year for three years and were a devoted pair, always together, even in winter. If one appeared at my window without the other, the bird would stay motionless and seem oblivious of tempting food offered it until the mate was in sight. Usually they entered and left my room together.

This female, called Jane, had the originality to sing a charming song during nesting season. Her gift was unique. Other female Great Tits do not sing although they have a variety of call-notes, a scold-note, etc.; but Jane's song was much superior to the male's. It varied a little from year to year and in these first years of her life it slightly resembled the male's 'tee-chū' song, but was much more musical. Instead of repetition of the same notes, she dropped down the scale in overlapping approximate thirds. The song was begun in gay, ringing tones and gradually grew softer and sweeter as it lowered in pitch. A chime of bells dying away on the wind was suggested.

The fourth year Jane's mate died of an injured leg. She mated another first-year bird, in appearance resembling her other mate, who was of exceptionally large build, with broader frontal markings than usual. She nested that spring in a tree trunk down the road, having been driven from her usual site in my garden by a pugnacious couple of Great Tits who greedily wanted the whole garden to themselves. When Jane's first brood by mate II was fledged, she tried to bring them to my garden, but the pugnacious pair chased them away. Even if I tried to give her food by the stream across the road, the pugnacious male would flash over my hedge with angry demonstrations to prevent Jane and mate II from taking food from my hand for their young. But while her second brood were nestlings, mate II was killed by a cat. She carried on feeding her young with increased effort and I often saw her pause on the threshold of her nest after leaving it, a worried expression on her face;* then she would fly to the tree-top and glance in all directions as if looking for her mate. As soon as her brood flew she again brought them to my garden. This time neither of the pugnacious Tits showed objection, although

---

* This may appear anthropomorphic, but her whole manner as well as her look showed she was worried. In my close observations of the tits I have learnt to tell by their looks and manner if they are troubled about something, and I am satisfied that in this instance it was the case.

they still would not tolerate other Great Tits entering the garden, for they also had a second brood. Sometimes the pugnacious male, with food in his beak intended for his own nestlings, would stop and appear to listen to the noise Jane's eight hungry fledglings were making, and instead of taking the food to his nestlings he flew to one of the widow's young and popped the caterpillar down its throat.

The following year Jane mated another first-year bird, offspring of the pugnacious couple. Again she had chosen a mate of big build and dark frontal attire. He was a very interesting character and unique nesting affairs followed. For some time Jane had been vying with another female Great Tit, called Grey, for a large nesting-box hung to a tree in my orchard. In early April both began bringing moss to the box, each working when the other was absent, but I think Jane removed Grey's contribution, as when she entered the nest with her own material she often threw moss out of the nesting-hole. Grey never did this.

I was at that time puzzled because Grey appeared to have no mate and lived either alone or with Jane and her mate III. A few days later I saw Jane enter the nest with Grey following. They remained together in the nest for several minutes, both making the continuous high-pitched noise, resembling nestling-cries, that is used by Great Tits in certain phases of nesting. Then they flew out together amicably. This happened many times while Jane completed her nest. Grey had now stopped bringing material.

Mate III was occupied meanwhile in strenuous song and defending the tree from intruders, which cost him his crown feathers. Henceforth he was called Baldhead. He occasionally went inside the nesting-box, as if to see how things were progressing. I have never seen any male Great Tit or Blue Tit help with nest-building, although many attentive males escort their mates backwards and forwards to the nest while material is being collected by the female. This attention of the male occurs in many species and gives a false impression that the male is also building.

Jane's delightful little song, now more original than ever, frequently rang through the orchard. She would fly from her nest to fetch more material, singing while she flew, as if with an overflow of happiness. Grey, like a silent shadow, would often fly after her.

When Jane laid her first egg, Grey was no longer allowed entrance to the nesting-box. With great rapidity she then built a nest for herself in another box in the orchard, a beautiful one woven in many colours, for she had tugged away at my rugs, coats and coloured blankets and flown out of the window with beakfuls of bright, fluffed-up wool. But I had not the heart to stop this destruction, for I knew she was in a desperate hurry. I had then found out that Jane's mate was also hers. With equal devotion, Baldhead guarded both of their nesting sites, followed them about, and inspected their nests. The females were still friendly and the three went about together. In three days Grey's nest was completed and her first egg laid. Baldhead attentively fed both his mates, on their nests when they were sitting and when they were off – which was often at the same time. Both fluttered their wings before him while uttering baby-cries, and in turn he fed them, always in a gallant manner and showing no favouritism. Sometimes he fed Grey in the trees near Jane's nest when she was sitting. There must have been a spy-hole in her nesting-box, for she always appeared to see this and, apparently to attract attention, she would sing her little song several times from her nest, afterwards popping her head out of the nesting-hole a few times, as if impatient. Grey waited her turn patiently when conditions were reversed.

On May 8th Jane's young started hatching, and from the day that Baldhead began feeding her nestlings, Grey was completely deserted. She fluttered her wings before him and made baby-cries as before, but he ignored her. On May 11th Grey's young also began to hatch. When off her nest she followed Baldhead to Jane's nesting-box with excited cries and wing quiverings. (This appeared to be giving information that nestlings were hatching.) Her mate still took no notice and Jane chased her away. She seemed greatly distressed, making queer cries and scolding-notes as she returned to her nest. For the next day or two, whenever she saw Baldhead the same pathetic appeals were made with no success, and on May 14th she flew into my room just as he was taking cheese from me for Jane's nestlings. At once she stood still, quivering her wings and wailing more than ever. Baldhead suddenly eyed her curiously, and with the cheese still in his beak, mounted her, but she angrily spread her tail and shook him off. He flew away and never again took notice of her. I enticed him to Grey's nest and made him look at the nestlings. He gazed at them a moment but flew off to Jane's nest, never returning to Grey's. Whenever the deserted mate saw Jane or Baldhead, she placed herself before them with distressed wailing and quiverings that grew more and more exaggerated and sometimes, when they had flown from sight, she would fly to my shoulder with wings still violently quivering and look up into my face with a pathetic, appealing expression. She had always fed from my hand and I was helping her with food for her nestlings but she would not eat anything for herself now. Her trouble was not to feed her young, for the female will carry on when her mate dies, as Jane had done when her second mate was killed, without expending energy on distressful display. Grey was apparently fretting at desertion.

On the morning of May 19th Grey did not come to me as usual to fetch food for her nestlings, but spent nearly all the time hovering near Jane's nest, with incessant exaggerated emotional display. It became very distressing to watch her, so agonised was her wailing cry and so pathetic her appearance as she kept quivering her wings with this unnatural effort. Even her nestlings were deserted while she made her last appeal. That afternoon she died, apparently of her grief. The nestlings survived only a few hours.

Jane and Baldhead brought off their brood and also reared a second one successfully, but Jane seemed very tired afterwards and never regained strength after her moult. She and Baldhead did not show special interest in each other during the winter, although they were often together. The sound of her wings in flight had altered and was heavier. She survived the hard winter, but died in early April, 1947, aged six.

2

Baldhead, even in his fledgling days, was an interesting bird of very definite character. His parents, the Pugnacious Tits, started preparations for a second brood two weeks after he was fledged, and Baldhead developed an unusual obsession for watching all the nesting affairs. Normally first brood Great Tits take no notice of the second brood (only some Great Tits are double-brooded). The rest of the fledglings never went near the nest, but Baldhead spent much time leaning over the nesting-hole, as if trying to solve the mystery of it all and why his father had suddenly taken to feeding his mother instead of him. When she came off her nest this inquisitive offspring would crane his head down the nesting-hole and stare at the eggs until she returned, often pushing him away and spreading her wings over the entrance in protest. Every day, as if magnetised by it, he returned again and again to the nesting-hole. It was funny to watch his start of surprise when gaping beaks first shot up at him from the nest. He drew back then ventured another look with head held first one side then the other, as if to make sure he was seeing correctly. It seemed the naked nestlings fascinated him; he continually stared at them, always starting back at first sight, when I presume their beaks shot up at him in expectation of food. He hindered the parents' work of feeding the babies, for when they took food to the nest he stuck his head down the entrance hole to watch, and the parents would come out with scolding notes to push him away. If they chased him he assumed baby ways, shivering his wings and making baby-cries. He rarely got caterpillars given him now, but he fed often from my hand and sometimes, while taking a favourite bit of cheese, he would look towards the nest then, dropping the cheese, hurriedly fly to it as if afraid of missing something that was going on down entertainment hole.

When the second brood flew and one fledgling was balancing uncertainly on a twig with the tendency to fall forward habitual to Great Tit babies on first perching, Baldhead flew up and went through an astonishing performance of Tit-antics in front of the baby, who stared at him with an expression of great interest. Having turned a somersault round a twig and hung on to it upside down with one foot, swinging the other in the air, also vigorously pulled off leaves and chucked them down, he finally hammered the bark with a loud tattoo then flew off, never again taking the slightest interest in the fledglings or the nesting-hole.

After Jane died in early April, Baldhead soon found another mate. She chose a new nesting-box on a tree in the orchard, but he showed no interest in this mate or her nest, and he rarely accompanied or fed her. He had now developed another obsession, this time for Grey's old nesting-box. With much display he had kept this from other Tits although he took no notice of Jane's old nests – for her second brood she had built in another nesting-box. Often when his new mate came off her eggs and called to him, expecting attention, he was absorbed in an excited performance with Grey's old nesting-box and ignored her. She waited nearby a moment, then her gentle call-note changed to a subdued scold-note as she flew away to fend for herself. Baldhead continued his frenzied behaviour over the empty nesting-box apparently without noticing his mate. She was called Monocle, one of her eyes having a rim, looking like an eyeglass. It is difficult to describe this queer behaviour because so much depended upon the excited manner and his absorption. He first peered through the entrance hole eagerly, as if expecting to see something, then with high-pitched nestling-cry sounds he entered the nest and worked up a great crescendo of urgent-sounding cries until he suddenly began hopping hurriedly in and out of the box, his movements getting quicker and quicker, as if his life depended upon the speed of this action. Occasionally he hopped on to the lid of the box with an odd little call, then back inside again, repeating the whole performance, although never in a set pattern. His frantic haste and urgent-sounding cries were abnormal behaviour. To a bird-watcher's eye his present mate, Monocle, had much less charm or individuality than Jane or Grey. Did Baldhead feel this and want Grey back in her old nest, or was he perhaps unsatisfied because this year he had only one mate? It is extremely unusual for Great Tits to be bigamists, but they have so much individuality that their nesting affairs have no set pattern, although it is more usual for them to have one brood and for the male to be attentive to his mate during egg-brooding, also to show enthusiasm over feeding the young, even two or three weeks after they have flown. But even these normal nesting affairs that are often termed 'instinctive' show great variation in detail and no two couples are quite alike in behaviour to each other while nest-building and rearing young.

Baldhead's frenzied performance over Grey's nest would cease suddenly, then he would fly off in a calm, leisurely manner in the opposite direction to his mate's nest. All this was very unlike his behaviour to the two mates the previous year. When they were both sitting, he fed them constantly, always accompanied them when off their nests and guarded their nesting sites with continual vigilance.

The obsession for Grey's nest lasted until his mate's eggs hatched, when he devoted himself to feeding his eight young. Also, he and his mate adopted eight young fledglings belonging to one of his and Jane's offspring.

It came about this way. One of Jane's second brood, called Fatty, was big and bold like his father and an interesting bird to watch. Like Baldhead, he remained in my garden all the year round and their nests were on adjoining territory. Baldhead possessed the orchard, Fatty and another couple shared the front garden. Baldhead and Fatty had many disputes over their boundary, with much display and odd language.

Their mates also had lively quarrels between themselves, sometimes rolling together on the ground with feet interlocked. The females' disputes were hot and sharp but quickly over, while the males appeared to enjoy making a prolonged game or fantastic art of their varied ways of displaying, sometimes for three hours at a stretch.

Fatty was a devoted mate, as so often with first-year birds. He accompanied his wife while she collected nesting material, watching all her movements though not helping practically. She pushed him out if he tried to follow her into the nest, so he waited outside patiently, with occasional glances through the nesting-hole, until she flew for more material. Perhaps the reason males of many species do not help with nest-building is that the females will not allow it.

One afternoon, while his mate rested on a branch above her nesting-box, Fatty ventured inside and made gentle nestling-cry sounds from the nest. She immediately flew to another tree and called to him. He joined her, and having got him off her nest she returned to the same branch above it, and perched on one foot, continued her rest. He flew to the nesting-box again, but this time stayed quietly on the ledge outside the entrance hole, often looking up at her.

On June 2nd poor Fatty lost his mate. There had been an intense heat-wave and she had seemed much exhausted while feeding her young through the heat. They were now within five or six days of flying, had things been normal. All that day and the next, Fatty carried on feeding the young, but seemed restless and unhappy. When he came as usual to my hand for food, each piece picked up was thrown down and, without eating anything, he flew away.

On June 4th he fed his young until 11 a.m., but his manner was strange and he looked absent-minded. He never came to my hand that morning – for the first time in his life he had taken no notice when I called him. Nor did he appear to see favourite tit-bits I held before his eyes – nuts and cheese that he had always before been eager to eat or take to his young. His eyes seemed not focusing upon anything close in front of him, and they had a strange expression. At eleven o'clock I went out and on returning at two-thirty I found Fatty had disappeared. The young cried ceaselessly until 5 p.m. Then Baldhead, no doubt attracted by their cries, looked at them through the entrance hole with an interested expression on his face, but he flew off again to feed his own young, who were fledged on May 31st and were still in the orchard.

Would Baldhead adopt Fatty's eight young if I gave them to him? The chances seemed small, for he had eight of his own, but I took two from the nest and placed them in his nesting-box. At once the bigger one scrambled out through the entrance hole, fortunately just as Monocle appeared. It fluttered to a nearby branch. Monocle looked puzzled, gave first a little scold-note then the gentle call-note used when young ones first fly. The hungry fledgling cried loudly and shivered its wings on seeing her. She glanced at the trees, apparently making sure no parents were coming, then she quickly fetched caterpillars several times, as if realising the fledgling's extreme hunger. She next went to her nesting-box and peered through the entrance hole. The other baby crouched silently in the nest but she did not enter. I placed it beside the first one on the branch. Being smaller and unable to fly properly it overbalanced and fell into the grass. Monocle showed much concern and hovered over it, calling in gentle tones, trying to coax it upwards to a safer perch. But it only cried, so she fed it in the grass.

I fetched two more of Fatty's babies. Baldhead arrived while I was placing them on the branch, beside the first fledgling. Like his mate, he looked bewildered at the sight of them near his nest. He first scanned the trees for parents, a scold-note, feebly begun, died away into silence and he looked at his mate, who exchanged his glance. She then turned to the fledglings and called gently. In a flash Baldhead disappeared and returned with a large caterpillar dangling from his beak, and although the young were not now crying he enthusiastically stuffed them with food, fetched at record speed. They both appeared to realise these young were starving although there were not now any outward signs that they were hungry.

All was going so well that I fetched the remaining four, two at a time. Baldhead and Monocle became more and more excited, calling and feeding them in a flustered manner and often exchanging glances. Then Baldhead flew to his nesting-box, his mate following, and with much subdued chattering, they examined the box behind, below and on top as well as inside, seemingly trying to account for these fledglings. As Baldhead had not seen them come from his nest it seemed his mate had communicated this to him.

By degrees they coaxed the bigger fledglings to join their own young on the trees across the orchard, but four were too small to fly properly and needed my assistance. So successful was this adoption that even more care was bestowed on them than their own fledglings. Baldhead seemed in his element with this excitement of adoption and even his behaviour to his mate altered. He now sought her company when she flew near their nest and they both displayed with vibrating wings, making nestling-cry imitations by the nest, which they had not done after their own young flew. This recapitulation of pre-nesting display, often with more emotion shown than before nesting, is usual with Great and Blue Tits whose nesting affairs have been carried on with enthusiasm. Although Baldhead had not displayed with Monocle after their own young flew, the previous year he and Jane had many wing-quivering displays after each of their broods had flown.

On June 29th, three weeks after Fatty's disappearance, he returned with three full-grown young, about five days younger than his own. He flew straight to his usual perch on my shoulder, then to my hand for food which he took to these adopted young. Some widow must have enticed him to help rear his family, but she did not appear with him in my garden.

Fatty's own young were by this time much reduced in number and being taught independence by their foster-parents. Because now seldom fed, they chased after Fatty instead, and tried to snatch caterpillars from his beak that were being taken to the adopted trio. Although he did not let them seize the food he was surprisingly good-tempered with these pestering youngsters, and never pushed them away with scold-notes as is usual when the full-grown young of one brood pester the parents taking food to another; but these clamouring young were Fatty's offspring and had more right to the caterpillars than the adopted trio. Whether Fatty realised this or not cannot be proved but, watching his tolerance when they persistently chased after him, it appeared that he did recognise his lawful young. They caused him so much trouble that he invented a clever dodge of taking the food a roundabout route through my cottage, these youngsters being less familiar with the bathroom and kitchen windows than he was. When one of his offspring was clever enough to follow this dodge he outwitted it by amazingly fast flight round trees, so the youngster only caught him up in time to see the coveted caterpillar being swallowed by one of the adopted trio.

Fatty had much to contend with on his return. Baldhead now seemed to bear him a grudge and fiercely chased him from the front garden whenever he saw him. As Baldhead's territory was the orchard at the back, this malice had nothing to do with territorial defence. The other Great Tits with young, whose nesting tree was in the front garden, never molested him, nor did Baldhead show anger to any other Great Tit except Fatty. By deserting his young, Baldhead seemed to consider he had forfeited the right to return to his nesting site and Fatty did not resist his angry demonstrations.

In the autumn a female – possibly the mother of the trio – often accompanied Fatty to the cottage and gradually Baldhead ceased to molest him, except that on very mild October and November days Fatty was attacked if he looked inside any of the nesting-boxes in the garden. He never nested here again, but is often with me out of nesting season.

Baldhead and his mate kept together during autumn and winter, although not showing much interest in each other. They had some disputes over new roosting-boxes put up for them. Baldhead expected first choice, but did not always keep to the same one each night, nor did he seem able to make up his mind which to choose. Monocle would perch on a tree and watch while he flitted from one box to another, poking his head inside them, but not entering. Finally, she would get impatient and try to secure a roost for herself. Directly she flew to her choice of roosting-box, Baldhead pushed himself in front of her, preventing her entrance with a noisy scolding. She flew away but appeared to have chosen for him, for he entered that box and she chose another. (Great Tits do not roost together usually, even when they are inseparable during the day.) I think this was a bedtime game, as I have often seen birds behaving playfully just before going to roost. When nesting time comes round again Baldhead will let his mate have first choice over everything she wants, but in autumn and winter the male always takes precedence – with species that keep together all the year round. I have noticed there comes a time of change-over between the precedency, when both mates hesitate in a polite manner, apparently waiting for each other to have first helping of food.

In personal intercourse with Baldhead I am sometimes outwitted. His favourite food is nuts and last autumn I brought some indoors in a paper bag, giving him one which he ate on the rungs under a chair. Knowing he would tear open the bag to help himself to another, I wrapped it in a double-folded teacloth, rolling this round the bag and turning both ends under securely in a way that seemed impossible for a small bird to undo. I placed this on a side-table. I had my back to Baldhead while wrapping the bag and he could not possibly have seen what I was doing from where he was, under the chair seat. He soon flew to my hand for more nut, but I gave him cheese – his second choice of food. He threw this away with an impatient toss and looked up at me expectantly. Again I offered him cheese. He made a curious sort of grimace with his beak half-opened, refused to take the cheese and flew round the room, looking for but unable to find the paper bag. I left the room for a few minutes; on my return he flew out of the fanlight window with the haste habitual to him after theft. Several nuts were rolling on the side-table. He had pulled the cloth undone and torn open the paper bag, helping himself to a nut. I had never before wrapped food in this cloth or in any other kind of cloth, nor had I ever put bird food on that side-table, which was used for painting materials, so he had no reason to suspect the cloth contained the paper bag, which was solidly covered with a double layer of cloth.

Baldhead also loves butter but knows he must not steal it from a plate and never attempts this unless given permission, as long as I am in the room. (Birds are so sensitive that they learn at once what is forbidden and what is allowed, although they have no conscience over disobeying when one's back is turned!) But in cold weather, when butter is hard and spreads nobbily, he flies up and snatches knobs off the bread with pick-pocket deftness, just as I am about to put it into my mouth. As he is encouraged to feed from my hand it would be unreasonable to scold him for this, but perhaps to be on the safe side, he always flies quickly out of the window with this spoil, instead of eating it indoors, as with food given him.

Baldhead, like many other Great Tits, soon finds out the correct way to open small boxes in which I keep tit-bits for birds. Instead of just hammering in an attempt to open, he carefully inspects any new type of box, the construction apparently being noted; he then tries to open it the right way, generally succeeding after a struggle unless it is too difficult for me to open easily myself. Match-boxes are held by the feet and pulled open by the beak; if the box is too stiff to pull wide open it is taken up, turned over and shaken to get out the bits. A tin lozenge box, hinged one side, on first being used, was examined all over with great care, then prised upwards, attempts never being made to lift the lid on the hinged side. The trouble with this box was that if he only opened it half-way the lid fell back before he could grab the food, but after some false attempts he got it farther open and quickly inserted his head before it shut. Sometimes he held it open with a foot. These are just a few examples of Baldhead's intelligence. Some Great Tits, equally at home in my cottage, never get beyond hammering on lids although they have had the advantage of seeing other clever ones opening the boxes. Intelligence varies a great deal within the species.

3

One of Jane's offspring by her first mate was another exceptional bird, who had the peculiarity of being unable to lay eggs. She was one of three females reared from a first brood. Her two sisters were attached to each other and always together, but this odd one seemed afraid of other birds and was always alone. When they came near her she flew away with a little squeak, then began nervously examining her toes. She had very small feet, this perhaps partly accounting for her fear, feet being used for defensive purposes. While still a fledgling she had some crown feathers plucked; afterwards she shunned other birds more than ever, but sought my company, spending much time on the rails underneath my chair. At night she roosted on the picture-rail above my bed, being the first of many Great Tits to do this. When her crown feathers grew again they had a ruffled look which earned her the name of Curley and like other of my birds, she soon responded to her name.

Like her parents, Curley had much individuality; I could never mistake her for others of her species even as a fledgling, and her manner sometimes suggested self-consciousness. When other birds crowded round me at feeding time she would disappear; when all had gone she stealthily approached me from behind, climbed up the back of my calves and nipped me gently underneath the knee, then flew to a perch opposite me, alternately examining her toes and throwing me quick glances. Directly I called her name she came eagerly to feed from my hand. This nipping developed into a game which was frequently played. When she saw me engrossed in some quiet occupation, she stole up behind me and gave a gentle nip in some unexpected place, or else hopped all over me, hunting for the most threadbare part in my clothes; when found she carefully parted the threads into a convenient hole through which to nip me, always looking up at my face afterwards as if to see the effect. This game continued until I gave an agonised squeal, and then I saw the light of contentment in her eyes as she perched opposite, alternately glancing at me and examining her toes.

If Curley was hungry and had failed to make me realise the fact, she either flew to the window-curtains and plucked out the velvet pile or tore at the pages of the telephone directory, eyeing me with an expectant expression all the while for she knew such destruction always attracted my attention and was not allowed.

Her adult plumage was sleeker and brighter than other female Great Tits, but in other respects she was decidedly female, both in appearance and in her ways. Her first mate was a fine-looking bird of the large type – Great Tits varying much in size. Curley gave him trouble, being slow over decisions always. He worked hard, trying to get her to decide upon a nesting site, but for several weeks she wavered between the choice of four nesting-boxes in my orchard, each box having to be defended from other eager Tits by her bold, determined mate. She would work hard at enlarging the entrance hole of one box, then look inside, give a little squeak, as if of fright, then fly away to another box. Her mate followed her, giving encouragement and persuasion by continually entering the boxes himself and calling to her from inside in nestling-cry imitations. All Great Tits do this but the female generally spends more time inside prospective nesting-holes and boxes than the male; also, she calls to him in the same nestling-cry sounds.* Curley popped in and out of each box hurriedly and silently, except for an occasional nervous sounding squeak before flying to the next box.

This indecision continued until all neighbouring Tits had hatched their young, then Curley's mate grew very restive and they both left my garden for a month. Curley reappeared afterwards alone and idled about in the trees, sunbathing and taking life easily. Her plumage was in excellent condition, and I was sure she had not brooded eggs while away.

The following year much the same nesting behaviour occurred but with a different mate. She had no young, was absent from the garden

---

* This nestling-cry imitation has been mentioned previously and is quite different from the fledgling-cry adopted by the female when she wants her mate to feed her.

for three weeks, returning with her crown feathers plucked, probably by her exasperated mate for he had shown much impatience before they left the orchard.

The third year she chose for her mate a queer, nervous bird with two large, horny whiskers that crossed over his beak, making it difficult for him to grip food. He was excessively nervous and excitable and when taking food from my hand, he usually dropped it in a flurry of agitation as he flew away. 'Whiskers' was untidy looking, his movements flustered and jerky, but he was a faithful bird and had reared his brood alone the previous year, his mate having died soon after the young were hatched.

Curley was now in beautifully sleek, bright spring plumage and she had gradually overcome fear of other birds. She stood up for herself and even took the initiative in small disputes. Judging from continual observation of both birds during winter and early spring they had paired with no courting display, just before nesting-time. This year Curley chose the largest and best-looking nesting-box in my garden without indecision and Whiskers, having strong feet and an alarming looking beak, appeared to defend the site by bluff and sudden nervous flurryings to and fro in front of the tree where the nesting-box was hung. Curley became brave in defence of this nesting site, her small feet seeming equal in strength to one or two larger females with whom she came to grips. So between them they kept the attractive and coveted nesting-box.

But the progress of nest-building was extremely slow. Curley gave the impression of playing at nesting. Whiskers, like her former mates, spent much time coaxing her to hasten building – so it seemed – by loud furores of cries like a chorus of nestlings, both from inside and outside the box, but Curley only occasionally made a little sound from the nesting-box and she never responded to Whiskers' display. Every morning she took a little moss to the nest, and between each lot there was a long interval spent in tearing bark from an apple-tree twig above her nest. Whiskers began to show impatience, continually chasing her, for he wanted coition, but she dodged away from him – I think, never allowing it.

Birds were very early over nesting that year (1946); on May 26th other Great Tits' young were fledged, while Curley still was bringing the few bits of moss each morning; every time, before going to collect more, she plucked leaves from a sweet-briar that grew by her nest and tore them into shreds, throwing down the pieces. There was so much impatience of manner in these destructive attacks that undoubtedly they were caused by frustration over her inability to produce eggs. From that date Whiskers began to lose interest in the nest and Curley was without his attendance for most of the day. She still vigorously defended her nest, and on May 28th Jane's fledglings were driven from her territory with much angry noise. By May 31st she had collected enough moss for the nest but it was not lined or neatly finished. She slept in it each night and every morning popped in and out several times, but no more nesting material was brought. Much of her day was spent twig-biting and plucking sweet-briar leaves more impatiently than ever. Whiskers sometimes appeared when Curley was absent. Her appetite had for some time been very poor, although she seemed quite well and looked in perfect condition. For the next fortnight either she or occasionally her mate kept guard over the empty nest, but they were never there together. He was more flurried than ever, snatched food from me spasmodically and generally dropped it as he flew away.

On June 14th I found an old Partridge's egg in a field and placed it in Curley's nest. She at once began to brood it, and although Whiskers had not been there when I put the egg in the box or near Curley before she began brooding, within one minute he arrived on the scene in a flurry of excitement, a caterpillar dangling from his queer beak. Curley put her head out of the nesting-hole to receive it and both birds seemed happy at last. How did Whiskers know she was sitting? He could not have known through sight or sound; he had never fed her before nor had she ever made the fledgling-cry sound that female's utter when ready for their mates to feed them; they had not even been seen together in my garden for two weeks, yet without having seen the egg or been near when she entered the nest to begin brooding, he came hurrying across my neighbour's garden with a caterpillar directly she brooded the egg. In his enthusiasm, he brought her food every few minutes that morning and Curley, instead of being intent on sitting, kept putting her head out of the entrance hole to watch for his arrival. In the afternoon she left the nest for three hours, much disconcerting her mate who arrived at the nest with caterpillars and seemed puzzled not to find her sitting. He flew round the garden, calling her in gentle tones; not finding her, he kept guard over the nest until her return, when he enthusiastically fed her again.

The next day she only sat half the morning and during that time was fed attentively; as before she did not sit closely, and frequently put her head out of the entrance hole. The following fortnight she played at brooding the large egg for an hour each morning, Whiskers entering into the spirit of the game by feeding her while she was sitting, then they separated for the rest of the day, taking turns at guarding the nest or leaving the garden. Curley's mate never offered her food off the nest as is usual when affairs are normal. I noticed her appetite suddenly became very hearty after the arrival of the Partridge's egg.

From July 1st to 6th both birds were often away; they always returned singly. Curley now made no attempt to brood, although she still guarded her nest noisily from other birds' proximity. She had grown fatter and looked in fine condition while all other females, exhausted from the labour of rearing families, were thin and bedraggled.

From July 6th to 31st Curley was seldom seen in the garden; she never entered her nest. Whiskers rarely appeared, when he did it was only to snatch food nervously and disappear again. As in former years Curley returned permanently in August, idled her time away in sunbathing and her old habits of examining her toes and playing nipping games with me. Whiskers did not return with her. Curley's moult affected her appearance much less than other Tits, as in previous years.

During autumn she again scolded any bird that went near her nest and she roosted in it at night. On warm October days she took a little more moss to the nesting-box which I have never seen other Great Tits do in autumn. Whiskers returned in October for spasmodic snatchings of food from me, which he generally dropped while hurrying away. In early winter he disappeared altogether.

One night at the end of December, poor Curley was killed by a neighbour's cat, her remains being found beside her nesting-box, which the cat had pulled to the ground after severing the thick rope that had fastened it to the tree.

4

Curley's two sisters, although inseparable as fledglings, parted company in autumn. One left the garden altogether – or was killed without my knowledge – the other, an especially intelligent bird, I always had under close observation. She was named Twist, because her tail had a peculiar twist from roosting with it pressed sideways. After her moult it was straight but gradually became more and more curved until it was sickle-shaped and ragged.

Twist always appeared to understand some things that I said to her and, unlike other birds, she seemed to enjoy being caressed when young. Like all Jane's offspring, she never had the least fear of me; when a full-grown fledgling she took naps perched on my knee or preened her feathers while on my hand or shoulder. I could raise my hand, with her on it, close to my face and gently rub my cheek down her back. She would turn up her face and look into my eyes, but never moved away while I continued the caress. Birds generally dislike being touched on the back, although they do not mind gentle stroking of breast feathers or downy sides. I think this is because parent birds sometimes stand on the back of their young to push them from an exposed perch if a Hawk flies overhead, also, when the young are full-grown and demanding food too roughly, the parent will occasionally subdue them by standing on their backs.

One day when I was caressing Twist in this way I said: 'Give me a kiss.' To my astonishment she quickly touched my nose with her beak – a bird's kiss. I thought her response was chance, but the next day she again responded to these words in the same way, and she continued to do so for the rest of her life. If I asked her a second time running she looked at me with a puzzled expression without responding, and if I repeated it, to try and coax her, she looked at me very crossly. But when an hour or two's interval had elapsed she was again responsive. When hungry, if she saw I had cheese for her she would often give three hurried kisses in succession, but even if I had cheese to coax her, she would not kiss if asked twice running. She never offered one without being asked, and other words did not produce a kiss.

Birds have different ways of asking for food. Twist always perched on my shoulder and looked up into my face with a pleading expression. If I said, 'Have none,' her expression altered, she looked annoyed, left my shoulder and perched opposite me with a fixed stare. If I said, 'Shall I get some?' she instantly flew to the door, her expression eager and expectant. While I went to the kitchen to fetch cheese, she either waited on top of the sitting-room door or followed me, and with head craned forward, watched for the cheese she knew I was getting for her.

She would only eat cheese or nuts; if offered bread or fat she looked at it a moment then picked it up and chucked it across the room, looking up at me afterwards with her pleading expression. If I gave her another piece of food that she disliked she swung round sharply on my hand so that her back was towards the food. She then turned round again and looked up at me, clearly expecting this time I should understand she wanted cheese or nuts. I did understand and this time she got what she wanted, but I did not encourage her to chuck food across the room by giving her cheese when she did this.

Many of my Great Tits are remarkably clever in finding out where food is kept, but Twist was particularly sharp. She had only to see once where I kept her favourite food and she remembered. I have seen her trying to push a saucer off a plate because, while waiting on the kitchen door for me to get her cheese the previous day, she saw me place a saucer over what remained on the plate.

Twist's mate was a bird from a copse over the fields opposite. He had an unusual variation of the 'Tee-chu' song:

This was sung very fast and repeated over and over again with wonderfully vital rhythm.

Twist, not her mate, chose her first nesting site. She fought hard to keep in my garden, but the pugnacious Tits drove her off and the nearest site available was in a vent pipe by some farm buildings over the road. When her young were nearly ready to fly she came in to roost on the picture rails above my bed. One evening she went to her roost earlier than usual. Three of her young had flown, the others were still in the nest. She looked dreadfully exhausted, and dispensing with her usual preening preliminaries, straightway settled down to sleep, her head tucked under her wing. But a minute later she stood alert upon her perch, head craned forward; next moment she had flown out of the window and over the road to her fledglings, apparently just for one more look to make sure all was well. In another moment she returned, this time not stirring until dawn, when, as usual, she flew over the top of drawn curtains and through the fanlight window.

The following evening she looked more fagged than ever. Her nine young had now flown and this is always the hardest day for a mother Tit with a large brood. That night Twist's exhaustion made her oversleep. She did not waken until I drew back the curtains at seven-thirty (D.S. time). Instantly she realised it was late and started up with an anxious expression; uttering a loud scolding-note, she flew hurriedly over the road to her fledglings. Never again did she sleep indoors. This was an interesting use of the scold-note; perhaps she was annoyed with herself or else feared harm had come to her neglected young.

The following two years Twist nested in her mate's copse over the fields, perhaps because the vent pipe had been removed and her mate favoured his little wood as suitable territory. When the white violets showed their bloom in the copse, Twist's visits to my cottage began to grow shorter and less frequent. By the time the bluebells were in full glory she was very hurried on her occasional visits, for there was an ash-tree in the copse with a neatly chiselled hole in its stem and now the interior of this hole had become the centre of Twist's thoughts. When cowslips covered the meadows her visits to my cottage ceased while she reared her young. With birds the time of nesting affairs is more correctly reckoned by the flowers in bloom than by calendar dates.

As I often walked to the copse it was easy to keep in touch with Twist, who came with her mate to my call. Sometimes she flew to meet me over the cowslip meadows before I called; perched on my shoulder, she ate the cheese I brought while her mate fed from my hand.

When nesting days were over Twist came back to my garden for many long visits each day and spent much time indoors with me during autumn and winter. Unlike her mother Jane, who was inseparable from her first mate, Twist generally came alone, her mate seeming to prefer the copse while she preferred my garden – the home where she was born. But I noticed sometimes when she was indoors she suddenly stood rigid, with a tense expression, and dropping food she was eating tucked between her toes, she hurriedly flew out of the window and across the meadows towards the copse. Occasionally she paused a moment on a tree outside the window, still with a tense expression, before hurrying off to her mate – for I sometimes followed her and found she flew to him. The sudden tension of her body and her facial expression, as if vision was centred inwards, her eyes not focusing upon what was in front of them, suggested she was responding to some form of communication from her mate. Perhaps her sensitive ears, through windows almost closed, could hear his call from far away across the meadows, his distant voice, tuned to her ears, piercing the louder intervening sounds of road traffic or tractors. Or had she and her mate some other vibrant or telepathic form of communication? Other cases of communication without sound or sight, such as Whiskers knowing Curley was at last brooding an egg, although he had not been near when I placed it in the nesting-box, nor within sight of Curley, who had kept completely silent, may point to the latter conclusion. Curley had been in her nest every morning on previous days, yet he never once fed her. How did he know the egg was there unless Curley had communicated this to him by some telepathic means?

In Twist's fourth winter her tail became more bent and ragged than ever from the heavy snows. In the intense cold of early February, 1947, she died, frozen in her sleep, five weeks after her sister Curley.

Curley and Twist had never been friendly towards each other and they always reacted in the same way when meeting in my room. Twist would fly into the crook of my arm and look very surly, while Curley flew to the top of a window curtain-rod. If Twist stayed with me for more than a few minutes, the velvet pile of the curtains suffered, for Curley began to tear it out and though I shouted at her she would not stop this destruction until I went towards her, Twist then flying away out of another window. Then Curley perched opposite me and examined her toes with her self-conscious air, and when I called her name, flew to my hand for food. They were both on good terms with Jane – their mother – and all other Great Tits, even the non-residents who only came to my garden and indoors during winter.

5

The following year, 1948, was Baldhead's third nesting season. He and Monocle brought off their first brood successfully, and a week after their young were fledged he became restlessly interested in nesting-holes again. His mate showed little enthusiasm for a second brood, but Baldhead's vigorous displaying over nesting-boxes eventually brought response, and she began to build another nest in a different box from her first. When the young were hatched Baldhead was far more attentive in looking after them than his mate. She took much time off, feeding and resting in the trees while he devoted himself to nursery duties, scarcely stopping to take food and never resting in daytime. At night he slept in a roost on the picture-rail above my bed.

Another pair of Great Tits, Puggy and her second mate, also had a second brood, a week older than Baldhead's, her nest being in the front garden. Here the position was reversed; Puggy was the attentive parent. She and her first mate were the Pugnacious Tits. They had been a very devoted couple – both first-year birds when mated. Perhaps Puggy was not naturally pugnacious but had adopted her mate's dominant and aggressive ways towards other Tits for when he died and she mated a peace-loving bird, who never fought, she became timid and nervous in her manner to other birds. After her mate died, watching her subdued ways it seemed she missed the spirit of the Pugnacious Tit. Although nesting in the same hole, she and her second mate allowed other birds to bring their young anywhere in their territory unmolested. But he did not show much affection for her. She often put her head out of her nesting-hole, expecting him with food when she was sitting; he rarely came, compared with her first mate. Nor did he show enthusiasm for feeding his young. She was always a devoted mother and for eight years had reared two broods. Perhaps Baldhead had inherited some of his nesting enthusiasm from her for she was his mother.

On June 24th Puggy's young of the second brood were fledged, all leaving the nest in an orderly manner, one after another taking flight without hesitation. They were well-developed fledglings with quite long tails, as Puggy never encouraged her young to early flight; she liked them to be strong on the wing. Some parent Great Tits try and coax them to fly when four or five days younger. The brood, on their first morning, were taken out of my garden into the playing fields for a few hours; in the afternoon they trooped back home, Puggy leading them along with the charmingly gentle language that parent Great Tits use. At roost hour she shepherded them into the oak tree that grows by my bedroom window, and there they spent their first night. Her mate took only a small share in looking after the family, a few days later he deserted them altogether and hid in bushes, resting himself while she did all the work.

On June 25th Baldhead's young flew, three or four days before their time. They were very small and weak on the wing. Their mother deserted them for an hour at a time, but Baldhead was a wonderful father to the brood; by degrees he coaxed them to safe perches in my orchard hedge, where he attentively supplied them with food all day long. On July 2nd his mate stopped feeding them altogether, but he continued until July 8th. Only two out of seven had survived; these were charming fledglings called Teaser and Buffer, henceforth much in my company.

In contrast to Baldhead's mate, Puggy was then still attentively feeding her four surviving young, although they were older by a few days. Even on July 13th she was occasionally supplying them with food and calling them to her in gentle tones for caterpillar hunts around the bushes. That day Baldhead's fledglings were feeding from my hand when she wanted cheese for her young. She perched on my wrist and, through a half-opened beak, hissed at them. They ignored her and went on feeding. But she was really very tolerant of all youngsters, and the hiss was never repeated when she stopped feeding her own. On that same day I have this note of Baldhead's behaviour to Puggy's young.

July 13th. Baldhead looks annoyed if fledglings are feeding from my hand when he wants food for himself. There is not room for him to get at the cheese on my palm when Puggy's four youngsters are surrounding it, so he perches on my arm and makes complaining squeaks with a little display which no one heeds. He then hops to my shoulder and pecks sharply at my cheek. I call out 'don't,' and he walks round the back of my neck, fussily tweaking me and pulling my hair; he then returns to my hand, stretching out his head and pushing aside the fledglings, in turn gives each one a light tap on the head. They still do not leave my hand, so I give Baldhead cheese on my other hand.

Both Puggy and Baldhead look ragged and worn in plumage while the inattentive mates are both in good condition and later, during moult, they do not suffer nearly as much as the others.

On January 9th of the next year I recorded the following:

Great Tits suddenly begin disputing in hottest form, male fighting male; female attacking female. The dispute is over Baldhead's roosting-box, which he has occupied since autumn and during last winter. It is hung to a tree by my window on the right side of cottage and is in

Baldhead's orchard territory. At midday I see him and his rival rolling on the floor, feet interlocked, and throw a match-box to frighten them apart. They fly out of the window, one in hot pursuit of the other. Half an hour later a lamed, ill-looking Great Tit flies in through the fanlight, landing in a gasping condition plop on my lap, unable to stand. At first I do not recognise Baldhead, so different does he look, his eyes dim with pain, feathers fluffed out and head bowed over his chest so the frontal markings are not seen. Every now and then he flinches, his body heaves with each breath. He is too bad to eat properly, but I get a little cheese into him as he lies there. Other Tits enter the room, he seems unconscious of them until suddenly, although I hear nothing and no bird enters the room, he cocks his eyes, an alertness of expression just visible through the look of pain; next moment he has flown into a corner and lies hidden behind a shoe against a wardrobe. Then his victor enters the room. This bird is very strong, powerful and dominant. He is called Inkey because of very black, wide frontal markings. He was not bred in my garden and only appeared last autumn; Baldhead, brave in defence of his roosting-box, has been defeated by this outsider; if he recovers he has lost his territory, owned all his life – for the orchard territory includes this side of my cottage.

January 10th. Baldhead is very ill, his eyes are clouded and he is still unable to stand on either leg. He flies in at the fanlight and flops on to my lap several times a day, choosing a moment when no other birds are in the room. If Inkey enters after him he quickly hides on the floor behind furniture but I am generally able to prevent Inkey's entrance by closing all windows directly Baldhead appears. He understands the safety of this, and if in hiding, immediately I close the windows he flies from cover and lies on my hand to feed. I keep him on my lap for as long as possible, but the other birds flying around the windows, trying to get in and tapping furiously at the panes, makes Baldhead restless; after a time I open the fanlight and he flies away to the trees. Other Great Tits never molest him in his weak condition. Inkey is sometimes outside when he flies away through the fanlight, but there is no chasing of the defeated by the conqueror.

After a week or two Baldhead began to improve. By February 7th he was able to use one leg quite normally, but the other usually hung down behind him when he perched. Since losing his old roost in his territory he had slept every night in a box hung to a tree on the other side of my cottage. But now all Great Tits began displaying over nesting sites so Baldhead had to hold his new box in his weak condition. It was interesting to find that although his rivals could easily have ousted him by brute force, they seemed to regulate methods of warfare to those of which he was capable, so he held his ground for some weeks. He worked very hard, displaying in many original ways and inventing much odd language, the trick of his fledgling days also coming into use again, for I sometimes saw him hanging to a twig upside down by one foot, swinging the lame leg in the air (page 16). Sometimes he would flop on to my lap, panting with exhaustion after his efforts, but as soon as he had a little recovered he flew out again to hold his nesting site. His mate, Monocle, had been very retiring since Baldhead's injury; she shunned the presence of other Great Tits but came indoors to feed a few times daily.

Baldhead, after struggles to keep his territory

On March 29th, Puggy started building in her usual tree-hole, the same side of my cottage as Baldhead's new box but about thirty yards distant. The oak tree where her fledglings had roosted last year stretched its branches over Baldhead's box. The next two days Baldhead only appeared in my garden three times to take food, his mate completely disappeared. On March 31st Puggy's mate chased Baldhead away from the left side of my cottage into Inkey's territory, on the right. I saw Inkey pursuing him up the orchard. A little while later Bald-head flew into the cottage, landing flop on the floor at my feet. He was breathing heavily, with feathers fluffed out, his crown feathers were plucked, the right side of his face was bare and a slight trickle of blood showed near his ear. At first I was afraid he was dying, but after a few minutes he took food and water which revived him; in ten minutes he was asking me to open the window – closed to keep others away – and although he looked a wreck with his featherless head and lame leg, his spirit was undaunted; he would yet hold his own over entrance to my garden and cottage.

He did not appear again that morning. I grew anxious, but after a search, found him with his mate in a large oak tree just beyond the top – or north – side of my orchard. He perched on my shoulder to eat cheese, then began flying around the oak with his mate, evidently searching for a nesting-hole, but there was nothing suitable. I fetched a nesting-box, first fixing it on the back of my orchard hedge too near the border of Inkey's territory. Baldhead showed great excitement when seeing the box but turned to me with a scold-note at watching where I fixed it and flew to the other side of the oak tree. I moved the box to his chosen spot, then he eagerly entered it, with the usual nestling-cry sounds. His mate gazed through the entrance hole, then grew fidgety, for she wanted him to come out so that she could try it for herself. She hopped restlessly from twig to twig outside, began pulling bark from a branch and hammering it with her beak, but Baldhead would not stir. Eventually she went inside with him, then both came out together, inspected the box all round and afterwards took turns at entering – Baldhead always staying inside the longest. They showed obvious delight at having this box; she began building that afternoon while Baldhead limped around, chasing any Tits who went near the box. I left food and water near their nest, but next morning Baldhead came to my cottage several times, choosing a passage along the back of the orchard hedge to avoid arousing Inkey's anger again by flying near his nest. Now Baldhead had begun nesting away from Inkey's or Puggy's territory no objection was made to his passing the front of the cottage and entering to get food whenever he liked, but his mate never ventured to enter my garden until her young were hatched.

Inkey and Baldhead spent hours displaying together over the boundary between their territory at the top of my orchard while their mates were building and sitting. It was interesting to note that the strong male never took advantage of his opponent's physical weakness in these disputes over boundary. Baldhead limped about, defending his rights by various methods of display, and now, for the first time this year he sang the 'tee-chu' song from tree-tops, in a voice rather feeble and cracked, but in a manner full of confidence and spirit. Although he looked a complete wreck with his featherless face and head he was livelier than at any time since his first defeat; his appetite increased and his leg strengthened a little, although he will always limp. The lamed leg appears to have been dislocated – it is not in normal position when he stands. He and Monocle reared their brood successfully, but this year he did not attempt a second for he was too exhausted. After his moult he looked beautiful again in new plumage and was perfectly well except for his limp.

Inkey's mate, called Smoke, had chosen to nest in a large petrol tin instead of the nesting-box taken from Baldhead, and now an interesting case of territorial behaviour occurred in connection with this box. A pair of Great Tits, who were complete strangers to my garden, surreptitiously took this nesting-box, which was in Inkey's territory while keeping a territory of their own beyond Puggy's, over the road. This they flew to straight from the nest, without ever perching in Inkey's territory except upon the nesting-box. While Smoke was busy putting finishing touches to her nest, the stranger female crept in silently from over the road, flying behind bushes and entering the box with her moss, then returning for more material, always collected from over the road in her land, although my garden was rich in moss. At first Inkey was so engrossed with Baldhead at the top of the orchard that he may not have noticed these stealthy strangers, but a few days after they took the box I saw Inkey peering inside with an expression of interest. To my surprise, he made no objection to these silent strangers, who never uttered a note or displayed when he went near their nest or looked inside the box. Not once did Inkey chase the strangers or display over boundary lines as he did half the day with Baldhead. There *were* no boundary lines, for the strangers made no claim to land, they never fed in my garden, even at the bird-table; all they wanted was the nesting-box, for they had no suitable hole in their territory over the road.

When their young were hatched, all food was fetched from their land, carried along the border of Puggy's into Inkey's territory to their nest. When Inkey's young flew they often perched on the strangers' nesting-box or the tree branch above and were fed by their parents, the strangers never making the usual protest at having chattering fledglings on top of their nest while the nestlings inside were only just hatched. They could not protest, for it was Inkey's land and his offspring had the right to perch on their nesting-box. If either of the strangers was in the nest when the Inkey family were surrounding it it stayed inside the box until the territory owners moved away. Their nestlings were very silent for Tits, the atmosphere in which they were reared perhaps subduing them, for my other Great Tit nestlings call out in chorus at entry of their parents and after they leave, the strength of their voices increasing every day. The strangers' brood began to fly two weeks later than Inkey's young, the former at an earlier age by four or five days. Only two flew the first day, these the father bird took straight across the road, for the first time perching on trees in my garden while coaxing his babies to follow him. Meanwhile, the mother bird looked after the rest of the brood. They flew two days later, and were quickly taken over the road by their mother. Inkey watched these young make their first flights with an expression of great interest and hovered near the nest, restlessly although not interfering, until all had gone. It seemed he had allowed these Tits to use the box under some understanding that no claim was made to land outside the box, and their young must be taken away directly they flew. Or perhaps it was because these silent strangers behaved as they did that they were never interfered with by Inkey and Smoke, who were both very dominant with all other Great Tits who entered their land.

In all other cases in my garden of stranger Great Tits trying to nest in boxes on territory belonging to other couples, they have been forced to abandon their half-built nests, but in these cases they used a small part of land surrounding their box.

When the silent brood had disappeared from my garden it was interesting to find that the parents, particularly the mother bird, often returned to fetch food for the young from inside my cottage and from the bird-table, which they had never done while using the nesting-box. All my Tits having been fledged two or three weeks before may have partly accounted for this, for strictness of territorial behaviour was then relaxed, but all the while these strangers were nesting I had seven pairs of Great Tits entering the cottage for food which they took to their young although their nests were not all in my garden, Puggy and Inkey being the only ones that owned territory surrounding my cottage. My Tits allow entry to be made to the cottage for food by those accustomed to using the rooms for the winter season. But the strangers did not risk entry while they were using the nesting-box within two feet of one of my windows, I think, for fear of being chased away from their nest if the residents objected. The very day their young had left my garden the parents returned to fetch food; they ran no risk then of being chased from their young.

NESTING NOTES, 1950

January 29th to February 11th. All the autumn and winter Baldhead roosted in his favourite box, taken from him last year by Inkey after the battle that cost him a permanent leg injury. Now these two Tits are again disputing for the box and surrounding territory. Inkey is big and strong, Baldhead is now physically weakened but his spirit is still indomitable. For a week he displays from morning till night in many original ways, the most prominent invention being a succession of flying leaps, two or three feet high, over Inkey while keeping in stiffened display pose and uttering many strange notes. Inkey merely struts along the ground in an elongated pose, head up, tail spread, wings drooped, while Baldhead leaps over him. Inkey then flies to the coveted box, Baldhead rushes at him, putting phenomenal speed into the charge and Inkey retires; B. repeating the ferocious charge. He has grown a spike on the tip of his upper mandible which makes his beak look very long and gives him an impressive appearance. Sometimes I see him lying on the window-ledge near the box, looking utterly exhausted and a queer strained expression on his face. But he holds his ground by incessant effort and vigorous display, hardly pausing to eat the food I give him – he chucks it away half-eaten.

Since the summer a grey-type female with a white star on her crown has followed him about persistently. His old mate, Monocle, never seeks his company. She had not enough vitality for Baldhead and had grown lazy over feeding their young. This new female, called Star, is full of life and she takes her share in fighting for the territory. Often she comes to grips with Smoke — Inkey's mate — and as they roll together on the ground, feet interlocked, Baldhead hovers over them, in agitation squeaking out high-pitched notes. His lamed leg was gained through this form of combat; he wants to separate the females, but is not always successful. They do not hurt each other and seem equally matched in strength. By February 15th Inkey and Smoke were ousted from Baldhead's territory. This year he has kept all his head feathers intact. His battle had been won without coming to grips with his opponent. He spent the next two days resting on a tree near the boundary of his land on Inkey's side. He now ate all the food given him with much eagerness and each night he retired very early to roost in the hard-earned box. He had been an early rooster since his lameness, for he gets tired sooner than other birds.

February 18th. Baldhead's new mate, Star, enters his roosting-box at 8 a.m., stays there a long while then enters another box nearby. On February 20th he as usual goes to his roost in good time, but he quickly flies away, showing signs of excitement, flicking his tail and wings, then breaking into song. From every tree-top in his land he sings, announcing his news to the neighbourhood — for his mate has chosen her nesting-box, and for the first time is roosting in it. He then returns to his box and looks through the entrance hole at his mate. He tries to enter but she turns him out of his roost, for Great Tits do not usually sleep together, and females often dislike their mates in their nesting-box (possibly a habit that has grown through having frequently to use narrow holes where space is very cramped, and there is need to keep the nest free of excreta). Baldhead shows agitation and insists upon entering his box, but soon reappears through the entrance hole, looking flustered and hen-pecked. He takes a turn round his territory then tries again with the same result. He impatiently hammers at the entrance hole, flies round the garden and tries once more. After he enters, there is a sound of fluttering wings inside the box and he emerges, looking very cross. This continues for an hour. All other Tits, who roost later than he does, are in bed, the Blackbirds seek their roosting perches, dusk is giving way to night, but Baldhead is still trying to get into his roost. He has tried dozens of times, always his mate forces him to beat a hasty retreat and he gets more and more fussed and worried, but will not give way. He goes through many frustration antics, consisting of restless movements, twig hammering, tearing leaves, etc., and gives whimpering cries, then at last, almost in starlight, he enters and remains in the box. All is quiet inside the roost.

February 23rd. Each night the same struggle at roost hour, although she gives in a little sooner, perhaps too sleepy to resist any longer. I placed another box, of similar make, just above the old one. Baldhead tried it but soon came out and persevered with his mate over the favourite box.

February 28th. The problem continues but B. is gradually winning. Last night, when Star thrust him out for the seventh time he flitted around the roost uttering long volleys of excited scold-notes. She jumped up and down inside the box, trying to catch glimpses of him without showing her face outside the entrance hole. He stopped scolding, flew to the box, intending to enter, but loud rapping noises came from inside, this driving him away. More scold-notes ensued. The new mate of the Robin Dobs, a sprightly young female, flew at Baldhead, gave him a peck on his rump and flitted hastily back to her roosting tree. This suggested, 'shut up!' He soon made a successful entry and all was quiet.

March 10th. Baldhead has gradually overcome his roosting difficulties. Star now lets him enter without any fuss.

March 24th. She begins taking moss into the box. All goes well with Baldhead at bedtime.

Baldhead's efforts of continuous display with Inkey had left him slightly lamer than before so he did not make much protest when some other nesting-boxes in his territory were taken by stranger Great Tits. The result was that altogether nine pairs nested in my garden. Besides this, Teaser, a Baldhead offspring, came to me with her young – she had always nested in the orchard next door. One day I counted sixty Great Tits in my trees and hedges. I could distinguish the different broods by their voices and details of utterance in their fledgling calls, for each family, when newly flown, had some characteristic feature in the call or cry, either of tone quality, pitch, details of rhythmic utterance or speed of repetition of the notes which constitute the fledgling call. In some of the broods there were one or two members that had distinctive calls of their own from the very first. As the fledglings grew the call gradually altered a little and then each bird's voice developed some degree of individuality. The parent Great Tits always knew the calls of their own young and there was never confusion over the feeding of these many broods. Each family of young kept together remarkably well and when occasionally a fledgling found itself among the young of another brood it first tried to get food from the stranger parents by crying and fluttering its wings; finding this unsuccessful, it called loudly and turned its head this way and that, to listen for the sound of its own family, and when the familiar notes of its own brothers and sisters were heard, it quickly joined them, never flying towards one of the other broods, who were calling from another part of the garden. Only once I saw Baldhead feed a small fledgling that was not his own, but directly after he had given the caterpillar he looked at the baby with a queer, surprised expression then gave it a gentle tap on the head which sent it flying to its own family nearby.

There is a good deal of variation in the shades of colouring among Great Tit fledglings, some having white cheeks, for instance, and some yellow, the latter being altogether more golden in hue in the parts where the former are whitish.

Naturally, there was a difference in the dates that the broods were fledged.

1. On May 28th Monocle's seven young flew. They were hatched on May 8th, so were all well-developed fledglings with fairly long tails. She took them away from my garden for several days to a hedgerow that was much haunted by Magpies. When she returned only three had survived. Monocle, Bald-head's former mate, had paired with a younger male and their nest was in orchard territory adjoining Baldhead's. Monocle kept away from their territory boundary and avoided contact with Star or Baldhead; she seemed very nervous of them. The two males frequently entered each other's territory when seeking food, the owner always displayed mildly but did not forbid entrance.

2. On June 3rd the Silent Strangers of last year brought off their brood from a nesting-box by my gate. As before, they took their family over the road, were very quiet in all their nesting affairs and their young very subdued in voice.

3. On June 4th the Back Wall Strangers' eight young flew, in very

orderly manner, one after another all flying to the same trees and shepherded to the back of my orchard hedge, away from Baldhead's nest. They had nested in a box tied to the back or north wall of my cottage – Baldhead's box being on the west side – and all their food had been sought from trees north of my orchard. They avoided contact with any of my resident Great Tits.

4. On June 4th Baldhead's ten young flew. Hatching began on May 18th. (Further details later.)

5. The same day two members from the Front Wall Strangers' brood were fledged. The remainder flew on June 8th. These strangers were so surreptitious that until they began feeding their young I never noticed that the box, hung under cover of japonica against the front wall of the cottage, was occupied. I had seen the male displaying with Puggy's mate outside the french window, but thought this stranger was the mate of a female called Tiptoe.

6. On June 11th Tiptoe's young flew. She was a gentle female who had been with me for a year. When she first came she was unable to use one leg; it healed with the foot a little twisted so she was unable to grip with it. Her mate was a newcomer who always kept in the background. Their nesting-box was on the apple tree by my west fence, so he sought all his food in the neighbouring garden. Tiptoe, perhaps because of her lameness, fed her young chiefly with food taken from me, after the first few days of hatching. The father bird supplied all natural food. Baldhead and Star made no objection to her presence although she frequently went near their nest, which was close to hers but hidden by an intervening macrocarpus tree. I think this tolerance was because of Tiptoe's weak leg, for I notice that Great Tits are usually tolerant of birds that are slightly hurt or lamed. Tiptoe kept her brood always in my garden, generally on the west side. The seven young used sometimes to perch on me while she fed them and when she stopped feeding them they followed Baldhead's brood indoors to take food from me. It was amusing to watch them all trooping in through the fanlight with much chatter. The members of each brood always kept together.

7. On June 11th Dimple's young flew. She and her mate nested the far side of my north hedge in the orchard. She had trouble with Monocle, whose territory adjoined hers, when she brought her brood to me. Dimple persisted although it cost her the loss of many feathers in disputes.

8. On June 14th Smoke's young were fledged. She had nested secretively, later than the others, in a nesting-box hidden among foliage in my east hedge in the orchard. Most of her nest-building was done in the evenings, when other Great Tits of my garden were taking time off to bathe and preen alongside the playing-field hedge, where there is a small brook. She worked very hard while at it, but took longer than the other females to build her nest because she dared not work if they were nearby. Inkey always kept the far side of the hedge, to avoid contact with the other males. By the time Smoke's young were fledged Monocle was no longer feeding hers and Baldhead and his mate too busy with their brood to notice Smoke, who had free run of the garden and orchard for the three young which she kept with her. Inkey took the rest of her brood away with him, and I have not yet seen him again.

Teaser and her mate, Timpano, adopted rather the same method of separation, although it is not usual with Great Tits. Teaser brought four of the young to my garden and Timpano reared the others in the neighbouring garden and beyond, in the playing fields. Teaser flew over to Timpano sometimes but he never came here; Baldhead and Puggy's mate objected to his presence in my garden. I sometimes took my Tit-box to the playing fields to give Timpano cheese for his young, then Teaser, who no doubt saw me from a tree-top in my garden, used to hurry towards us, her four fledglings following after her. She then took turns with Timpano in flying down from the trees to get cheese from my Tit-box for her young.

9. June 18th. Cross and his new mate brought off their young, who were hatched on May 30th. This bird was Puggy's second mate. His ways were peaceful while she was alive, but his next mate did not give him an easy time and, evidently through frustration at her lack of response, he became bad tempered towards other Great Tits, so was given the name Cross. On March 24th Puggy had started to build her nest in her mate's roosting-box outside the east window of my bedroom. Ten days later she disappeared and probably had become the victim of a cat, for the previous day I had twice chased one who was stealthily watching her collect moss for her nest. She was ten years old and had recently become less alert and her movements slower. Her nest was almost complete. Unlike some other female Great Tits she had made no resistance to her mate's entry into her nest at bedtime and so he slept with her after she started to build in his roosting-box. After

Cross lost Puggy he made many entries to the nest during the day, but he now would not roost in it and slept down a gutter pipe nearby.

Cross's new mate was an old-looking bird with no sheen on her plumage. She was nervous in manners and a complete stranger, who somehow knew that Cross needed a mate. She turned up within two days. The mystery is how it comes about that a bird suddenly appears when a vacancy arises for a new mate. After Puggy's disappearance Cross had continued to sing from exposed positions in his territory in the manner usual to Great Tits who are nesting and exactly the same way as he had sung when Puggy was alive and building her nest. So how did this stranger know he now needed a new mate? Cross evidently wanted her to behave like Puggy, but she was very different. He expected her to take on the ready-made nest and did all he could to persuade her to enter, but she would not do so. For a fortnight he spent much of the day hovering over the nest, making nestling-cry sounds from inside and outside the box, trying to get his new mate to take interest in Puggy's nest, but after watching him for a moment she would fly away to the trees. Sometimes he fetched a caterpillar, called her to him then held it out to her, but before she could take it he flew to the nesting-box, turned round to see that she was watching, gave another call-note, then entered the box and quickly put out his head through the entrance hole, showing her the food, and again withdrawing into the nest; he repeated this several times, all the while giving excited little call-notes. She never showed the least sign of response and always flew away, leaving him inside the box. He made distressed cries when he found she had gone and, dropping the caterpillar, he went after her. He became fidgety and restless; he would not eat, the food he took from me he chucked away after taking one bite. During this fortnight she spent much time at the window, clinging to the frame and looking at her reflection in the glass. Sometimes she displayed at it a little, being the only Great or Blue Tit among my many residents and strangers that has done this: nor have I ever found other Great or Blue Tits take any notice of their reflections in mirrors. On the first time of seeing the reflection they usually look behind the mirror, after this they appear satisfied and no more interest is taken in the reflections. Cross's mate evidently was puzzled and twisted her head into every possible position while examining the reflection and often tapping the glass. When she found this noise attracted my attention she tapped for purposes of getting food. As soon as she started nesting, the window-pane ceased to interest her.

After a fortnight she began to build in another box I had put up close to Puggy's, but until she brooded her eggs she slept in a little roost fixed close to my east window. This worried Cross, for most females roost in their nest after starting to build, if not sooner. Every evening he tried to coax her into her nesting-box by making baby-cries and flying backwards and forwards from her roost to the nest, but as usual she was unresponsive, so he tried to enter beside her in her chosen bed. This she would not allow. He then restlessly flitted around, giving odd call-notes every few moments, first looking inside Puggy's nesting-box then inside his new mate's nest. This always went on for half an hour after she had gone to roost; finally, he began calling her in very gentle tones then flew to her roost and peered in at her, but she spread her wings in protest against his entering. Again he visited both nests then at last popped down the gutter pipe to bed. When she began sitting he slept in her small roost by my window. He had become fidgety and was by then bad tempered with all other Great Tits except his mate. He looked very off colour and bedraggled as if beginning to moult prematurely, but his restlessness ceased after his mate began to sit. She has never come into the cottage through the fanlight like the other Tits and seems dull-witted, compared to them, in many ways. She feeds from my hand out of doors or just inside the french window.

Her young were only sixteen days old when they flew. Monocle's were three weeks old when fledged and Baldhead's three weeks all but one day. The ages when Great Tit broods leave the nest show much variation. The three mentioned above had exactly the same type nesting-boxes, with entrance holes the same height from the nests. I have watched some parents push their young back into the nest with gentle scold-notes if they try to fly a little before the parent thinks fit.

Baldhead's brood of ten all flew on the same day, although they varied much in size. Some of the bigger ones were more nervous of the plunge than the smaller ones. I watched them leave the nest, some in the morning, others at different intervals during the afternoon. First came two well-grown male fledglings, who made strong flights to the trees. The third to appear at the entrance hole was the smallest of the family. Her behaviour differed from the others, instead of looking around at the trees and distant objects within her view she kept her eyes fixed on the ground and for five minutes gazed at the earth beneath her while her larger brothers and sisters jumped about inside the nesting-box, impatiently awaiting their chance for exit. At last she spread her wings and half-floated, half-fell to the ground on the spot that she had stared at so intently. She was odd looking, with a completely bald forehead but a thick crop of feathers that rose to a peak on her crown. Her wide baby beak nearly reached to her bright eyes. As she scurried along the ground on legs that looked very long in proportion to her tiny body she looked so like a queer goblin that she became Gobline – the 'e' to denote her sex. She tried to hide in a clump of flowers while her mother called her from above, trying to coax her upwards to a safe perch, but Gobline was not yet able to fly. I put out my hand, intending to assist her to a branch, but she turned round with an indignant air, hissed at me loudly and snapped her beak many times in defiance. As she wished no interference I let her alone; she then ran into cover of long grass beneath a tree.

The rest of the brood flew at different intervals of the day, to safe tree-perches. At roost hour the parents showed much concern over Gobline, for she could not fly to the bushy tree where the others had been safely settled for the night on thin twigs and branches where no cat could climb. Gobline slept on the ground, the tall grasses and wild flowers surrounding her. I was careful not to walk near so that no trodden pathway should help cats to discover her. Next morning she was alive, vigorously calling for food. She still could not fly, but by aid of little fluttering leaps she managed to perch on a low fork of a cow parsley branch, a foot above ground, looking more goblinish than ever in this raised seat among the flowers. I guarded her carefully so that no Magpies or Daws should seize her in this rather exposed perch. Her second night was again spent hidden in long grass, but the following day she was able to fly to the trees. Her forehead was now covered with feathers, but the peaked crown still remained. Her quaint ways and appearance were fascinating to watch. She was still very tiny compared to all the other Great Tit fledglings in the garden, in fact I have never seen one so small that survived. She had a big appetite for natural food but disliked cheese and spat it out. Baldhead and Star remembered this when feeding her, and it was very rarely that they took her artificial food, although the others of the brood were by now having much cheese and bits of peanut given them – the peanut first nibbled by the parent to make it softer for the fledglings. Gobline was determined to get her fill of natural food, and she sat wing fanning and calling for attention until she had got more than her share. Often I saw Baldhead trying to stuff large moths down her throat; she liked moths, but even in the first days of being fledged, if given food that was too big to swallow easily, this precocious fledgling preferred to eat it in the grown-up Tit fashion, tucked between the toes. So these large moths always ended by being eaten in this way. Usually the young Tits do not learn to handle food between the toes until several days after they leave the nest. Long before the others she was finding moths for herself, hidden beneath low-growing plants in the flower-beds.

On June 11th, five days after the young flew, Baldhead's lame leg gave way again; how it happened I do not know, but it may have been through overstrain of the apparently dislocated joint. At seven-thirty that morning I noticed Star was rushing about in a rather hysterical manner, seizing food from me in much more haste than usual, but Baldhead did not appear for the next hour. Then he flew up, and flopped on to my lap, unable to stand. I held water before him and he drank thirstily, afterwards eating some cheese. He lay still for ten minutes, then Star flew to him and, in an excited manner, began displaying – quivering her wings and making nestling-cry sounds. Baldhead responded by a faint sound but lay still until she had flown to the young. A moment later he resumed work on his one leg. Although obviously in pain and often balancing by the aid of a spread wing for support, he struggled to stuff food down the fledglings' throats. He showed much courage, for he looked very ill and was not able to eat much himself for the next few days. Star stimulated him by displaying frequently with much wing fluttering; she worked far harder than before and took the main share of feeding the young while Baldhead took occasional intervals of rest that he so much needed. They never left my garden. Their brood was alternately kept in the front part or the orchard.

On the day that the parents ceased feeding their brood, Gobline also strained one leg and she could not get about to find food for herself. For several days she was dependent upon me, but I could not supply the natural diet that she liked. She developed an unusual cry that sounded like sobbing, whenever she saw either of her parents, but they did not give her food. Often Baldhead and Gobline were perched side by side, both holding up their game legs in exactly the same manner. She kept uttering her sobbing notes in his ear while her wings quivered slightly; Baldhead never repulsed her but he did not respond to her cries. I caught green flies and grasshoppers for her and also occasionally a few small spiders which she liked, but when I offered her a large black one she and all the other fledglings shrank in fear from it. The spider escaped across the room, to be devoured by an adult Great Tit with much relish, for this is one of their favourite foods. Gobline was still very undersized and now she had to spend her day either sleeping or remaining motionless, hunched on a perch. Two of her big brothers noticed this and often tried to urge her into movement by sidling towards her along the branch where she was perched and, with much chatter, giving her gentle pokes. She held her own, turning upon them in the same manner as she had once repulsed my effort to assist her to a safe perch. Her brothers drew back when she snapped her beak and hissed at them, but they soon came forward again to continue their teasing. They were very gentle with her and probably this enlivened her day so I never interfered with the big brothers' playful behaviour.

In a fortnight the leg had quite recovered. She had grown rather snappy towards all the other fledglings, probably as a result of the troubles she had encountered through her handicaps. This snappiness ceased after several days, during which time she grew quickly to the average size for a female.

Gobline never quite lost her sobbing note, which she later used in an abridged version when wanting something. She had for some time slept every night above my bed, alternating between two boxes, one round and one square, that the other Tits had not tried to occupy. But one evening at the end of July, another youngster Great Tit was in her round roost-box when she came to bed; she hesitated a moment, then hopped into the square box, apparently unperturbed, but the next second she flew out and, like a whirlwind, fluttered her wings over the entrance of the occupied box while making fierce pecks at the occupier until he came out and the two birds, with feet interlocked, rolled together on my bed. I called out, 'Stop it!' then both flew to the window-ledge, shaking their ruffled feathers and uttering scold-notes, which were taken up by several other birds, indoors and outdoors. For ten minutes Gobline and the male Tit she had attacked remained a few feet apart on the window-sill, both looking up at the roost and apparently each waiting for the other to make a move. Finally, he flew to the same roost again, then Gobline flew off, out of the window. A few minutes later she returned to the window, glanced up at the roost, gave a nervous squeak, shook her feathers and disappeared again. That night she slept outside. The following evening the other Tit went early to bed in another box, adjoining Gobline's two roosts. When she came in a while later she appeared nervous of going to either box, perhaps not knowing whether the Tit was again in one of them. After hesitating for several minutes, perched on the window curtain-rod, she crept along the picture rails towards the roosts and quickly slithered into the square box. She did not look to see whether her other roost was occupied, and I fancy, if it had been, she would not have made objection, for since that sudden outburst her behaviour had been very meek and mild with other Tits. It is usual for Tits to keep their own roost and try to expel others who occupy it, but I have not before had a young Tit try to keep two roosts, although adults will keep others from entering roosting-boxes in their territory.

The next evening the male again took Gobline's round box and she crept along the picture rails to her square roost. No sooner was she settled there than he stampeded out of his box, noisily giving warning of an attack and when he spread wings in display at the entrance of Gobline's square roost she remained quietly inside. Then he began to try and turn her out by entering it. I said, 'Stop it!' He took no notice so I stood on the bed and touched his tail. At once he left Gobline alone and returned to the round box. For many nights afterwards the male youngster occupied the round roost and Gobline the square one. She always waited until he was in his bed before seeking hers.

Of other Great Tits under observation during ten years at Bird Cottage, I noted the following: Knicky's first mate died after three years. They had always been together, winter, autumn and summer, perched upon the same bough or bush, calling to one another if moving from tree to tree. They were single brooded and always nested in the same hole. Knicky's second mate, Tapper, was not often with her out of nesting season, but they nested in that same hole for two seasons. Then Knicky died. Tapper always tapped at my french window to attract my attention before he came indoors through the fanlight to feed from my hand.

Snatch and his mate, called Grab, were two lively birds and inseparable mates, with character and appearance much alike. The male had narrow frontal markings which were more characteristic of a female. Both seemed always in a terrific hurry, they flew faster than most Great Tits and their movements were jerkier. They snatched food from me in a wild manner although not afraid, for they entered the room, but as if they had urgent appointments and must seize all the food possible in their only spare moment. When Grab died, Snatch chose a completely different sort of mate, who was quiet mannered, smaller in build and greyer in plumage – where other Tits are greenish. She was so tame with me that she would sit on my hand and pull strands from a ball of wool for her nesting material. She clung to my sleeve and called to me gently when I had not the wool in my hand which she wanted me to fetch. The next winter Snatch disappeared. He had never been very attentive to this mate. She chose Whiskers – he was later Curley's mate – for her second mate and died while the nestlings were tiny. Whiskers reared them with great difficulty and they obviously were not fed enough, but he did his best for the large brood. I think one of this grey female's offspring was Baldhead's mate called Grey, her appearance and ways were so very alike, and I find these small variations of colouring and size are often inherited, as well as gentleness, bold manners or other characteristics.

Another couple, especially devoted in their ways and very emotional over nesting affairs, brought disaster to their young by their enthusiasm. Their voluble excitement and displaying when rearing young was so noticeable that it attracted the attention of all their enemies, so their young came to grief. Three times they tried the same nesting-hole with failures, then left the garden and never returned. Their nesting-hole was afterwards occupied by the Pugnacious Tits who successfully reared two broods each year for many years, but their ways were completely different.

I have never found two females laying in the same nest. The average clutch has been nine with one egg often not hatching, or eight with all eggs hatching. Almost always every nestling is successfully fledged but about half of the brood usually fall victim to their enemies within two or three days of leaving the nest. Blue Tits have sometimes had twelve all hatching from one female, so probably most of the larger clutches that are seen occasionally are from one exceptionally prolific bird.

GREAT TITS

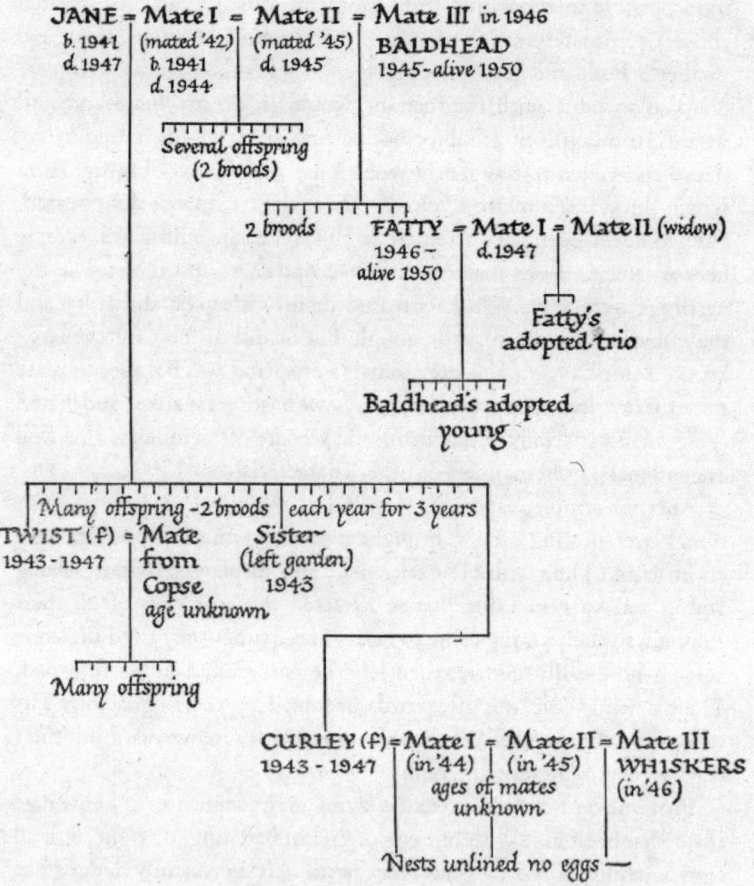

GENEALOGICAL TREE

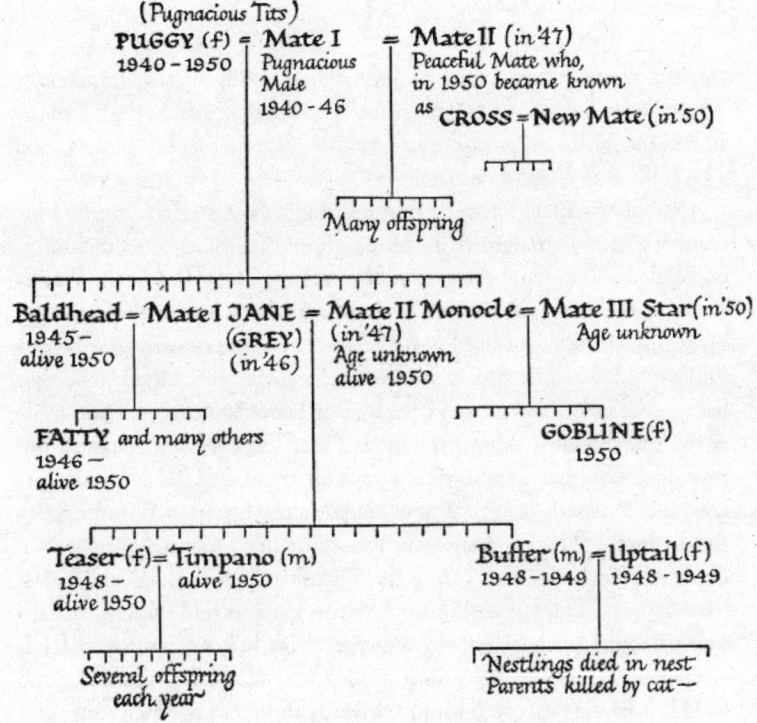

CHAPTER 3

Bird Biography: Blackbirds

1

In part one of the previous chapter, when telling of the Pugnacious Tits' altered behaviour to Jane after her brood was fatherless, I mentioned that birds will adjust their territorial laws to meet circumstances. The following is another case in point.

One of my Blackbirds, during nesting season, strictly guarded his territory in my orchard from all neighbouring Blackbirds including one called Thief, from the next-door orchard. Because I mowed paths through the long grass of my orchard and threw scraps there for the birds, my Blackie had hard work to keep the others away, but he did while food was plentiful elsewhere. His mate was unlucky, an egg being taken from her clutch by a Rat or Daw. She deserted and built again, but the same thing happened. Thief's young were hatched and he made many attempts to steal scraps for them, but Blackie was vigilant and chased him off. When Blackie's mate started brooding her third clutch, Thief's mate was brooding her second. Owing to a drought, food now was scarce for Thrush tribes, the clay soil being hard as iron. Thief was finding it really hard to find enough for his three fledglings and then my Blackie, who had no young to feed, altered his territorial behaviour. Thief was allowed to come for the food but Blackie escorted him backwards and forwards each time, and always stood over him while he fed the fledglings.

Thief normally kept Blackie out of his territory so both had adjusted their behaviour to meet the circumstances. It was amusing to watch Blackie accompany Thief into his domain, wait beside him wherever he perched and, as soon as the young had been fed, the two would return for more food, Thief first and Blackie close on his heels. In a couple of days the three fledglings were following their father along my orchard paths, always with Blackie bringing up the rear. Each time Thief picked up food the fledglings clustered round him with open beaks and Blackie stood beside them, head tilted forward, his expression alert while he watched the food being swallowed by a fledgling. All other neighbouring Blackbirds were still refused entry into his territory – but I think their young were not fledged.

Then the drought ended, and with the softening of the soil came the hardening of Blackie's territorial defence. Thief and his family were chased off every time, but Blackie still had no young to feed. I have known many other cases of relaxation of territorial behaviour during drought, and in snow or prolonged frost. My Blackbirds normally are very strict over their boundary defences, perhaps more so than is usual because of the extreme popularity of my garden. The sensible discrimination over relaxation of this strictness seems to prove territorial behaviour is not wholly automatic, as some ornithologists maintain, but adjusted by minds with good reasoning power.

Thief's mate was an unusual bird with white edgings to her wings and tail, and a white star on her forehead. She was always very trim, with every feather in place and altogether a remarkably lovely bird. He was usually disgracefully untidy, with feathers looking as if never preened and his eyes had a battered look, the yellow rims being incomplete. She never appeared to have any of the usual intercourse with other Blackbirds, her decorative touch of albinism perhaps making her aloof and others avoid or respect her.

The ragged Thief well deserved his name. I never saw a Blackbird so sharp at thieving. In summer I had meals in the orchard while watching the birds. At lunchtime Thief would choose a perch in his orchard where he could overlook me and keep his sharp eye on my plate. If it contained meat he waited until my head was turned away to watch some bird behind me, then he swooped down silently but quick as lightning and, before I had realised what was happening, had snatched meat from the plate and flown off with a loud chuckle, my Blackbird in hot pursuit. The rapid pickpocket action of a really first-class bird-thief seems a gift which cannot be acquired; I find some Great Tits have this natural talent, others are always comparatively clumsy over their many attempts.

Even Thief's songs were stolen tunes, cribbed from neighbouring Blackbirds with little embellishment added – as is usual when one Blackbird copies from another. (See Bird Song, Chapter 11, pages 150 and 153.)

For six years Thief and his pretty mate reared their families next door in the same rambler bush. Then she died and he mated an ordinary female who carried on in that same bush. He died two years later.

One of Thief's offspring had some odd characteristics, and as this bird chose to include part of my front garden in his territory I have had him under close observation.

2

Thief's son did not gain his territory easily, for the old Blackbird, who owned all my front garden, was very tenacious.

While the old bird was in moult he allowed many youngsters to feed on his lawn, among them Thief's son, still in fledgling attire. When autumn came the old Blackbird, in his new plumage, was vigorous and strict over possession. All the young ones left except Thief's offspring, who hung about at the far end of the lawn under cover of bushes and the hedge bordering the road. The tall apple-tree there was his favourite perch; here he preened himself and basked in the sun, also he sometimes sang a very quiet subsong, only audible quite close to the tree. He kept a watchful eye on the old Blackbird, seizing opportunities to trespass on the lawn for food or running up to the bird-table by my window when the old bird was occupied with other neighbours at the back of my cottage.

It was a mild winter and in January the youngster began efforts to gain half the front garden for nesting territory. With care this original bird selected a large oak-leaf from the many dead ones on the ground and, with this in his beak and head held up high so the stiff brown leaf was very conspicuous, he rushed to battle with the old Blackbird in the middle of his territory. There was a scrimmage in the flower-beds as they chased one another in and out of the bushes then flew up, beak to beak. Suddenly the youngster turned tail and ran quickly back to the far end of the lawn. Carefully he placed the oak leaf on the grass then rushed back to combat. The battle was long and fierce. The youngster came out of it looking battered but the old Blackbird, who was the first to give up, looked in perfect condition.

An hour or two later the youngster picked up the same oak-leaf and, brandishing it high with a confident air, strutted right across the old Blackbird's territory. They fought less fiercely than before, much being the usual Blackbird walking chase, backwards and forwards and in and out of the bushes, the youngster brandishing his oak-leaf with a cocky air. Occasionally they flew up beak to beak, and after a little the young bird retired to change his war-worn oak-leaf for a fresh one, again running to attack with neck stretched high, the stiff brown leaf prominently held in his upraised bill.

For many days the two Blackbirds fought, always the youngster with his oak-leaf, like a talisman, held in his bill. Once he tried carrying several oak-leaves, but found they hampered him and soon put them down, selecting one large, stiff leaf. He never chose any other kind of leaf although there were many on the ground. At the end of a month Oakleaf, as he was now called, was a battered-looking bird, but he had won half the lawn. He now turned much attention to song and nesting affairs.

Oakleaf's originality again was shown in song, for he made a more effective use of vibrato than I have ever heard before. His phrase was

superbly sung, and the tone of his long-held final note with the impassioned vibrato compelled concentrated listening and much thought about the soul of a bird. Perched high on the tall old apple-tree, this odd-looking, battle-scarred Blackbird sang by the hour, perfecting a variety of original tunes. Unlike his father, he never copied a phrase from another Blackbird, but went on composing his own melodies, embellishing them, turning them all ways and experimenting in different tone effects, tempo and pitches.

Nesting days began and one fledgling was reared from his first brood. Although the old Blackbird also was feeding his young, Oakleaf often encroached on his territory, unearthed a worm and held it up high, as if swaggering before his old enemy. Their battles went on and before Oakleaf's mate hatched her second brood the old Blackbird had died of wounds inflicted by the strong beak of the impetuous young battle-scarred bird. He was now grotesque looking, with the feathers all plucked from his crown and bare patches above his eyes.

Up to the first week in August, Oakleaf continued to sing, but his mate failed to rear any young from their second or third broods. Perhaps his exceptional powers of song attracted attention of enemies to their nest. The rest of August Oakleaf spent much time squatting on the lawn, his bald head upturned with his beak pointing to the sky and a dazed expression in his eyes. Unlike most Blackbirds, he did not hide among bushes or trees during moult, but posed like a scarecrow in a prominent position, apparently to keep away others from his hard-earned land.

On September 4th, in the early hours of a wild, windy morning, Oakleaf was absent from the garden, and I saw a young Blackbird with adult plumage not yet complete performing a very unusual dance on his lawn. She chose a sheltered strip, surrounded by flower-beds, with a rose pergola behind. Lifting her wings high so the pale undersides were seen, she flickered them rapidly and gave a little leap into the air, then darted forward a few paces on the ground and, with more quick wing flickers, turned sharply round, darting, leaping and turning again, with occasional light wing-flicking. Every movement was at lightning speed and full of airy grace. Suddenly she stopped and pecked the lawn vigorously, scattering small clods of clay soil. Snatching one, she threw it with a sharp twist of her head, darted after it, seized it again and threw it as if playing a rapid game with a ball. Again she made a springing leap, and flicking high-raised wings at intervals, she whirled round three times in a circle of a few feet, keeping to the ground but with motion too rapid to know if she was running, hopping or propelled forwards by the curious wing-flicks. Suddenly she stopped, her body sunk on the ground, her head upturned.

It was the most surprising performance, for the dancer's movements were not typical of a Blackbird. To the bird-watcher, this exuberant dance was in keeping with the spirit of the wild, south-west wind. In a moment she rose again, stretched upwards her wings for the flicker, gave one springing leap and repeated a quick circling spin, as if bouncing round aided by occasional wing-flicks. Then she stood still with lowered head, as if intent on looking for food, and another young Blackbird, son of Oakleaf, flew up to her and began pecking the earth. For a moment the two birds stood back to back and vigorously pecked the ground, then the dancer sprinted across the lawn and flew up to one end of the pergola. Oakleafson followed and flew to the other end. But the dancer turned her back to him and in an absorbed-looking manner, plucked leaves from the rambler and chucked them down, while young Oakleafson slowly hopped towards her. Suddenly the dancer turned and with one quick wing-flickered hop, she landed the other side of him. For a while they stayed back to back, still as effigies, then the dancer flew to the lawn and again began her graceful, wild dance, this time watched by Oakleafson from above.

Once more the two young Blackbirds stood back to back on the lawn, Oakleafson vigorously pecking the earth, the dancer turning dead leaves over and over as if absent-mindedly. Suddenly she flew rapidly to a tree, he following a moment afterwards.

Later in the day she again flew to the lawn. Oakleafson watched her from behind the pergola as she began her light wing-flicker and leap, but this time the grotesque-looking Oakleaf appeared, a drab creature with bald head and body dwarf-shaped with no tail, yet still possessor of a strong yellow beak. At sight of this queer-looking bird the dancer hastily disappeared. Perhaps she knew Oakleaf with his golden bill had slain her father two months ago, after many battles waged with an oak-leaf held in his bill.

So this remnant of a Blackbird strutted slowly up and down the lawn alone, proud possessor of the land perhaps, but with no spirit left to enjoy. In the background remained Oakleafson, for whose sake all the battles had been fought. He, too, now feared this battle-scarred bird of original ways and great power of song.

3

Oakleaf's behaviour was quite different in his second year. In October another Blackbird of his age, who had nested in my orchard, took possession of the old Blackbird's territory and Oakleaf gave up half his lawn to this bird without fighting. They appeared to settle matters by mild, friendly games around the new boundary of Oakleaf's territory, a flower-bed jutting out as a sort of no-man's land. The new bird, called Darky because he sang into the dark after other Blackbirds were asleep, would walk towards Oakleaf, who hastily picked up a piece of apple from under the tree and stalked round the flower-bed, holding the apple high, with head upraised and tail outspread like a fan. Darky rushed at him, he eluded the attack, dodged round the bushes and deposited the apple in Darky's territory just beyond the flower-bed. Darky ran after him, also with spread tail, upraised head and stiffly poised body. He pretended to grab the apple, but let Oakleaf intercept. Then the two birds paraded after each other in comically affected-looking attitudes, in and out of the flower-beds. They returned to the apple, which Oakleaf snatched and held erect cockily in front of Darky, who chased him back to his side of the boundary, where he dropped the apple and pretended to eat it. Darky dashed at him and they flew up together, snapping at the air playfully, so it seemed. Then the game began again as before. They spent many hours over it in October and November, apparently enjoying it and never suffering even a ruffled feather from their intercourse.

In January Oakleaf started running away from all Blackbirds, especially Darky, who frequently chased his flying form, for Oakleaf hurried off at first sight of Darky even if he was on Oakleaf's territory. In February (the year was 1947), during the prolonged snow Oakleaf seized food from my window-sill every day and when Darky protested he held the food high, quivered his wings, dramatically in effect, and spread his tail. This performance stopped Darky's protest, but Oakleaf always hurried away after eating and never appeared on the lawn until March 23rd. That day he crouched under a may-tree the far corner of the lawn, in his typical attitude, body low on the ground and head upturned, beak pointing to the sky. Suddenly his mate appeared and simultaneously Oakleaf disappeared over the hedge into my neighbour's garden. This was now the main part of his territory, but he still owned the corner of my lawn under the may-tree and a narrow strip of lawn behind the pergola, culminating in the apple-tree – his old song-perch.

The next day he again crouched motionless under the may-tree, his back towards his mate who pretended to feed behind the tree. Then she flew right up to my window in Darky's land, Oakleaf immediately following in curious looping flight, with an original high-pitched chuckle. He alighted behind her. She turned rapidly, jumped over him and flew back to the may-tree, he following. Then Darky appeared, running up in a consequential manner and standing nearby with flared tail and cocked-up head, rudely staring at the lovers. Oakleaf was too engrossed in his mate to notice, so Darky returned leisurely to his own land.

On March 26th, Oakleaf paid a return visit to Darky, armed with a beakload of leaves and a long strip of paper dangling from his high-held bill to the ground. This load hampered his progress and he kept tripping on the paper-end, but his slow advance had a humorous, mock-triumphant air. He appeared to be enjoying himself immensely, his manner and expression being quite different from when he attacked the old Blackbird to gain territory. Darky ran forward and they flew up together in the flower-bed, but Oakleaf found his beakload tiresome. He flew back to his may-tree, carefully deposited the leaves and paper under the tree, then came forward again, but Darky meanwhile had flown back to my window-sill to feed. When he saw Oakleaf advance he ran towards him, Oakleaf hurriedly picked up two leaves and rushed to meet him. Beak to beak they flew up several times, posturing in between, then Oakleaf returned to his may-tree and placed the leaves on the ground, afterwards wiping his beak on the turf, opening and shutting his mandibles in a queer way, as if the taste of the leaves had been unpleasant. He and Darky had no more encounters.

That spring Darky sang better and more continuously than any other Blackbird but failed to rear any young. Oakleaf, who had failure the previous year, now reared all his broods, but had very little song. His voice appeared to have cracked; when he tried his old tunes there was no beauty in his feeble tones. This, and other cases, seems to show that song is detrimental to nesting. Also, this year Oakleaf was a more devoted parent. He often brooded the nestlings himself, even when they were nearly ready to fly, which I have not found usual with male Blackbirds. This extra precaution was no doubt to protect the young from marauders. The nest was in the same hedge as before, but when Oakleaf attempted to sing he chose a perch farther away from the nest. This sobered and sensible bird had also this year kept all his feathers intact.

Birds learn from their mistakes, quickly gaining wisdom from experience, which surely shows that their actions are guided by reason, not merely instinctive and automatic.

Oakleaf, in his third year, reinforced the oak-leaf with a stick which he brandished high as he ran to meet Darky in their boundary disputes. In his fourth year this original bird had yet another brilliant idea. He added a peculiar flight attack; when Darky approached his territory he seized his weapons, including the stick, ran to meet him and when close, put on a sudden spurt that ended in circular flight at terrific speed just above and round his charging opponent's head, landing again about two feet away from him, then running quickly back into his own territory and turning round to repeat this attack, which bewildered Darky until he got used to it. The flight charge was exceedingly clever, for hampered with leaf and stick, Oakleaf had found the usual beak-to-beak encounter unsatisfactory, he had to drop his weapons when they flew upwards with clashing bills. But his new swift flight finish gave no chance for beak encounter. Darky rushed forward on the ground to meet him, charging empty space while Oakleaf, with his weapons, did his quickly rounded aerial finish to the attack. Eventually, Darky took to dodging round bushes when Oakleaf began flight attacks, the bushes hampering this modern method of warfare and favouring the old-fashioned stalking chases. When Oakleaf's fifth nesting season arrives perhaps he will invent yet another surprise for Darky, as there seems no end to the originality of this Blackbird.

CHAPTER 4

Autumn Robin Notes

The autumn of 1946 preceeded an exceptionally hard winter. There was an unusual influx of Robins to my garden in September, battling for possession of a winter territory that would include the bird-table or part of my cottage. The following extracts from my autumn notes were written while watching the Robins or directly afterwards. It was interesting to find that my Robin, named Dobs, acted differently to each intruder. Dobs was in his second year.

August 26th. Dobs is now in bright new plumage, his manner is defiant and he seems equal to tackling anything. He has greedily taken both sides of my cottage, not leaving his mate the east half as he did last year. She has retired next door, to East Garden and has not appeared in mine for some days. Two new Robins are trying to advance from the west and south-west. They are antagonistic to each other as well as to Dobs. These two Robins are rarely seen, but from cover of the tall macrocarpus tree near the west wall of my cottage, one bird shoots menacing notes at Dobs, who warbles back quietly but threateningly and bristles all over until he looks enormously big. The other new Robin is attacking from south-west, by my garden gate. From cover of trees she shouts loud, hard, spasmodic notes, occasionally flying to the ground to pick up something, then hurrying away with 'tic, tic, ticks' before Dobs has time to attack. My garden 'ticks' all day long.

August 27th. Dobs's mate walks across the lawn with her head held high and mincing steps – the slim, long-legged female again. Dobs appears and she retreats slowly, now assuming a heavier figure, with shortened legs and rotund body. Muttering something under her breath, she retires to her next-door territory. Dobs warbles very quietly to himself – or her – from the hedge which separates the two territories. He keeps stretching up his head, alert to the possibility of repetition of his mate's boldness – sauciness better describes it! West Robin threatens fresh attack; fierce notes come from behind

Trees left unshaded are those of especial mention
in the chapter and elsewhere in the book

macrocarpus tree. Dobs settles with him quietly but firmly in Robin language.

August 28th. Dobs is on bird-table with his mate, apparently friendly. He takes food from my hand, she picks up crumbs that are dropped. She seems a little nervous but Dobs is all smiles this morning, and no scolding ensues.

August 30th, and until September 4th. Dobs always comes alone, his mate not visible. Afternoon of 4th he chases her along their boundary hedge.

September 4th to 8th. Trouble with west Robin increases. Continuous flow of language from Dobs, and shouts from west Robin in the macrocarpus tree. Sometimes they roll together under the tree with locked feet but do not hurt each other. Dobs's language is superbly controlled; west Robin's hysterical sounding, spasmodic shouts do not seem nearly so convincing as Dobs's steady flow of language, sometimes uttered under his breath but sounding full of threatening meaning. In the early morning Dobs sings a beautiful song, but he can also sing in very different language when occasion demands. A Robin's song is more expressive in autumn than in spring. It has many more moods, sounding to me like fierce, threatening, coaxing, relieved, content, triumphant, morbid, conceited, wistful, determined, bored, hopeless – giving the impression his adversary is a fool and the world a hopeless affair! Garstang, in his book on bird song, called him the Chopin of bird music, but Chopin is frequently sentimental. Robins never are.

September 9th. South-west Robin has encroached towards Oakleaf's may-tree and the pergola. The south of garden is now her territory. She has little song and has the long-legged female appearance. She trips about very daintily. Dobs does not fight her, he is too busy keeping his mate from east side of cottage and west Robin from the west front of lawn. This afternoon Dobs has been singing from the top of east hedge plum-tree, a monotonous, loud song that sounds unlike his usual varied performance and seems just a noise to keep away the other Robins. He has grown very portly, weighs more than most Robins when on my hand, and his red breast is exceptionally brilliant, his mate pale in comparison.

September 12th. Dobs seems to have settled his territorial affairs to his satisfaction for the present, for he has been singing sweetly all day and has had no trouble with other Robins. West Robin sang a little from the macrocarpus, which is now apparently his territory boundary. Perhaps they are influenced by this fine, calm day – the first without wind for many weeks. Yesterday a party of Long-tailed Tits, perched on the wires alongside the road, had their tails blown backwards over their heads. They seemed nearly to lose balance. Today not even a high-perched Long-tailed Tit could have had the least trouble with his tail. Much of Dobs's day was spent perched low in the bushes, singing a continuous subsong which sounded like a long tale unfolding; sometimes while singing he half-closed his eyes and seemed unconscious of the world around him. How different his song and manner from that of previous days of dispute.

September 24th. Dobs is busy again over matters connected with his mate. South-west Robin and west Robin are sparring at each other by song and sighing notes, loud and hopeless sounding. Dobs pays no attention to them, he is concerned in keeping the back door, east side of cottage – which is the kitchen door – from his wife, who has been trying to edge her way into this crumby portion of territory. He is perched on the filbert-tree by the back door, his song quiet but ominous sounding, his eyes focused on his mate behind the tree, who retorts by loud 'tic, ticks.' With the loss of this door her last hopes of future crumbs would fail, but she is obviously afraid of coming too near Dobs; her strategy is a determined effort to take advantage of his need to defend the other side of the cottage. Every time his back is turned she edges slowly towards the back door, pretending to pick up food on the way, but not really eating or hunting for food. Her eye is always upon Dobs; if his attention is turned to her again she slowly retreats. He never attacks her and his song in dealing with her is always very quiet. He often pauses in these back door disputes to take food from my hand in the front garden, at the same time cocking his eye at west Robin, who sings much from the border of his territory. Sometimes Dobs perches opposite him for a few minutes to sing loudly, then he hurriedly flits back to the filbert-tree, for it seems he is particularly anxious to keep that kitchen door in his territory. His mate gives him more trouble than the two new Robins, perhaps because he is driving her from last winter's share of my garden and cottage front. But a fresh complication is developing from the west, for yet another Robin is pressing into west Robin's territory, from the sound of his voice, a strong male with much determination. West Robin is therefore tempted to try and encroach on Dobs, beyond the macrocarpus boundary. As the situation develops, Dobs leaves the back door and comes to deal with the other Robins, who fall into vulgar-sounding splutterings noises, as if losing their tempers. Dobs has a certain dignity about his methods of warfare. He uses strong language, but never resorts to mere vulgar splutterings or squeaking sounds.

A sudden silence from all the striving Robins while a party of Long-tailed Tits flit through the garden. It seemed the carefree atmosphere of this wandering flock affected the Robins, the breezy air of the Long-tails cooling the heat of the fiery Redbreasts' dispute. A sunny autumn day to these Tits means pleasant roaming along bright-coloured hedgerows, the rich spoil shared in friendly companionship, while to Robins such days seem to bring an urge for solitude, resulting in strife for sole possession of a strip of land where they can feed well in lonely retirement from others of their kind.

The Long-tails have passed by but their voices still ring from the distance, like many tiny, high-pitched electric bells. A long silence from the Robins, then Dobs begins to sing, three emphatic notes followed by one questioning upward scoop, which fritters away into rippling notes, the cadence four long, loud notes, dwelt on with increasing length and emphasis, sounding – anthropomorphically interpreted – as if that settled everything worth bothering about. The other Robins are silent except for a few desultory 'tic, ticks.' There is no more strife that afternoon. Dobs warbles quietly by my side, a gentleness in his character seeming reflected in this charming subsong.

September 26th. Dobs's song, to the accompaniment of pattering raindrops, is interrupted. The situation of west Robin is becoming serious. The new west-west Robin has encroached on west Robin and threatens to oust him from his territory. He has actually appeared beyond the macrocarpus on the lawn in front of the cottage in conflict with west Robin. Dobs, in fury, left his song-tree on East Hedge and, with feathers upstanding so that he looked enormous, flew at the two encroachers, sending them over the west fence. When he returned to his song-post his notes were long drawn and emphatic with one or two chuckle explosions interspersed. (The Robin has in his repertoire something similar to the Blackbird's well-known chuckle, although of course much higher pitched.)

Afternoon of same day. The two west Robins are again in conflict with each other under the macrocarpus-tree, but they chiefly sigh, squeak and shout, with much display and chasing. South-west Robin edges closer, seeming to wonder if she can gain ground from this new disturbance. She ventures nearer than ever before towards cottage on west side. Dobs gets annoyed and keeps flying down with ruffled feathers, singing from the ground near the macrocarpus – the west Robins' tree of dispute. But he dare not leave the East Hedge for long as his mate waits her opportunities from that side. It is a busy day for Dobs. He pauses a moment to drink from the bird-bath; between each sip he sings a spluttery phrase, sounding as if the water was bubbling in his mouth. He has to sing incessantly now, having to deal with four Robins.

Same Afternoon, 3.30. Yet another couple of Robins are pressing on west Robin and trying to get near the cottage via macrocarpus-tree and surrounding lawn. Four Robins are now disputing for this tree. From 3.30 until 5 p.m. a chase goes on, round and round the tree and its neighbouring apple-tree on the south-west. Dobs is furious; he sings incessantly with loud emphasis, often flying to the top of the bird-table to display, red-hot anger gleaming from his eyes. His head is enlarged, his body seems shrunken and his figure deformed. He is too agitated by this influx of Robins to take food offered him, he fears to stop singing or displaying for one moment, even to feed. South-west Robin is still trying to take advantage of west Robin's predicament; she now comes right to the flower-beds in Dobs's and west Robin's territory. Previously her boundary was Oakleaf's may-tree and the pergola adjoining. For many hours the flutter of Robin wings is heard, hitting against the leaves as they dash headlong in and out, round and through the trees. Dobs does not enter the chase, but sings continuously from the bird-table, with flashing eyes and alarming contortions of his usually attractive form; also, he now resorts to the splutter-note, which had not hitherto demeaned his song.

At 5 o'clock there was a plague of flying ants in my garden and probably high above, for the sky overhead was literally swarming with Martins and Swallows. Looking upwards, the masses of circling birds, crossing and recrossing each other at different levels, made a curious revolving motion so that one felt as if going round with them. As they circled higher and yet higher, seen far up in the heavens these hundreds of tiny specks looked like black snowflakes whirling upwards until almost lost to sight. Then a downwards motion began and a few swept close to earth, all gradually becoming visible as slender-winged birds with graceful, curving flight. Those that flew low looked surprisingly large – an illusion created by the smallness of others at higher levels. Again the masses of Swallows were wheeling upwards, forming innumerable gigantic patterns of intricate design, ever changing as they flew in rapid convolutions far into the sky above. Half an hour later this great migration assembly drifted eastwards, only leaving a small number hawking the flying ants at low levels over the garden. Willow-Warblers and Spotted Flycatchers also seemed enjoying the plague; even Sparrows were snapping them on the wing. When the Swallows had gone the plague increased still more and occasionally one of the four Robins paused in the chase to pick some from the trees or ground, but immediately it was pounced upon by another bird of the chase and dragged into the whirl round the trees again. Sometimes one Robin stood still to sing a phrase suggesting a Blackcap's cadence. His was no ordinary Robin song; perhaps he had lived away from his kind, with many Blackcaps around him. The others never stopped for real song, although there was much spluttering, squeaking or shouting of single notes and sometimes a long squealing note, ending in sighing sounds. During the evening Dobs entered the chase and when too hard pressed he resorted to something resembling a spit – excusable under the trying circumstances, for he had south-west Robin and his mate at the back door to cope with besides these four interlopers.

After dusk that night there were many agitated, defiant little Robin forms flitting about my lawn. The darkness gave them a chance to feed unmolested perhaps.

September 27th, 7 a.m. (Summer Time). The seven Robins are all busy again. Only Dobs has sung the Matins this morning. The rest began their day by 'ticks' and shouts that sounded like swear notes. The invasion of these new Robins is causing Dobs much uneasiness. The first new one, described previously as a strong-sounding male or as west-west Robin, has ousted west Robin from the macrocarpus and adjacent apple-tree and taken possession of the west front of lawn. This bird, in future called New Robin, is fiery and a match for Dobs.

September 27th (continued), 10 a.m. The glorious day of brilliant sunshine and clear blue sky seems to have made the Robins for a while forget their quarrels in a chorus of song expressive of the golden autumn morning. I notice, however, that Dobs sings louder than usual and without pause, as if wishing to hear only his own voice. His notes are also shriller than before the influx of Robins. He sounds at tension, but is singing well.

At 11 a.m. the chorus ceases and New Robin advances to the lawn on west front of cottage. He hops about jauntily, with bluff-swagger gait, on this new piece of ground, his eye cocked at Dobs on the bird-table, who glares angrily at him for a moment then flashes down to the lawn beside him, his body contorted, his head extended as if to bursting point and his language frightful. New Robin continues to hop jauntily, but keeps opening his beak wide to let out an amazingly loud and prolonged gutteral hiss, given with graduated intensity. As the hiss gathers vehemence the beak opens wider until the tongue is visible. His beak is scarcely closed again before this devastating performance is repeated, but he retreats slowly, so Dobs flies to his favourite song-perch, a tall plum-tree on East Hedge, commanding a good view of his mate's territory as well as being conspicuous to all the other Robins. He sings lustily until occasion demands another pounce on New Robin.

I am sitting close to the bird-table on the lawn. New Robin comes up to me and hints for food. Dobs shoots down from his high perch like a flashing meteor, in fury striking the intruder. They roll together on the lawn, feet interlocked, the grip of their clutching claws firm and evenly matched. At last one bird gets his beak at the other's throat. This seems a death struggle, so I separate the furious Redbreasts. But Dobs's blood is up, his flaming eyes match his fiery-coloured breast, and he at once attacks again. Loud hand-clapping at their ears frightens them apart. New Robin retires behind the macrocarpus-tree with a few desultory 'tic, ticks.' Dobs seems to think himself the victor, for he flattens his ruffled feathers and putting on his pleased expression, flies to his perch to sing sweetly, all shrillness gone from his voice.

September 28th. The Blackcap Robin is now singing from an apple-tree west of the macrocarpus. He has a mellow voice for a Robin, with Blackcap quality, and constantly repeats his phrase of a few notes resembling the Blackcap cadence. For ten minutes he sings this; it seems he has nothing else in his repertoire. Then come three low-muttered notes followed by long silence; New Robin is chasing him.

Dobs is singing from the back door filbert-tree, to keep his mate away. The four new invading Robins start 'ticking' and spluttering like a lot of alarm clocks. All are striving for possession of the apple-tree west of New Robin's macrocarpus and they start a swinging chase around and through the tree. Their flight is soft and silent, but as they dive in and out of the branches the flutter of their wings against the stiffening texture of autumn leaves makes a curious rattling sound. There now seems to be no anger in this chase, and I could believe it to be half-fun. If the Robins extend their chase to the pear-tree south of the apple-tree, the demure south-west Robin flies up, full of protest; this pear-tree is the border of her territory. The Blackcap Robin sometimes pauses to sing his recurrent phrase, but any of the four that perch to sing are flown at and pushed into the chase again. For over an hour this game continues, if game it is. Then the four Robins all start singing, the Blackcap Robin's mellow notes sounding like a tenor in a chorus of sopranos. Dobs flies to the front garden when the chorus begins, but this time, instead of singing shrilly, he warbles an exclusive, shimmering subsong, which stands out as definitely amongst the full-throated singers as one muted instrument does in a quartet of unmuted strings. At sundown the 'ticking' of all six Robins is heard at intervals. Dobs, who is used to having the bird-bath to himself at dusk for a lengthy splashing bathe, now finds it necessary to keep up breathless 'tic, ticks' during a very hurried dip. From the way he keeps looking about him it appears he is nervous of other Robins interfering with his dusk-hour bath. After he has finished, New Robin occupies the bath for a long while.

September 30th. Robin-song rains down on me from every tree while I sit on the lawn. Blackcap Robin's song is now richer and includes more phrases imitative of a Blackcap. It is an unusual song, with few ordinary Robin passages. The south-west Robin has become more assertive for Blackcap Robin flew right across her territory and now seems trying to squeeze himself into a portion of her land. A long chase ensues on this southern part of the lawn.

I take my chair to the orchard, where I have not sat for many weeks. A Blackbird is singing subsong there, and I want to listen. Directly I sit down, Dobs appears and perches on my knee. Then New Robin comes 'tick-ing' along, looking like an artificial clockwork toy bird, the way he jerks up his tail and flicks his wings. Dobs bristles, the red flame gathers in his eyes, he flies at the intruder and a chase begins around the orchard trees near me, three of the other invaders joining in. Apparently they all want to possess the orchard because I am there, for they have not disputed over this territory before. I begin to fear the object for possession that causes much of this strife is myself. When I return to the front garden the Robins follow and sing from trees surrounding me there. This seems to show that territory is not the whole cause of their determination to get near my cottage. A power of reasoning seems indicated, for they all discern where the source of food comes from and wish to secure ME, not only the land for their winter territory.

October 3rd. New Robin now displays a draggled, loose feather, waving behind his rump – a sign of further encounters with Blackcap Robin, who still sings in the adjacent apple-tree. Dobs, looking spick and span, seems now to have settled his disputes. New Robin has gained the west window of the cottage and nearly half the lawn in line with this window. Beyond this he is not allowed to encroach, with one exception. The bird-bath is just inside Dobs's territory. New Robin is allowed an evening bath, taken always *after* Dobs, apparently by arrangement.

The above settlement between New Robin and Dobs proved final. Blackcap Robin was pushed farther away from the cottage by New Robin, and he finally settled at the back of West Garden orchard. The demure-looking south-west Robin held her added portion up to the flower-beds. Dobs was successful in ousting his mate from the kitchen door. She retreated into East Garden and even through the bitter frosts and snows of almost the worst winter within living human memory, she never ventured to seek crumbs from the cottage back door.

The difference in Dobs's method of dealing with each intruder was always noticeable. As my notes reveal, he was constantly on guard against his mate but never attacked her. The means employed to keep her away were calm song, determined and persistent; occasional chasing or very mild display consisting of puffing out his feathers – which to the human eye made him look an important bird not to be disobeyed! Yet he seemed more concerned over keeping the back door from his mate than in attending to west Robin's threats of intrusion on the west side of the cottage. These he settled surprisingly quickly by song sounding fiercer than he ever used for his mate. West Robin and Dobs rolled together under the tree once or twice, but there was not vicious action in this conflict and Dobs's expression did not show fury as with New Robin. With west Robin his song was loud and emphatic, but he never resorted to spluttering notes or hysterical-sounding shrillness. From the first his manner with New Robin was altogether different. Directly he sighted New Robin he became agitated, his eyes flamed, his voice became shrill, he spluttered and used distortion display to its fullest extent. He pounced down and attacked so violently that I had to frighten them apart for fear death would result from his vicious action. But the attention he payed to south-west Robin's encroachment on his land was scarcely worth mentioning, so mild was his expostulation. Going from one to another of all these intruders he always changed tactics according to the individual. This seems to show that display is not only an automatic reaction but a controlled proceeding, used with judgment according to assessment and knowledge of the opponent.

The following autumn, which preceeded an exceptionally mild winter, Dobs had an easy time. There were no battles for territory in front of my cottage and his mate retreated to East Garden without giving any trouble. I noticed that Robins were more evenly distributed over uninhabited surrounding land. I comment upon this because the influx of Robins to my garden in autumn has always appeared to be in relation to the hardness of the coming winter. I also notice that Tits and other individuals under close observation will choose more sheltered roosts when bad weather is ahead, although at the time of going to roost no sign is apparent of the sudden change, which comes after midnight. Another case of precognition of weather changes is that they will suddenly eat much more about two days previous to a cold spell. At the time of their sudden appetite the day may be very mild and humans unaware of the severe weather ahead.

CHAPTER 5

Recognition, Friendship and Games

The following spring, although Dobs then had all my front lawn and half the orchard, his mate nested in East Garden. I saw very little of her, but Dobs sought all his food in my garden, only entering East Garden for necessary visits to the nest. On the few occasions when she tried to take food from me Dobs interfered, pouncing down and chasing her away then returning to get some cake himself. If it was the period of feeding his mate he gave the cake to her, but later, when she was feeding the young, he still drove her from me and snatched the food she wanted for her nestlings, either eating it himself or taking it to the young.

It amuses me sometimes to work Dobs up into a fury. I know some of the things that set him off! When many birds are crowding round me, waiting to be handed food, I hold out one bit of cheese to a Tit who quickly takes it from my hand. Then Dobs sees me produce a pellet of bread, which I offer him. His look of anger is worth studying. He stays where he is, glaring at me and watching for cheese to replace the bread. If I then hand a Tit another piece of cheese the fat is in the fire! Dobs starts attacking first one bird then another, charging about like a madman until he has cleared all the birds away. He does not then come and ask for cheese, he is also angry with me, so turns his back with a flick of his tail, shakes his ruffled feathers and flies to a tree where he sings loudly, his back still towards me. After a little he returns in a good mood and even if there are many Tits around he waits very patiently until every bird has had cheese before taking some himself.

He knows I object to his attacking other birds, especially when they are on my hand. These attacks appear to be jealousy, as Robins always like to have the field to themselves. I find all tame ones are liable to sudden tempers when they see other birds on my hand, but this angry charging of other species is quite different from their reaction to another Robin. They try and ward off one of their own species with much display, before it has a chance to perch on my hand.

I find from close observation that birds have no difficulty over recognising and remembering each other individually. They also can distinguish individual humans, as the following will show.

When Dobs's offspring were fledged he tried to prevent their going near me – unlike some parent Robins who have liked me to help feed their young until the time came to drive them away. One of the young from his second brood caused him much trouble and refused to leave for some weeks after Dobs had got rid of the rest of the brood. Whenever chased by his angry parent, Dobs's son flew to the top of my head or avoided trouble by retreating next door until Dobs was out of sight, but little Dobson always returned, especially if I called his name. When his red breast-feathers began to appear Dobs grew really fierce and eventually the youngster had to leave. I completely lost sight of him for nearly three months then news came that a ringed Robin had been seen near a farmhouse about a mile from my cottage. I hurried there and was told the pink-ringed Robin had appeared the previous week when the farmer's wife was mowing the lawn. It had flown along in front of the machine just as the youngster used to do when I was mowing. He had later flown across the lane to a small enclosure and had not been seen since. I went into the enclosure, calling his name. Almost at once Dobson appeared on a tree beside me, his head-feathers raised, his eyes glittering, apparently with excitement. He may also have associated the sight of me with Dobs pouncing on him, hence the raised head-feathers, for I noticed he looked around carefully with an expectant pose and head stretched right up so he could get full view over the branch on which he was perched. Immediately I held out my hand he flew to it with his former confidence, ate some cake and returned to the bough where he warbled a quiet song with eyes fixed upon me. He did not again look around for Dobs – if this was his reason for that action at first – nor were his head-feathers raised any more. When I walked away he hopped to the end of the bough where he could get the best view of my retreating figure; on looking back before turning the corner I saw him craning his neck out to keep me in sight. A month later I went again to visit him. The farmer's wife had once or twice seen him in the interval, but he would not perch on her hand. This time he met me in the lane outside the enclosure as soon as I called his name. He sang a few notes, looking at me with the same excited glint in his eye but this time without raised head-feathers, nor did he stretch up his head to search the distance as before. At once he flew to my hand with accustomed familiarity. Afterwards I visited him at intervals of a month, six weeks and four months, and although my clothes in winter were completely different and new to him, this did not affect his immediate recognition. Once he flew to me in the lane before I called him, proving my voice was not his only means of recognition. He did not always keep to the same part of the enclosure or lane, his winter territory was very extensive and he encroached on that of other Robins at times, especially near the two farmhouses – a second farm being four large fields away from the enclosure he had at first occupied. Several other people, when seeing me with Dobson on my hand in the lane, tried to coax him on to theirs but without success, this leaving no doubt that he remembered and recognised me individually. An interval of eight months had elapsed the last time I passed along Dobson's lane. When near his territory I stopped to talk to someone. A minute later he flew towards me, straightway perching on the hand held out to greet him. He ate ten pieces of cake instead of the usual three or four, his eyes glittered with excitement and his head-feathers were slightly raised as he looked at me and sang subsong perched very near. There were no signs of another Robin in the lane nor did Dobson look around as if expecting one to appear; this time I think the head-feathers were raised because of my presence.

Birds are able to distinguish individual humans from afar, for those that are tamest often fly across meadows and along roads to meet me, apparently spotting me from tree-tops. It is not my clothes that are responsible for their ability to recognise me, for on one occasion I left home by the road, wearing a blue coat and head-scarf and returned across fieldpaths in a green mackintosh and hood, purposely pulled low over my face. Both had been purchased while out, but the birds flew as usual to meet me, recognising me from across two long fields. In winter, when very hungry, several Great Tits have sometimes flown to a nearby bus stop to meet my return bus on the rare occasions when I take this double-decker which passes my house to the county town. I presume they watch me get into it and remember this when two hours later the bus returns.

Close watch is kept over all my movements, and I find they often know what I am going to do from seeing my preparations. For instance, one winter when my hot-water supply failed I took weekly afternoon baths at a friend's house. After the third time Great and Blue Tits had learnt where I was going when they saw my basket filled with bath gear; directly I started out they flew on in front, along and across the road, and perched in my friend's garden to await my arrival, their purpose being to get a feed from my hand before I disappeared. (Wherever I go the Tit-box is taken, so they are not disappointed when they do clever things.) The birds never flew in advance to this house except when I went out prepared for a bath.

Their reaction to humans varies according to the person. Some people who come to my cottage always induce fear, others they treat with comparative friendliness and enter the room while they are there without concern, although they never behave quite normally until alone with me again. Two people entering the room generally frightens them away for a few minutes, and it takes them longer to gain courage to enter again when two people are with me than when there is only one. Three strangers they fear still more, which shows that up to a point they are aware of numbers. This applies to whether the people are speaking and moving or quiet and still, it seeming the sight of the extra person that disturbs them. There have been some exceptional occasions when birds have entered the room confidently before two or even four strangers, and it is curious to find that their reactions to people are frequently in sympathy with my thoughts.

Among themselves they also have likes and dislikes. Sometimes special friendships between the young of a brood are formed as soon as they leave the nest, if not before. The two birds become inseparable companions, doing everything together until one or both leave the territory. Twist and her sister was one example of this – page 26. Two fledgling male Great Tits were another example. They were like twins, indistinguishable from each other in appearance and always together. Among their games was the following, played with much twittering. One twin would lightly touch the tip of his brother's wing, which sent him hopping quickly a few twigs away – this game being always played in the trees. Twin I followed him, twittering excitedly and again touched his wing-tip, the game continuing like this until Twin II, with much sign of merriment, changed over and became the toucher. Fledgling Great Tits, when playing with each other, have a delightful laughter note, soft but unmistakably the excited chuckling of enjoyment over their game. This note is not used for other occasions. The Twins were always playing together with 'laughter-notes' and I never saw them apart until one day an accident happened to one of the brothers. All day long he had to keep quiet and still, holding a broken leg tucked between feathers underneath him. This puzzled his brother, who at first kept trying to entice him to play by touching his wing-tips and pulling his tail. Then he attempted to pull the injured leg down in a gently playful manner. This obviously hurt the injury and brought a sharp scold-note and peck of reproval. The uninjured Twin stared a moment in apparent astonishment then flew away, all playfulness gone from his ways. After this he kept apart from his brother and moped by himself with as forlorn an air as the twin who had suffered the fracture. I once saw him place food within reach of his injured brother, afterwards quickly flying away. In ten days the fracture was healed but a callus, looking like a false joint, had formed in the centre of the tarsus, the lower half being set out of line. The leg seemed strong and normal except in appearance. The brothers never resumed their friendship, both seemed dissatisfied with remaining in my garden and they left separately, first the one who had been injured, a week later his brother.

In winter, two years later, a strange-looking Great Tit appeared, with feathers artificially blackened as if he had been bathing in black ink. He flew straight to my hand, as if he had never been away, the peculiarity of his crooked leg making identification unmistakable. He disappeared again in spring and never returned. This was a good test of bird memory. I think those who are tame when very young never forget. This may account for some old, ill or injured birds who occasionally appear on my doorstep, astonishing me by coming straight to my hand. I have lost identification of the individual but their memory serves them well when needing help.

I find the various males and females of my garden know each other even at a distance, also, the males who are mated never respond to the mating signals of a female not their own although they may watch her with interest. In a garden like mine, where as many as possible of each species stay to nest after winter hospitality, their territory is generally not large, so frequently males come into contact with females mated to a neighbouring male. The Chaffinch is the only species in my garden who has attempted coition with a female who was not his mate. She was slightly injured and had difficulty in flying. The Chaffinch pursued her on the ground, uttering the note peculiar to mating season. She tried to dodge him, but he got on her back and was shaken off. He became persistent and I interfered, the male then returned to his own mate.

Parent birds also never mistake fledglings of a neighbouring brood for their own. They will sometimes show concern for a straying youngster of a very tender age, but older fledglings are generally chased away if they are of an age when their parents still feed them.

Birds, like humans, need occupation as an outlet for their vitality and for a pastime. Many Great Tits are indoors with me for much of the time during autumn and winter, and I find it necessary to provide toys for them, otherwise they choose a pastime that inflicts damage to something of value to me. Before I knew that Great Tits liked toys I found one of four celluloid parakeets (from a Christmas tree) missing from its perch on a holly bough in my room. That same day I saw a Great Tit fly to the holly, knock one of the remaining parakeets on to the floor, then, holding it with one foot, begin hammering, pecking and pulling the bird in mock-ferocious manner, often picking it up and turning it over, probably because this made it rattle. Having succeeded in tearing its side open, the Tit flew with it out of the window. Until all these toy birds had been disposed of, the Tit had no eye for anything else in the room. Some clever imitations of Blue Tits, made in felt, were ill-treated in the same manner, but if nothing as realistic and exciting is in sight, Great Tits will seize my ink-bottle stopper and, knowing this to be forbidden, fly quickly out of the window with it while I am filling my pen. When wanting to cork the bottle I see the Tit on the lawn or a tree branch, ill-treating the stopper like he did the toy parakeets and stuffed birds. These were not regarded as live things, merely as toys that amused him and something on which to vent high spirits. Their violent attacks upon these toy birds had resemblance to the reactions some birds show to stuffed hawks.

Unfortunately, it is not only the ink-bottle stopper they destroy. When they see me writing, dipping my pen in the ink-pot, their favourite way of attracting my attention is to upset the ink. They do it deliberately, then escape my wrath by quick flight out of the window. They have various ways of trying to divert me from writing, often hammering on my skull, and sitting on my shoulder to pull my hair and tweak my ears, this meaning they want nuts and cheese. If I refuse to be bullied into noticing them sometimes one of them will walk on to my page and carefully lift my nib from the paper, looking up at me while doing it. This forces me to stop, so the Tits have won! The writing of this book provides good Tit sport. Many of my notes are on loose sheets; these they watch me place in order on the table beside the typewriter, then they fly up and purposely scatter pages to the floor. They have developed a technique for upsetting things by landing with a rush and quick skidding of their feet. Together with the breeze made by their wings, it scatters pages with effective speed; also, large cake-tins they send crashing to the floor by this quick skidding method; with luck the lid falls off through the force of the crash and after a hasty flight to the window, because of the noise – they return to eat the contents of the tin. Another game is to perch on the roller of the typewriter when I pause for thought, and if my hands are not held over the page, they tear a hole in the last sentence while I am thinking of the next! Occasionally a Tit taps a key sharply with his beak but, luckily, the resulting movement he finds alarming.

Close observation of bird-life reveals that many species, especially when young, spend much time in play. The young of some species associate with other species in chasing games and other recreation. Especially young Willow-Warblers and sometimes Chiffchaffs, delight in chasing other species, often much to their annoyance. A Blue Tit is the Willow-Warbler's favourite for this game, perhaps because this Tit is responsive. In my orchard I have seen these two chasing each other around the trees until the Blue Tit, less active on the wing, retired to rest. The young Willow-Warbler paused only a moment to look for the next most suitable victim. He saw a Spotted Flycatcher perched on the fence with dark eyes intent on choosing a fly, a bird light on the wing and worthy of chase. Before the chosen fly could be snapped the Willow-Warbler was after him, the sober grey Flycatcher swift and silent in flight, the sprightly young Willow Warbler, in fresh plumage of primrose and green, noisily snapping his beak as with agile flight he chased the Flycatcher around trees and across the orchard. Directly the Flycatcher alighted on another perch, the Willow-Warbler turned to race after a Chaffinch who was pursuing his mate. But the Chaffinch was engrossed in his own affairs so attention was turned to a Great Tit, flying from her nest to find food for her young. The Tit scolded angrily for parent birds have no time for play. The game often lasts a considerable time with scarcely a break, for when other birds fail there is always a Sparrow to chase.

Occasionally Willow-Warblers and Chiffchaffs will keep to their species for the chasing game, but usually in their case, a different species is chosen for play. When chasing Swallows the Willow-Warbler meets his match in sharp turns of the wing and swiftness of flight. One day five baby Swallows were perched close together on the wire outside my window. A young Willow-Warbler was perched on the tree nearby, watching as eagerly as the baby Swallows for the parent birds to fly back with food. Each time they returned, the teasing Willow-Warbler chased them, making so much confusion that the Swallows dropped half their beakful of flies in their haste to stuff them down the babies' throats and get away from the Willow-Warbler. Sometimes the Swallows snapped at the teasing imp but it made no difference. The Willow-Warbler seemed in his element, matching his swift flight against a Swallow's. The plumage of these two species made a lovely contrast; the delicate spring-like colouring of the small, slight Warbler against the deep night-blue of the larger long-winged bird. Yet the Willow-Warbler's wings sped him as quickly as the Swallow's longer ones. This can only be for short flights, the Warbler putting forth all his strength.

Swallows and Swifts, in chasing games, keep to their own species. I have seen Swallows play a wonderfully graceful game of catching a feather. It was one August afternoon when I was sitting at the top of a steeply sloping farm field in the uplands of Devon that I noticed more Swallows than usual were wheeling close together over one part of the field, presumably an abundance of flies on the hot, sunny day being the cause. Ducks and Geese roamed in this field and the grass was sprinkled with a few white breast-feathers. I then saw a Swallow dip to the ground and sweep upwards with one of these feathers held in his beak and, circling above the other Swallows, he let it fall. As it floated down it was caught by one of the wheeling birds who then rose above the rest and again the feather was let loose, to float down through the many circling Swallows. This time it nearly reached earth, then one bird swept down with graceful dip and flicker of wings, rising aloft with the feather, to drop it once more. Sometimes their wayward toy would fall uncaught, perhaps too worn for further use; then quickly a bird swooped to the grass, seized another feather while on the wing and the play continued as before. It was a beautiful game to watch in the setting of hills, with a background of wild moorland and far away the blue haze of distant sea meeting the deeper blue sky.

The Swallow's game may be evolved from the simple one, common to many species, of picking up things, dropping and watching them fall, although I have never seen a Swallow do this. An untamed Jackdaw once took a fancy for entering my bedroom down the chimney at dawn. Several mornings he came, and getting familiar with the room, he flew to my dressing-table. In spite of difficulty in balancing on the polished surface, he skidded about and picked up small things, dropped them over the table edge and turned his head sideways with an intent expression, to watch them fall. Eventually, he knocked over a photograph frame, and the crash sent him flying out of the window.

One of my Great Tits' toys is a covered glass jar containing seashells. They pluck off the lid, pick out the shells and chuck them with a sharp twist of their heads either down on the floor or across the room, always watching them fall with interest. Matches are treated in the same manner and often when I have been out I return to find matches strewn all over the room, the box having been pulled open and lying in two halves on the floor.

One of the great charms of House-Martins is their playfulness. They have fun even in the cradle. I have watched a young one stretching half its body out of the nest to play with a smaller Martin in a neighbouring nest. Twittering excitedly, with head craned forward, it just managed to touch the tip of the other baby's beak. The smaller one entered into the fun and bobbed up from its nest to take the kiss, both withdrawing directly afterwards. Then the bigger one, behaving excitedly, began poking its brother – or sister – as if trying to egg it on to join in the fun, but getting no response, the merry Martin again turned to the neighbouring baby and, with a terrific effort, heaved almost all its body outside the nest, with eager twitterings touching the small one's beak. This touch or kiss was received with obvious amusement by the little one, who repeatedly retired into its nest then bobbed up again to thrust its head forward for another touch of beaks. The game continued for some time, the enjoyment of the Martins so infectious it was impossible to watch without laughter. The elder one, in its eager excitement, made stretching efforts that could easily end in falling from the nest and the parents evidently disapproved. When preparing for their second brood they wisely sealed up the old entrance hole, making another on the opposite side of their nest where there were no neighbours, so the young of their next brood were not tempted to play risky games with neighbouring young before they were fledged.

Many birds play in a puppy-like manner at shaking and biting of things inedible. I once watched a young Herring-Gull on the bank of a Cornish estuary treating my small umbrella in this manner. After a droll examination he played for a long while at shaking and biting it, then began pulling and letting go the elastic band, watching the effect with keen interest. Previously he had investigated my satchel, pulled out the contents, discarded some sketching materials but seized upon my lunch, taking a bite from a sandwich which he surprisingly spat out – this was before food rationing! His attention then turned to my bare legs which he pecked several times and the buttons on my plimsoles catching his eye, he tried to pull them off, diving first at one shoe then the other in playful manner. When tired of playing with the umbrella he fell asleep beside it, enabling me to make a quick sketch of him before he awoke. I learnt afterwards the explanation of his tameness. A month or two previously he had been rescued from the river, coated in oil and unable to fly. Someone had cared for him, cleaned his feathers and given him food.

Although the Song-Thrush is not a playful bird, a youngster in my garden spent so much time shaking and pulling at some rope attached to a stick that he unravelled it, and I removed the rope lest he entangled himself.

The Blackbird is an individualist in all his ways. His idea of a game seems to be property ownership, and he plays with a chosen friend. If either friend is prevented from playing, the game does not continue with another Blackbird neighbour. For three years, at all seasons, one Blackbird in my orchard played with a neighbour friend at owning a small tree-stump. As the stump was the opposite side of the orchard to the neighbour's territory, this was not a dispute for land but a game that both birds appeared to enjoy spending much time over every day. Even in nesting season they played for a short while in the evenings. If the neighbour did not turn up, my Blackbird flew next door and they returned together to the tree-stump. The game began by typical Blackbird stalking, taking turns to be leader or follower. Then one bird flew onto the tree-stump, the other quickly chased him off and perched there himself, with tail outspread, head upturned and humorous cockiness in his erect posture. In his turn he was chased off, the stalking began again and the game was repeated, often continuing for hours with slight variations. There was some resemblance to the children's game of 'I'm the King of the Castle.' I have seen many other male Blackbirds at similar play, always with a chosen friend, other neighbours just as accessible being treated differently and generally chased right off the territory. Darky and Oakleaf were another example of this (page 59).

In all these things there is much evidence that the mind of a bird works according to the individual as well as to the species.

Birds sunbathe frequently in summer and autumn, often using certain sheltered tree-stumps or dead branches for this purpose. In my orchard a half-fallen, dead apple-tree is one of the chosen sun-traps. I first discovered this one midsummerday morning, just as the sun reached its zenith. In the leafy orchard, where the grass was almost shoulder high, this half-fallen, bare-branched tree stood out like a grey rock does in a deep green sea. Along its sloping trunk and bare arms there were several sunbathing birds lying flat on their breasts, their wings and tails outspread so each feather shone with the full light of sunshine. Their heads were all turned to one side and slightly raised to the sun, their beaks held half-open as if to let the sun shine inside too. Three Willow-Warblers were on the upper branch, some Great Tits and Blue Tits lay on the gnarled stump, while the thick base of the sloping trunk had been chosen by two young Blackbirds.

Sometimes a familiar bird will spread wings and tail to sunbathe on my lap or in the crook of my arm. Every feather on the head and body is raised and the beak is always held half-open, perhaps for breathing reasons, as in heat waves they occasionally fly about with beaks agape. Goldfinches in sunbathing pose are a very lovely sight.

I once saw two Herons sunbathing in a buttercup meadow, near a river. Their long necks were stretched out to the full and pointed upwards with heads held aslant and beaks open, their half-spread wings held low and away from their sides. Against the golden background in the bright sunlight these queer, white, snake-like necks, toning into pale grey at the back, looked indescribably odd. They remained motionless for so long that it seemed they were not birds but some form of symbolic statue, expressing something weird and remote.

Along that same river there were Lapwing and Redshank associating in mixed parties, bathing and splashing together in the shallows and sunning themselves side by side on the stones at the water's edge. Certain striking contrasts in these two species make this friendly association very beautiful to watch. I made the following notes at the time – Lapwing hover with flapping wings and legs dangling over the silken sheen of the water which reflects them perfectly. How they enjoy the water, bathing and splashing then shaking their ragged wings to dry. Some chasing each other excitedly and tumbling close above the water with wild, wailing cries, sweeping upwards in a curve then dropping sheer, wings aslant, broad petalled and ragged tipped as if torn by winds. The Redshanks are slick in flight, their clean-cut, pointed wings taking them with swift precision. They call in pure, liquid sounding notes while skimming the water's surface in rapid zigzag shoots, or swinging upwards in wide sweeping curves, over and down the grassy bank, their legs sticking out behind like little tongues of flame. They perch among shining wet stones at the water's edge, suddenly becoming almost invisible, their colouring changed from the dazzling white and tortoiseshell shades seen in flight, to a dull greyish tone, matching the stone's shadows. They pause motionless for a while as if dozing, then suddenly one or two arise, shoot across the river, calling and trilling; others follow in twos or threes to settle elsewhere and, when they alight, their long wings are held suspended upwards a moment then folded in orderly manner by bringing them forward, round and down to their sides.

Flight and song is used by many species as their principal form of recreation. This will be referred to in separate chapters.

CHAPTER 6

Roosts, Food, and Nesting-Boxes

Birds look ahead more than is generally supposed. They often hunt for and test roosts in the morning; if the roost is later occupied by another bird, fighting will follow with fierce attack by the original owner and poor defence by the new occupant. Once a Great Tit, hard up for a bed, found a Blue Tit roosting in a box hung to the window-frame. He went through threatening fight displays and pecked the Blue Tit in her bed. She put up hot defence, the Great Tit failed to get the roost so flew away. Soon he came back and started a violent attack on the box from the back end, where the wood had rotted and was reinforced with cardboard. His onslaught was effective, the back end gave way and the Blue Tit was forced to leave her roost; so did the Great Tit, for it was now of doubtful value. I hastily repaired the damage. The Great Tit immediately flew up and sat inside the box. Blue Tit followed, squealing loudly and butting with lowered head at the Great Tit in the usual manner of 'Billy Biter' when determined to win a fight. The Great Tit did not defend himself, and in a few seconds flew off, the Blue Tit entering her roost. It seemed the Great Tit knew he had done wrong; all his fury was spent, he looked guilty and drooped his tail as he flew away. On following evenings he made a habit of peering inside the roost to make sure the Blue Tit was there; she always was, so he hopped on to the roof, gave one or two sharp raps, as if for fun, then flew elsewhere to bed. Sometimes he glanced with a queer expression at the back end before leaving the box, perhaps remembering but never repeating his onslaught.

Where to find safe shelter for the night is the first great problem the young fledgling has to face. One morning I watched a young Great Tit spend a long time trying to widen a narrow hole in a tree. He managed to get out a few bits of rotten wood, but his beak was not yet strong enough for the job and he could not widen the hole sufficiently for turning round inside it; a bird will not roost back to the opening. There was only one possible solution for the young Tit, he tried entering the hole backwards. It was amusing to watch his efforts, for steering the tip of his long tail into the opening proved very difficult and he went through many antics, always with his head turned round to keep an eye on the troublesome tail, before he successfully got the tip into the hole. Then he slowly squeezed the rest of his body backwards along the narrow, level crevice. It was obviously a tight fit and his head came too near the entrance for safety as a roost, but he stayed there for some minutes then came out and went in search of a better one, which later was found and he slept in it at night. He had worked very hard for his bed.

I sometimes find the smallest member of a newly-fledged brood – various species – at dusk seeking cover on the ground under leaves of plants or old tree-roots. Its parents make every effort to entice it to safe roosting perches, but the fledgling perhaps feels the earth provides more warmth and shelter from wind. I have tried placing these small fledglings on safe tree-perches, thinking their difficulty might be to fly upwards, but they leave the high perch and immediately seek ground cover again, although they are birds of the trees. They seem not to have instinctive feeling for roosting above ground, but gradually learn to find safe cover at night in such places as are typical of the species.

One evening at dusk, ten-thirty Double Summer Time, I had just got into bed when a baby Great Tit, with a tail barely a quarter of an inch long, fluttered in through the window and settled on my chest. After close inspection of my face it cuddled down within an inch of my chin, head tucked under wing. It was such a tiny ball of fluffed-out feathers and light as thistle-down. After a while I tried to lift without wakening it, but resenting interference, it quickly scrambled still farther underneath my chin, so my head had to be held up while it continued to sleep for an hour. Then I made another attempt to lift it, but at the first touch it fluttered to my shoulder, falling asleep again instantaneously. Finally, I put it into a little box by my bed. This was not to its liking, it became wide awake, flew to the window and slept until dawn, clinging to the inside of the frame, then I put it outside so it could join the rest of the brood. (It was one of Jane's smallest from a second brood.)

Blue Tits have less difficulty in finding a roost because, being so small, they can squeeze into such narrow crevices. But the very young fledgling sometimes underestimates its size. One evening at sundown nine babies fluttered into my sitting-room and tried to find roosts in cracks of doors or other such crevices too narrow even for a newly-fledged Blue Tit. One fluttered up to my handbag which hung on a door handle, and made many comical efforts to squeeze itself under the flap. This also was unsuccessful so the whole brood trooped out again with much chatter, and were led by their parents to the trees.

Sometimes it happens that one of my youngster Great Tits, instead of coming to his accustomed roost in a box on the picture rails above my bed, goes off roaming in the early hours of evening and does not get back till morning. Directly he enters the room – about 7.30 a.m. – he flies straight to his bed and stays there some minutes, perhaps having missed the comfortable roost on his night out! He goes early to bed that evening.

There is much variation in the hours birds go to roost. Some individuals in a species seem to need more sleep than others, they not only go to bed sooner, but often sleep later in the morning. With Great Tits the variation may be as much as two hours – this having nothing to do with age. Some also sleep more soundly and wake up less often in the night. Curley, for instance, slept through the short summer night without once moving on her perch, while others may turn about many times, even pecking the bottom of their roosts in the night. Curley was the first to sleep above my bed on the picture rail; soon both my sitting-room and bedroom had young Great Tits roosting along the rails, the corners being favoured and fought for. One night Curley fell from her perch in her sleep, for the rail is slippery and no interlock of feet is possible. She was rather frightened for a moment, but directly I turned on the light she flew up to the rail again and slept. Next night I gave her a cardboard box on the picture rail, many more of these afterwards supplied to meet the Tits' demands. Instead of hanging pictures on my rails, the walls are hung with sugar and cereal cartons; often by day the Tits hammer on these boxes in play and make holes in the roofs of their roosts, but I never interfere as it keeps them employed upon damaging their own beds instead of my curtains, armchairs and other furniture, which they pull to bits. They become very possessive over these boxes and the owners fly at any other Tit who by day hammers at the cardboard for fun. After they have grown adult plumage they dislike sleeping near each other and short squabbles arise every evening over the roosting-boxes. Those most determined to remain take possession of the rooms, and the others are driven away by degrees. If the weather is very bad some often return to their old boxes and no squabbling occurs, those who have taken possession becoming tolerant. Great Tits are so individual that there is an infinite amount of variety over roosting behaviour as in everything else they do, this making it very interesting to watch. At daybreak every morning I waken to the sound of birds' wings as they flutter through the darkened room and fly out of the window over the top of drawn curtains.

One wet winter night at one o'clock, a very strong wind arose, driving the rain through the open window. I got up, turned on the light and my hand was on the latch to close the fanlight window when one of my Great Tits flew in from the dark night and went straight to his roosting-box above my bed. It was a strange and lovely sensation to see a bird fly in from the darkness of the wild, wet night.

In autumn and winter my male Blackbird, Darky, and his mate sometimes take no notice of each other during the daytime, but this is what I often see at roost hour. The female appears on the lawn at sundown, looks up at a tree, gives a few wing twitches or cocks her tail upwards. Darky then flies down to a different part of the lawn, he eyes her from the distance. Both feed for a while then she flies to roost in a macrocarpus near my window. He slightly tilts his head towards her, showing consciousness of her movement, but continues to feed and hop around the lawn in the fading light. Eventually he flies to roost on another branch of the same tree. She may go to bed half an hour before him or wait until dusk, he following almost immediately afterwards, for roosting hours vary. Weather affects this, also if there are other Blackbirds on the lawn they stay longer, perhaps finding their presence of interest. I made the following notes on September 23rd. – At sundown, seven Blackbirds were feeding on the lawn until too dark to distinguish young birds from old, or sexes. They flitted about with quick movements, in the darkness looking like a lot of gnomes, fascinating to watch. Suddenly one bird struck up a piercing 'tchink, tchink' and still 'tchinking,' he flew to roost in the macrocarpus. Directly he flew up all the rest flitted silently away to bed. It is the first time this autumn that roosting has been advertised by this call; probably it now will continue, roosting territory being of importance in autumn and winter.

On the rare occasions when I get on my bed in the afternoon, the Great Tit who sleeps above me perches for a moment on the screen beside the bed, surveying my recumbent form; then he flies to his roost on the picture rail above. I hear him give a few preening movements before he settles down quietly for about three minutes. After that he becomes restless, begins tapping the bottom of his bed in play, then flies off out of the window or comes down to my bed to amuse himself. The birds appear to regard the bed as my nest, for I have sometimes had twenty or more playing on it when I have been ill and, instead of making messes on sheets and blankets, they fly to the window-sill or screen, where newspaper is spread for sanitary purposes, returning again to the bed directly afterwards. Only if they are suddenly annoyed or I speak to them severely for tearing at my book or pulling a blanket to pieces, they retort by making an immediate mess on the bed then flying to the window. They never play about on the bed unless I am on it.

One winter, when I was ill for two or three weeks, Tits amused themselves on the bed every day in a variety of ways. Some played at possession of me, so it seemed, and displayed while walking about all over me, tails fully spread, wings half-opened and drooped, heads stiffly held up, their beaks pointing to the ceiling. They muttered queer language to each other while displaying, and their expressions were so humorous it was impossible to watch without laughter. It was obviously all in fun, the birds entering into the game were not at that time disputing for territory, for it was early winter. Another amusement was to slide down the slopes of my pillow, which miniature alpine sport some seemed to enjoy. They climbed to the top, then slowly slid down without moving their feet. Occasionally they rolled on the bed, two together with feet interlocked, quarrelling over a piece of cheese. They became very tyrannical when I had no more cheese to give them, especially Baldhead, who is a determined bird with a sharp beak. When he stood over me with his threatening look, demanding what I was unable to give, there was need for complete submergence under bedclothes. If I put out my head to breathe he pounced at my nose and gave a few sharp pecks to my cheeks so the sheet had to be quickly pulled over my head again. But his wits were as sharp as his beak; he tried to get at me by tugging at the top of the sheet, lifting the edge and squeezing himself underneath until he reached my hair which he pulled vigorously, while the other Tits walked over the sheet above my face, giving occasional pecks to try to remove it. This type of treatment is always inflicted upon me when my supply of cheese and nuts runs out – in these days of rationing and food scarcity too often occurring.

If they think I have any peanuts they start chucking away other food given them and pester me persistantly for nuts until I take them to the cupboard where these are usually kept, and let them see for themselves the nut-tin is empty. They then understand and remember there are none until they see a fresh supply arrive. When Baldhead is shown the empty tin he looks very cross, the sudden change in his expression very noticeable, and he flies out of the window with a peculiar twitch of his tail which he gives when annoyed. But he soon returns to perch on my shoulder and accept some cheese. I used to keep the few peanuts obtainable in a table-drawer, but some of the Great Tits found a way of getting at them, even when it was closed. They climbed up underneath the table and entered the back end of the drawer, pulled out some of the many folded papers and letters which blocked their way and heaved these over the back-end to the floor. This was a hard struggle and took them many minutes. Then they squeezed themselves along the drawer from the back to the front, where the nuts were kept. It was an astonishing feat, for the folded papers almost filled the rather long but narrow drawer. They deserved the nuts for their effort, but because the floor was always being littered with papers, that had to be replaced in the drawer many times a day, I had to keep their nuts elsewhere.

When my Great Tits want to get a nut that I am gripping firmly between my fingers, they first make efforts to pull it out, if this fails to release my hold they try to pull my fingers away from the nut, between whiles throwing me many impatient glances.

Birds, like humans, have individual tastes in food. One Thrush likes dried currants but will not eat bread unless snow covers the ground and he is desperately hungry; another Thrush refuses currants and likes bread. One Blackbird would not eat worms but lived on insects, fruit, etc. Darky sometimes eats a wasp after pulling out the sting, but I have never seen one eaten by any other Blackbird. Great Tits eat bees;

only one of my many Great Tits likes wasps; the sting of bees and wasps they always extract with much dexterity before eating.

Once I watched a youngster Great Tit cautiously approach a huge Bumble-Bee, gorging a fallen pear on the lawn. After a moment's hesitation the Tit gently tapped the bee's furry body with his beak. It made an angry buzz and tried to fly but could only crawl, which it did apace, the Tit hopping close behind and repeatedly prodding it on the back. They went half-way across the lawn in this manner, then the bee flew heavily away; the Tit gazed after it and gave a double-noted call. The young Great Tit is full of fun and curiosity; this incident, which was amusing to watch, had no connection with food, he was playing with the bee and, judging by his expression and manner, he was sorry when he lost his toy. They never eat Bumble-Bees.

Cheese is a popular food with Tits as with most birds, yet one or two Great Tits refuse it, liking animal fat and nuts, while another likes cheese but will not eat animal fat. Weather affects their choice of food. In cold spells they want more fat and cheese, in hot weather fat is not eaten, but heat does not put them off cheese and nuts. A few are fussy over the type of nut, but I have never yet had a Tit refuse peanuts. I recently obtained a coconut, for the first time since the war; the Tits looked at it nervously and did not begin to peck it until two hours after I hung it outside. Even when they did try eating it, to my surprise many of them were not keen on this type of nut; two or three Great Tits made a grimace and wiped their bills after pecking it, not returning for more. My birds are all well fed, probably they would devour the coconut if very hungry. I found the Blue Tits liked it better than the Great Tits, but even the Blue Tits were very moderate in the amount they ate, and they took plenty of bread and fat in proportion to the coconut. I believe the latter is rather indigestible food for birds and when giving one to the Tits care should be taken to supply fat and bread as well, otherwise from hunger they may eat too much of a food that is not good for them in large quantities.

I have some Great Tits who are fussy over the type of cheese I offer them. Process or Dutch is taken up and chucked across the room, while the kind to their taste is eaten with relish. A few individuals seem unable to digest fat. It is harmful to give this to small nestlings, especially Great Tits and probably all species of Tit nestlings. I once had a pair of Great Tits who fed their brood with much enthusiasm on large quantities of mutton fat. To my horror as well as the parents' distress, the nestlings never grew any feathers of the normal kind. When it was time for them to leave the nest they clambered out and fell to the ground, unable to fly. They were horrible-looking objects, dun-coloured and looking as if they had been dipped in grease, their undeveloped quills without a single coloured feather. Only three left the nest, I presume the others had died beforehand. These miserable fledglings were devoured by cats within half an hour. Their inexperienced but enthusiastic parents were both first-year birds — I also was ignorant over nestling diet in those days. This is the only case among all my birds, even first-year couples, of mistaken choice over food for their young. Always they give natural food entirely for the first few days after hatching, then they may add a little cheese, gradually increasing this. Tits will not give the nestlings any other artificial food except cheese or carefully selected peanuts, which they first chew into small fragments. In bad weather Great Tits sometimes overdo the amount of cheese they give their nestlings, with the result the babies shut their beaks tight, refusing to be cajoled into swallowing any more. The parent gives a gentle scold-note, tries every member of the brood, and if with no response, scolds them softly again and leaves the nest, either eating the cheese or chucking it away. Then the parent goes in search of a caterpillar, which the nestlings usually accept, but if too gorged with cheese even to manage this natural food, the parent leaves them for a while until their appetite returns. They are more careful afterwards not to overdo cheese, learning from experience. The same sort of thing happens with Blackbirds, but it is always the father bird who overdoes artificial food. I sometimes watch him trying, for five minutes on end, to stuff bread down a fledgling's closed beak, when it has been so overgorged with this type of food that it tries to escape its tiresome parent by flying away, but the father pursues it and persistently proffers the unwanted bread. Eventually the parent picks up an insect and this is generally accepted. The father Blackbird does not behave with quick understanding like the Great Tit parents, but he learns slowly what the Tit grasps at once.

There was an experiment made of trying to rear Bearded Tits in captivity. Here the parents behaved abnormally, as in most cases of birds who are not free. When their nestlings, from being overfed, did not open their beaks to take food, the parents cast them from the nest instead of waiting for them to get hungry again as my parent Tits have always done. The Tit nestling, if healthy, digests its food so quickly that it very soon gets an appetite again even if overfed; the Bearded Tits' nestlings may perhaps have been unhealthy through unsuitable food in captivity.

Robins and Sparrows seem to thrive on artificial food after the first few days. When Dobs's young are a week old he grabs all he can get of cake, bread, cheese, fat or lean meat, currants and sultanas, etc., and stuffs it down the throats of his nestlings; they never seem to refuse anything. The young Thrush seems not to thrive on such a diet and soon begins to spit out artificial food, gaping again at its parent who quickly seems to understand. Often in droughts, when there are few snails or worms obtainable, my young Thrushes will squat on the ground so their parents can more quickly pop quantities of ants into their beaks.

When I started putting up nesting-boxes for the birds I did not clean the used ones, thinking they would prefer them left undisturbed. Experience taught me this was wrong. I found the Tits who used uncleaned boxes were very restless at night and continually woke up to preen, while those from clean boxes were free of parasite troubles and never needed night preening. I used to watch Tits go to their uncleaned nesting-boxes, peep inside then hurriedly make one or two preening movements and fly away without entering. On examining the boxes I saw lice round the interior of the entrance hole. Directly I cleaned the boxes (a kettle of quite boiling water poured over all sides the surest and quickest method), the Tits occupied the boxes, and preening movements were not again made on looking inside. All the boxes I clean are used for roosting in winter and nesting in spring, those left uncleaned are not entered again, unless driven by necessity through scarcity of safe nesting-holes. Some people think 'leaving it to Nature' is best. But in supplying birds with artificial water-tight boxes we encourage them to use something not quite natural. The hole in a tree probably gets enough moisture through it for cleansing purposes. Also, I notice ants enter tree-holes where Tits have nested, not to nest there themselves, but for some definite reason. This, I think, may be for eating the lice. I have good reason for thinking this as the other day, when cleaning out the Tits' roost-boxes, some ants appeared and I watched them walk off with the bird lice I was scraping out of one of the boxes. Many species of birds, when suffering from this pest, pick up ants and place them between their feathers.

It is important to have the entrance hole of a nesting-box not less than nine inches from the bottom, for the cat's paw, when determined to claw out nestlings, is long and supple. The Blue Tit incident related on page 5 of Chapter 1 could only be accounted for by a cat getting at the nest; here the hole was five inches from the bottom. I have seen a cat get its paw to the nest of a six-inch length also. Since I took to making them at least nine inches there has been no more trouble with marauders. Tits like to have two or three inches of moss foundation to their nest so that, even apart from cats, the deeper boxes are much better. The young are apt to clamber out too soon if they have an entrance hole within easy reach from their nest, and an extra day or two in the box means their chance of surviving is more than doubled, for the fledgling weak on the wing is sure prey for its many enemies. They like plenty of room to stretch their wings before they fly, so the box should not be cramped in width. I make mine about seven inches by five inches or larger. Petrol cans are popular with Tits and I have had several occupied, but the young are, I think, better off in wooden boxes. Unless shaded from the sun, nest boxes should not face south or west. I find sunlight on the entrance hole late in the day encourages the young to flight at the wrong hour. Parents like them to fly from the nest early in the day, this giving time for them to find their feet and learn a little about safe perches before roost hour.

People frequently bring me birds they have picked up; some are badly injured, but more often they are suffering from a minor injury with shock and they would have recovered soon if left on a safe perch close to where found. The fright of unaccustomed human handling and being taken away from its home, although kindly meant, often results in its death. Sometimes, too, the bird brought me is merely an immature fledgling, which always is better left in a hedge or bush close to where it is found. If taken away from its parents it has little chance of survival for it is deprived of its natural food. People sometimes have told me they tried to revive the injured bird by giving it brandy, but this is very bad for birds. Water should be given as soon as possible and a little later some milk, bread, dipped in milk, and cheese, grated or broken into very small fragments. The bird may not be able to eat for a time, but the food can be left within its reach and then the quieter it is, the more chance it will have of recovery. The wild bird does not understand caresses, so there should be no petting and stroking of feathers. This may only aggravate the bird's fright. Alcohol is considered very bad for human beings in cases of head injuries, and it should be remembered that the same applies to birds, whatever their injury, but especially this should not be given to them when stunned.

CHAPTER 7

Finches and Others

BULLFINCH

Bullfinches inhabit my garden for the larger part of the year, only wandering farther afield during autumn and early winter when I do not see them for a few weeks. One spring I made the following notes of my Bullfinch, called Chanter because he sang a lovely little chant.

March 22nd. This morning I heard Chanter calling unusually loudly from the trees, so went out to watch. He flew round the garden, perching conspicuously on the tallest tree-tops, calling his loudest while jerking his tail and lifting his head, showing the full beauty of his glowing breast which was lit to intense brilliance by sunshine. Presently another Bullfinch appeared, I think Chanter's son for this male has always accompanied him and his mate since last summer. He flew close to Chanter, perching opposite him on the branch and seeming to communicate something to him. Chanter nodded his head several times while jerking his tail rapidly. Both birds then nodded, facing each other with heads nearly touching. Then the second Bullfinch flew off, over the trees to a meadow beyond. My instant impression was that this little ceremony meant they were parting company – whether correct or not the other Bullfinch was not again seen in my garden. Chanter's loud call-notes were resumed and soon his mate appeared on an adjoining tree. He flew towards her and perched on a bough a few feet away, looked at her a moment then flew right up and delicately touched her on the beak – a bird's kiss – flying back to his perch directly afterwards. She leant forward to receive the touch, carefully wiping her beak on the branch as soon as his back was turned. She then flew to a tree farther off from her mate, he followed to perch opposite, as before flying up in graceful manner to touch her bill, held out to him. For half an hour I watched them go from tree to tree, where always in the same way this one gentle touch on the beak was given and received without more bill-wiping from her in the intervals.

Later they flew to their last year's nesting site, a tall, thick bush in my neighbour's orchard.

March 25th. Progress seems to be made in Chanter's wooing. He and his mate were this morning perched a foot apart on the bough of a tree and he kept dancing up to her with quick eager movements, now giving her several billings each time. She was perched with her back to him, but always turned her head towards him for the billings. Later they fed on their old nesting-tree where now they are often seen. Chanter stretched out his head to peck a budding leaf on a twig almost out of reach, lost his balance and tumbled over, landing lower down on the bush. Completely unconcerned, he continued feeding from another twig above him as if the fall had been intentional. I have several times seen Bullfinches lose their balance and fall in disorderly manner to lower branches when trying to peck buds out of their reach.

On the days following the above notes, Chanter and his mate were always seen in close company; if she lost sight of him for a moment his piping notes quickly led her to him. The charming tune of his full song is recorded in Bird Song Chapter 12. Although the whole tune was not often sung, he frequently piped the opening notes or the cadence, the soft tones of his voice and dignity of his plain song in keeping with the character of the gentle-mannered Bullfinch.

When Chanter's young were fledged these quaint babies, with stout little bodies and as yet scarcely any tail, were brought to my garden, the parents spending much time on the flower-beds, extracting seeds from forget-me-nots which were fed to the fledglings, who perched in a row on the pergola. Chanter and his mate also were often to be seen clinging to cow-parsley, arched under their weight while they plucked the ripening seeds. Their young, calling softly and persistently, fluttered round them when hunger made them impatient; often they attempted to alight on thin stems of long grasses or wild flowers that would not hold their weight, many swaying perches being tried before they found one where they could settle with closed wings.

I think the damage Bullfinches do to fruit-buds has been exaggerated, for it is a fact my trees bear crops equal to those in orchards where no Bullfinches feed. In early spring these birds take mostly green salad in the form of leaf-buds, this thinning of leaves seeming to improve the quantity of flower-buds. When blossoming starts they first choose wild plums and crab apples that grow in the hedges of my orchard, then they work at pear and apple-trees, particularly the former, yet all these trees are heavily laden with fruit each year (except an occasional miss when the tree is resting). I have come to the conclusion the Bullfinch must only take diseased buds. The only time noticeable damage has been done was one year when a mischievous Bullfinch nipped off every flower from three artificial crabs, the ground beneath becoming white as snow, but the sight of this beautiful bird in the blossom well repaid the early loss of bloom. This year my cherry crab-apples bore much fruit (as well as all the other fruit-trees in the orchard), and these decorative bright-red little apples were sought by Blackbirds, Thrushes, Robins and two Blackcaps. The latter spent five days in the last week of September feeding almost continuously on this fruit, before leaving on their journey. A more charming bird picture cannot be imagined than these Blackcaps, male and female, bending their dark, glossy heads over the little red apples that glowed like miniature Chinese lanterns and often swung to and fro at the first touch of their beaks if they pecked the sides without holding the apples, for they hang on long stems. The Blackcaps watched intently until the swinging ceased then gave another sharper stab, finding this made more swinging, they ended by perching where they could attack the crab from above, steadying the stem at the same time. When the apples were hollowed to the core the Chaffinches had their turn, for their chosen portion of fruit is always the pips.

CHAFFINCH

At one time I had several Chaffinches who took, or rather snatched, food from my hand. Once they discovered food could be got in this way their demands became persistent and they were so boisterous over their snatchings, flying up like whirlwinds while shouting shrill call-notes, that they created a commotion which upset the Tits, who perch in friendly manner and were continually being swept off my hand. The result was that the Tits started quick snatchings, merely to avoid the Chaffinches, so I had to give up encouraging hand-tame Chaffinches excepting one called Chink, whom I have now had constantly in my garden for nine years. He flies down straight from the trees at my call of 'Chink, Chink,' in a voice made as sharp as possible. But he, like the others, snatches the food, taking three or four pieces if possible, though dropping some as he flies away. He has never perched to eat on my hand like the Tits, Robins and some Blackbirds. Chink only comes for food and unlike the other species, shows little interest in my company. He appears not to have the intelligence to find his way in and out of the windows to get food, however hungry he may be, but he flies to meet me along roads with the Tits and follows after me a little way when I go out in winter-time. Early in spring his demands become exorbitant. If I am sitting in the garden he perches on the back of my chair and shouts call-notes and song right into my ear until more food is forthcoming; if I refuse to pay attention he persistently calls until I grow deafened by the loud, shrill tones close to the drum of my ear, so when I have no more food I offer him a leaf to every few call-notes, which displeases him, his expression looks bored and at about the tenth leaf he darts off at great speed, as if to make up for lost time. He then starts chasing his mate or intruding birds, leaving me in peace to watch and admire the slick cut of a Chaffinch's flight.

Chink's nesting territory varies between the orchard and front garden. All the year round he stays with me, but his mate and the other females, who nested or were bred in the garden, leave in the autumn except for occasional return visits. Some of the young males bred in the garden remain for the autumn, or even until early spring, although they are away some days, when I presume they join flocks. I generally see more females than males in my garden in early spring, some I recognise as the returned females who nested the previous year or the young reared the previous summer. But some are, I think, strangers to my garden.

Chink kept to the same mate for six years, although he must have had plenty of choice with all these females around, apparently anxious to stay in his territory where some of them had been bred. His mate was very tame and followed me about but she would not come to my hand and every time I threw her food in the presence of Chink, he snatched it from her and hurriedly ate it himself. I never saw him feed her or stand aside for her to take food she was given. Another couple of Chaffinches, whose nest was on a bare branch just above where I habitually sit in the orchard, were also very tame, and I had good chances of close observation. The male never fed his mate while sitting or when off the nest, but like Chink, he fed the young attentively. Another pair that I was less familiar with and only occasionally watched, had a nest high up in a hedge. This male seemed often to feed his mate while sitting, for if I watched a short while he was sure to appear and fly to the nest with food. (*The Handbook of British Birds* states male Chaffinches feed females while sitting. From my observations it seems according to the individual.) The mate of the former bird bound the moss of her nest with long strands of sewing cotton stolen from me. She found for herself the method we use when carrying a long rope; she looped it into a coil, first picking up one end then taking up the rest of the yard-long strand at two-inch intervals until she had it all neatly coiled in her bill. Carrying the cotton uncoiled it would get entangled in twigs surrounding her nest, so be difficult to use.

One year Chink's mate built her nest on my pergola. The nestlings were amusing to watch when nearly ready to fly. The neat little nest being too small for the fat-looking babies, they bulged over the rim and kept standing on each other's backs to stretch or preen. One morning four flew boldly from the nest, following quickly after each other without a moment's hesitation, and landing in trees across the lawn; but one was left behind, afraid to take the plunge. It stood on the rim of the nest, giving an interesting study of quick-changing poses and facial expressions. First upright with outstretched head looking for the others, then crouching low, its face contorted with fear. After a moment it began to preen, looked comfortable and fluffed out its feathers, a fat, contented babyish expression on its face, next moment it drew itself up to full height, raised its wings slightly, looked upwards, then sank down on the rim of the nest, misery in its attitude and on its face. The parents kept away from the nest; they had not been near when the others flew. At last the lone fledgling stood bolt upright and with a confident expression fluttered its wings and was off on a long flight, terminating inside a bedroom in my neighbour's house. Chink followed directly afterwards, the window was wide open at the bottom and he hovered on the sill, calling in gentle tones or fluttering in front of the window until at last the fledgling flew out to the sill and was fed. Afterwards it perched on a creeper by the window, apparently afraid to risk another flight. It was not the smallest of the brood and it was very strong on the wing for a fledgling, but in temperament it was nervous and for some days it remained apart from the others, clinging to the wall creeper or nearby tree. The nervous baby bird does not only fear flight but the difficulty of landing on a perch has to be overcome. I think this baby flew on and on, past bushes and trees into the bedroom, because it could not face alighting once it was on the wing. I have seen other newly-fledged young of various species wanting to follow after the rest of the brood, but obviously having too much difficulty over judging where to perch and how to do it. Even hopping from short distances to perch on my hand causes fledglings some trouble. They are not afraid of my hand, for they are tame and fearless of me, but it is a question of measuring the distance accurately and knowing what to do with their legs. They often alight more awkwardly from a short distance of about a foot than from farther off.

Expressions of fledgling birds in all species are fascinating to watch. A baby Green Woodpecker came last summer to my garden for two days. It was plump and fluffy and kept looking for parents who were slow to come; its poses of expectancy and sudden relapses into a bored stare when the supposed parent turned out to be a Starling or Blackbird were suitable for filming. I made the following notes:

June 18th. A fledgling Green Woodpecker close to my cottage resting in a fork against the tree-bole, feathers fluffed out, looking rotund in shape instead of the characteristic long bodied Woodpecker appearance. It frequently called for food but no parent came. After an hour it suddenly held erect its head and called 'pee, pee, pee, pee, pee,' in a high-pitched voice, its pose the pleading baby with helplessness in its attitude. Then 'Yik, Yik,' loudly and peremptorily, its pose now very expectant, with neck fully stretched out and head craning forward, eyes goggling with excitement. For that moment it became long-shaped like an adult, although its tail was so short. Then it suddenly subsided into fat fluffiness again, its face dejected, for the expected parent had passed across the garden, but would not feed the fledgling where it was perched. Next moment the baby flew to the orchard, its flight slow but the wings flapping at a quick pace. It did not dip, with closed wings, like the adult Woodpecker. Very young fledglings in all species make a vigorous effort of continuous fast wing-flappings; only when experienced do they adopt the alternate closing and beating of wings in flight, making the dip which is habitual to many passerines.

GREENFINCH

My first year in Bird Cottage, when hemp-seed and peanuts were easily obtainable in unlimited supply for about fourpence a pound, I was able to attract and tame more species than has since been possible. Greenfinches, as well as many others, have a passion for hemp-seed, and they were amusing to watch when I could supply this on the bird-table. While the parents perched on the hemp-bowl, eating large quantities, their young used to climb on their backs, calling noisily and impatiently, pushing each other off and taking turns to scramble up with much wing-fluttering. The parents stolidly continued eating as if unconscious of their chattering fledglings who tumbled about on their backs. Then suddenly the whole family flew to another perch, where the clamorous young were fed.

In winter one particular Greenfinch installed himself as owner of the hemp. When the Judge (so called because of his expression) had eaten his fill he continued to sit on the small seed-container, preventing any other bird from taking its share. One after another the hungry birds attempted to snatch a seed, trying many dodges, particularly attacks from behind, but the Judge always swung round and faced the other bird. There was much excitable display from the attacker, but the Judge was calm, he merely thrust forward his head and snapped his strong beak several times at the heads of the hungry birds. They were nervous of him and never could shift him from his seat on the container. At his own time he flew off, perhaps to stretch his wings and get up another appetite, for he was generally back again before long. The moment he left the hemp-bowl it was surrounded by a dozen birds, Greenfinches, Sparrows, Chaffinches, all jostling each other in eagerness to seize some grains of seed, but the Great Tits, who also love hemp-seed, kept aloof until the mob had dispersed. Sometimes I pushed the Judge off the container, both for the good of his soul and because of the hungry birds. If the container was empty the Judge sat on the window-sill, his beak pressed against the glass, watching my movements inside the room with embarrassing intentness; every few moments he gave one small tap on the pane, his persistent concentrated gaze and quiet, determined tapping impossible to ignore. So after a while he got what he wanted and it caused me much distress when the Judge tapped in vain, for I could no longer buy the seed. He then withdrew from the bird-table, as did all other Greenfinches. Since then I have had no intimacy with this species, although they nest in my garden and feed on the anchusas, growing under my windows, when the seeds are ripe.

GOLDFINCH

All round my cottage I have grown teazels for the Goldfinches. Sometimes twenty of these birds have been perched on them, extracting the seeds. In summer and autumn my garden is enlivened by a continuous trickle of their family chatter as the young flutter over flower-beds while the parents are gathering seeds of various plants, corn-flower and michaelmas daisies in their season being a favourite choice.

When extracting seeds from teazels they make a curious buzzing sound, suggesting a zither accompaniment to their musical twittering while they feed. A vibratory movement of the head when the beak is inserted into the seed-pocket seems necessary before the seeds can be pulled out, unless they are very ripe. This produces the buzzing, which carries a long distance, like the Woodpecker's drumming. I recently watched some young Goldfinches try unsuccessfully to extract seeds without the vibratory movement. Puzzled at their failure, they kept watching their parents' neat action but could not copy the vibratory trick and only moved their heads from side to side in the teazel pockets. This accomplished nothing, it made no sound, also failed to entice the seed out, although they got their beaks well into the pockets. It was amusing to watch the puzzled expressions of the young birds, who kept turning to look at their parents then trying to imitate the actions. It reminded me of beginners at the violin who attempt to make vibrato, but the fingers will not vibrate. How the accomplished teazel performer made such a loud buzzing that carried so far at first puzzled me, but undoubtedly vibratory beak action on stiff surface has the effect of producing life and strength to the sound just as the violinist's tone gains life through use of vibrato, which intensifies vibrations and brings more natural harmonics into play.

My Goldfinches always nest high up in evergreen trees, where little can be seen of their nesting affairs. A friend once brought me a nestling picked up in the road of a country town. It was only a few days old, still in down with half-open eyes, but black and gold was just beginning to show on its wings. The vitality of this immature bird was astonishing. When I put it into an improvised nest it scrambled out again and came towards me across the room to climb into the palm of my outstretched hand, there snuggling down to sleep. I fed it every hour during daylight on bread and milk, but the second day it shut its beak tight when I tried to give it this unnatural food, which disagreed with its digestion. No bird-seed of a suitable kind was then available. There were many Goldfinches in the garden and the nestling stretched up its head and cried at the sound of their voices, so I put the improvised nest on top of a hedge, leaving the nestling for an hour in the hope that some parent Goldfinch would hear its cries and, like Baldhead and his mate, adopt the orphan. When I returned the nestling had disappeared, nor was it to be found anywhere near the hedge.

SPARROWS AND SWALLOWS

Because Sparrows, with their ill-mannered, pushful ways drive other birds away, I keep them at a distance as far as possible, but there are always numbers of House- and Tree-Sparrows around my hedges. Perhaps because of this, Swallows or House-Martins do not build near my cottage. When, in late summer, a few perch with their young on the wires over my garden, often these rude Sparrows drive them off by flying up and squawking scold-notes close to their ears, much to my annoyance, for there are no birds more beautiful to study at close quarters. Last autumn a family of full-grown young Swallows were perched on the rails of some steps and when I walked up to them, putting my hand on the rails, they did not fly away but looked up into my face, as if inquisitively, then seemed to forget my presence altogether although the nearest one was within an inch of my hand. I shall never forget the lovely look in its eyes, wild and intent yet with a far-seeing expression that was indescribably touching, as was the beauty of its fresh young plumage. The sheen in the sunlight of its dark blue wings and wonderfully soft-looking breast-feathers tinged with a faint flush, the lovely-shaped head and glowing, deep-toned colours all made such a setting for those expressive eyes. One of the great joys of close and intimate bird-watching is learning the expressions in their eyes, also seeing the texture and colours of plumage, the reflections of light on their feathers giving an infinite variety of shades in colour to each bird.*

THRUSH

I find it difficult to study the Thrush intimately chiefly because the Blackbirds push them into the background. The latter become possessive when encouraged to tameness and the Thrushes, who seem nervous of their big, black relation, allow themselves to be chased away unless they are very hungry. But sometimes they find ways of dodging the chaser. I have one Thrush who gets the better of Darky, the Blackbird, by darting up from behind, sweeping round him and seizing food so quickly that Darky's heavier chasing movement misses fire; he turns first in one direction then the other and ends by tilting up his head with a queer expression in the direction of the departed Thrush, who by nature is slow in movement when seeking food, but can learn to outwit his troublesome relation by bringing into play the quick action of which he is capable.

Last summer when food was very scarce for Thrush tribes owing to prolonged drought, my Blackbirds relaxed possessiveness and let all Thrushes take food without molestation. Then it was the Thrushes who went for each other, heads lowered to the ground, bills snapping and backs raised in the attitude of combat. Neighbouring parent birds who needed food for their young boldly defied the residents and much sparring occurred. When the two young of one brood were old

---

* There are two kinds of colour in birds' feathers, namely, pigmentation and structural, the latter arising from the splitting up of the white light at the fine feather structure. The surface of minute air bubbles inside the tiny barbules of the feathers splits up the light, giving rainbow reflections like oil does on the surface of water.

enough to fend for themselves they used to wait by the kitchen door while calling me in sharp clicking notes until I fed them. The young of my resident Thrush went to the front of the cottage and were fed by the bird-table, while another youngster called me to feed it on the orchard side of the cottage. The parent birds sought me and were fed wherever I happened to be, perhaps at the top of the orchard or down the garden, but the young ones always called me to them in their chosen places, thus settling their own disputes – for the residents still chased the young of neighbours if they came into contact. The young Blackbirds used to follow me wherever I went, like their parents, for Blackbirds seem to relax territorial behaviour during drought or other times of need.

SPOTTED FLYCATCHER

One year a Spotted Flycatcher nested outside my window, between the top of some trellis-work and the wall. The male took no practical share in the building, but he fed her frequently at the nest while she was working. I made these notes at the time. – The Spotted Flycatcher is very agile over her building, she collects much of her material on the wing, pulling at cobwebs while hovering on fluttering wings before tree branches and fences, her flight quick and soft as she returns to her nest. She also binds the moss to the trellis-work with coloured cotton strands – gathered from my chair after I have taken tackings from sewing. She has to hold her wings and tail straight upwards in order to turn round while moulding her nest in this narrow site. Her mate often flies up while she is working, hovering close to the nest as if to watch its progress and encourage her with many softly-warbled notes, quietly and hurriedly sung. When he presents her with flies they twitter together in a charming manner after each fly is swallowed. He warbles in a Martin-like way at times, this song very sweet and soft, so different from the emphatic notes more frequently heard ... The Spotted Flycatcher and Dobs, my Robin, have just been rolling together on the ground at my feet. The Flycatchers seem to feel the cottage is theirs now she is sitting on her nest beside the french window. Not only am I reprimanded when entering this window, but she attacks the Tits, Robin or any other bird who flies through the front windows; she darts from her nest to fly fiercely at us with half-hissed, half-whispered swear-notes! It is an awkward situation, this newcomer taking possession and my old friends driven away! Fighting sometimes follows, my residents giving way after a short tussle, for nesting sites have to be respected. My Tits have the sense to enter mostly by side windows, but Dobs, with slower wits, never thinks of doing this. The Flycatcher sits restlessly, her white chin always craned up as she looks for her mate or watches what goes on within her view. Every movement of mine she follows, her head turning about and eyes intently gazing as if with the interest of a bird-watcher! I feel she gives back in good measure the staring I have done while she built her nest.

Before the Flycatcher's eggs were hatched I went away from home for a fortnight. On my return she was sitting on another clutch, her nest now on trellis-work against the back wall of my cottage instead of the front. Her first nest had been robbed; it lay in two pieces on the ground. Anxious lest the robber should return, I kept close watch over her nest. This time the Flycatchers did not once fly at me with hisses of disapproval even when I arranged wire netting round the nest. It seemed, by their altered friendly manner, that they understood I was giving them protection, which luckily proved a success. The family were a delight to watch, for baby Flycatchers have much charm.

When the time came for fledging, as with Chink's young, four made bold flights but one was left behind in the nest, too afraid for flight, its sensitive face even more expressive of changing emotions than the baby Chaffinch's. Often in overcoming fears courage is developed. Perhaps this may apply to the baby bird's first struggle against fear of leaving the nest and trusting to untried wings. I watched this struggle working in the baby Flycatcher, clinging alone to its nest after the others had flown; the terrified distortions of its face in the effort to overcome fear and the sublime moment of standing up, wings opened and no trace of fear left on its face – trusting at last. It was a miniature heaven from hell and a grand sight.

CHAPTER 8

The Mind of a Bird

When trying to form some estimation of the mind of a bird it must be realised that there is an immense amount of difference in the character and intelligence of individuals both within and between the species.

Examining the physical structure of a bird's brain it is found that the corpus striatum – connected with emotional activity – is very highly developed, with relatively many fibres compared to man, but the cortex of the brain is not so highly developed. This might be expected since birds' emotions are much in evidence, a lesser amount of intelligence being shown.

They are very sensitive and highly keyed, with quicker pulses and warmer blood than man. Added to their keen sight and hearing, they have a well-developed sense of direction, necessary because of their powers of flight, also probably some other senses which are undeveloped in man.

EMOTIONS

Fear

Fear and suspicion of their enemy man, who so often harms and tortures birds, naturally plays a large part in their life. They are always alert for danger when the human who has not gained their complete confidence is in sight, so it is hard for us to watch their behaviour intimately, which is necessary for a fuller understanding of their minds. At the slightest suspicion of fear a bird entirely alters its natural behaviour; it becomes hesitant, its actions cautious and guarded, this often creating false impressions about the bird.

Some are by nature far more nervous than others, it is a question of temperament. This was seen in the fledging incidents related in the last chapter. Often those who are most timid when very young prove the most intelligent and interesting characters; being more sensitive, they are more responsive once fear of the human is overcome. The Great Tit Curley was an example of this.

Nestlings seem free of all fears until parents have taught them to crouch at warning notes or they have had some frightening experience, in which case they afterwards crouch at any unfamiliar object moving above or near their nest. So many hazards beset a bird and discrimination must be used to decide which are dangerous, which can be ignored, and this the young bird gradually learns after leaving the nest, from watching other birds and from warning notes. Their parents teach them to keep off the ground and under cover from above. The temperamentally nervous fledglings cautiously keep to safe perches, but there are bold ones whose interest in the world around them at times makes them disregard safety precautions. If one of these continues to make itself conspicuous by chattering or moving about after a warning note that a cat is near (ground danger warning is generally different from an air warning), the parent may give a subdued scold-note accompanied by a tap on the head with its beak. This immediately silences the youngster; if a nestling, it crouches, if a fledgling, it stays rigid upon its perch until it sees from other birds that danger is over. If the warning note to take cover from above is unheeded, the parent Great Tit sometimes pushes the fledgling from its exposed perch by kicking from above with its feet, scold-notes accompanying the push.

Once the young have witnessed the terrifying sight of a fledgling being carried off by a Jackdaw, cat, or bird of prey, they become excessively cautious, taking fright unnecessarily many times a day. If nestlings, they crouch at every movement above or near their nest; if fledglings, they rush to shelter with sharp cries of alarm, though the supposed dangers may be such things as the neighbouring Blackbird swooping down to steal food from another's territory or a Swallow sweeping low overhead. Anything suddenly passing near them causes alarm, for they have not yet learnt to distinguish what is harmful to them. Especially they fear aeroplanes at this stage, even the sound of one is recognised without seeing it approach. Sometimes when a fledgling Great Tit is in rigid pose, freezing at the sound of a distant plane, its parent arrives with food, and although the parent keeps pushing the caterpillar against the closed beak of its frozen offspring the food is ignored and the fledgling keeps rigid on its perch while looking upwards with the blinking eyes that denote fear. At last it relaxes enough to take food, but stays motionless upon its perch until all sound of the plane has died away. By degrees they learn the real dangers, their terror of planes or sweeping Swallows is first reduced to a suspicious stare then gradually these are disregarded altogether – although the roar of a plane very close overhead always alarms my birds.

Their ears as well as their eyes are alert for enemies and they connect sound and sight of anything suspicious even from the first time of appearance. They also learn to distinguish between the dangerous Jackdaw seeking prey and the one flying overhead for other purposes – perhaps the tense pose of head being the danger signal, for I can judge by this myself.

Birds have numerous ways of showing their fears. It is only in acute fear the posture is rigid. Frequent head-turning of a certain kind denotes suspicion, but familiarity with the individual is often necessary before all the nervous mannerisms and fear reactions are recognised as such.

Parent birds are always alert for possible danger to their young, but cease at this period to heed danger to themselves. It is noticeable how much more intense their suffering seems when afraid for their young than when fear is on their own account. Mortality among very young chicks is appallingly high, so their difficulty in rearing a brood with so many creatures against them – man included – would account for the extreme fear of parent birds.

When birds take cover at warning notes which prove false alarms, from watching the expression in their eyes and their rapid recovery to normal behaviour, it is evident fear is only felt momentarily; if danger has been real, a hawk flying overhead, etc., then complete recovery from fright takes a few minutes, even after the danger has passed.

State of health affects fear; in moult, illness or any disability they generally become painfully nervous for their weakened physique makes them lose confidence in themselves.

The courage birds show through the dangers and difficulties of their life is immense, especially when protecting their young – their bravery the greater because they are sensitive and alive to danger. Some show more courage than others, for, as in all things, it rests much with the individual.

General Emotions

Many ornithologists at the present time say that bird and human mind are completely different, and that the former have not such emotions as love, hatred, jealousy, etc., clearly defined. It is thought they react automatically in set patterns of behaviour according to the stimulus. Details of such theories will be known to the readers of recent literature on this subject, but I wish in the following pages of this chapter to give reasons why I think that this view is inadequate to explain the nature and behaviour of birds.

It is probable I shall be accused of some anthropomorphism in the bird biographies and other accounts in this book, but all my descriptions of how the birds behaved are strictly accurate although it is difficult to give detailed narratives of bird behaviour in natural language without a little anthropomorphism. If a specialised ornithological vocabulary existed, full enough for describing their ways, it would sound less anthropomorphic, but it would then be as unintelligible to the ordinary reader as a lawyer's document! Besides this, after the incidents I have witnessed during eleven years of observation of individual birds at close quarters, I cannot think that their mind is so remote from ours. It seems reasonable to think that they have some resemblances although, of course, many differences. I should like to stress the point that birds have a language for their needs, they have recreations, even taking the form of definite games something like ours, they have developed song and use it as a means of expression. In some cases their music is akin to ours (see Blackbirds in Chapter 11).

All my evidence is from watching individual birds at close quarters when they are free. With patience it is possible in this way to learn much from the expression in their eyes, and inflections of movement and of voice which together form their language. For instance, in the gaping displays common among many species of birds, there are inflections of gape that, together with eye expression, give different meanings to the gape. With birds that I know intimately, the meanings of their various gapes is apparent to me, because I know their expressions and understand the small inflections in their manner of gaping, this being in many cases essential for correct interpretation. There is often a faint, almost inaudible sound, only heard when very close, or there may be a loud hiss in the case of a threatening or angry gape, with blazing eyes. The beak, in spite of its hard texture, quickly shows emotion, for it has subtle variations of movement and these movements can be read when intimate with a bird – as with humans we get to know and read the expressions of their mouth. Birds, when wanting something, often give slow gapes; if it is food they want the beak may also be quickly opened and shut, perhaps several times. They may make the same kind of slow gape with a different eye expression and posture when suddenly warm sunshine is felt on their feathers, suggesting sunbathing to them. If quite close to the bird a very slight wing-twitch will also be seen, then if circumstances are favourable the bird retreats to a suitable spot for spreading wings and tail feathers to sunbathe. An amusing gape to watch is the one sometimes given when a bird is suddenly frustrated by another bird forestalling him unexpectedly. A faint sound generally is made, like a suppressed exclamation, and the eyes have a comical expression, for a mixture of emotions cause this gape. The bird has been surprised and thwarted, momentarily he seems undecided how to act; he may be left gaping with this queer expression and a hesitant pose while his forestaller gets off scathless. Another gape that seems really a grimace is made by Great Tits when they are expecting a nut and are given something less to their taste. The beak is half-opened and a faint sound made, resembling air coming out of a bottle when uncorking it. The whole expression is one of disgust. There is, of course, the well-known gaping accompanied by baby-cry imitations, used by the adult at certain periods of nesting season. In all these cases and many more, the emotion can be identified by the eye expressions and different inflections and manner of gaping. The same applies to all other forms of display.

The intimate knowledge of a bird needed before a correct interpretation of its behaviour can be given is evidenced by the following instances.

1. The Blackbird, Oakleaf, picks up a leaf to go into battle. He runs across the lawn, disappearing behind bushes, the oak-leaf held in his bill. The bird-watcher unfamiliar with this Blackbird might well think the male bird was participating in nest-building; but Oakleaf carries leaves for purposes entirely his own. (See Chapter 3, Part 2.) He also has occasionally been seen to hold up a leaf before his mate when

wooing, but from the different facial expression and manner of displaying it I know which purpose is meant by his action. If the human who is intimate with the bird can distinguish subtle differences in similar actions or displays how much more apparent these distinctions would appear to their own species or race.

2. One Great Tit used to ask for food, as I first thought, by the incongruous action of a persistent flea-hunt in his breast-feathers. Birds have various ways of asking for food, but this extraordinary display gave an impression the bird was half-witted. After fixing his eyes on me intently for a moment, he bent his head down and hurriedly poked his beak in and out of his breast-feathers like a dog snapping at fleas. The action was curiously jerky and never used when preening. At intervals he stopped to fix his eyes on me with a pleading expression, then the flea-hunt was resumed. When this bird got to know me well this curious performance ceased. It was only a nervous habit brought out by shyness in asking for food. This bird was Whiskers, Curley's mate, and he again showed this nervous habit when Curley could not lay eggs and he was growing impatient. Birds are very prone to contract nervous habits which can easily be misconstrued, this often creating a false impression of stupidity or indefinite emotion.

3. An instance occurred recently that appeared like parental stupidity and lack of recognition, but proved to be the reverse. A brood of Great Tits had flown in the morning, all except the smallest who clambered from the nest, clung to the bole of the tree and fell to the ground. The parents tried to coax it up again, but its wings had not strength to fly upwards. It found a secluded spot under the low sheltering branch of a very young lawsonia tree. Long grass around it gave some protection, but I was afraid of neighbours' cats who devour many of my garden fledglings. So towards evening I placed the baby bird on a wide branch of another small tree nearby, being afraid to move it far away in case the parents had difficulty in finding it. Soon the father bird came with food and although the fledgling cried lustily the father only gave one glance at his offspring, then agitatedly hopped around under the first tree as if concerned about the fledgling's disappearance. He then flew to the tree where it was perched, crying for food, but immediately returned to the ground under the other tree and, looking up at me, gave several scold-notes. I understood the meaning of his behaviour at last; where I had placed the fledgling was

exposed from above and it would be easy prey for the Jackdaws and Magpies who pick off many young from my garden, so it was safer on the ground under cover of the other tree. A parent bird will not feed its young on a dangerous perch because this entices it to remain there instead of seeking safer cover or following after its parent. While the father bird flew off to feed his other fledglings, I took the small one right across the garden and placed it on the branch of a tree that had very dense foliage. The fledgling was now concealed from above and below, but far off from its original spot under the lawsonia near its nest, so this would be a test of recognition. It continued to cry and next minute the father bird flew up in a pleased manner, fed the baby without hesitation and gave two or three gentle notes (the usual soft notes given when the young first fly). Then he flew to the tree-top and gave loud call-notes to which the mother bird responded. She came hurrying to the tree and together they flew to their youngest fledgling, obviously delighted that it was at last on a safe perch. They fed it several times then displayed together excitedly on the bough beside the fledgling, in a manner usual when all have flown from the nest. If I had not understood the father bird's behaviour and the reason for his scold-notes when he refused to feed the baby in response to its cries when on that exposed perch, it would have appeared like a case of lack of recognition of his own young, whereas it was an example of sensible behaviour. My birds can make me understand by their notes and actions or inflections of movement what is passing through their minds. If I do not get their meaning at once they soon find a way of communication, often acting like in a dumb charade, which is a way frequently used among themselves for explaining what they want.

There is much variation over display with species and with individuals, some displaying far more than others, the intelligent species varying most.

Some of the reasons given for thinking birds have not our clearly-defined emotions is that their displays – including gaping – do not seem to have any single identifiable emotion, that in some species threat and sexual display is alike, in some distinct, and that they are able to switch suddenly from one emotion to another and back again according to the other individual's response. But the human being is just as indefinite if we judge from outward display. Some races and individuals blush, gesticulate, or make other manifestations of emotion much more than others, but the extent of their feelings cannot be assessed by these outward signs. It may be the same with birds.

Threat and sexual display would not seem alike to the birds themselves because of the different inflections of movement, etc., that act as a language, some of which even the bird-watcher can understand if intimate with the individual. But probably there are many details in display which have significance to the birds, which no human could possibly follow or understand.

Time goes at a different pace to birds, they have faster pulses, higher temperatures, their sight and hearing quicker and their actions often at a pace we cannot follow with our eyes. Their reactions would not seem quick-changing to them, and it is natural their spontaneous natures would react instantaneously according to the behaviour of their associates. So these quick-seeming changes are no proof of indefinite feelings.

Their emotions may be clearly defined when the action seems inappropriate, for instance, when the bird sings from shock. It has been stated a bird is incapable of love, or heartless, because he may sing when his mate is killed even before the warmth has left her body. When this happens it is because his emotions are violently stirred and he must give them outlet. I have known birds sing loudly directly their mates have been run over by traffic outside my gate. When this outburst of agitated song is over they will appear to be moping at their loss, and cease singing altogether for several days. The reaction depends upon the individual, some recovering sooner than others, perhaps because there is much more attachment between some mates.

So that from all one witnesses of bird behaviour, there seems no reason for assuming they have not these simple emotions clearly defined.

MEMORY AND RECOGNITION

I find birds remember each other when they meet at my house after several months separation during nesting season. There are some who have special antipathy for another of their species, and this is always shown in exactly the same individual manner. For instance, Curley and Twist were apart for three months each nesting season yet, when meeting again, their antagonism, which was noticeable as fledglings, was always shown in the same ways; but they were not antagonistic to others of their species. (Chapter 2, Part 4.) Similarly, Baldhead became intolerant of Fatty after the unusual nesting affairs related in Chapter 2, Part 2, his intolerance being shown after each period of Fatty's absence from the cottage. There are some birds who are especially friendly towards each other, and this same immediate recognition applies. Strangers are tolerated or not, according to circumstances and individuals. Even in the distance, recognition and remembrance of each other is shown by their different reactions, without a note having been uttered. They distinguish me from other humans across two or three large fields, even in clothes they have never before seen me wear. (See page 76.)

They have no difficulty in distinguishing their own fledglings from those of others, for in my garden it often happens the young from one nest stray near the nest of another brood, the same species and age. The trespassing fledglings are driven away at once by scold-notes if very close to the strangers' nest – unless circumstances are unusual as in Baldhead's adoption of the orphans.

As before mentioned, one Great Tit recognised me after two years' absence, and various other tests show that my garden birds remember me after several months' absence, Tits, Robins, Blackbirds, Chaffinches coming straight to my hand, although some may flutter round me hesitatingly just at first even after a week's separation. It depends upon the individual. (See Chapter 5.)

INTELLIGENCE

Because, at the present time, it seems the tendency is to underestimate bird intelligence, I am purposely giving most attention to this subject in writing of bird mind, choosing an intelligent species for many examples.

1. The Great Tit Jane, whose biography is given in Chapter 2, showed much agitation the first time her fledglings flew close to the windows of my cottage. Young birds often bang against glass, accidents occurring if they enter a room before understanding window-panes – for the fledgling easily succumbs if its head is hit, the older bird being able to stand a much harder blow. Jane must have realised the danger

of glass for, after a few moments of agitated fluttering over her fledglings, she seized some food, called her young to the open fanlight – where there is a perch for birds – then quickly placed herself so that she could hold the food to her young with the glass intervening. They tried to get it and, of course, pecked the glass. She next put her head outside the window to show the food to her fledglings without the glass barrier, but before they could take it she withdrew behind the window-pane and held it so they pecked the glass again. She repeated this three times; by then her young, with characteristic quickness of Great Tits, had understood and were examining the window-panes with quaint expressions of interest on their faces. There was no trouble when they afterwards followed their parents into the room because Jane had taught them to know glass; they were cautious when approaching the windows, found their way out of the open ones and never banged into those that were closed. What else except reasoning power could have accounted for Jane's action?

Parent birds teach their young many things. Although some of their lessons are simple compared to the above, teaching, even in its simplest form, is beyond the field of automatic behaviour. That a bird has the perception to foresee the necessity of teaching her young to know glass, shows that reasoning enters into their intelligence and that this is of a higher order than is generally supposed.

2. One December day a Blue Tit, new to my cottage, flew into the room through the small fanlight which in winter is usually the only open window. It tried to get out again by a closed one on the opposite side of the room, fluttering and banging itself against the pane in panic-stricken efforts. Another Blue Tit, familiar with my room and the fanlight, saw from outside the closed window this frightened Tit struggling against the panes. After watching a moment with a worried expression,* the outside Tit flew hurriedly round to the other side of the cottage, entered through the fanlight, paused a second on the sill to call gently, but finding no notice was taken the rescuer flew across the room and touched the fluttering Tit, who immediately turned round to follow the rescuer back across the room and out of the narrowly-opened fanlight. In going to fetch the stranger-Tit the rescuer showed thought amounting to reasoning power. The less intelligent bird tries to contact the frightened one inside by flying to the outside of the window-pane, this happening sometimes in similar

cases. Great Tits also occasionally help each other to find their way out of the fanlight in much the same way as did the Blue Tit. Being highly nervous, excitable birds, the stranger Great Tit flies wildly from window to window, banging into the panes with such force it may be half-stunned on a sill by the time its rescuer arrives, sometimes clinging to the curtain and gazing with a worried expression* at the gasping, half-stunned Tit. When the latter shows signs of recovering the rescuer may have to fly backwards and forwards from the fanlight to the sill several times before it quite recovers consciousness, then the two birds fly through the fanlight, the stranger following with a deliberate flight quite different from the panic-stricken plunges it had made without the guidance of a rescuer.

I am continually seeing birds faced with situations new to them and it has been my experience to find that unless they are paralysed with fright they act intelligently, the degree varying according to the individual as well as the species.

Birds have applied their brains to the craft of nest-building with wonderful skill and although we loosely say that they build by instinct, this does not cover many of the things that go to the building of a nest. They have to overcome such difficulties as the following:

One of my Great Tits, Smoke, this year chose a large petrol tin for her nest. It being hung aslant, she skidded on the slippery surface when she took in her first bits of moss, so she began bringing some small sticks for a foundation. This is unusual for Tits; they choose moss, wool or other flexible material easily taken through the small entrance of a nesting-hole. These sticks presented a problem that Smoke had to solve for herself; they were longer than the width of the entrance to the petrol tin. The first one she brought was held in the middle and three unsuccessful attempts were made to force it through the hole, but she found it was too long and would not yield to pressure. She hopped to a perch in front of the tin and stared at the hole with an intent expression for a moment, then went back and deliberately stretched her head back – away from the hole – turned it to one

---

* In both these instances their expression, fidgety manners and strained poses showed they were really worried.

side so the stick was in length-wise position instead of across the entrance hole, and successfully got it through. It could not possibly have been chance, for the pose of stretching back and twisting her neck was most unnatural. It must have been a deliberate action, which appeared to be the result of her concentrated stare at the entrance hole. Every stick was then taken through in this same manner. Many such problems are continually confronting the nest-builder; they are solved by the individual intelligence of the bird. House-Martins have arrived at the same method of plastering their clay pellets as man uses in laying his bricks – overlapping the joins. Other species weave with the skill of basket makers and embroiderers, utilising with sense and artistry materials they can find and think fit. Intelligent application of their minds to nest-building is necessary to accomplish the work with so much perfection, variation in detail occurring although the pattern of the nest conforms to the species. And how is it the forefathers arrived at the wonderful patterns if not through using their intelligence?

Naturally, many actions in the daily round of a bird's life are automatic – so are many of ours. With birds or humans, actions become automatically performed through constant repetition. For instance:

1. A bird may take the same route to its nest, choosing exactly the same perches mechanically while mind and eyes are alert for enemies who may be watching their movements. When I am doing a garden job necessitating many journeys to the same spot, I find myself taking exactly the same route each time; by so doing the job is more quickly and easily performed. Birds likewise are helped by this routine, but if occasion makes it advisable they will alter their route although the habit of certain perches may have become very strongly formed. Sometimes no habit is formed, the bird always varying its route to the nest.

2. It may happen a bird continues to look for its nest in the accustomed place after someone has removed it a short distance away. Again there are similar traits in human behaviour, for if something is removed without our knowledge we may continue to search for it where we think it should be found and has always been kept although the thing in question may be easy to see in its altered position.

The above two points have been given as reasons for the automaton theory of bird behaviour. My experience of the latter has only shown that the bird becomes very distressed if her nest is moved a little way off, perhaps more because of the danger that interference might bring to the young than difficulty in seeing the nest a few feet away. Fear nearly always makes a parent bird afraid to go to its nest even if it has not been tampered with in this manner. Artificial tests for intelligence are generally misleading because of the complete alteration in a bird's behaviour under influence of fear.

Birds are also said to be lacking in intelligence because they seem not to recognise their own nestlings if they fall from the nest to the ground below it or are removed to another position nearby. But I have found they continue to feed their immature fledglings when they fly or fall from the nest too soon, or even if I place very immature young, fallen from a nest, into another improvised nest nearby. (See Chapter 1, a Robin incident. In this case it must be taken into consideration the bird has no fear of me so its actions are normal.)

If a naked nestling falls from the nest it is deserted by its parents. It would have no chance of survival in its exposed position, and it could not be brooded without neglect of those in the nest. If not consciously deserted it seems likely the completely naked, immature bird has not yet developed personality for recognition away from its surroundings. Instinct alone does not seem to account for birds' behaviour over deserting young. For instance, judgment often seems shown over giving the weakling a chance to recover, the parent distinguishing between accidental injury, causing temporary deformity and the incurable case. Fledglings in my garden have occasionally got their legs injured, but the parents continue to feed them during temporary deformity although they may seem hopelessly crippled. Often they recover after a day or two, but if good progress is not made the parent gives up feeding it. The Blackbird Oakleaf gave a good example of this. One of his newly-flown young broke its leg and seemed very ill for a day or two after the accident, but Oakleaf continued to feed it for a week in spite of its appearance being abnormal. At the end of the week it looked better, but the leg was permanently twisted; the bird was weakened and could never be strong. Oakleaf deserted it, despite cries for food, yet he was still feeding the rest of the brood. I took pity on the invalid and it was well fed for several weeks, but never became normally strong in the leg, and it was undersized and weakly. When driven from my garden in autumn it was incapable of fending for itself through the hardships of winter. Oakleaf had given the fledgling a chance to recover from the injury, and it seemed reasonable to think he acted with realisation of the facts. If he acted only on instinct why did he not desert the fledgling at once, when it seemed very ill and the foot was quite unusable?

I had another Blackbird who fed an undersized offspring much longer than those who were stronger and full-sized. I have seen other cases of this with many species, which shows that the parent does not necessarily desert the small fledgling who may never reach quite full stature.

Birds accidentally caught in a net or imprisoned in a room, etc., show panic when the human stranger approaches and they struggle more wildly to free themselves, making it harder to release them unharmed. But the person who has gained their confidence finds their behaviour intelligently responsive towards efforts to free them – not always easy if toes are entangled. Here is an incident that occurred recently. House-mice were doing much damage in my room, including an attack upon a new coat, strips being torn off the pockets to get at a nut inside. (My pockets generally contain bits of food for the birds.) In despair I set a mouse-trap in a corner, shielded by tin tray fortifications I thought no bird could move, although I intended to take away the trap at dawn. But I forgot. The following morning, while gardening near the window, I heard the terrible sound of a struggling creature in the trap – though it was supposed to kill instantaneously. Entering the room, I found a Great Tit had managed to pull aside a tin tray and had spotted the cheese on the trap, with the result he was caught round the neck. He had fluttered his wings and struggled desperately to free himself until I walked towards him repeating soothingly, 'It's all right, I'll let you free' – for birds understand the meaning of speech by its tone. Then he stopped struggling, and when I bent over him he looked up at me without any sign of fear or pain but an expectant expression in his eyes. Still talking softly to him, I pulled the trap and the bird very gently towards me, this being necessary before I could get both hands on the spring. He kept perfectly still and relaxed, his eyes on mine with that waiting expression. I expected he might struggle while I was lifting the spring, and this would make it difficult to free him without injury. But he had the intelligence to realise I was releasing him and kept quite still, his eyes calmly watching mine while I lifted the spring. He was freed unharmed. He gave a quick little shake to his ruffled feathers then flew out of the window with a subdued scold-note. Examining the trap to discover why he was not crushed, I found a small bend in the wire just where it closed over his neck; but for this he would have been killed outright. After a short preen outside, he returned to take food from my hand as usual, apparently none the worse for his experience. I am haunted by the sight of his lovely head pinned down on the trap, but grateful to have been spared causing a bird injury or death. The mice may do what they like, for I cannot set another trap in my rooms.

With birds continually flying round me, spying into everything I do, it is impossible to avoid catching their toes occasionally in shutting tins or drawers. Often Great Tits perch on the rim at the last moment before closing and I see them just in time to prevent serious damage, but sometimes their feet get a little hurt. They perch on me directly afterwards to examine their toes, passing their beaks down each toe, probably to moisten it with saliva. The accident never makes the bird fear me, he does not even fly out of the room for he realises it was not an intentional hurt. I have even gripped a Great Tit's head between my fingers once or twice when I was picking up something and the bird suddenly pounced at the same time. The Tit gave a short shriek but, directly I let go, with softly spoken apologies, he just gave a shake to his feathers and calmly looked up at me without the least suspicion of fear, although the sudden gripping of his head cannot have been comfortable and must have been a shock. Yet if I speak sharply to the bird – when no physical hurt has been suffered – he will be afraid and fly away from me until I change my tone of voice. How do birds come by such discrimination if not through using their intelligence?

Just as it is possible to assess from facial expressions and slight movements what a bird wants or is going to do, the bird can assess the human. I gave illustrations of this in Chapter 5 (bath preparations), and Chapter 1 (butter-dish tests), but here is another. If I hold out an unshelled nut to some of my Great Tits they look at it eagerly then up at my face with an expectant expression, watching for me to show signs of cracking it for them. I sometimes do this with a hammer, and directly I take up this tool certain intelligent ones fly to the window, waiting outside until the crack is over, when they immediately return with great eagerness of manner to receive the nut. They realise I am going to make a noise directly they see me with hammer and nut; the hammer alone or the nut alone never makes them fly to the window. Only certain Great Tits understand the sharp crack is going to happen, others hurriedly fly away when the noise is heard, except a few who are insensitive to the bang. The most intelligent and sensitive birds watch my face and actions, putting two and two together with astonishing speed in many such things as the above, even after once or twice seeing the action. Great Tits are especially full of curiosity at an early age, as seen in Chapter 2, Part 2 – Baldhead's curiosity over his parents' second brood. This may help to develop their powers of observation and intelligence. The same applies to some of the crow tribe, etc.

Birds understand the importance of watching eye expressions, not only among themselves but with the human. When my birds want me to throw food I am holding in my hand, they do not keep their eyes upon the food or the hand that throws it, but gaze searchingly into my eyes, this keen scrutiny being kept up until I either throw the food or move away. As well as fixing my eyes, they ask for the food to be thrown in ways that vary with the individual, but they never pay attention to the hand that holds the food; they are concerned only with how I am going to act, and their contact with the human is made through the eyes. In Chapter 1, I have already referred to their being able to interpret correctly my tone of voice or movements, in butter-dish experiments, etc. If they want to steal food, and I keep silent, they watch my eyes for signs of objection while going towards it and helping themselves. The birds who do not know me well behave in the same manner. If a piece of cheese or bread is on the floor near the window, a hungry stranger Blue Tit spies it and wonders if I shall object to his taking it. He cautiously enters, eyes fixed on mine while he takes the food then flies away. One Blue Tit coveted a large piece of bread-and-butter placed on the floor, which he was unable to lift, so by degrees he dragged it along with his feet, all the while fixing his eyes on the human's face until he got it outside and could eat without fear of disapproval. Blackbirds and other species generally behave in much the same manner.

This winter, for a week or two, I did some typing every day at a table beside my bed. The Great Tits have always before kept off the bed unless I am in it, although they hop over everything else in the room. But because I was busy so close to the bed two or three of them began hopping along it and perching there to eat food I gave them.

Directly I called 'Get off the bed' – the first time in rather a commanding tone – they obeyed and hopped either farther from me to their favourite screen perch, or came closer to me, perching on my chairback or the table. After the first time, I repeated the words without a commanding tone yet they understood, at once leaving the bed for some other perch nearby. I then tried, in the same tone, saying other words such as ' poke the fire,' but although they glanced up at me they did not move from the bed. I tested them too often for it to have been chance. Always they obeyed the words, 'Get off the bed,' or just, 'Off the bed.' After three days they had reverted to their old habit of never perching on it.

Birds have certain codes of behaviour which make their actions appear to conform to a set pattern, but each bird has a personality of its own and, if we study bird-law carefully and intimately, comparing behaviour within the species, we find continual relaxations or elastic variations of laws according to individual circumstances. (Chapter 3, Part 1, Thief being allowed to bring his young into Blackie's territory; Chapter 2, Part 1, Jane allowed into the Pugnacious Tits' territory when she lost her mate, etc.) Sensible discrimination is shown over many things in bird behaviour. These codes seem sometimes based upon general recognition of the character of an individual, for I have known a Blackbird, who was an exceptionally fine singer, keep order in the garden as if he had some recognised influential position; whenever he saw two birds fighting – of any species – he stalked up to them and immediately they stopped quarrelling. Having settled their dispute he flew back to his song perch and continued singing. Another example, a Thrush, also a remarkably fine songster, who had such distinction or social superiority that even Blackbirds gave way before him. Usually the Song-Thrush is chivvied by the Blackbird if both come into close contact on the feeding-ground, but if something special in the way of food tempted this Thrush, he could walk calmly in front of any Blackbird in my garden and they gave way before him. It was an astonishing sight to see the Blackbirds allow this precedency. In both cases it appeared to be the personality and perhaps special power of song that gained this distinction, for neither were ever seen to fight or display physical strength to gain superiority.

Bird behaviour is much dependent upon the character of the individual. Even finding and securing a mate is a varied process within the species. It may be accomplished with very little display or preliminary courting or there may be much conspicuous wooing and ardent display, according to individuals and to circumstances. As will be mentioned in the following song chapters, there is infinite variation over quality and quantity of song within the species – as well, of course, as between the species – the same applying in the art of flight performances. All these individual differences must be taken into consideration when trying to get nearer an understanding of bird mind. The more familiar one becomes with each bird, the more noticeable it is that in all things birds have individuality. These differences may be great or they may seem to us very slight, but the fact that all this variation of intelligence, memory, emotions, etc., occurs within the species, affecting their behaviour, shows that although certain fundamental laws are obeyed instinctively, in the main, actions are not automatic, but controlled by the mind of the bird according to its character. To me, the grounds never seem secure for the definite statement continually made at the present time, that bird-mind is completely different from ours. Their sight and hearing has resemblances although some differences. (Birds give imitations that show they hear the sound as we hear it.) And if we compare reactions of birds to those of men, especially the human child, there are many points of resemblance, particularly where emotions are concerned. Bird-mind, within its limitations of intelligence, may have resemblances although naturally many differences. Development is, of course, on entirely different lines, but if there are not resemblances how is it that bird and man can arrive at as much understanding of each other when they become intimate?

Man has developed his brain at expense of the senses and lost some natural faculties or senses possessed by primitive tribes. Birds, in their wild, free life have these senses highly developed, particularly the sense of direction or homing sense, necessary because flight gives them power to travel vast distances away from their breeding grounds.

FLIGHT PERFORMANCES

Birds not only use flight as a natural means of locomotion, but in beautified forms as a means of expression, some species combining it

Coming through the fanlight. A Blue Tit and Great Tits, hesitant because a huge camera is focussed upon them. *September 1950*.

Great Tits and the script! The bird in flight has just left my hand. *July 1950*.

Two youngster Great Tits, aged four months. *September 1950.*

A Blue Tit family.

Offspring of Baldhead on my hand. Age nine weeks. *July 1950*.

Great Tits in flight.

Opening a matchbox. *July 1950.*

Great Tit tearing a telephone directory. *July 1950.*

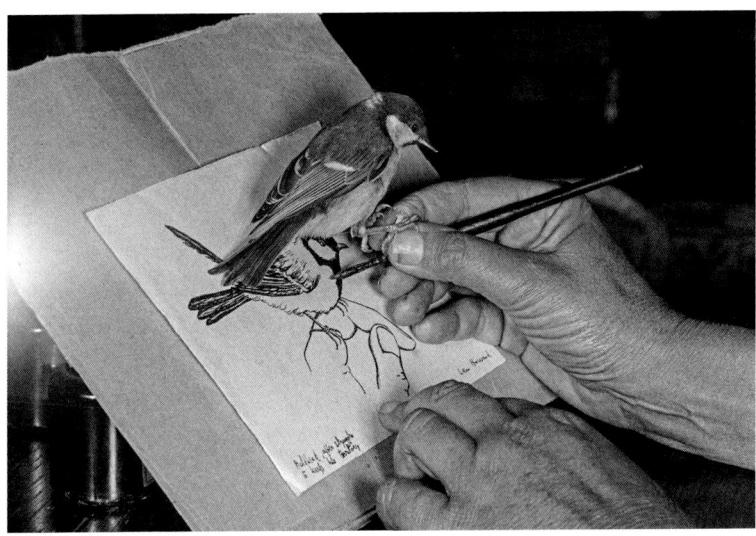

Interest in art! (The actual sketch is reproduced in the text because it is distorted through being photographed on a slant.) *July 1950*.

A youngster about the same age as the inquisitive one (above), but very different in character and appearance. *July 1950*.

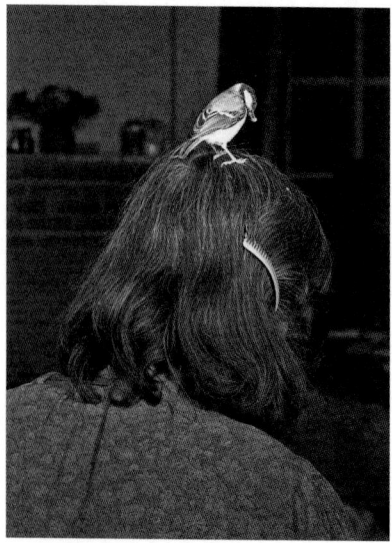

Often Tits, several at a time, hop on my back when I stoop. The youngster below is an offspring of Cross. *July 1950.*

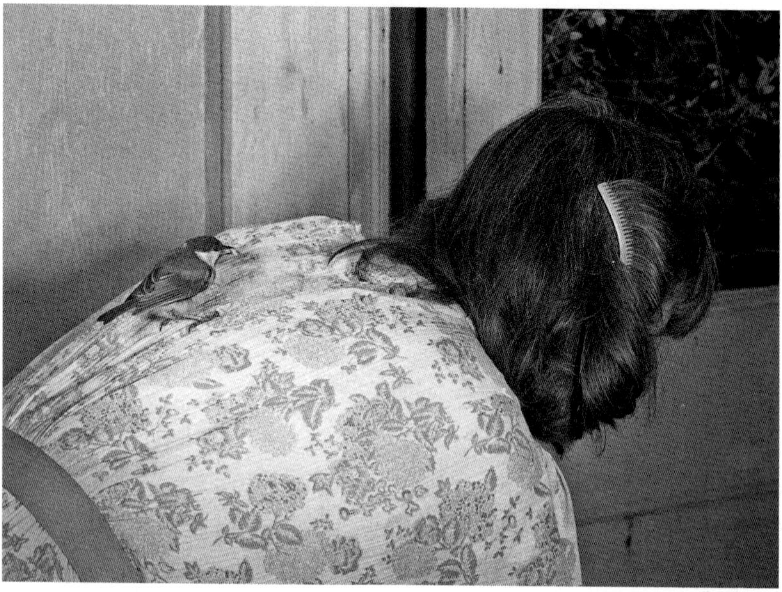

Robin at nest.

After a bathe. An adult Great Tit, in moult, taken by the bird-bath. *July 1950.*

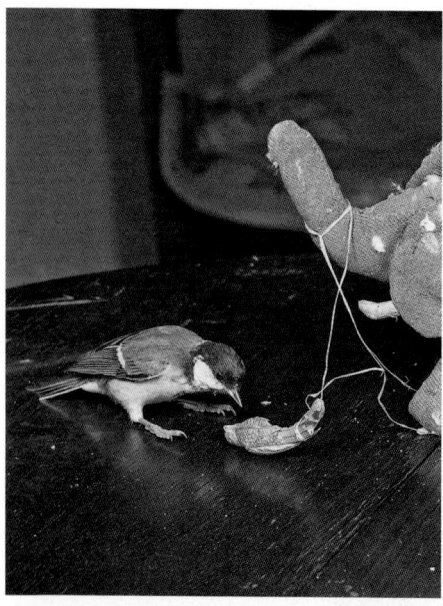

A toy Parakeet fascinates the youngster Great Tits, but their first approach is usually cautious. *September 1950.*

A favourite toy of the Great Tits, which they attack vigorously then pull out the stuffing. *September 1950.*

Great Tit choosing a shell. *September 1950.*

The shell game interrupted as the camera flashes. *September 1950.*

Great Tit, looking to see if anyone is occupying his roost-box and entering his roost. *July 1950.*

Great Tits, young and adult, like getting at books. *September 1950.*

A young Cuckoo brought to me while Eric Hosking was photographing my birds. It was injured and died that night. Its skin has been preserved in the British Natural History Museum, South Kensington. *July 1950*.

Spotted Flycatcher.

Spotted Flycatcher hovering before nest.

Parcels are always examined and torn open by Great Tits. These are two adult males. *September 1950.*

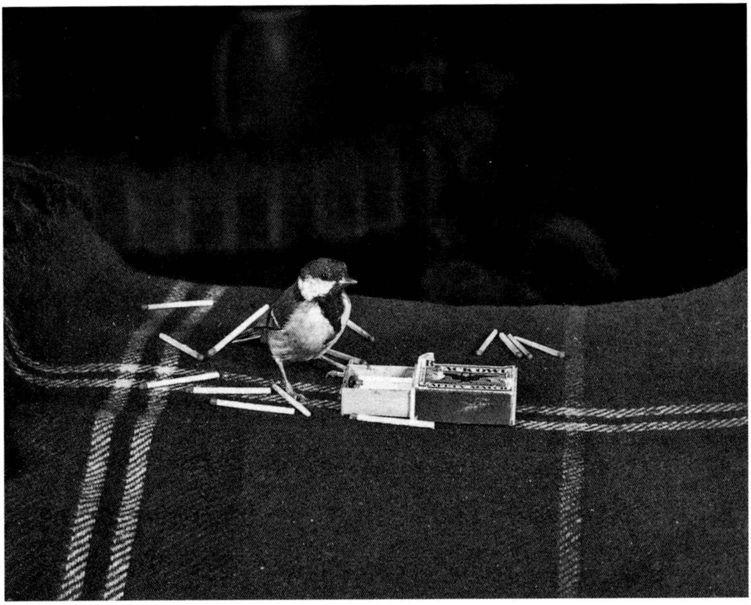

Great Tit throwing matches. *September 1950.*

Great Tits in their nest.

Willow-Warbler singing.

Sedge-Warbler

Nightingale.

The same bird in an aggressive display.

Sky-Lark

Song Thrush

with song. (See Chapter 12.) Many species spend hours of the day in the recreation of flight, as others spend hours in song. Flight is an art akin to music, with rhythm and feeling of movement as its foundation, a glorious means of expression that birds, with their emotional natures, know well how to use.

Some species, social in their habits, such as Waders, Starlings, etc., have developed flock-flight in unison to such perfection that the inquisitive human is for ever wondering how they achieve this simultaneous movement without a conductor to assist. Much has been written about this interesting subject. E. M. Nicholson in *How Birds Live* suggests that all birds in the flock are 'keyed up to a state of quickened responsiveness,' and 'like a dog waiting orders from a master' their minds are blank and alert to take leadership from any one bird in the flock who happens to turn. But the flocks vary from a very few birds to hundreds, and why should there always happen to be only one among them who turns, or perhaps two, the flock splitting? In my opinion, flight performances may be achieved in a manner comparable to musicians performing together. Musicians when playing are keyed up to a quickened responsiveness as birds are during these flights, and in good chamber music performances – without a conductor – the players feel together as one, not as separate individuals each playing a different part. They concentrate upon the music as a whole, not on their separate parts alone. All are swayed by the same impulse or inspiration, and each feels a supersensitive consciousness of the other player's interpretation, often to the point of feeling it slightly in advance. In playing, as in all actions, the mind must work in slight anticipation of action and this is particularly an important factor in quick passages. One might argue that it is the score from which musicians play that is their guide, but Zigeuner Bands play without written music, extemporising their different parts yet achieving the effect of a whole, all being inspired by the same wave of feeling. This also applies to Welsh part-singing, 'hwyl' is the Welsh term for this inspiration. Since musicians do not always play a composition exactly in the same manner, ensemble performances are ragged without this supersensitive anticipation. This might be described as intercommunication between individual minds under extraneous impulse.

As it is possible for humans of special sensibilities to combine together under the same emotional sway, it is likely that this would apply even more to birds, for they are admittedly quicker in emotional reaction. When under the excitement of performance, musicians are carried along by a living current that is a sort of life in itself, and they are not only thrilled themselves, but their audience can feel the thrill of their performances. When birds pass close to us, flying rhythmically in these simultaneous flights, the effect upon humans sensitive to such things is very strong; there is a thrill and excitement emanating from the flock; the birds' flight is felt as well as seen.

But when birds are flying to their feeding grounds or for other such practical purposes, there is not concentration upon flight as a performance and no tenseness of application to flight movement; they are not keyed up to emotional responsiveness and the result is not rhythmical as a whole. They then fly as if following one after another and no emotional thrill is felt emanating from the flock as they pass near the watcher.

There is much evidence that thought transference occurs among humans, this being generally accepted by scientists because of much existing proof. It is thought to be a natural faculty much neglected and decayed in modern man. There is reason for thinking birds possess this extra sense, intimate observation bringing cases that cannot be explained otherwise. (See Chapter 2, page 31.) Birds' senses play a large part in their lives; they have developed to a high degree sense of direction and of time; with the exception of smell, they have all the senses normally possessed by man in a well-developed form and there seems no reason to exclude the probability of their having this extra-sensory perception or telepathic communication in a simple form, by which many things in bird behaviour could be explained that are otherwise unaccountable.

Part Two
BIRD SONG

CHAPTER 9

Atmosphere and Song

It was a bleak December day and no birds were on the wing in the valley of the Sussex Ouse. Dejected-looking groups of Daws and Rooks were straddled upon the fences, and many Gulls sat hunched along the riverside. All looked too depressed for flight or food and not one bird-note was to be heard. The still air was damp and shuddery, a grim sulkiness seemed settled upon everything. The grey downs looked toneless and dead, fields and marshes were drab and cheerless, and the river flowing between them was lifeless, dark-coloured and oily.

Slowly the grey sky darkened with gathering clouds and by the time a distant bend in the river was reached it seemed night would fall at noon. Firle Beacon and Mount Caburn were like shadows of themselves, while towards the sea and westwards the downs were blurred and indistinguishable from the blackness of overhanging clouds. There was an eerie quiet that did not belong to day.

Then suddenly a Thrush broke the heavy winter silence by a full, rich song and at the same moment a small shaft of sunlight fell on the smooth peak of Mount Caburn so that its shadowed form was crowned with gold, which slowly spread until this shapely hill stood all alight while everything around as yet remained in gloom.

The Thrush, in his tree near the river, sang as if spring had come, while the sun stretched long silvery feelers from under the great cloud-bank that was gradually drifting apart, and through a widening rift the sun's face was slowly revealed. Firle Beacon was touched with sunlight which crept along that whole range, then into the Ouse valley, turning fields from drabness to glowing green. The grazing cattle, before unseen in the gloom, stood out in rich colours against the grass, and the river, now rippled by a faint breeze, sparkled and became alive.

Two horses, lying in a field across the water, stood up, stretched themselves and swished their tails as if expectant of summer flies. And, indeed, it seemed that the sun, blazing through the rift in those sombre clouds, had an intensified brilliance unknown to mid-winter.

Now all birds found their voices and wings. Cries of Peewits came from over the marsh and a flock wheeled high in the air; many Fieldfares called as they passed overhead, flying to the trees where the Thrush still sang; the forlorn-looking Rooks roused themselves and took to the wing, cawing eerily as if shaking off evil dreams; the crouching Gulls arose all together and as they sailed and circled above, it seemed they expressed by flight what the Thrush was saying by song.

A Great Black-backed Gull was there, majestic in movement, slow and powerful in his measured turns, as if he timed his flight of slow planing in small circles for some momentous purpose ordained by the world above. A small bush-covered headland jutted out close to the river and over this he curved his flight, always rounding with slow precision, his great wings and tail full-spread.

Thick clouds soon covered the sun again. Elation passed, but the effect of that rift was still felt all around. Eagerness replaced gloom. Two Snipe flew swiftly across the marsh, all birds sought their feeding grounds and now not one Gull or Rook remained crouching forlornly alongside the river.

Perhaps the most wonderful thing about birds is their song. The more one listens to their music, gathering knowledge and understanding of their musical language, the more beauty the subject holds. Song is an emotional outlet, a bird's heart goes into his music, so by full and intimate appreciation of his song we get nearer understanding a bird's nature.

Being highly strung and easily roused, many different kinds of emotions will make them break into song. They are very sensitive to atmosphere. Especially the transitional lights between day and night rouse a bird to his fullest expression by song. When the stars are fading the dawn-chorus begins. Lark, Blackbird or another the first to sing – for dawn-song has no set rules – and while the earth gathers light more and more birds fill the air with stirring song, giving their fullest to the awakening day. At sundown their song has a quieter tone, in keeping with nature's mood of peace and beauty as evening falls.

Sudden and unexpected changes of atmosphere, such as sunlight after storm, also bring response from birds even in mid-winter, as shown in the above episode. That song in the sunlight on December 21st was the only bird-music heard until the turn of the year, a long spell of exceptionally bleak and gloomy weather having lasted for most of that month.

Birds love the sunlight. Towards sundown in my garden many will perch where they can face the sinking sun, as the shadows spread to them they shift their positions, perhaps a few twigs higher catch the sun's rays for a short while. But the shadows creep after them so they move again, the trees keeping the last rays of sunlight being full of birds preening or just watching the sun going down. For a while they are very quiet, not one bird will feed or sing during these moments of hush that precede sundown. When the sun has sunk very low on the horizon the atmosphere changes and birds are stirred to music while the skies grow brilliant and earth slowly darkens, the last notes of Thrush and Blackbird falling with heightened beauty on the gathering dusk.

In spring it may happen that bird-song is silenced when, for some days, an easterly wind clings like a blight over the land. The Blackbird, an especially sensitive singer, is often the first to go silent. Although, by the calendar, the time is ripe for him to unfold the great talent he hides under dark feathers for so much of the year, precious days of his fulfilment are lost. The east wind seems not to have affected the organs of his voice, for his chuckle and call-notes are loud and clear. His mate may continue nesting and brooding her eggs, which is her creative work, but his creative spark is put out by the chill of the atmosphere. When not parading his territory, stalking the neighbour Blackbirds, he spends much time perched motionless and quiet on a tree. At the first sign of change in the weather, often sensed by birds many hours before the human, the Blackbird and all other songsters take to music again in full measure, while the kindlier wind brings softening of atmosphere and the sky is swept clear of the east-wind blight.

The quality of bird-song is also affected by their surrounding atmosphere. Birds bred and remaining in the confinement of large towns have less spirit and variety in their songs than those who have the freedom of the countryside and choose leafy gardens or wild woodlands for their homes. Partly, this is because they are influenced by the sounds they hear around them. A thrush may sing better for having heard a Nightingale, and the Robin whose home has been where Warblers' sing sometimes blends a little of the beauty of their songs into the phrases of his own. I think this applies to many species, for musicians learn from one another and birds have ears alert for every sound. But besides this imitative influence over their phrases, the actual atmosphere of scene seems to affect the quality of song. My earliest impression of the Willow-Warbler was that he sang best in quiet places where many flowers grew. (He is not, of course, a roadside bird like the Whitethroats, some Finches and Buntings.) I have noticed since that he appears sensitive to surroundings, and it seems his song varies emotionally according to Nature's mood. Although his music is usually gently reflective, I once heard him entirely change the character of his song.

It was in April, but a heavy snowstorm had covered the South Downs. Sunshine had thawed the snow in a sheltered hollow under Ditchling Beacon, but the blossoming blackthorn, which filled the hollow, rivalled the dazzling whiteness of the snow-clad hill above. The only sound, ringing through the stillness, was the voice of a Willow-Warbler, incessantly shouting a triumphant song as he flew backwards and forwards with unusually buoyant flight over the tops of those snow-white bushes. His loud, exultant tones were not characteristic, but the shape of the song and purity of voice remained unchanged. It seemed the brilliance of the scene with the first blossoming of spring had made him shout his song of exaltation while making joyous flights over the flowering bushes. If it was merely that the thaw had freed his lungs, why should he always choose that aerial pathway across the blossom for his song?

A few days later I returned to the same hollow. The snow had melted from the downs, the blossom faded from the bushes, and the soft greens of downland turf and unfolding leaves replaced the dazzling brilliance of the former scene. Among the same bushes the Willow-Warbler was singing, but this time there was no buoyant flight above them and the spirit of love and tenderness shone through his mellow notes. A gentleness, born of the maturer spring, was in his voice as in the scene.

All these things show a high degree of emotional receptivity and responsiveness – perhaps best appreciated by the artistically susceptible mind. In bird-song there is evidence of so much that is beyond the limits of automatism, and those who have not the sensitive ear or opportunity to acquire really intimate knowledge and understanding of bird-song are much hampered in their power to estimate a bird's nature. The fact that musical talent varies individually – within species – as much as among human performers of music is not compatible with the theory of minds that only work automatically, without individual intelligence. This variation of talent is not only a question of voice quality, but such things as the material of the song or musical composition; the interpretation of the composition, especially with Blackbirds; and the technical ability, for there are some who have to work much longer than others to acquire song-technique, various degrees of proficiency being finally achieved. Also, the way birds work shows much musical intelligence.

Illustrations of all these points will be given in the analysis of bird-song that follows. These analytical chapters, beginning with technique of bird-music approached from a new angle, may perhaps help some readers to explore for themselves the vast field of interest that lies behind listening to bird-song. The following chapter is entirely technical and analytical, but can easily be skipped by those not specially interested in this subject.

CHAPTER 10

Analysis of Technique in Bird Song

Analysis of technique in bird-song is helpful for learning to follow the rapid intricacies of many songs so that individuals within the species can be distinguished by subtle differences in their song. Recognising the individual Blackbird or Thrush by his particular tunes or phrases is not difficult, provided the listener has a good ear and is alert for imitations within the species – for a good singer, especially among Blackbirds, often has his best ideas cribbed by neighbours. (See Imitation, page 153.) But the song of many species is of such fine texture and the pace so quick that the human ear if untrained, has difficulty over following the song in detail, many listeners even being unable to distinguish between different species whose music has some slight resemblance, as for instance, the Blackcap and Garden-Warbler. But the more familiar one becomes with these rapid and complicated songs, the more apparent are the individual differences.

The birds themselves would not have our difficulty in recognising individuals by their song. They are more sensitive to sound and degrees of sound within their range. As already mentioned in a previous chapter, time to them is slower than to us, their pulse faster, their temperature higher and their emotional reactions quicker. So, to them, the pace of their fastest musical phrases would be easy to follow and their sharper hearing would make the subtle inflections of voice easy to distinguish. But we need to learn these subtleties of their musical language.

Realisation of the following technical points is, I think, helpful for better understanding of bird-music.

1. Birds use a musical scale containing more intervals within the octave than our scale, which is adjusted by temperament to twelve notes – the chromatic scale of semitones.* Our ears are accustomed to

---

* Definition: 'Our scale is modified by a system of compromise whereby the tones, generated with the vibrations of a ground tone, are mutually modified and

this scale, with a semitone as the smallest interval, but birds use freely many notes in between the semitone, even smaller than the demi-semitone, as can be most easily noticed when they sing a rapid phrase of many notes descending down the scale, yet the passage has only fallen one or two tones, according to our musical notation. These intervals, smaller than semitones, I term intertones. Birds, therefore, have an infinite variety of notes, each with its harmonics or secondary notes which accompany any single note, their scale, in fact, being the natural unlimited scale of Nature. Larks and Warblers employ to perfection numbers of intertones; they sound natural to our ears although impossible to transcribe accurately, for our scale and musical language is different.

2. Timbre is one of the most important factors in recognition of the songs of different species, but birds make continual alterations in the sound of their notes without alteration of the timbre (apart from change of interval), just as a human singer alters his words yet keeps the same quality of timbre or voice. As we cannot say that birds use different words or vowels, this alteration is, I think, best described by the word phone.* For instance, when the Chiffchaff sings, the chiff is a different phone from chaff, although the timbre is unaltered; similarly, the Cuckoo uses two phones, but many species employ a great number of different phones which give colour and variety to their music. Transcribing phones into such sounds as 'pee, tee, tew,' etc., never seems satisfactory because people appear to hear these phones differently, 'tee' to one person being more like 'chew' to another, and so on. But whatever the phones sound like to each person, if these are consciously noticed and the phone changes memorised, it assists the mind to take in the details of bird-song, this making rapid passages easier to follow and identification of individuals within the species then become possible, even with the most complicated songs.

3. Birds, like human musicians, make much use of accelerando, ritardando and tempo rubato. The musical term, *rubato*, means an elastic treatment of the notes without disturbing the rhythm, some notes being accelerated and others retarded so that the balance is kept and

---

in part cancelled, until their number is reduced to the actual practical scale of twelve tones.'

* Definition: 'Voice sound as vowel or consonant.'

the rhythm as a whole unaffected. It will often be noticed in listening to bird-song that a sudden or gradual accelerando – or hastening – of quick notes is followed by dwelling on long notes or one long note elaborated by a trill. For example, the Wood-Warbler, with perfect artistry, makes a very effective use of a gradual accelerando that leads to a sustained note with an exquisite trill.

I find that listening to bird-song occasionally with an analytical mind helps appreciation of the perfection of their music without detracting from the emotional pleasure.

In the following pages much use will be made of the words intertone, phone and rubato, so it should be remembered that

intertones mean intervals within the semitone;

phone means type of sound that alters within the timbre;

rubato means elastic give and take of note values within the rhythm.*

4. Rhythm is the foundation of bird-song as of all music. The character and emotion of the music depends to a great extent upon the rhythm. Each species of bird seems to be born with a rhythm of its own – which shows even in the fledgling cries – as with human races there is characteristic rhythm in their native music.

For purposes of technical analysis the following classification into types of rhythm is, I think, helpful, but the unavoidable imperfections of such groupings must be taken into account. Naturally, there is overlapping of types and no exact line can be drawn between them.

TYPES OF RHYTHM AND TECHNICAL ANALYSIS OF SPECIES

TYPE I. – CUCKOO (male); CHIFFCHAFF; DOVES, etc. Birds who have only one song in a set rhythm of the simplest possible form.

They hardly achieve rhythm in its bigger sense; it might be described as expressing a few notes rhythmically. Their song depends much upon phone; for example, 'cuck-cuck' would be feeble but 'cuc-koo'

---

* Rhythm definitions:
 'The united sum of different parts into a unit.'
 'An expression of the instinct for order in sound.'

is a masterpiece considering its simplicity. Timbre, phone and delivery make the character of these songs even more than the simple rhythm, for the phrases 'cuc-koo' and 'chiffchaff' are rhythmically of the same balance yet totally different in effect. There are many people who mistake a Great Tit's 'tee-chū'* song for the Chiffchaff's, which is really not alike. Both birds use two notes and two phones, but these have not any resemblance, and the timbre of these species is very different, as is the style of their delivery. The Chiffchaff sounds controlled and quietly precise, the Great Tit recklessly bold, as if flinging his all into every note. The Great Tit should not even be included in this type, often four notes or more are used, making the 'tee-chū' song very variable in rhythm, and it depends upon the individual bird what tune is sung. Also, this Tit has many other songs and conversational pieces. (See page 164.) Some Chiffchaffs have original ways of grouping their two-noted phrase in its repetition, this making recognition of the individual possible.

It is often possible to distinguish individual Cuckoos by consistent choice of certain intervals, pitches, and slight variations of the two phones. The Dove species have monotonous songs and, I think, their dreamy crooning does not vary enough with the individual for recognition to be possible by song, although I have heard Turtle-Doves whose notes had some distinctive peculiarities. Besides the 'turr-tle-dove' song from which the name is derived, this species croons on one upturned note evenly repeated, and also one note upturned followed by two downturned notes, all evenly repeated.

TYPE 2. – CHAFFINCH; YELLOWHAMMER; WREN; DUNNOCK; CORN-BUNTING, etc. Birds whose song conforms to a set but much more elaborate rhythm.

The rhythm of these songs is outstanding, the balance of long and short notes being musically perfect. (Without balance there is no 'order in sound,' and good rhythm depends upon perfection of balance.) Owing to the speed of these songs phone plays a less important part than in Type 1, except in the finale of Chaffinch and Yellowhammer. Song abbreviations and shortened variants are heard especially in

---

* Handbook term.

early spring and late summer, but during the height of the season each bird usually repeats his full song without varying the set rhythmic pattern. Individuals in these species are often distinguishable for they do not all sing quite alike in detail. Chaffinches are distinguishable by distinct differences of intervals in the trills as well as the cadence (or finale). But each bird repeats his own version in full song. Some Chaffinches sing their trills descending in approximate thirds, and finish with extra brilliance, others keep to closer intervals, and a few seem unable to achieve the customary flourish at the cadence, the song being rounded off lamely or clumsily. Their delivery is always boldly rhythmical. As with the Chaffinch, the Yellowhammer's song at its fullest has a cadence of very definite changes in intervals and phones. Their songs bear no resemblance, but in both cases the cadence is the feature of the song, although some singers in each species seem incapable of performing both of the final notes. The Yellowhammer, in the fullest edition of his song, finishes with two notes that form a rallentando, dreamy in effect. Although the individual varies the detail and interpretation of the song at times, it is always kept within the same set rhythmic pattern. Both Yellowhammer and Corn-Bunting sing in an easy, effortless style suitable to the heat of summer afternoons when they alone keep up continuous song.

The Wren's delivery is so bold for such a small bird that it is sometimes startling if heard very close. The strong rhythm of the full song is set to pattern without much individual difference even in detail. They sing many abbreviated variants. The Dunnock's (Hedge Sparrow's) rhythm is rather sing-song in effect, and he sings in a neat, precise manner, a little as if repeating something learnt by heart. Both species are hard to distinguish individually by their songs.

TYPE 3. — REED-WARBLER; SEDGE-WARBLER; BLACKCAP; GARDEN-WARBLER; WILLOW-WARBLER; LARK; LINNET; GOLDFINCH, etc. Birds whose rhythms are free and varied, the accented beat changing – especially in subsong. The delivery of these elaborated rhythms is also complicated by the use of tempo rubato.

The Reed-Warbler's song is a good example. He sometimes works up an accelerando of quick notes to a great speed then balances the whole by proportionately retarded slower notes. He often changes the accent, thus making cross-rhythms. Here is an example of one

Reed-Warbler's rhythm, to show changing accents. This was rapidly taken down while he sang. The accented beats are correct as far as it is possible to notate, but there were, of course, many notes between these crotchets. The bird-scale intertones make any transcription of the notes in their song impossible except for rhythmic outline.

The delivery is intensely rhythmic and full of energy, the outstanding feature being rhythm, but the more familiar one becomes with individual singers the more conscious one is of phone changes, which heighten the colour effect of the song. Many of the phrases contained in his song are imitative, but he weaves them with continuity into an original composition with rhythm that is entirely his own.

The Sedge-Warbler is very much more imitative and he uses much irregular rubato which is not always well balanced – but this is often exaggerated by nervousness of the listener. He has not such a strong and decisive rhythm of his own as the Reed-Warbler.

The Blackcap and Garden-Warbler also create in free and varied rhythms, sometimes with use of rubato. The Garden-Warbler uses more trills but has less variety of interval and rhythm than the Blackcap, whose timbre is purer and rings more clearly, the notes usually lengthening towards the cadence with a crescendo. Individual Blackcaps are much easier to distinguish than Garden-Warblers because their song is more melodic.

It may be thought by many that the Willow-Warbler repeats one phrase in a set rhythmic pattern as do birds in Type 2. His song is of such delicate texture that only the experienced listener will realise this is not the case. His song of varying, falling intertones on a diminuendo seems to be sung with one phone of many inflections that gradually lead into the phone being changed at the cadence – on the last two notes. Much rubato is used, the song beginning slowly and accelerating as the tone diminishes.

Distinguishing all these Warblers within the species is possible by noticing their individual rhythmic patterns, phones, cadences and other details.

Sky-Larks and Tree-Pipits have great freedom of rhythm, the former, of course, having many more tunes woven into their song. The Tree-Pipit gives a wonderful example of ritardando as he glides down to a tree-top singing 'seea-seea-seea.'[*] There is much individual variation in the material of the Lark's song. The Tree-Pipit varies more in the way he sings and individual birds make curtailments of the full song, many phrases then never being sung (see page 177).

Both Linnet and Goldfinch use rubato and crescendos in their songs. The Goldfinch's gay and spontaneous-sounding song with its sparkling rhythms is more brilliant than the Linnet's gentler and more subtle music. The delivery is fluent and light, a Linnet's more serious.

The Greenfinch's heavier, monotonous song seems to verge between Type 2 and Type 3, for it is not quite set in rhythm nor is there much freedom or change. But he has a way of singing his song in fragments; when he gives it in full it has some variation although he is not a good example of Type 3 rhythm.

TYPE 4. – BLACKBIRD; THRUSH; ROBIN; NIGHTINGALE, etc. Birds whose song consists of many distinctly different phrases in different rhythms, sung with a moment's pause between each phrase. In their subsongs the separate phrases are all woven together into one continuous stream of song, often lasting several minutes and sung very quietly.

Blackbirds are composers of many phrases or tunes of entirely different rhythms, sung with slight pauses separating the tunes. Each bird composes his own melodies, although much cribbing goes on especially among the less gifted singers (see page 154 on cribbing). Their song is much more akin to human music than that of any other species, some of their tunes being in approximately correct classical notation of interval and time signature (using compound and simple time). Each bird appears to try for variety of effect by singing his tunes at different paces, adding embellishments, altering the key, singing in major and minor modes, using staccato and legato.[†] The Blackbird even tries turning his phrase upside down. All these ways of treating a

---

[*] Handbook term.

[†] Staccato definition: sharply detached – legato; smoothly slurred.

tune are in the human composer's technique. He varies phones and has a wide range of intervals in his songs. His delivery is calm and controlled. Vibrato* is used effectively and with great discrimination. Blackbirds are very easy to recognise individually by their song because of its more human technique and the difference in each bird's tunes.

The Song-Thrush also composes many phrases of different rhythms, but they are shorter than the Blackbird's and sung twice or three times consecutively before he makes a half-second pause then begins his next phrase. This repetition gives rhythmical balance to the song as a whole; without it the effect would be choppy because of the shortness of each phrase and the different rhythmical beats between one phrase and another. The song depends much upon delivery, which is always boldly rhythmic. Some phrases in the song are common to many within the species, but each bird composes original ones as well and even those not invented by the singer have individual touches so that recognition by song is very easy. The Thrush sings with little variation of tone level – crescendo or rubato, etc., being hardly consistent with the shortness of each phrase.

Both Blackbird and Thrush have quiet subsongs, consisting of the material used in full song, but strung together without any break, excepting some connecting notes which are dwelt on. These linking notes are call-notes, chuckle-notes and occasionally an imitative phrase from another bird is included. All is sung very quickly and quietly, concentrated listening being necessary to pick out the details for analysis.

The Mistle-Thrush is a much less enterprising composer than Blackbird or Song-Thrush, but his type of song and quality of voice more resembles the former species. The rhythms of his song are comparatively simple, the range of intervals usually smaller and there is less change of phone and length value of notes, compared to the Blackbird. Individuals can be distinguished by their tunes, but recognition is not as easy in many cases as with Blackbirds, for although each bird makes his own tunes there is similarity between them very often and also much imitation within the species.

---

* Vibrato is often incorrectly termed as tremolo and perhaps better understood by this misnomer.

The Robin has much variety of rhythm and phone. The type of rhythm in his song as a whole is Warbler-like, but the form is different and corresponds with the Thrush tribe. His delivery and rubato vary according to his state of mind when singing, for he uses song more than any other species for a variety of territorial purposes, singing during autumn and winter as well as in nesting season. In calm moods his cadenza-like passages of chromatic intertones are often accelerated, followed by dwelling on long notes at the cadences, the rubato being well balanced. But in autumn disputes for territory his rubato runs riot and his delivery sometimes becomes strident and forced, he uses marked inflections of voice, accentuating certain notes in some phrases so that they convey totally different effects than when sung at ease after the dispute. Much of his song is common to the species, but some Robins have original ideas.

His subsong has great fluency of rhythm and contains a number of imitations from other species' songs and call-notes, as well as a miniature representation of all his own phrases, often linked together with two or three sighing notes, the first slightly accented, but all in the same whispered tones as the rest of the subsong.

Like the Thrush, the Nightingale depends much upon delivery and technique for the effects of his song. He sings many phrases in different rhythms – a slight pause between each – these being common to the species, although there are variants of the set phrases. Outstanding features of his song are the uses he makes of crescendos, phones and trill technique. Owing to the set pattern of each phrase, individuals cannot so easily be distinguished as in the case of Blackbirds and Thrushes, who compose their phrases individually. Occasionally a Nightingale may be heard to give an imitative phrase.

As with all songsters, there is much variation in ability, some Nightingales singing much more beautifully than others, so that recognition of the bird individually is by his way of singing the phrases, more than by the music he sings.

The Wood-Warbler and Tree-Creeper are both overlaps between types, for they sing two set songs, each in a different rhythm, and these two songs are sung at different times, quite separately. The Wood-Warbler's second song is not performed as often as the trill song previously mentioned on page 138. It consists of one note – the phone 'tway' – repeated with a big crescendo-ritardando, a perfect contrast to the trill song, which works up an accelerando on one note. It is remarkable that the timbre of these two songs is quite different, the trill song being high-pitched and a little thin-sounding, the 'tway' song mellow and exceptionally full-voiced.

The Tree-Creeper has one song which he sings fairly frequently and it may be heard all the year round. The rhythm is very definite and he sings it with much emphasis, making it sound like a miniature bugle-call. The other song is only sung during mating season – at least, I have only heard it at this time – and the tone is soft and secretive-sounding. It is a rhythmical grouping of notes that resemble their main call-note. Unlike the other song, there is no change of phone, but some slight variations of interval occur. The few notes of which the song consists are usually sung on an accelerando.

The Redstart and Pied Flycatcher overlap between Type 2 and Type 3. Both commence their song in a set pattern and rhythm, but finish in free style with much variation – often imitative, but I should mention that I have only heard one Pied Flycatcher, so am not able to judge if this is usual to his species. The following pages, analysing the songs of many species separately, will include a variety of things I have noticed about these songsters.

CHAPTER II

Songs of Warblers and Thrush Tribes

CHIFFCHAFF

Bird-song, like all music, impresses according to the receptive ability and mood of the listener. Associations often influence our feelings towards the song of a species. For me the Chiffchaff's song is coloured with remembrances of childish visions. I first heard it from bed one early morning when very young and the mysterious tip-tap puzzled me much until I decided it came from a fairy blacksmith, hammering on a miniature anvil, making tiny horseshoes for fairy steeds. Listening to the song brought much delight to me and I continued to picture the fairy workman until some weeks later I heard an older member of the household say rather peevishly, 'I suppose that monotonous sound must come from some bird or other. It's been going on all day and gets on my nerves.' What a difference between the two impressions! It seems general for the Chiffchaff's song to be welcomed chiefly because this is the first migrant voice we hear in the woods and the sound is so essentially associated with early spring. But to me, there is still an air of mystery about this bird's song, some fairylike charm in his voice and in the restraint of his rhythmic beats, suggestive of secrets that belong to the woods.

A few individuals break away from the set song of the species. I have heard a young bird in autumn venture upon a few imitative phrases and call-notes of other species, which he inserted between 'chiff-chaffs.' The following spring the same original song came from a copse a quarter of a mile distant from where the young bird had sung the previous autumn. It was probably the same bird. The Chiffchaff, like many other species, includes the baby-cry in his song during a certain period of the nesting season.

WILLOW-WARBLER

The Willow-Warbler's song has, I think, the most intimate appeal of all the species. It goes straight from heart to heart, where there is true sympathy between bird and man. Each note seems to be delivered with loving care, especially after nesting begins. The rapidity of utterance and strength of tone sound thoughtfully graduated as the pure, sweet notes gently fall, then rising a little, fall again to a softer cadence. Often two or three repetitions of this diminuendo phrase are linked as if sung in one long breath, the tide of song smoothly ebbing and flowing, and sometimes sinking to the softest murmur. The purity of tone and exquisite simplicity of utterance make it the most perfect bird-music.

It is interesting to hear the young bird gradually shaping his song. The Willow-Warbler's fledgling cry is a wispy note like a gentle sigh. When he leaves the nest he repeats it continually but without sound of urgency, already showing the characteristic gentleness of the adult's rhythm. As the fledgling grows the cry strengthens very gradually, the Willow-Warbler's voice always being fairly soft. Usually in June the young bird begins to shape this note into a halting phrase of five or six notes, roughly outlining the future song. These notes have not yet purity or sweetness, nor is there control of tone value or free use of gracefully falling intertones. But the youngster seems practising towards this end. One or two notes are sung proportionately too loud, making the phrase sound jerky. He tries again and again, giving slow emphasis to each note as if to gain control of tone value. Gradually the slow emphasis turns into a caressing note and the husk of song has more of the adult's appealing sweetness. The youngster sings fitfully, but soon the caressing notes flow freely, the phrase is now expanded and the husk filled in with gently-flowing intertones that fall on a diminuendo, the line beautifully softened by varying little upward curves. The full beauty of expression and tone is not heard until the bird returns the following spring.

Then the Willow-Warbler sheds his lovely song all day among the fresh spring greenery, and when his mate starts to brood her eggs a careful listener can often hear the wispy baby-cry that seemed forgotten long ago, reappearing attached to the beginning of the perfected song, now sung more gently, but more beautifully than ever.

BLACKBIRD

As well as possessing the most lovely mellow voice, the Blackbird has imaginative genius. The moods of his tunes are very diverse, most often beautiful, calm and reposeful, sometimes drolly humorous or weird in effect, and often they are pastoral in character (these being usually in six-eight time). Each bird's song is compiled of many such tunes, composed by himself then sung with improvised variations of the original idea if he thinks fit. Sometimes he leaves the tune unaltered when he has it perfected.

One Blackbird actually composed the opening phrase of the Rondo in Beethoven's violin concerto. (This was not imitation; I can vouch for his not having heard the concerto played.) At first he sang:

Then a few days later the last note was altered and he sang the complete phrase twice, exactly as in the beginning of Beethoven's Rondo, only of course higher pitched.

For the rest of the season this tune often figured among others in his song. Sometimes he sang the phrase only once and he occasionally reverted to his first idea, making a pause on the long-held last note, to which he added an effective vibrato.

His interpretation of the Rondo varied. If the tune was sung only once he took it slowly, with smooth phrasing; when sung with the repeat, the pace was quickened towards the end each time of singing the phrase, a rubato effect that added brilliance to the performance – when sung by a Blackbird.

Perhaps it is fair to mention that in the score of Beethoven's Rondo the first crotchet – the note marked *slow* – always has *Tenuto* written above it, an indication that the note must be held, this being what the Blackbird did with exaggeration at times.

Blackbirds' tunes often do not come to them complete the first time of singing. It is interesting listening to touches being added which make the half-formed idea musically complete. Here is another example. This tune was first sung:

After a few days the Blackbird introduced a chromatic semitone which formed an effective triplet in the last half of the first bar:

This alteration made an incomparable amount of difference; the effect was graceful and charming, and it was sung with excellent musical interpretation, from a human standpoint. The downward slurred octave in the second bar was sung glidingly, giving a caressing touch that was in keeping with the chromatic triplet. He sang this for several days, then came a test of his musical judgment – to a human musician extremely interesting to witness. He tried the effect of altering the triplet into four semiquavers, making the tune:

He sang this a few times, but discarded it, returning to the triplet which he stuck to for the rest of the season and following years. He was absolutely right, for the last alteration was an overload which completely spoilt the feeling of the tune, whereas the triplet had made it perfect. This bird, called Fields, was full of original ideas and some of them were weird, humorous and mysterious, through the introduction of low-toned staccato notes and other technical experiments not usual in a Blackbird's song, but the good composers seem to try everything within range of their voice.

Listening to the Blackbird composing, it seems some intellectual understanding guides his musical gifts. He has certainly advanced along lines of classical human music far more than any other bird. As with most species there is much individual difference in ability. One Blackbird sang a Bach phrase, which may have been copied from hearing me play Bach on the violin. There was a short trill on one note which he had some difficulty in singing neatly at first, but after much practice he got it slick and clear. Then he began experiments of embellishing Bach's music by doubling the length of the trill and adding a similar trill to another note in the phrase. He was an exceptionally fine singer and the result was very lovely – flute-like in effect. He included this elaborated tune in his repertoire for three years. The second year a neighbour Blackbird, Thief, tried to crib it, but the trills were beyond his vocal technique. After a squeaky struggle he abandoned the attempt. (Thief's fondness for stealing tunes was mentioned in his biography.)

The Blackbird's trick of ending some of his phrases with high squeaky notes reminds me of certain human composers who formed a habit of declaring the finality of a movement by some untoward flourish, often high harmonics in violin compositions. But the finest

Blackbird singers usually end their melodies suitably (without use of artificial harmonics!).

The adult Blackbird's warbled subsong has a deeper, more tenor sound than any other bird's subsong and the smoother melodies he weaves into this music stand out clearly, with legato effect, among the embroidery of 'chuckle-notes,' 'chooks' and other notes which bind together his tunes into one long, continuous song. These 'chuckle-notes' are rather clumsily conspicuous at times in the subsong, for they are higher pitched than the rest of this music. (Thrush and Robin include chuckles that are imitative into their smoothly-flowing subsongs without these being noticeable – for their subsongs are higher pitched and taken at a faster speed.)

Youngster Blackbirds have little melody in this soft music when first they begin to croon to themselves. They sometimes listen to adults and soon their subsong contains one or two tunes that later are voiced aloud. The following incident is an example of a listening youngster – written on the spot, while watching the birds.

September 25th, 1948; 5 p.m. An adult Blackbird, Fields, is perched high on a tree-branch, facing the evening sun, warbling a continuous and beautiful subsong, many full-song phrases interwoven between other notes. A young male flies to the same tree, perches within three yards of Fields and gazes at him with a listening expression. Fields stops singing and turns his back to the youngster. All is quiet for a few minutes. The youngster shows impatience. He turns round on his perch, keeps looking at Fields and opening and shutting his beak. (Birds often do this when wanting to be given food or other things. In this case, as subsequent behaviour showed, he wanted song.) Presently Fields begins singing his quiet song again. The youngster edges closer and, facing the same direction, fluffs out his feathers in exact imitation of Fields' pose. Again he has the listening expression; I feel sure he is taking a lesson from the older bird's singing. Always any slight alteration in Fields' pose is copied by this youngster. The song continues for half an hour, both birds remaining almost without movement, except that the black-robed tutor sometimes turns his head slightly while still singing and his eyes rest on the listening youngster, whose gaze is always upon the master musician. There is an air of deep content and absorption on the faces of both birds. The youngster's newly-grown black attire has less depth of tone than the older bird's richness of hue and the young Blackbird's beak is dark while Fields' is golden in colour. At last Fields stops singing, stretches himself and hops to the very end of the bough; the youngster copies this stretch exactly, in every detail of movement then hops slowly after him. Fields calls loudly, 'Shreeeee!' and flies off, the youngster at his heels. 'Shreeeee' is a note used on certain occasions, when wishing to be conspicuous, etc. (See page 156.)

I have heard an unusual song, of an entirely different type, come from a Blackbird. It alarmed me on first hearing for it sounded like a hysterical Song-Thrush going mad through some kind of torture and hoarsely shouting a jumbled medley of song in reaction to fright. Hurrying to the bird with ideas of saving it from disaster, I discovered it was the passionate love-song of a Blackbird in the last throes of wooing a provocative female, who led him a chase, round and round in small circles, on the roof of my wood-shed. He was getting more and more excited as the chase grew faster; his neck was stretched out, head-feathers were ruffled, eyes glittering and beak opened to let fling this volley of explosive-sounding song. She often threw glances over her shoulder in return, while leading him this last dance, the culmination of many weeks slow stalking chases up and down the lawn. Suddenly she flew to a branch beside the shed and mating took place.

The curious thing about this song was that it consisted of many short notes and phrases typical of a Song-Thrush, not Blackbird. There was no repetition, as in the Thrush's song and not a moment's pause; the voice and delivery were uncharacteristic. The whole performance was like an operatic scene with the performers overdramatising their parts, the roof-top in its setting of tree branches making perfect stage scenery. The few times I have heard this dramatic love-song it has always been directly prior to mating, but it does not appear of common occurrence. This Blackbird did not commence his ordinary song until a week later. Usually I find Blackbirds have mated before giving time to full song. Contrary to the theory that one purpose of song is to attract females to the territory of males 'in a position to breed and ready to receive mates,' the female comes to the male often many weeks before he commences song, this applying to many species. (The Chaffinch uses call-notes for communication when his mate is first seen on his territory – but I notice the female appear occasionally before the double-noted call begins. His song commences soon afterwards.)

It is usual for each Blackbird's song to consist of many different original tunes with sometimes a few imitations from neighbours of the same species. But a bird living over the fields opposite my garden composed one beautiful melody and sang it exclusively the whole season, never varying this tune or attempting to sing anything else. His constant repetition never jarred for he sang the lovely melody so perfectly. Towards the end of the season another Blackbird added this tune to his own collection and the following spring it was echoed by a dozen more, within a mile radius, perhaps some of his offspring. Not one imitator really got the spirit of this melody, it was a lame affair interpreted by them in comparison to the composer. I have often noticed that Blackbirds sing their own compositions much more expressively than those they crib from neighbours.

As mentioned in the last chapter, the less gifted Blackbirds do much cribbing. For instance, Thief and two others were bad composers, their original efforts were without shape or rhythm, and I could not find a single phrase that could be put into notation because the material was too indefinite. It consisted of one or two notes with a finale comparable to a high-pitched falsetto of a short chuckle-note, or that type of unmusical invention. These birds had some good tunes in their song, but they were cribbed from the Blackbirds named Fields, Blackie, Darky, Oakleaf, etc., and sung badly in comparison to these composers' performances. Listening to the latter four Blackbirds, I could fill a page with the original tunes of each bird and know that they were not imitations, because I had followed their way of composing and knew all the birds intimately. Very occasionally these good singers included an imitation in their song, but this was exceptional, the main bulk of their music was entirely original. Darky has taken an idea from Fields, but almost at once the idea was altered and made into an original variation and later discarded. An especially good melody may be taken up by any singer and when distinguishing an individual by song it must be taken into account that Blackbirds imitate each other's tunes sometimes so that much of the material in a song must be recognised before certainty of the individual can be established. They do not imitate songs of other species.

SONG-THRUSH

The high-voiced, spirited song of the Thrush is very different from the music of poetical moods sung by the mellow-voiced Blackbird. A Thrush, when at work finding food or nesting, is a gentle, retiring bird; often so slow to move, he seems dreaming or half-awake. All the more wonderful is the contrasting character of his song, when perched high on a favoured tree-top, head upturned to heaven, he shouts aloud in clear ringing tones his vigorous notes. A song full of life and energy that can cheer the dullest days, for he sings in November, December and January as well as in nesting months, giving fresh heart to the listener longing for spring.

The Thrush's gift lies in his power as a performer; his short, clean-cut phrases depend for their beauty upon the spirited rhythmic delivery and lovely tone of his voice, the impression being how finely he sings more than how fine his song. As with most of the best singers, some individuals are incomparably superior to others.

Many Thrushes include imitative notes in their song, not only of other species, but of sounds that take their fancy. One gave a clever imitation of my lawn-mower, another produced a rhythmical hammering phrase that appeared to be copied from hearing a roof being tiled. Their choice of imitation from other birds is of rhythmical calls such as Tits, Nuthatch or Woodpecker and some of the Nightingale's forceful notes.

Their quiet subsong consists of many phrases and notes strung together without pause – as with the Blackbird's subsong. Sometimes, with both species, it includes a new phrase that the bird has not sung in full song and, as if practising it for performance later, this is repeated many times over without break, often the whispered tones suddenly giving way to a louder trial of the tune, as if the bird wanted to hear how it sounded in full voice. Young Thrushes and Blackbirds, also some other species, begin singing a simple subsong when a few weeks old; later they select bits from this subdued singing and in louder tones practise them for public performance. Their voice production and technique soon improves, and they gradually add more tunes, giving their voice full play.

MISTLE-THRUSH

The beautiful tone quality of the Mistle-Thrush's voice has a little resemblance to the Blackbird, but less depth and variation. It has the throaty sound of a tenor or viola, less brilliant than the Song-Thrush, but strong and rich within its own more limited register.

Being a rover by nature, his song-perches are often two or three fields apart, usually the topmost branches of certain tall trees, the sound of his plain-song carrying far in leafless days. His song ceases soon after the trees are in leaf. He sings in a bold and direct manner, this wild music of simple line and firm strength seeming the embodiment of sincerity and truth.

Mistle-Thrushes occasionally sing quiet phrases, that may contain imitations of other species, between their full-voiced song. The fledgling-cry is a high-pitched edition of the adult's churring note – which gives him the title of 'Schreecher,' among many countryfolk. This note seems to serve many purposes. I notice when alarmed the tone of their 'churr' becomes harsher, and different inflections of tone quality can often be detected.

In early autumn it is interesting to watch the roving parties of old and young birds together. One September I saw an assembly of eleven in a long, very narrow field bordered with many trees. One bird appeared to be leader, he always perched most prominently on the tallest tree-tops, churred loudest and kept flicking his wings. Two others kept his side of the field, each perched behind him on a different tree, the rest were on the opposite side, also perched apart on bushes and trees. The leader flew forward to the next tree-top and the rest moved up correspondingly, all perching facing the leader, who also faced them while vigorously flicking his wings and churring. Then the bird on the tree behind him flew to his tree, instantly two birds from the opposite side began churring, and also flew to this tree, at which the leader became very excited, turned round on his perch while wing flickering and calling loudly. All were so absorbed that I was able to walk very close to any of them without their seeming to be aware of my presence. It was either some kind of ceremony or a game.

Blackbirds include something of the sort among their many

pastimes. Often a female is the prominent bird who leads off the ceremony – or game – by perching conspicuously on a tree-branch, while wing-flickering and calling, 'Schreeeee' – a note used only for certain occasions (see page 152). At her call other Blackbirds of both sexes gather on her tree, gazing at her while she turns her back to them and flicks her wings. I have seen fourteen Blackbirds, many first-year but some older ones, collect to the tree, keeping as far apart as possible, but all watching the female intently and occasionally answering the 'schreeeee' in a mysterious tone of voice, unlike her vigorous summoning call. Sometimes a male is the prominent bird. These ceremonies may have something to do with pairing; it may be that the leading bird is playing the part of instructor to first-year birds.

To return to the Mistle-Thrush, I have noticed this species has become much scarcer of recent years. Also the 'storm-cock' is now seldom heard singing through wild weather in my district. A Mistle-Thrush nested in my garden for some years and I found it was the Song-Thrushes who sang through bad weather, not my Mistle-Thrush. On fine November or early December days both sang, the Song-Thrush fairly frequently, the 'storm-cock' a very little. Song-Thrushes continued all winter unless there was prolonged snow or frost. My Mistle-Thrush and others in the district stopped singing in mid-winter, starting again about the first or second week of February.

NIGHTINGALE

Although the Nightingale sings by day he needs the mystery of night for his song. He is a great dramatic singer, with more technical ability than any other species. His mysterious note, repeated on a crescendo, is both wonderful for its emotional effect and for masterly control of technique. The poise of that first suspended note has much of the mystery and remoteness of stars on a still summer night; from these heights the dramatist, with his intense vitality, brings the song back to earth by a contrasting brilliant display of dynamic rhythm; heard close, the effect being one of powerful mechanism. Forceful rhythmic phrases and bubbling trill crescendos are performed with amazing skill and driving power, the bird's vitality seeming inexhaustible. There is hardly a moment's break between these phrases; then comes a longer pause, a pause that is part of the song, when the stillness and beauty of night are felt with growing intensity, then the wonderful note is heard and it seems sprung from the poetry of night.

Imagining that note in the hands of a Willow-Warbler, one feels the poetic beauty would be held all through the song, but a Nightingale has other ideas of getting effects, he is a brilliant performer and brings his powerful voice and masterly technique much into play. Each individual does not compose his own tunes – as do the Blackbird and both Thrushes; the material of their song is common to the species. Individuals put some variation in how they sing the set phrases.

ROBIN

In style, Robin music is romantic and rather florid. His voice can be sweet and his subsong is especially charming. When he uses song for disputing with other Robins his timbre often becomes shrill and he distorts phrases that in gentler moods are sung musically. Especially in autumn territorial battles, when song seems used as a language, certain phrases sound threatening, abusive, triumphant, etc.; according to how the battle with his opponent progresses. This may sound anthropomorphism, but it is a fact that one can tell without looking when the invading Robin is giving trouble and follow much that is happening by the sound of the song – the voice, phones, phrases used, and accentuation of certain notes in these phrases.

Although most of the song is common to the species considerable variation occurs with some individuals. Occasionally imitative notes can be detected – from other species – such imitations most often included in the fascinating flow of murmured subsong. Listening intently to one Robin, I heard what sounded like faint echoes of a few notes of Linnet, Goldfinch, Blackcap, Thrush, Great Tit and Blackbird's chuckle-note, all these interspersed without break into the running stream of subsong. So rapidly and smoothly did the song flow that one was only conscious of these imitations by intense concentration, for they were woven among the rhythms of Robin's own song. The clever blending of miniature imitations within his own rhythms made the especial beauty of this bird's subsong.

To me, the music of running brooks and fast-flowing hillside streams is suggested by Robin's subsong. Long ago, before humans built houses and handled a spade for his benefit, he perhaps sought the sheltered streamside banks for territory, for Robins seem bred to the art of fishing. I have seen one fly out to a floating reed on a pond, and from this unstable perch spear food from the water with all the skill of a water-bird, but I was not able to see what he caught. Another time, when I threw bread on a lake for the Waterhens, a Robin flew out, and perching precariously on weed, fished out some of the bread as if he was a born fisher. Most birds who are not waterside species do not show this deftness on the water.

When singing this whispered subsong, Robins often close their eyes and the sound seems to come from far away. At other times they may turn their head from side to side while singing this almost inaudible song, with the air of a public speaker addressing an audience. Sometimes, too, their head-feathers are slightly raised, but there is no other Robin in sight or anywhere near, nor is the display aimed at me, for I have noticed it when I am inside the cottage, and the Robin just outside.

Except in subsong Robin is not a good imitator, although a few individuals sing short cadences resembling notes of some Warblers, and in exceptional cases – as with 'Blackcap Robin' – really good imitations form part of the song to the exclusion of Robin tunes. Attempts to copy other species seem to show up the limitations of Robin's voice, making it sound high-pitched and thin. He has cultivated a decorative style of technique suitable to his timbre and when he tacks these Robin frills on to some imitations they sound out of place – feeble in effect. For instance, if he tries a Tit's song, which depends upon freshness of voice and spontaneous-sounding rhythm, his voice sounds thin and whiny, his rhythm weak and indecisive compared to the Tit. Possibly he is aware of failure, anyway he quickly smothers his effort by a sad-sounding trickle of falling intertones, making a laughably unsuitable ending to the Tit's joyful phrase. Similarly, he makes a hash of the Goldfinch's gay music by falling into a minor key – a mournful streak in Robins being their persistent use of a minor key. (I mean in effect, for literally our major or minor mode is not applicable to bird-music of Robin and Goldfinch.)

I have so far found female Robins sing less full song than males and their song and voice is inferior. Some females sing more subsong, but the quality is not as good. They sing most in autumn when first settled in their territory and do not of course sing at all while nesting.

BLACKCAP

There is no music more lovely than the Blackcap's song. One day, in early June, a Blackcap was singing on the verge of a little wood where white-willows and ash trees blend their soft greens with the deeper shades of alder and oak. At first he flitted from tree to tree, his clear silvery notes, in short phrases, seeming flung to the air as lightly as the wind tossed the willow's long silvery leaves. Then he sang his full song, perched low on a branch with head upturned to the sunlit foliage, and it seemed the bird and the trees were inseparably linked in one great harmonious inspiration. Together they expressed to perfection the music of colour and sound, for the windswept leaves in the sunlight were continually weaving fresh patterns of tone-colour that seemed a complete counterpart to the Blackcap's beautifully woven song. Phrases that began delicately were worked up to a finish on a gust of impetuous force, then a subdued, undulating song with notes flowing faster, until the finely turned fall of the cadence.

Close beside the wood was the Kingfisher's pool, where bright blue dragon-flies darted over the water like sparks struck from the Kingfisher. From the trees above the pool came the slower, deeper notes of a Blackbird. When Blackcap and Blackbird are heard together in full voice there seems no resemblance between their songs – the smaller bird naturally moulds his music on finer lines. But the quality of his song as a Warbler species corresponds with the Blackbird's as a Thrush species. Both are lovers of a tune on large lines. Blackcaps do much finely-woven warbling, but the greatest part of their song is when they break through this into a lovely, ringing tune. This may be sung without preliminary, but they often get a wonderful effect by working up their song, the big melody being held in reserve for the climax.

The subsongs of Blackcap and Thrush tribes have some similarity in mode of expression. One September a Blackbird and Blackcap, perched a little apart, were singing subsongs. The latter included imitative phrases among his own warbles, linking all together and singing in subdued tones until he sang a Blackbird imitation twice, with raised voice and timbre so exactly like a Blackbird singing softly that it seemed the two birds had suddenly changed places. He resumed the subdued tones, but every time the Blackbird imitations were sung he broke into a louder voice. I think this was not in compliment to the nearby Blackbird but because he liked singing the tune and it suited him, for I have at other times heard emphasis given to Blackbird imitations as if they had special appeal. A Song-Thrush may also be well imitated, but his sharper rhythms seem less often favoured.

GARDEN-WARBLER

The Garden-Warbler's long-sustained warbling song is beautiful and rich in trills, but he has not the Blackcap's lovely melody or clear, silvery tones. Many people seem to have difficulty in distinguishing between these two species. There is some resemblance in the warbling part of a Blackcap's song to the Garden-Warbler's luscious, more trilly music, but the latter has not the fine tune referred to above, which Blackcaps sing with such abandon and is really the greater part of their song. There is nothing resembling this in the Garden-Warbler's music. He has concentrated entirely upon rich, decorative warbling, this being much like his subdued, continuous song we term subsong. Exactly where subsong ends and full song begins is difficult to define with some species.

WHITETHROATS

The two Whitethroats, besides their main song, have a varied, long-sustained warbling on the same lines as a Garden-Warbler, but inferior in quality. It is unsatisfactory to call this subsong, for it may be sung quite loudly and is more musical, both in composition and tone quality, than their more dramatic and better-known performances. The shy and charming Lesser Whitethroat has a surprisingly loud, bubbling trill, all on one note, for his main song, attached to a quieter prelude, sung from cover of hedgerows or low bushes. This prelude is really part of the sustained song just mentioned; the length varies and may be anything from three soft notes to a long warble, worked up to a crescendo from almost a whisper. The loud rattling trill may also be heard without any prelude, especially late in the season.

The Greater Whitethroat's best-known song is his flight-dance tune, when he leaps high above the hedgerow, straight and quick as an arrow, dancing down again to the light, springy rhythm of a short song, rather scratchy in tone compared to his long-sustained warbling. As with many species, the fledgling-cry is a sharp double-note, 'chik-ka, chik-ka, chik-ka, chik-ka,' jerked out with sharply-accented rhythm, which suggests the bird is dancing up and down on springs. This fledgling-cry soon grows loud and is full of vitality; already the springy rhythm seems closely related to the adult's song-dance tune. One feels the notes have only to be freed from their monotonous pitch to be irresistibly suitable for the accompaniment of flight. In the mature song the fledgling-cry is noticeable.

Their long-sustained warbling song sometimes contains many imitative notes.

WOOD-WARBLER

Listening to the Wood-Warbler's trill song without seeing his accompanying flight is like hearing Schubert's songs without the piano accompaniment upon which the beauty of the vocal part depends. Yet too often this bird is hidden from view, for his flight-song is set among leaf-covered trees, a sublimely graceful aerial glide timed to the tense rhythm of quickening notes which, as he alights, are resolved into the trembling motion of a trill. This fine trill is uniquely sung on a curve which heightens expression and gives to the straight line of the song – all on one note – the rounded cadence it needs. The following is a diagram of the song:

The sinuosity of the curve is very variable. This song is often repeated many times, only a momentary pause between the repeats. Without seeing the flight it sometimes begins to sound rather mechanical, then comes a wonderful change. There is a short pause and another most beautiful song is intoned, just one note of strangely appealing tone quality, many times intoned on a persuasive rallentando. The earnestness of this song is deeply moving. The bird remains perched while singing with head upraised and sometimes when the song ceases he turns his head searchingly this way and that, as if expecting some effect from his song. He then resumes the flight-song for a while, until again the deeper note is intoned, This song is precious, there is no repetition as with the trill-song.

REED-WARBLER

Heard at his best the Reed-Warbler is among the most wonderful of bird musicians. A good singer has endless variety of effect, he works up great crescendos and his imitations are so well blended into his own rhythms that his song always sounds strikingly original. It varies much with individuals, some being far better songsters than others.

I first heard his song in ideal surroundings at a lake where a Black Tern halts for a few days on his migratory passage both in spring and autumn, and the following extract is from notes made at the time:

Water lilies have now spread their white and golden cups on the smooth surface of Lye Mere and among them Great Crested Grebes have built their island nest. In company with Coots, both parents and young are floating lazily around; the Coots rap out their metallic note, which rings sharply, now loud and close then like an echo faintly sounding in the distance. Two Herons, like age-old guardians, stand high on a forked branch of an old tree overlooking the lake. From the reed-bed far across the mere comes the throbbing of a rhythmic song, suggesting a wild barbaric dance in drum-beat rhythm of primitive tribes. A Willow-Warbler is singing in the trees beside the lake; there is striking contrast in the music of these two birds. The Willow-Warbler's restful song is smoothly rounded, his voice pure-toned and sweet all through the song. The Reed-Warbler's restless music is of an angular type and although there are many lovely-toned, concordant phrases, the pulsing note is often harsh in tone. This rhythmic reiteration of angular or discordant notes gives a wild energy to his song, the rhythm also suggestive, in miniature, of music by certain modern composers who sometimes revert to percussion effects of primitive drum-music.

An example of a Reed-Warbler's rhythm is given on page 141.

SEDGE-WARBLER

To me, the Sedge-Warbler's music is less original and not so strong in effect as the Reed-Warbler's. Most of the Sedge-Warbler's phrases are imitative and he does not usually blend his mimicry into such a well-balanced song sounding like a composition of his own. He seems to be deliberately caricaturing the originators of his imitations as if doing a comic turn, with generous encores for favourite items! I have, however, heard some very finely-balanced, musical song from Sedge-Warblers soon after their arrival, and I think this species becomes more of a caricaturist under the excitement of territorial defence. He is a delightful bird to watch under stress of nesting affairs, when from the top of a reed stem he hurls at his opponent, the Reed-Warbler, a volley of excitable song, phrases and scold-notes culled from a dozen species and sung with exaggerated emphasis.

CHAPTER 12

Songs of Tits, Finches, Pipits, etc.

BLUE TIT

Blue tits have three main songs, one of them often sung with a gliding flight resembling the Wood-Warbler's aerial glide. The songs vary considerably in detail with the individual; the lesser-known one is, I think, what I call the fledgling-cry tune – for Blue Tits are generally thought to have only two songs. This tune consists of the double-noted fledgling-cry several times repeated in joyful manner and strung together in many changing rhythms, varying in length according to the rhythmic pattern. The effect is a roundelay of many fledgling-notes which follow on and overlap. Tits are especially devoted parents and, being temperamentally lively and emotional, they show delight and excitement over nesting affairs more than most species. Hearing this song of the Blue Tit, sung at the very top of his voice from the tallest tree-top within sight of his nest while his mate is sitting, it seems he is overflowing with joy while he spins gay music from the notes that will soon be uttered by the coming brood. When his young are hatched this song is not continued.

His mood seems different in his flight-song. He spreads wide his wings and floats down rapturously through the air while a sparking spray of notes fall from him. Some individuals have more than three songs. Both sexes have many call-notes and a scold-note which is much in evidence if anyone unfamiliar approaches their nest. The male also uses his aerial glide without song – it is known as the 'ghost flight' – but I find some individuals always put this flight to music, although the accompanying song is often sung without flight.

GREAT TIT

Great Tits have much variety of song and conversational notes which are used for certain occasions. Some are common to the species but many are individual inspirations, for this bird is strongly individual in all his ways and full of invention. Sometimes he will take it into his head to give an excellent imitation of another species – Wagtail, Thrush, Hedge-Sparrow, Blackcap, or whatever takes his fancy for the moment. This imitation is generally not repeated. Watching the bird singing his imitation, he occasionally seems doing it for fun and his performance may have an audience of several other birds who hover around, gazing at him while he repeats the imitation many times running, with head and neck outstretched in humorous attitude, and in dancing manner hopping backwards and forwards from one twig to another. He appears to be playing the fool and enjoying himself immensely while the audience watches with interest. This happens in autumn when Tits mix together amicably, and often invent ways of passing the time. Once this performance is over the audience disperses and the imitation is not again repeated.

The phones of many Great Tit phrases stand out clearly like words. As a greeting among themselves and to me, they call 'Hee-hoy.' Those that know me well often call this when meeting me along the road; if I don't stand still and look at them they repeat it loudly and persistently until I do take notice. But if this fails to attract attention the female gives a scold-note; the male more often tries one of his other very dominant-sounding phrases. One day I was gardening when a Great Tit tried to attract my attention by flitting about in front of me with call-notes. Not wanting to stop work and put muddy hands into my pocket for his tit-bit box I pretended not to see him and kept my eyes on the ground. But a Great Tit is never at a loss unless frightened. In a few moments I heard a Wagtail's double-noted call coming from just above my head. Astonished at the perfection of the imitation, I immediately looked at the Tit – he had won, he nearly always does! With airy confidence, suggesting slight swagger, he perched on my hand to eat his tit-bit. I never heard that Wagtail note from him again, it was his inspiration of the moment and done to force my attention.

One delightful song, common to the species, has an accompaniment of wing tremolo – the same kind of ecstatic tremulous movement as in a Lark's soaring flight, only the Tit remains on his perch for the performance. This song, in effect, is slightly like the sound produced by quickly and lightly running a finger backwards and forwards across the strings of a guitar – only, of course, much higher pitched – and there is a slight breath taken before the reverse movement, which gives the song a rocking rhythm of great fascination to me. It is always sung from cover – under a bush, among foliage, or from underneath a chair in my room sometimes. But this, like their other songs, varies in details of intervals, etc.

The well-known 'tee-chū' song has much variation among individuals, each bird sticking to his own version. Here are two examples (Twist's mate's song and Timpano's song):

These songs rapidly and continuously repeated with much verve.

Another song common to Great Tits is:

Whatever his tune he makes the notes ring with life and good cheer.

Young Great Tits in summer and autumn sing a soft, continuous song, a little resembling the Robin's subsong. It is a pity adult Great Tits discard this lovely little song. Females share in some of the conversational notes or phrases and the gentle-toned long spun call-notes she utters when shepherding her young make as charming a piece of music as can be heard from any bird. Although its gentle delivery makes it completely different from any of the other songs, it is a form of miniature representation of the above notation.

Last summer when I was sitting in the orchard listening to a Blackcap singing from the hedge, the Great Tit Inkey flew up to me to get cheese for his young; he perched on my hand and was about to take food when he suddenly drew back, looked towards the warbling Blackcap and remained transfixed in an alert, listening pose, his eyes on the warbler. Then, instead of taking the cheese he flew to a branch beside me and sang an excellent imitation of the Blackcap's warbling. He repeated it several times, then shaking his feathers, as if to throw off the music, he returned to duty, took the cheese and fed his young. I never heard him sing that song again, it had taken his fancy for the moment and it was the rhythm he imitated so well, getting it almost exact only with a little more accentuation of beats. This was no mean achievement, for the Blackcap's warbling is intricate.

Great Tits seems to share one or two phrases with Marsh-Tits, for these are included in the repertoire of both species.

MARSH-TIT AND COAL-TIT

Marsh-Tits and Coal-Tits have several song-notes common to their species, also a variety of phrases are heard from individuals that are totally unexpected. Especially this applies to Marsh-Tits, who may spring a surprise on the listener by a fine, bold imitation of another species. The following unusual incident occurred on April 7th, 1948. (I quote from notes made on the spot.)

From where a Nightingale nests each year a Marsh-Tit sings two of his song-phrases, a trill-note and the loud note that increases in speed until a vibratory effect is achieved. The Marsh Tit's power in this imitation is amazing. He repeats these Nightingale phrases many times from a high tree-branch, with much wing-flickering. He then sings his own songs in his ordinary tones of voice while flitting about the tree. He calls 'Fitz-e-deu, fitz-e-deu,' two or three times, and says 'Bubble-na-na-na.' He has a lot of song today. Then he flies to the tree-top again for the Nightingale notes, ten times more loudly sung than his own songs and the timbre completely different. An astonishing performance for a Marsh-Tit. It actually deceived me at first, for migrants were early that year, Chiffchaff singing on March 7th, Willow-Warbler on 23rd, and I was expecting an early Nightingale. I accounted for the voice sounding not in good form by imagining the bird had just arrived and might be tired after his travels! This is the only time I remember being deceived by an imitation, and it is curious that the Marsh-Tit, who has no reputation for being an imitator, should be the deceiver. But individuality among birds is so strong that they are for ever overstepping their reputations and putting wrong all formulated theories.

CUCKOO

The Cuckoo sings his name in any interval from a second to a fifth. I think each bird generally keeps to his own interval but, when under excitement of pursuing the female, stammering often occurs and other variations of the normal song. It is said, 'In June the Cuckoo changes his tune.' I think it is emotion more than calendar dates that make changes temporally take place. However, the most striking change in tune I have heard was both in June and under excitement. On June 11th the two Cuckoos that had been constantly in the neighborhood of my garden were joined by a third one. The three birds for the next three days behaved very excitedly, displaying and giving chase while uttering odd gutteral notes. One bird continually sang this song, with its two unusual phones and changes of interval.

I came to the conclusion the third bird was a female, this song being sung by the male who had previously haunted my garden, for the other two had no 'Cuckoo' song. The bubbling note was sometimes heard and other odd sounds such as Cuckoos make under excitement of their changeling escapades. After June 14th no Cuckoos were again seen near my garden.

I once saw a female Cuckoo fly to a tree-top with her bubbling note, and perching on a prominent fork of a dead branch, perform actions of nest-building on the bare fork. She turned round very slowly, pressing her breast on the fork exactly as if moulding a nest, sometimes standing up and making actions with her beak as if arranging nesting material round the nest-cup. Her mate watched from a hedge nearby. Presently he began calling and flew to her, perching on one fork-tip. She continued nest-moulding movements, he began displaying in usual Cuckoo fashion. Then he flew off, she following. A few minutes later they returned to the hedge where he had before perched while watching her. As they were often near the same hedge afterwards I am sure some nest there became the first egg depository, for this was early in the season. I was unable to follow up close observations owing to the farm owner objecting to bird-watching on his land.

BULLFINCH

Bullfinches have an original song of a style quite unlike any other species. I believe each individual sings a slightly different tune. The following beautiful little chant was sung by Chanter in my orchard. It was possible to notate it because he used the human scale correctly and had a sense of key, for there is a definite feeling of progression to the tonic – or keynote.

Sung in April:

Sung in May:

He repeated these two notes  as if he had satisfaction in his cadence which ends on the keynote. Often he piped this cadence alone – as do other Bullfinches. Sometimes he sang only the first half of the tune, and he gave me the delight of hearing his full chant only a few times, always between 1.30 and 2 p.m. (Summer Time). He also made some other variations of the tune later in the year and the following year.

It is a great pity Bullfinches are lazy over singing their full song since they can compose such good music. It is usual for them to pipe bits of their song as they move about the trees, and their way of doing this reminds me of people who hum fragments of tunes absent-mindedly while going about their work.

Another Bullfinch in my garden sang the same sort of melody, but inserted a double-noted call-note instead of the rests, which gave a very different effect to the song. The first tune (Chanter's) was better music from a human standard because there the bird seemed to have realised that rests in musical phrases are sometimes as important as notes. Filling up gaps with call-notes is decorative, but musically not so strong, although the female Bullfinch perhaps would not agree!

Their piping notes have a distinct resemblance to pan pipes, very softly blown. Bullfinches unfortunately have a rather hesitant delivery which does not do full justice to their compositions. If they had stronger voices and more rhythmic delivery they would truly be great and famous as songsters. But their soft tones are lovely and watching this charming bird while he pipes his plain-song is one of the really great pleasures of life.

LINNET

It seems incomplete to write of the Linnet's song without mention of his mate for he sings his 'love-song' to her during nesting in a more pointed manner than most species. It is very pretty to watch. The following account is of a pair quite fearless of my presence, so very close watching was easier than in some cases.

Two Linnets flew out of a gorse bush, keeping close together and twittering softly. They alighted on the slopes near their chosen bush, the female collecting nesting material while her mate followed behind, not working himself but watching her and seeming to notice all her movements with great eagerness. When her beak was stocked he accompanied her back to the nesting bush; while she started to build he perched close by and, with the sun lighting his crimson breast and crown, he sang a mysterious musical language of phrases half-whispered, half-sung, intermingled with bell-like trills and wistful-sounding, caressing notes. The female often paused in her work to look up at him. The song rose to a fuller, more sustained trill and before this subsided both Linnets again took to the wing, with lilting flight and song. Thus the nest was built, the male always following close behind his mate and singing nearby while she worked. When she brooded the four eggs in her neat little nest, he always faced her while singing continually from perches visible to her. The nest was rather exposed from above and, when the downy grey nestlings felt the sun's heat, their mother perched on a twig jutting over the nest and spread her wings as a sunshade over the brood, her mate supplying food and full measure of song. But a Jackdaw spotted the nest and one morning the poor Linnets were fluttering over the gorse bush, searching and crying for their lost young. The whole morning they cried, hovering over their bush, a piteous sight to watch. Then the male began singing, his voice louder and fuller than before, and in response to his song the mother bird abandoned her search and flew to him; with twittering notes, they remained on the bush a while, then suddenly rose of one accord and with eager, purposeful flight, left the scene of their loss, never to return. Wisely, they had chosen to seek another site for their second brood.

The Linnet's music has much variety of tone colour, from the softest of delicate notes to the brilliance of trill crescendos. When, in flocking season, numbers gather to sing in chorus the concerted effect of rise and fall of tone is very wonderful, and it seems the Linnets do their utmost to produce this effect. It is interesting to watch and listen to flock performances. They may begin by about thirty birds flying to a tree in an excited, purposeful manner, all alighting simultaneously and near together. Then one bird starts singing, by about his third note another joins in, the rest following in quick succession, perhaps six at a time entering the chorus, some trilling, some twittering, some singing upward and downward slurred notes until all voices combine in a great crescendo held for a few moments. Then the volume of tone gradually sinks while over the fields another flock is seen heading in rushing flight for the Linnets' tree. They settle beside the singers and now the chorus again swells, the two flocks by degrees uniting in song until every bird has joined in a redoubled crescendo. The sound of this chorus travels far, stirring other flocks feeding in more distant fields. Before long there is another hurried rushing of wings, and the tree, bare of leaf, becomes laden with Linnets on every twig, all voicing their loudest fortissimo. The song reaches its climax which is held for a time, then the tone falls and rises again, until suddenly, all together, the birds take to flight, their minds tuned to one accord in song now act under one impulse to fly. The deserted tree, standing naked, seems strangely silent and bereft of life.

The Linnets' gradual entry into the chorus is undoubtedly for the purpose of working up a crescendo since these effects of crescendo and diminuendo play a large part in bird-song.

SPARROWS

In autumn large flocks of House and Tree-Sparrows congregate for singing in chorus. Naturally, a rough-toned result is produced from their harsh, chattering notes, but at least they seem striving for an effect of volume of tone. Unlike Linnets, their unruly natures are unable to concentrate long upon music, for throughout the chirruping chorus many ugly squawks can be heard as some members of the choir roughly peck their neighbouring singers in an attempt to bag their perches. Sparrows always want what the other fellow possesses, even if it is the twig upon which he stands! Their chirping chorus is a better musical effort than the solo chatter or chirrup, which can hardly be called song.

GOLDFINCH

The song of a Goldfinch is a musical picture of himself; full of gay charm and brilliance artistically blended with quiet tones; light, quick and spontaneous in movement, lively and light-hearted in effect. Thrush, Blackbird or Blackcap sing with head raised to heaven, not calling attention to their fine feathers while lost in song, but the Goldfinch makes sure the bright colours he wears are seen while singing his full song from a tree-top in spring. Bending low, he rotates his head to show off his crimson head-dress; still singing, he turns round on his perch, slightly spreading his wings so the gold bars he possesses are seen while he works up the trills of his song to a suitable brilliance.

Like most species, his song is fullest in spring, but Goldfinch's fluent, gay music can be heard all summer and autumn, then doubly precious because bird-song has become scarce. They give an impression of happiness perhaps more than any other species; all their actions seem set to music, for their call-note, repeated continually by young and old, is daintily musical and a pleasure to hear. The phones of this call-note sound something like 'wait-a-bit, wait-a-bit,' and often these words seem fitting, especially in flight when they look as if trying to catch up each other by taking light, springy air-leaps while calling 'wait-a-bit, wait-a-bit.'

Young birds, called 'grey-pates,' soon begin to practise their song, at first rather scratchy and unsteady in tone, but they work hard, perched high in some quiet corner, refining their tone quality and by degrees adding more notes to their song.

A charm of Goldfinches will sometimes alight on a tree-top and perform part singing. Their idea of concerted singing seems different from Linnets'. Each bird accentuates his phrasing, phones and cadences so the different voices stand out clearly in counterpoint. This part-singing seems to be intentional and is unlike the sound made when a number happen to be singing between feeding on wayside thistles. Listening yesterday to this part-singing, the following phrase – usual to Goldfinches – was very prominent from one bird:

It sounded most effective against the quick-noted passages and trills of the other birds. They had learnt the value of making short rests all together after cadences, this perhaps being the most definite proof that they were making music together in sympathetic accord, not each bird singing his own song as a solo performance.

The Goldfinch's song is sometimes described as resembling that of a Canary, but Goldfinch music, like his personality, is far daintier than the Canary's.

GREENFINCH

The Greenfinch should take some tips from Goldfinches especially on daintiness! His sturdy full song, heard at its best early in the season, is pleasantly musical, but he soon gets lazy and stolidly grinds out, monotonously as a pedlar calling his wares, the least musical part of his song – two or three notes ending in 'breeeese.'* As the season advances, he cuts out all notes except 'breeeese,' which is persistently repeated in a voice grown coarser and more drawling. This peculiarity may arise from a cumbersome trait in his character, shown when he becomes fearless and intimate on the bird-table, but it is a pity he gets into this rut of droning the least musical portion of his song when possessing trills and other musical notes that are very pleasant to hear. In early spring he sometimes sings while hovering over tree-tops or bushes.

One of his call-notes is a neat little trill which varies in length. When nest-building both male and female extend it considerably and use this note often for calling to each other from the nest; the quick, close trills, held at an even tone level, sound very like electric bells in miniature. When one bird utters the trill-note it never fails to bring a similar response from the mate, either called from a distant bush or while quickly winging towards its mate.

In writing of the Linnet and Goldfinch I mentioned the upward and downward slurred notes in their songs. The Greenfinch's 'breeeese' is drawled up or down, and sometimes drags itself both ways on a droning glissando. This appears to be a Finch-note in common, which each species sings according to his temperament and taste. All three species use the phrase a great deal, both in song and by itself as a solo performance. The Linnet, between his quick passages, often whispers this Finch-note phrase or sings it in the most delicate tones ever uttered by bird, with changing phones for the two notes. Goldfinches sing as if calling brightly:

---

* Handbook's 'Tswee'.

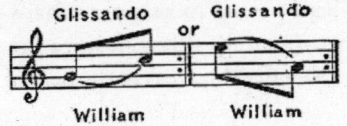

and in each case a glissando up or down is used, sometimes alternating the two, sometimes repeating one way only. This is the same with all three Finches. An apology is now due to Greenfinches for my rudeness over his drawling version of the Finch-note. The Green Linnet is a fine singer at times, and I am very fond of watching this bird.

CORN-BUNTING

I first heard a Corn-Bunting's song one August day when sitting under the lee of a wheatfield on high downland. A strong, gusty wind blew with a cutting sound through the hard, stiff ears of corn; apart from this it was very quiet, and no birds were in sight. Then came a lull in the wind and another sound, unknown to me, came from across the wheat-field. For a moment this, too, seemed the wind playing on the stiff, ripe corn, then I stood up to search the great field for a first glimpse of the bird. He was perched on a tall thistle surrounded by a sea of golden corn, wheezing out his song every second as if breathing life into all the ripening grains of wheat. 'Ticker, ticker, dureees-er; ticker, ticker, dureees-er' – a small sound in the vastness of the open downland space yet it seemed vital heard in that field of growing corn.

Autumn flocking season is another time when this species can be fully appreciated. During September and early October they congregate in large numbers on reedy marshland several miles from my home. A flock of sixty or more will perch on a bush to wind up their little clocks – for so their song sounds. They seem too preoccupied to notice or fear the bird-watcher within about six feet, but one step nearer and a few fly off with their call-note 'ticker, ticker, ticker,' others follow on until all are flying, ticking like a lot of busy wound-up clocks. 'Ticker' is their flock call, but also it often begins their song. Even their flight has a suggestion of clockwork, the whizzing movement of their wings looking like a flywheel spinning round at a tremendous pace, hard pushed to keep the heavily-built body on the move! But the Corn-Bunting, although not a great singer, seems of vital importance to that marshland as in the field of ripening corn.

YELLOWHAMMER

The Yellowhammer's song depends for its beauty upon a wonderful cadence which is not always sung, especially in some northern districts, where I believe the song frequently falls short of its perfection. Perhaps the climate there is less favourable, for this species sings best in warmth and sunshine, choosing mid-morning and afternoon for music and singing all through the heat of summer days.

From some high perch the Yellowhammer sings his little song of a few quick, level-toned notes leading to the cadence of one note poised high and a sheer drop to the final note, this rise and fall of interval very beautiful when the bird sings his best, the good singer putting just the right balance of tone and pronouncing clearly the lovely change of phone on the high note 'no.' The rise and fall of interval and phone-changes are evidently hard to accomplish, and it takes the young bird a long time even to attempt the cadence. The quick opening notes are first sung and after some weeks the high note may be jerked out in clumsy fashion as if the bird found it beyond his technical ability; the last note of sudden fall in pitch is not attempted until the following year. I once heard a young and an adult Yellowhammer singing from adjoining trees. The contrast was interesting. In this case the youngster pitched his song approximately a fifth higher and his immature effort ended on the high note, squeaked out as if his voice had broken. As his song was pitched so high perhaps the top note was beyond the compass of his voice. The mature bird's performance showed what artistic perfection can be reached even in the Yellowhammer's little song.

CURLEW, REDSHANK, ETC.

Birds can create a remote atmosphere just by one or two notes. This applies most of all to the Curlew's lovely call and to his music of crescendos and diminuendos, an air-born song with travelling trills that seem to come from infinity, linking the unknown beauty with all that we know of loveliness. The Redshank's notes and trilling have something of the same far-reaching quality, as also the other smaller Waders, who set the air trembling with their chorus of clear, piping notes while they themselves remain invisible as spirits against the dun-coloured feeding ground until suddenly their music ceases and they appear as one flickering-white form, moving fast above earth – the song-chorus embodied in flock-flight. With electrical precision the flashing white form changes colour to dark grey as it twists and turns rapidly over the feeding ground. Then flight ceases and the fast-moving flock looks to have flown beneath earth, so invisible do the Waders become as together they touch land, again making soft music with their clear, liquid voices that have such a strangely moving quality. The bond between music and flight is strong. Both are arts belonging to the freedom of air and space, both have movement formed into rhythm by balance of time.

TREE-PIPIT

The Tree-Pipit and Meadow-Pipit are among those who combine song with flight, both birds' performances being beautiful, but the Tree-Pipit's music is far richer. His song varies much in beauty for some individuals dispense with the flight; they then sing only a stilted edition of the song, full expression never being reached without the usual combination of flight. The two are so interdependent that the best songs have the best flights. An abridged song is sung to a very short, fluttering rise and gliding return to the same perch, but the flight-song can reach superb perfection.

For me, one individual Tree-Pipit shines out above all others I have heard. It was one spring day when the beech trees on the slopes of Wolstonbury Hill were just ready to break into leaf – a small spray of green showing here and there. From one of these trees rose the small brown bird, the sun lighting his plumage to a bright russet-brown exactly matching the sheaved buds of the beeches, while his pale underparts shone the same colour as the silvery stems of the trees. Like a Sky-Lark he soared on vibrant wings, then in exquisite full song he hovered a moment and floated down on wide-spread wings in a perfect spiral towards another tree, caressingly intoning 'seea-seea-seea,' his notes coming slower, slower, until he alighted with one last lingering 'seea,' then changed his tune to 'e-chuff, e-chuff, e-chuff' – these last notes sounding as if letting out steam after perching. Soon he rose again and many times repeated this perfect flight-song with an aerial curve over the trees, always gliding in caressing song to a different beech. This gave me the fanciful impression he was performing some wonderful rite of blessing the beeches of Wolstonbury Hill while they began to unfurl their leaves. It is a pity this beautiful flight-song is so often abridged by lazy or incompetent performers.

SKY-LARK

The Sky-Lark seems to belong more to heaven than to earth. When he sings near to earth without soaring the song lacks its fervour. Always a wing tremolo – or vibrato – accompanies his flight-song. I have seen a Lark singing his full song facing a strong breeze and drifting slowly backwards on tremulous wings. When the field hedge was below him the song and wing fluttering suddenly ceased, and he flew quickly forward against the wind, with fast but firmly-beating wings alternating between rests with wings closed, a dipping flight accompanied by his call-note, 'seep, seep.' They have a short little song, sung close to the ground or when chasing each other, this seeming conversational and an extension of one of their call-notes – the trill call-note.

Lark music has special significance for me. One of the great experiences of my life was when I first heard the song, at the age of about eleven, with full realisation of its beauty. I was lying on the slopes of a sand-dune, a book opened to start reading, when the Lark's song suddenly held me; while the bird soared far into the sky overhead his music brought a glorious revelation of beauty, not only for its own sake, but because it seemed the true meaning of life. Certain details of the scene remain vividly clear, especially the marram-grass tufts on the high sand-hill above me, the last pinnacle of earth beyond which was the blue sky, the Lark's world.

A bird, in spite of the inspirational power of his song, is generally supposed to be devoid of the immortal soul accredited to man. Among those who feel strongly the spiritual appeal of bird-song there must be some who ponder this question: How can bird-music have this great power to move a human soul unless a bird's spirit, released in song, is component with the Divine?

> The starry voice ascending spreads,
> Awakening, as it waxes thin,
> The best in us to him akin:
>   •   •   •   •   •
>
> Our wisdom speaks from failing blood,
> Our passion is too full in flood,
> We want the key of his wild note
> Of truthful in a tuneful throat.

LIVING WITH BIRDS

AUTHOR'S NOTE

Thanks are due to the editors of *The Countryman*, *Out of Doors* and *Countrygoer* for permission to reprint various passages in Chapters 10 and 12.
Also I wish to thank all those whose photographs appear in the book:
Mr S. Bayliss Smith, Mr Eric Hosking, Mr John Markham, Mr Owen Martin, Mr L. Hugh Newman, Mr J. M. Simpson and Mr C. W. Teager. All the remaining photographs were taken by me.

Contents

Preface	185
1 Star, a Great Tit of Genius	187
Introductory	187
Courting and Combats	188
Talent is Revealed	192
2 Star's Talent is Developed	201
Nesting Problems	201
The Talent is Developed	210
3 Star's Further Amazing Achievements	218
Progress Continues	218
Rivals on the Screen	224
Perseverance despite Interruptions	235
Final Achievements	242
4 Beauty Brings his Lame Fledgling	254
5 Illness and Injury	266
6 Great Tit Parents and Young	278
7 Youngsters (*continued*)	290
8 Blue Tits and Coal Tits	313
9 A Hedgehog Comes to Call	320
10 Robins and Others	328
Robins; Dobs, Turk, Stalky and Co.	328
Wrens, in Snow and Sunshine	333
House Sparrows; Grimes and Nogood	335
Nuthatches, in Garden and Wood	337
11 Taming and Attracting the Birds	342
12 Migrants in the Garden	349
Blackcaps	349
Garden Warblers and Lesser Whitethroats	352
Willow Warblers and Spotted Flycatchers	354
Turtle Doves	358
Swallows and House Martins	360

13	Blackbird Behaviour	364
14	Young Blackbirds, in Drought, Wind and Rain	383
15	Codes of Behaviour and General Conclusions	391

Photo Credits 398

Preface

Fourteen years ago I left London and began living with wild birds flying freely in and out of my small cottage in Sussex. Because the behaviour of the Great Tits was so intelligent and each individual so different in character I became especially interested in studying this species and recording their behaviour in detail. Some of their life histories were given in my first book *Birds as Individuals*. After I had written this I discovered that one of the Great Tits had a remarkable talent which she developed with keen interest. Much of my time for the three following years was given to watching this bird, whom I had named 'Star,' and working with her to develop her gift. The results were so astonishing that I decided upon this continuation of bird biographies.

This talented Great Tit was the third mate of a bird called 'Baldhead,' whose biography up to June 1950 was recorded in *Birds as Individuals*. A few incidents of their nesting season in that year have to be repeated in the opening chapter of this second book, otherwise the biography of this remarkable bird would be incomplete, but I have told them here from the point of view of Star's behaviour instead of Baldhead's.

All the material in the book is accurately compiled from notes taken at the time of the events. No scientific terms have been used as these would not be understood by many readers. In my former book I stressed the fact that much intelligence and individuality exists among birds. Also I said that their natural behaviour is suppressed at the slightest suspicion of fear. By living with birds I gain their complete trust so that they can reveal the extent of their intelligence and individuality which in this continuation of biographies is still further proved.

Len Howard

CHAPTER I

Star, a Great Tit of Genius

1. INTRODUCTORY

For many years about forty Great Tits, twenty Blue Tits, Blackbirds, Thrushes and other species have been in and out of my cottage all day, some of the Tits also roosting indoors. The interior of the cottage is arranged to suit them and my life has become more or less regulated by theirs. Great Tits fly around me whatever I am doing so that work needing concentration is better done after dark.

This evening, before beginning to write their biographies I stood at my window, watching the autumn sunset fade into dusk while the last 'tchinks' of a Blackbird came from his roost in a tree by the cottage. A Robin, in the dim light, flitted hastily to the bird-bath on the border of his territory, cocked his head saucily towards his rival already roosting in a tree, then he flew back to the inner precincts of his land. A faint 'tic, tic,' was heard as he sought his roost. All was now quiet in the garden; the Wren was asleep in a coconut-shell hung to the window-frame. Indoors, the Great Tits and Blue Tits turned in their roost-boxes as I drew the curtains and switched on the reading-lamp; they were used to this and soon fell asleep again, but the noise of typing disturbs them; if continued for long they become restless and hammer on their roost-boxes until I stop tapping the keys. How to get a book written under these conditions is one of the many problems of living with birds.

Although completely fearless with me, my birds are often slow to appear before human strangers, but it is curious that on occasions when their immediate appearance was most helpful they have come at once. During the war some Canadian troops, stationed nearby, came swarming across the field behind my garden hedge and started to break through it, until I called out to them to stop. The men waited while their leader came forward and said sharply, 'Private property can't be considered. We are practising getting to the village without going on the roads. We must go through your garden and hedges . . .' He stared at me in a puzzled manner and left his sentence unfinished, for birds were flying down from the trees and perching on me. 'That's funny,' he said. 'I've been in England a long time and never knew English people had their garden birds behave like that. I've been all over England too and never seen this before.' When I told him a little about my birds he stared at me all the harder. 'Then it's not an English custom? It's your own idea to live with these birds?' I said that it was their idea to live with me and that I had to protect them. 'I like to see them tame like that,' he said. 'If we come tramping through your garden we might frighten these little birds. We'll go another way.' As he retreated through the hedge he called out, 'I'm lucky to have seen this. I'll be telling them about it back home. Wonder if they'll believe me.' A few days later the nameplate, 'Bird Cottage,' was missing from my gate. At dusk the previous evening I had seen two Canadians stooping over it. Perhaps the cottage name was wanted by one of them as a backing for the bird-tale he had to tell.

The cottage is on a main road at one end of a fairly large village but thick hedges and trees surround the garden, and the gateway is kept overgrown to make it inconspicuous. The nameplate was never replaced, for too many people were coming in to see the birds and this upset them. In spring and summer especially, Bird Cottage must be kept very quiet.

2. COURTING AND COMBATS

In the early spring of 1946 a distinguished-looking Great Tit, with a small white star on her crown, appeared in my garden. She and her mate were strangers who had taken a territory in the neighbouring West Garden, but they had secured a nest-box hung to a tree in my west hedge. My resident Tits kept them from encroaching beyond this so I rarely saw them. Unaware that this Tit with the white star was a bird with an astonishing talent, I unfortunately chose Star, as I called her, for an experiment of moving her nest-box while she was absent, to see whether she knew it elsewhere, as I would not inflict this upon any bird whose confidence in me was absolute. Directly I took down her box she reappeared and hovered over me, crying so distressfully that I hurriedly replaced the nest-box on her chosen tree, leaving her to brood her eggs in peace.

This interference with Star's nest-box made her cautious of close intercourse with me for three years. It was not until the early autumn of 1949, when she was determined to get a bird called Baldhead for a mate, that she lost her shyness, perhaps because she saw that Baldhead had complete confidence in me. This male's biography, up to 1950, was given in my previous book *Birds as Individuals*; a short repetition of some facts in Baldhead's 1950 nesting season is necessary to make Star's biography complete.

Star showed much determination of character from the beginning. All the autumn and winter she persistently followed Baldhead about, entering the room directly after him and watching from a perch nearby while he fed from my hand. If he left the room directly afterwards she ignored the nut I offered her and flew after him, so keen was she to keep him in sight. For some weeks he seemed not to notice her; his mate of the previous season, called Monocle because of a rim round one eye, was still alive. If she had made efforts to keep him probably he would have remained faithful to her, but she never sought his company, so by mid-winter Star had won Baldhead for a mate.

She now put all her energy into helping him regain his old territory and nest-box by my cottage, which he had lost the previous spring to a Great Tit called Inkey, after desperate struggles that had cost him a leg injury and the loss of his head feathers. These had grown during the summer and he was again beautiful in appearance, but he was slightly lame.

Baldhead had roosted all the autumn and winter in the nest-box which Inkey had won from him; his victor had made no objection to this, but when territorial disputes began at the end of January 1950, Inkey and his mate Smoke again wanted the nesting-site and box. The previous year Baldhead's mate, Monocle, had left all the fighting to him. While he struggled with Inkey, even after he was injured, she cautiously hid in the bushes and flew away from Smoke, but Star's character was quite different; she was full of life and determination, and when there was something of importance to be done she worked hard until she had achieved it. Fearlessly she took a large share in fighting for the territory and nest-box. Often she came to grips with Smoke and as they rolled together on the ground with feet interlocked,

Baldhead hovered over them in agitation, squeaking out high-pitched notes. His lamed leg had resulted from this form of combat. Star and Smoke seemed equally matched in strength, both were vigorous birds, eager for conquest, but Star showed more persistence and after some days her ceaseless efforts wore out Smoke's resistance, she then became nervous of approaching Star and hovered in the background, while Star joined Baldhead in display by the nest-box. Baldhead also worked continuously at displays of various original kinds; he could not come to grips with Inkey because of his weak leg, but his spirit was indomitable. He invented a special form of high-speed attack which he used whenever Inkey perched by the nest-box. Such phenomenal speed was put into these charges, which were accompanied by high-pitched squeak-notes, that Inkey retreated every time.

Baldhead had grown an abnormal spike on the tip of his upper mandible, which made his beak look very long and gave him an impressive appearance. In these charges at Inkey he held his head well forward, thus making his beak conspicuous.

When Star saw Baldhead making these flashy attacks she flew to his side as Inkey retired into the background, then she and Baldhead made a show of examining the nest-box inside and out, with fussy, exaggerated movements, no doubt meant to impress Inkey and Smoke who watched from behind a tree.

By mid-February Baldhead, with Star's constant help, had won back his old territory and nest-box. This year (1950) he had kept all his head feathers intact. Now the battles were over, his previous mate, Monocle, appeared and for a few days made cautious efforts to get near the box. Baldhead took no notice of her. In the heyday of his youth he had been a bigamist and this had ended in tragedy (as related in *Birds as Individuals*). Bigamy is rare among Great Tits. Star, however, was continually on the watch for Monocle, and when she was seen edging her way slowly through the bushes towards the box, Star quietly approached her and she retreated. One day, instead of retiring, Monocle dodged round the adjacent macrocarpus-tree and tried to get to the nest-box from the other side. Star's manner changed, she grew angry, did many chin-up displays, then flew at Monocle with loud scold-notes, driving her from my garden and pursuing her beyond West Garden. Monocle did not again attempt to enter Star's territory. She mated with a first year bird who took the adjoining territory. She never went near their boundary and avoided all contact with Star and Baldhead, leaving my room at once if either of them were there. Her mate, called Peetur because he sang what sounded like 'pee-tur,' many times repeated, was on good terms with Baldhead. They often overlapped their boundaries when feeding.

On 20th February, Star for the first time roosted in the nest-box. It is not usual for Great Tits to sleep together so when Baldhead tried to enter soon afterwards she jumped up and pushed him out. He showed agitation and insisted upon entering. There was a sound of fluttering wings inside the box and he reappeared looking flustered and annoyed. After a turn round their territory he tried again with the same result. He looked cross and made whimpering sounds, hammered at the entrance hole and poked his head inside, but Star again jumped up and pushed him away. From Baldhead's point of view this large box had been his roost since last summer and he preferred it to any other; Star's viewpoint would be that nest-boxes had to be kept clean and having a mate roosting there would mean more work in removing excreta, also it was not the custom for Great Tits to share roosts. But Star gave way in the end, and almost in starlight, Baldhead entered and all was quiet inside the box. For several evenings the same tussle occurred but Star gave in sooner each day. On 27th February, when she had thrust him out for the seventh time he flitted round their box, uttering loud scold-notes while she jumped up and down inside, trying to catch glimpses of him through the entrance hole without being seen by him. When he again tried to enter she loudly rapped the floor of the box and this drove him away. A few minutes later he made a successful entry. After this Star made no further protests and he slept with her until their young were several days old, when he roosted elsewhere of his own accord.

This domestic disagreement was amusing to watch; possibly Star, too, got some fun from it, but Baldhead found it no joke, judging from his behaviour and expressions!

The abnormal spike on Baldhead's upper mandible had continued to grow and it curved downwards, evidently from pressure put on it when he was trying to pick up food. He now had learnt to turn his head sideways while feeding. When he first brought Star food he had difficulty in handing her his offering because of this projection. She shrank back in fear of contacting the spike and both birds stood facing each other with troubled expressions. After a minute Baldhead had an idea; he went up to her with his head turned sideways and she neatly took the caterpillar from the side of his beak. He must have realised that he could not feed his young in this manner, for two days before they were hatched he began vigorous bill-wiping, working at it for much of the day with difficulty because he had little grip of his perch owing to his weak leg. Sometimes he nearly fell over in his efforts to break off the projection, but he persevered and got rid of his impediment the day that the young were hatched. The theory that birds are conscious only of the present moment cannot be correct; there is much evidence that they make preparations in advance over things that apply only to the individual bird, therefore these cannot be instinctive actions.

Early one morning, five days after Star's fledglings left the nest, she kept rushing to me in an unusually excited manner, to fetch food for the fledglings. Normally she gave them mostly natural food. Baldhead did not appear for an hour, then he flew to me and lay on my lap, unable to stand. His lame leg had been strained again. Star showed much agitation, and began displaying before him, quivering her wings and making nestling-cry sounds. He responded by a faint cry but lay still until she had flown to her young, then he bravely resumed work on one leg, often supporting himself by aid of spread wings while putting food into a fledgling's mouth. After this Star took the main share of feeding the large family, working from morning until night, while Baldhead took intervals of rest. She stimulated him by frequent wing quivering displays. They never left my garden, their brood being kept alternately in the front part or in the orchard at the back of the cottage.

3. TALENT IS REVEALED

After this strenuous nesting season was over Star and Baldhead spent restful days sunbathing and preening. The white star on her crown reappeared after her moult, and she again looked trim and elegant. There was always a neatness in her movements which gave her an air of competence, but her outstanding feature was her eyes, which were exceptionally bright.

STAR, A GREAT TIT OF GENIUS

In September and October, like many of my other Tits, she spent much time over the seasonal pastimes of paper-tearing, hammering at my furniture and ripping the upholstery. Whatever Star set her mind upon she did thoroughly, to the best of her ability, so the holes made by her were larger and deeper than those made by the others, her paper-tearing was done quickly and efficiently and, listening to this demolition squad at work, it was Star's hammering that stood out the loudest. Although admiring her efficiency I had to discourage her from hammering because of the damage she did. Often I chased her to the window, saying 'Stop it!' but directly I was not watching, she flew back with renewed zest to continue her occupation.

It was not chance, but through noticing Star's character, that I chose her for the experiment which follows.

By the end of November, all the Tits had given up their hammering and paper-tearing pastime, the days being short and the natural food which they needed – besides what I provided – taking longer to find. Star was not one of my indoor roosters, but she was always the first to enter my room when I drew back the curtains. One morning, the 6th January, the idea struck me of trying her with a counting experiment.

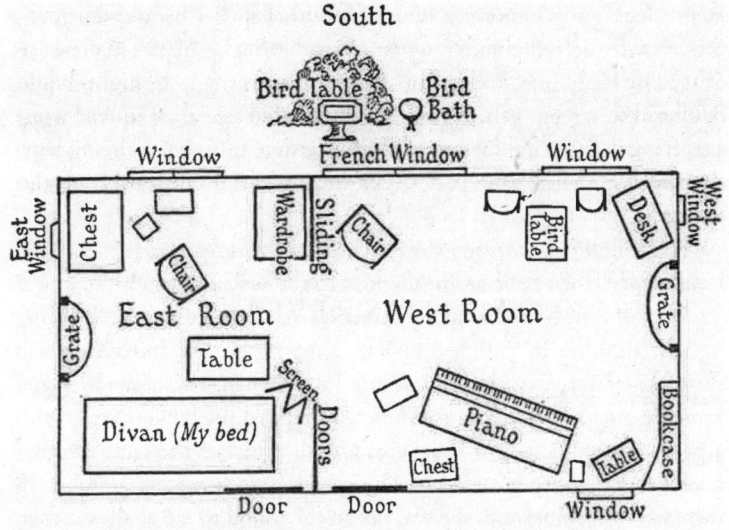

M *Star's tapping perch on screen frame*

When, as usual, she flew to my hand for her nut, instead of giving it to her I held it up in my other hand and said, 'You must tap for it.' Looking at her intently I called in sharp accents, 'Tap, Tap.' While I spoke her eyes were fixed keenly on mine, then she immediately flew to the top of a wooden screen-frame – a favourite bird perch – and deliberately rapped out two taps on the wood with her beak, copying my speed, she then flew to my hand for the nut. An hour later I tried her again with the same number. She responded correctly in exactly the same manner, flying to my hand directly afterwards for her nut. She had never been given food for hammering at things, on the contrary, as already related, I had tried to stop her indiscriminate hammerings in the autumn.

The next morning, the suggestion to tap three times was given her. She at once made three resounding raps on the screen. This test was successfully repeated four times during the day. She always copied my rather slow speed. On two occasions I attempted to get her to repeat the series of three taps twice running. This resulted in her leaving the room at once, but after an interval of about an hour she was responsive.

The third day a difficulty arose. Directly she appeared, she flew eagerly to the screen and instantly gave three rhythmic taps, then came to me for her nut. I withheld it because I wanted to try her with four beats. Seeing my hesitation, she angrily turned her back towards me then hastily left the room without the nut. She kept away for an unusually long time, four hours. When she returned, she again flew at once to the screen, instantly rapped out three taps then looked up at me, hoping this time for her reward. I gave it to her, for she thought she had done what was expected of her and I did not want to annoy her again.

The following morning she perched on the screen, gave me a sidelong glance, then bent her head close to the wood without tapping. I rapped out four beats, using my knuckles on the table instead of giving her the number by calling out 'tap' four times. She looked up and stared at me intently but did not tap. Probably the sound made by my knuckles was too muffled, for directly I tapped the table sharply with a pencil she got the four beats correctly. I repeated the same number several times during the day. She never gave a wrong number in response, but sometimes she was not in the mood to tap at all, she then turned her head upwards, to show that she was not interested; I gave

Star's pose to show me a lesson is not wanted

her a nut without trying to force her attention as a bird must be humoured to get good results in an experiment of this sort. When she was in the mood for a lesson, she either bowed her head close to the screen or looked at me with a very intent expression. If other birds were in the room she was unable to concentrate, and it was not often I had her alone for more than two minutes. When others entered just as we were beginning our mathematics I sometimes handed them food quickly to try and get rid of them, withholding Star's nut for the lesson. This made her angry, she gave a short chin-up display, then flew off without the nut or the lesson.

I now wanted to increase the number to five, but she forestalled me; for the next few days, 10th to 15th January, she flew to the screen-perch, instantly tapped four, threw me a quick look, tapped 3, 5, 2, glancing at me in between each number. The whole performance was very rapid, the tapping done at a much quicker pace than when she had copied mine, which she must have found laboriously slow, for birds' movements are far quicker than ours, and Time, to birds, goes at a much faster pace. This tapping was done three or four times each day,

Star's pose when wanting a number

the sequence varying between 4, 5, 5, 2 and 4, 5, 3, 2, sometimes the 2 being omitted. When I did not give her a nut for this brilliant exhibition of numbers – hoping she would then listen to 6 taps – she became very cross, swung round on her perch so that her back was turned towards me, then flew down from the screen and in stiffened poses, began a pretence search for food in all the most unlikely places in the rooms, where she had never before looked for food, such as the inside of a bedroom slipper, the top of the wardrobe, the bookcase, the fireplace, giving sharp pokes with her beak here and there but never going to the bird-table in the west room where food is always kept, as she normally would when hungry. This was a kind of annoyance display, aimed at me, for she kept throwing me sidelong glances. She would not come to me when I called her, holding out a nut. Directly other birds entered the room I handed them food and suddenly she flew to me for the nut. Her display had some resemblance to the false-feeding displays in my rooms between rival male Great Tits, when territorial disputes are in progress, but her mock search was much more extensive. Star never went through her tapping performance except on the screen in the east room, and, so far, it was only done when I stood near it, intending to give her a lesson.

On 16th January she perched on the screen without tapping and looked at me intently. I tapped five, which she copied correctly, then I tried six and she instantly got this. She was now copying my pace again and it was fascinating to watch her intent concentration as she bent her head to the screen, slowly and deliberately, then, at a perfectly even measure, and with firmness, tapped the given numbers.

Later that day I gave her six again. This time she tapped five and then started to fly to my hand for her nut, but, as if realising her mistake, turned back to the screen and gave one loud rap, flying to my hand directly afterwards for her reward. This incident of adding the one to the five was the most interesting evidence so far that she was conscious of the numbers she was tapping. Star had never on any previous occasion given a single tap, nor had this number ever been given her to copy. Twice afterwards during that day she responded correctly to six without this slip. This behaviour over her mistake corresponds with a Jackdaw's behaviour in one of O. Koehler's experiments with caged birds. The Jackdaw given the task to secure five baits went back to its cage after only securing four, but immediately returned and completed its task, then went home to its cage with an air of finality.

The following week lessons were impossible, for territorial chases and displays had begun. When Star came indoors, her mind was centred upon watching for rival Tits to enter the room; directly they appeared she flew at them and chased them away from the cottage. She was worried, for this year Baldhead was making no efforts to win their territory and the coveted nest-box, which the young male called Peetur had used as a roost all the winter. Baldhead was now too lame and physically weakened for the exertions of displays and chases, and Star, by herself, was ceaselessly struggling to keep Peetur and Monocle, his mate of the previous year, from the nest-box, by chases, chin-up displays and scold-notes. Monocle was easily got rid of, but Peetur was tenacious. It is very unusual for the female to tackle the male over territorial disputes.

So now all Star would do when I began tapping a number was to cut me short by hammering furiously on the screen, only pausing to insert gimlet-action digs into the wood, as if trying to wrench it. Attempts to gain her attention only resulted in her digging into the wood with fiercer twists of her beak so I gave up bothering her and handed her food quickly. She did not as usual wait to eat her nut on my hand, but seized it and hurriedly flew out to her territory.

One wet, windy morning a week later (23rd January) there was a lull in the disputes. She flew to the screen, looked at me, then bowed her head and in a painstaking manner gave three deliberate taps, afterwards looking up at me with her intent expression. I tapped six, she got this correctly but instead of coming to me for her reward, began tapping of her own accord, rapidly, one number after another with slight pauses in between, 5, 4, 6, 7, 5, then she flew to my hand for her nut. After this, for three weeks, territorial affairs took all her attention.

Baldhead still made no effort to gain the territory and several times, when Star saw him perched listlessly indoors she tried to stir him into action by an exact imitation of the original highspeed charge he had invented the previous year for disputes with Inkey. While she rushed towards him, she used his high-pitched squeak-note, but she stopped a foot away from him, stood still, and looked at him keenly. He did not move away from her but uttered some feeble notes and fidgeted on his perch. She never used this imitation charge in her disputes with rivals or for any other purpose and I am convinced that her intention was to rouse Baldhead from his torpor and make him use his high-speed charge which had previously been so effective with Inkey. Birds frequently use acting to show other birds what they want done. They sometimes use this miming method of communication when wanting something from me. But Star's performance was an exceptionally interesting and intelligent use of this method of intercourse. For three days she repeated the performance, using it only when Baldhead was idling on his perch with a vacant expression in his eyes, unusual to him. Her action may have helped him, for he began to show more liveliness and took interest in the nest-box, making chin-up displays before Peetur, but he continually flew to me for a nut and stayed with me a long time, while Star held on alone with frantic efforts of display, scarcely pausing to eat the food I offered her. It seemed, during these days, that they were holding the site by day but Peetur still slept in the box at night.

On 13th February there was another lull in the disputes. Star perched on the screen and fixed her bright eyes on me with the look that meant she was in a mood for tapping numbers. I gave her 7, and she responded correctly, in her former deliberate manner and at my speed, which to suit her was now much quicker. She accented the first and fifth beats, making the rhythm four and three. Four times during that day and three times on the next, I experimented with different accents in beating 7, but at present she always kept to her own rhythm of 4 and 3, which was the natural one to the human ear as well as to the bird's. Sometimes she tapped much faster than I did. The only time she got the number wrong was when I gave her 7, accenting the second and fifth beats, 1,111,111. She very naturally tapped 6, divided into triplets, 111,111. I had been aware that in giving 7 with an accent on the second beat, I had made the first beat fainter than it should have been. After this, Star tapped of her own accord 6 beats in triplet rhythm. She had before done it in three twos, 11,11,11.

On 15th February I tried Star with 8 beats and each time she did it correctly, dividing the number into 4, 4. Once I gave her the number too slowly and she began tapping before I had finished. I called out to her 'No! Wait a minute.' She stopped and looked at me. (I talk to my birds in ordinary language and find they often get some understanding of my words by the tone of voice, although in this case it was probably merely hearing my voice that stopped her.) I tapped 8 very fast and she got the number correctly. Twice that day she tapped of her own accord, at a faster pace than she had ever done before, 7, 7, 7, 6, 6, or 7, 7, 6, 6, 7, and it appeared she was trying to work up her speed to the fastest possible to achieve. She now kept to the rhythm of 3, 3 for 6. This was the last day of the experiment; the development of Star's talent had to wait until the autumn, for her mind became entirely engrossed in nesting affairs.

I had made several attempts to get some of my other Great Tits to tap numbers, both when Star was doing it and when I had them alone on the screen perch. They had not responded and most of them hastily left the screen when I tapped a number, but I determined to try them and their young in the autumn.

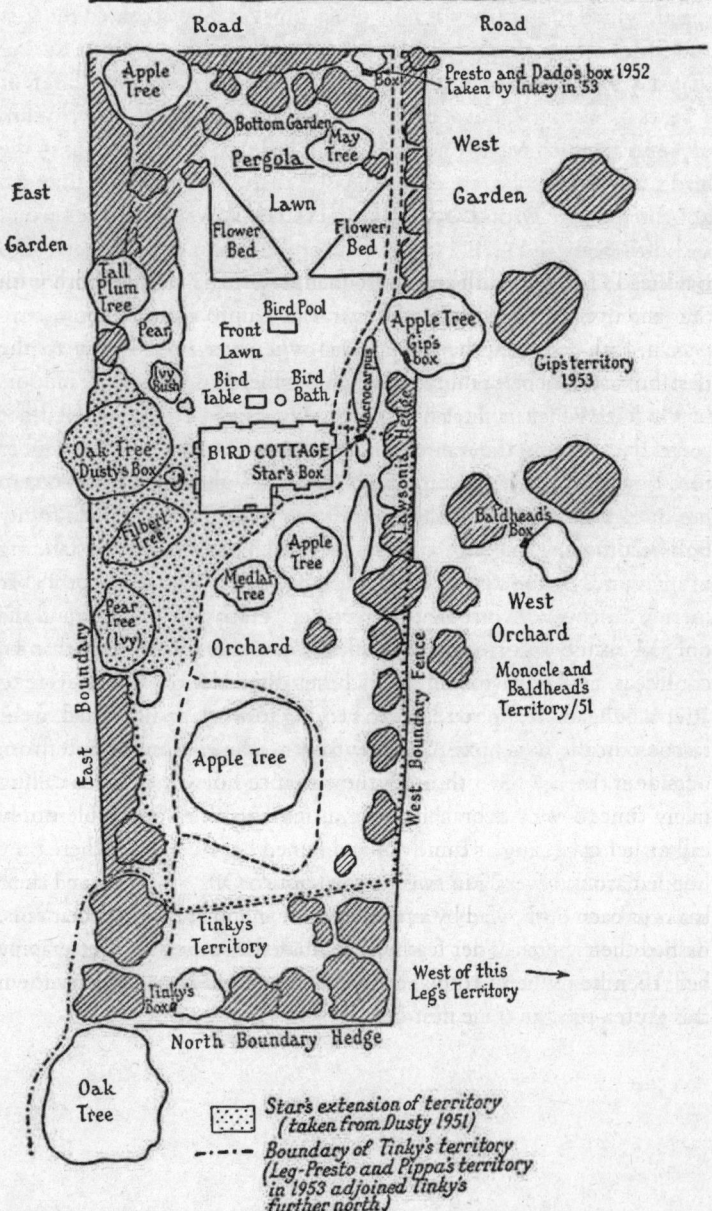

CHAPTER 2

Star's Talent is Developed

1. NESTING PROBLEMS

Baldhead's failing health and consequent erratic behaviour, both with Star and over territorial affairs, now created a problem for her.

On 16th February he disappeared whenever Peetur flew to the nest-box, and the next morning when Baldhead and Star were indoors he made a sudden rush at her with a chin-up. She hurriedly left the room with a protesting note. Later in the day he was with her by the nest-box and they both displayed at Peetur when he flew to them while they were hopping around the tree to which the box was hung. Baldhead's efforts of display were very limited and he came to me for food whenever Peetur became possessive and threatened to go for him. He wanted the protection of sitting on my lap and feeding was only an excuse to get away, for he flew to me more frequently than he could eat, and asked for nuts which he chucked away! That evening after Baldhead had retired early to bed, Peetur, as was now usual, went to roost in the nest-box. A moment later, Star gave a call-note from outside it, then looked through the entrance hole, afterwards calling many times from the branch above, using an attractive double-noted call of her own. Peetur came out and joined her on a tree, where they hopped around calling in sweet-toned notes. Often they turned their backs to each other, and by a rapid spreading and closing of their tails, flashed their white under feathers. In dusk she sought her gutter-pipe bed, then he returned to his roost. All the winter she had slept down this gutter-pipe near the nest-box.

The next day or two Star was with Baldhead, backing him up while he made mild efforts to keep Peetur away from the nest-box, and when Baldhead came to me for food, she very often accompanied him. They seemed on friendly terms. Then suddenly Baldhead appeared angry and flew at her in the same manner as previously. She left the room without any retort. The following day, 23rd February, Star rushed at

Baldhead with a high-pitched squeak-note and an imitation of his charge at Inkey. She stopped a foot away from him as before; they looked at each other, then both flew to the nest-box and examined it together, behaving as if they were mates. Peetur was absent, but presently he flew up in a possessive manner, thrust them away from the box and spread his wings over the entrance hole. Star, in a frustrated manner, tore bark from the tree and made gimlet action digs into the wood while Baldhead and Peetur mildly displayed at each other and uttered odd notes. The next day Baldhead made no attempt to display over the nesting-site and he stood nearby unmoved while Peetur looked inside the box. That evening Star called sweetly to Peetur and cocked her tail at him. He responded and they hopped round the tree, as on the previous evening. He watched her go down the gutter-pipe to bed, then sang facing her roost before he retired to his nest-box. But it still seemed that Star did not want to give up Baldhead, for she was with him by day and tore bark frantically every time Peetur appeared and found them together near the nest-box.

On 25th February, Baldhead again flew at Star; this time she retorted by a chin-up display. They were together again later, and that evening she kept with him until roost hour. Peetur took no notice of them. When Baldhead flew indoors to bed Star went down her gutter-pipe roost without paying attention to Peetur.

The following morning when she was perched on the screen, Baldhead flew at her again, then they both swung round, back to back on the screen. That night Baldhead roosted in a nest-box I had hung to a tree in West Orchard, a few feet beyond my fence. Star, as usual, slept down the gutter-pipe near the box for which Baldhead had now given up disputing. On 28th February, Star entered Peetur's box; directly she came out he went inside and made nestling-cry sounds, which she afterwards gave from inside the box. This is usual behaviour for paired Tits when choosing their nesting-box or hole. For several days Baldhead was often with them near the box, apparently on friendly terms. At that time it seemed he would not be capable of entering further into nesting affairs. He spent much of the day with me indoors, listlessly perched on my lap or on top of the window curtains.

Peetur now spent much of the day at the far boundaries of his territory, which extended up the orchard; Star zealously guarded her nest-box, only leaving it when feeding. Monocle as usual had remained cautiously in the background where she could wait and see the result of the disputes; now these were over, she made a few attempts to get near the box, but Star prevented it. Monocle then tried hard to win Peetur back again; she always flew to him when he was in the orchard, cocked her tail at him and used all the female charms that she possessed for wooing a male. Peetur was always a good-natured fellow, even in his dealings with males, so to outward appearances, Monocle met with some response, for he took a little notice of her, and sometimes they exchanged sweet notes when hopping around the trees together, but this quickly brought Star to them in fierce protest, and Monocle rapidly retired, leaving Star displaying angrily on her territory boundary. Star then called to Peetur, using her attractive double-noted call, and he followed her back to her box. Two or three days later Monocle tried again with the same results and she made several more attempts in the first half of March, then Peetur began to shun her presence. Star was now seldom out of his sight, so Monocle had no further chance to woo him.

On 23rd March (1951), Star began to take moss to her nest-box. Peetur had the same difficulty at roost hour as Baldhead had the previous year. Peetur's frustration antics were amusing to watch, for he was a lively bird. He adopted different notes each time Star turned him out of the box and repeated them continuously until his next attempt to enter, one to three minutes later. As he tried thirty times the first evening before he was allowed to remain, his vocabulary had become extensive by dusk, when he at last gained his bed. Star gave in by degrees as she had done with Baldhead. It appeared that she enjoyed hearing the language Peetur invented, for she often put her head out of the nest-box to listen when he was taking a turn round his territory while uttering the latest invention. Once she came out of the box and called to him in her special notes, which brought him hurrying to her, but she had quickly slipped back into the nest-box before he could reach it, and she did not at once let him enter. After the first night, it seemed Peetur also was enjoying this bedtime performance; he knew she was going to give in eventually.

I have noticed that when a Great Tit's winter roost is chosen by his mate for her nest, he always wants to continue roosting in it after she has begun to occupy it herself. Usually he cannot persuade her to allow it and she sometimes pecks him fiercely if he tries persistence, so he has to roost elsewhere. I have not found the male trying to roost with his mate if she chooses a box or hole which he has not occupied up to the time she starts to roost or build in it. She does not always roost in the nest herself until it is nearly completed. The behaviour of Great Tits is according to the individual and it varies greatly because their characters are so different.

April 2nd was the first fine day that spring, the weather having been exceptionally bad that year. Star worked at nest-building every morning and she now sang 'tee-chu' three times in succession to attract Peetur's attention if he was not near her. He used the same song in the same pitch to answer her, but he repeated the notes more times. It was a shortened version of his full song. Often they used a phrase sounding like 'he-hoy' for communication with each other.

Baldhead still spent much of the day indoors. His appetite had been exceptionally good for the last month and he was becoming a little more lively. Monocle, who liked taking the easiest course, now came forward and joined Baldhead at his roost-box which no other Tits had tried to take from him. He showed no interest in her but did not drive her away, nor did she take much notice of him and never came indoors with him. Monocle soon started to build in his box while he spent the days feeding and resting, and acting as if unaware of her existence. By the end of April her nest was built and she began to brood her eggs, but I never saw Baldhead feed her, either off the nest or on it. He was not fit to take part in rearing a family but he seemed happier now making some effort. Often he sat on my hand for a long while, his expression vacant, as if he was losing consciousness and I knew that he would not live much longer. The abnormal spike on his upper mandible had been gradually growing again and it was now as long as in the previous spring. It had been straight when only a small protuberance, but pressure had again made it grow curved like a Curlew's beak. As before, he got rid of it before his young were hatched.

Star characteristically took infinite pains over building her nest, selecting the very best material she could find. Seeing that she was taking beakfuls from my rugs and wool mats, I rolled up my best rug when she was not there and put it in the passage. She quickly found out where it was and, standing on top of the roll, plucked at the edges within her reach. I replaced the rug in the sitting-room, for completely bare patches on the borders would look worse than thinning out over a large area! The weather was so bad that she wisely delayed laying her eggs, and was behind most other Tits over this.

On 23rd April, after her territory boundaries had long been settled, Star suddenly became possessed with the idea of expelling the Great Tits, Cross and his new mate called Dusty, from their territory on the east side of my cottage. Cross was one of my resident birds. He was retiring by nature. (His previous nesting affairs with his former mate, Puggy, were related in *Birds as Individuals*.) Although this had been his territory the previous year, now, whenever Cross and Dusty were absent for a few moments, Star flew to the oak tree, below which was Dusty's nest-box, attached to a small fruit tree; Peetur followed when Star called to him in her special double-noted call, and directly Cross and Dusty appeared, the latter with nest material in her beak, Star took the lead in chasing Dusty away, Peetur then chased Cross; neither of the owners made any resistance. This happened many times that day.

The next day Cross took to hiding and avoided Peetur but Dusty had to complete her half-finished nest although this was difficult against Star's opposition. She tried the dodge of waiting, with a beakload of material ready collected, on the west side of the cottage just beyond Star's territory, where she could watch her movements. Directly Peetur and Star went to the orchard, Dusty made a dash along the front of the cottage and round to her nest. But Star soon discovered this, then she only went with Peetur as far as the medlar tree, and while Dusty hurried round the front of the cottage, Star rushed round from the back even more quickly and, spreading her wings over the entrance hole of the nest-box, prevented Dusty from entering. Instead of showing spirit and standing up for her rights, Dusty flew away to wait until Star returned to her own nest. But she stayed there only a second, her nest was completed and her whole attention now was centred upon preventing the box under the oak tree from being occupied. So she rushed back, and if Dusty was inside the box, Star clung to the entrance hole, and holding up her chin, waved her head slowly from side to side; after this threat display she entered the box, the timid occupier fled and Star came out with a beakful of her nest material, flew with it to the oak tree and there let it drop. For three days this behaviour continued.

It was then that I fell out with Star, for I tried to intervene. With stupid human lack of perception I had not foreseen the impending food crisis for Tits' nestlings and the consequent necessity, from Star's point of view, for her behaviour. I thought that her vitality was leading her into abnormal desires for possession, and that she would do better to get on with her own nesting affairs. She had not tried to take Cross's territory the previous year and this year she had more land in the orchard. She was already later than my other resident Tits in laying her eggs, and she was hindering Dusty who was the latest to begin building. So although I rarely interfere with my birds, the next time she entered Dusty's box I rapped loudly on the roof of it, thinking it would frighten Star away. She came out, but only to stand on the box facing me, her bright eyes flashing as she angrily rebuked me by a long volley of scold-notes, then she hopped back into the box and quickly reappeared with a beakful of nest material; still scolding me, she flew with it to the oak tree and let it fall. I persevered with the rapping for a day but it had no effect, for Star had too much at stake, as I afterwards knew. I then tried putting long straws into her own box hoping she might think that a Sparrow was stealing her nest because of her absence. I always did this while she was in Dusty's nest the other side of the cottage, where she could not see me doing it. When she returned she never even glanced at the Sparrows near by, but quickly removed the straws from her nest, chucked them away with an impatient gesture, then turned towards me, shouting many fiercely uttered scold-notes. I felt she might reasonably mean, 'Stop interfering, you fool!' My interference had done no good, for she desperately needed possession of the east territory if she could get it from the timid owners. Star now refused to take food from my hand and whenever she saw me go near Dusty's nest-box or her own she scolded me furiously; it was a long while before she was friendly with me again.

Towards the end of April Star began to lay her eggs, yet she still spent all her spare time at Dusty's box. On 5th May she started brooding; that day I made the following notes: every time Star came off her nest she flew straight to Dusty's nest-box and hammered at the entrance hole. If Dusty was inside she displayed at her, then entered and drove her off. If she passed me she scolded loudly. Once she took a beakful of Dusty's nest-lining (wool stolen from my rugs) and carried it back to her own nest. After staying there a minute she rushed back to Dusty's box, and peered inside; it was empty. She entered quickly, seized more wool, flew to the oak and dropped it, then hurried back to her nest. This behaviour continued for three more days. Before Star began to lay her eggs, Peetur had stayed near Dusty's box while Star was there, but directly she had eggs in her own box he did not seem enthusiastic over her obsession for interfering with Dusty's nest. Although he followed her to that side of the cottage he did not now go near the box, but stayed in the trees near by or, if I was there, he fed unperturbed from my hand while Star hurled scold-notes into the air, and carried on frantically with her task of interference.

Cross had not shown himself for many days; probably he was in West Garden, where Dusty flew when chased from her nest. Peetur always accompanied Star back to her own nest and was a very attentive mate. On the morning of 11th May, Star clung to the entrance hole of Dusty's nest-box, peered inside but did not, as usual, enter. Scolding furiously, she returned to her own nest but came out the next moment and, as if possessed, rushed back to Dusty's box and looked inside for several minutes, again not entering, which was now unusual. She was agitated and restlessly flitted round the box when not staring into it. She would not eat the food which Peetur gave her; chucking it away, she once more peered inside Dusty's box then returned to brood her eggs, the good-natured Peetur following and seeing her into her nest. He showed no interest in Cross and Dusty's box and may not have understood why Star was so perturbed. Later that day, directly she came off her eggs, she hastened to their box and straightway entered, as if she had determined beforehand upon a course of action. A moment later, Dusty flew off the nest; her plumage, which had always looked dusty, now had feathers missing from the nape of her neck. Star had attacked her in her box, and now chased her into West Garden. Scold-noting frantically, Star then returned to her eggs. I looked inside Dusty's box. Star had resorted to this personal attack because there was now an egg in the nest.

Dusty did not return for many days. Star had won the battle but until her young were hatched she continued to fly straight to Dusty's nest-box directly she came off her eggs and, taking a rapid glance inside, made sure that it was unoccupied. Then she joined Peetur for a feed in the orchard trees.

On 13th May Monocle's young were hatched. The weather remained bitterly cold and leafing was very late. As I watched

Baldhead and Monocle searching in vain for food for their starving nestlings I realised the wisdom of Star's unusual behaviour. There was a food famine for Tit nestlings; without the addition to her territory of the oak tree, she could not possibly rear her young. Owing to the exceptionally late leafing of trees that spring, the oak had no leaves on it at the time of Star's fight for possession; later it provided the best supply of caterpillars in my garden. Star's remarkable foresight enabled her to bring off a brood of eight, while only two of Monocle's nestlings survived. The food famine was general for Tit nestlings that spring; I watched parent birds searching for twenty minutes before anything suitable could be found, and they even resorted to catching gnats on the window-panes and in the air; these, too, were very scarce. It will later be seen that Dusty benefited by Star's interference, for my garden had not enough food to supply the young of all the nesting Tits.

Baldhead often encroached on Peetur's orchard territory to hunt for caterpillars for his nestlings. Peetur made no objection but if Star was near she chased him over the fence – their boundary. Usually Baldhead came when Star was out of sight, for he knew that he had no right in my orchard now his territory was next door. In this last effort of Baldhead's life I tried to help him by putting cloths and planks of wood on the grass, underneath these a little food, suitable for his young, collected overnight. I put the catches in a box then called over the fence to Baldhead, who came instantly to fetch the contents, taking one grub at a time and flying backwards and forwards to his nest until all was finished. I had to hold the box over the fence otherwise Star objected. Occasionally she flew up and, perched on the fence, did a chin-up at Baldhead, who uttered a high squeak-note in reply. Star had not yet forgiven me for my interference and she still refused food from my hand.

Baldhead was too exhausted to continue feeding his young for more than three days after they flew. Monocle then took their two fledglings to the trees north of the orchard. When they had gone Star made no objection to Baldhead's presence in her orchard and he spent much time there, resting in his old territory where he could feed from my hand and sit on my lap or arm. He had become slow and sleepy in his ways, he even ate slowly, taking rests between each bite. Often his expression was dazed and he frequently bumped into his perch and stumbled when alighting, as if unable to see. His strength was rapidly failing and he was heavy on the wing, only flying a few feet at a time. On 21st June he was missing. He had died during the night, aged six years.

On 20th May Star's young were hatched. Bad weather continued and even with her additional territory she and Peetur found it hard work to feed their brood. Star often uttered a little cry of distress after searching for a long while without finding a single grub or caterpillar; the oak tree territory that she had worked so hard to secure was the main source of food, and owing to her foresight she reared her eight nestlings. They flew on 10th June. She kept them in or near the oak tree for two days, then took them over the road. I did not see them again until she brought back the three fledglings that had survived the usual dangers that beset a brood of newly fledged young. Peetur returned to his territory for part of the day and was always there in the evenings.

Monocle came to me several times a day for food for her young. When she saw Peetur, she flew to him and displayed with shivering wings. He ignored her but showed excitement at sight of Star, who was often away with her young. He followed her about and tried enticing her with baby-cry notes to the nest-boxes in their territory. Star was not interested and did not want a second brood; she stayed on the oak tree, calling Peetur away from the nest-boxes to join her there. I then discovered that Dusty was sitting on five eggs in her nest-box below the oak. Star now took no notice of her or of her nest and Dusty never perched on the trees in my garden. Cross did not appear until the young were hatched, all food for them being fetched from beyond West Garden. This gave her a better food supply than she could have got in my overcrowded garden.

Tiptoe, a female (mentioned in *Birds as Individuals*), nested in her usual box a few feet away from Star's, on my West apple tree, her territory being in West Garden, but she was often in mine and frequently fed her young with food taken from my hand, her mate supplying the natural food. Star never resented her presence and even allowed her to hunt for food in some of my orchard trees, which were Peetur and Star's property. Tiptoe was an old resident and had one foot twisted, and I find that the lame bird, contrary to popular belief, usually meets with special consideration from others of its kind. (See page 88, Tippett.)

There were other nest-boxes, occupied by Great Tits, near my north and south hedges, their territories being beyond my garden. A pair (called the 'Silent Strangers' in *Birds as Individuals*) had taken a box by my gate, their territory, as before, being over the road by the stream. The female was now tame and I called her Dado. Another couple of newcomers took an old petrol tin tied to a tree-stump; they owned a few feet of territory at the top of my orchard, the main part being beyond my north hedge. The male I called Tinky; he and Dado enter into later chapters as prominent figures.

2. THE TALENT IS DEVELOPED

On 24th June Star returned permanently, bringing her three youngsters, the only survivors of her brood of eight that had left my garden the previous week. That year there were even greater losses than usual among fledgling as well as nestling Tits, but mortality soon after flight is always very high. Star and Peetur fed them lavishly for another ten days, then he ceased to take interest. Star always looked after her young longer than other Great Tit parents; that year she continued to feed them for a month after they left the nest. She snatched food from my hand for her fledglings but, contrary to the previous year, she kept them away from me. She had not forgotten my interference with her nesting affairs, her manner with me was aloof, she frequently turned her back on me when I offered her nuts and there seemed nothing I could do to appease her. I had to take this severe punishment for my human stupidity over meddling with her efforts to combat food famine for her coming young.

In August I began trying to interest her in mathematics but every time I tapped a number on the table she flung scold-notes at me, then flew away. It appeared this reminded her of my rappings when I interfered over Dusty's nest-box. Fearing that she thought I now meant to drive her away, I stopped the experiment and tried to win back her friendship by feeding her lavishly with cachews and peanuts, her favourite foods, but still no progress was made over interesting her in tapping, until one day in late September she entered the room without my paying her any attention. She hopped from perch to perch near me and uttered soft notes to tell me she was there, but I pretended not to notice her. She perched opposite me for a few moments then flew to the screen and, of her own accord, tapped 4. I at once gave her a nut. Later that day I tried to get her to respond to my taps, but other birds were in the room and she seemed not to notice me. She could never concentrate in front of others.

The following day I got her alone and gave four taps, she tapped 4 in response and, instead of flying to me for her nut, looked at me with a cross expression and did a chin-up display, then swung round on the screen to turn her back on me, afterwards flying to the top of the wardrobe nearby, where she looked at me in an inquiring manner. I tapped 4 again, she flew back to the screen and bent her head low as if going to tap, but without doing so, raised it and looked at me, this time with an annoyed expression, her head feathers flattened as in a Great Tit's aggressive display. It seemed that a conflicting emotion of annoyance kept her from tapping, although she wanted to do it. I rapped four again, this time she bent her head low, her beak touching the wood, and after keeping in this position a moment, she slowly and softly but deliberately tapped four, then flew to my hand for a nut.

During October I had little time for the counting experiment. Star still seemed unable to forget our quarrel of the spring; she acted perversely with me. If I tried to get her to tap by holding up a nut and giving her a number, she turned her back and left the room, but often when I was busy she tried to attract my interest by flying to the screen and rapping a number of her own choice – varying from 3 to 7 – giving only one number, then looking at me expectantly. The position between us seemed to have become reversed, she now appeared to be the experimenter, waiting to see what response I would give! If I tapped the number she had given she seemed pleased and repeated it again after me, but if I gave a different number from the one she had given me she did a slight chin-up display. Sometimes after the chin-up she gave the correct response to my number, but in a half-hearted manner, with hesitating taps.

One day, late in October, I was speaking on the phone to a friend, Mr Garth Christian, when Star flew to the screen and tapped, to attract my attention. (The phone is near the screen.) I interrupted our conversation to rap 5 beats on the table. Star at once bent her head to the screen and laboriously hammered the correct number. My friend, a bird lover, was thrilled to hear this clearly through the phone.

In November I had more time to give to counting experiments, and on the ninth I began trying to get other Great Tits to tap. First I tried two females, singly, with two taps. Both ducked their heads nervously, one flew out of the window, the other hopped around the room, eyeing me suspiciously while I repeated the two taps several times. She did not understand and I could get no response; she soon flew off, disgruntled.

A male Great Tit (called Beauty, an offspring of Star and Baldhead), then entered the room and, as is his custom, perched on my shoulder. Instead of giving him a nut I held it up and tapped 2. He looked at me in a puzzled manner. I tapped again. He seemed trying to understand and searched my eyes every time I repeated the two taps. After the sixth series of two taps had been given him he gave two pronounced bill-wipes on the screen. I gave him a nut. He soon came back, and instead of flying to my shoulder as usual to him, perched on the screen and gave two bill-wipes without my having tapped. He had never done this before. I gave him a nut, hoping to get him to respond in bill-wipes. But all further efforts led to no results. Bill-wiping is often done when a bird is at tension. My tapping upset him.

While I was trying a fourth Great Tit, without getting any response, Star entered the room, flew at the fourth bird and took his place on the screen, then looked at me with her intent expression, which meant she wanted a number. I gave her 7 beats. In a masterly fashion she rapped out the correct number, loudly and deliberately, then flew to my hand for her nut. It was the first time she had given such a hearty response to my tapping since the spring. It seemed that competition was good for her and that she wanted to show off her special talent.

After this, for several days I tried these and other Tits, including some Blue Tits, but could not get any response. Even the bill-wiping ceased and when the Tits entered the room they became nervously expectant of my tapping; directly I began it they flew outdoors hastily so I had to stop the experiment. Rapping, in the bird world, can be done to show annoyance, although they also hammer things in play. The distinction is that one bird rapping *at* another bird means an annoyance display, but random hammering, not aimed at another bird, is done for entertainment and often if one Tit does this it starts many doing the same thing to amuse themselves. These other Tits were puzzled and afraid, for I was rapping at them; only Star understood the significance of my taps.

On 14th November I tried two more females who left the room in nervous haste. Peetur then perched on the screen. I gave him two taps. After a pause and repetition of my taps he gave me two bill-wipes. I gave him a nut and after eating it he did two more bill-wipes of his own accord. As with Beauty, he had not done this before and it was probably a nervous reaction to my tapping at him. Later that day I gave him three bill-wipes, done with a pencil on the table. He looked searchingly into my eyes, as if trying to understand but uncertain what to do. He flew to a lower bar of the screen, fidgeted uneasily on his perch and stared intently at me, turning his head from side to side as was his habit when contemplating a dash to my lips for his trick of taking nuts from my mouth. I let him do this, giving him a very small piece of nut. Then I repeated the three bill-wipes; after my third repetition he gave three hasty bill-wipes, eyed me nervously and flew away. Star then flew up and, in her most efficient manner, tapped 6 in response to my six taps. Her talent seemed all the more remarkable in contrast to these others.

Two hours later she again flew to the screen. When I began tapping she turned her head towards some Tits in the west room and did chin-ups at them. She wanted to keep them away from the screen. It seemed she was jealous or felt possessive over the lessons and the following year I had confirmation of this. (Page 41.) I repeated a number for her, but she could not get the other Tits off her mind and after giving a few disjointed, feeble taps she began displaying at them again. I gave up the lesson and she had her nut. On 15th November I got her alone and she tapped 6 correctly in response to my beats.

On 16th November she flew to the screen and tapped of her own accord, feebly and hesitatingly, without giving any definite numbers. I called her name and hammered a number loudly on the table; she went on with her faint, jumbled tappings, stopping sometimes to cast glances at some Tits the far end of the west room. I said sharply, 'Star, you are not listening.' She stopped her vague hammering and looked at me intently. This meant that the right response would come when I gave her five taps. She rapped them out decisively, in a competent manner, then came for her nut.

Star does a chin-up display at the other Tits

I could not get any results from the other Tits, even Peetur's bill-wiping ceased and was replaced by a hurried exit from the room directly I tapped. The experiment was producing a nervous atmosphere among them and by trying to interest the others in mathematics I was upsetting Star. So I gave up experimenting with all except Star for that year, and let a month elapse before resuming her lessons, to enable her to forget the disturbance over the other Tits. This break proved worth the lost time, for her mind was fresh when on 15th December I gave her a lesson. First she got 4 correctly to my taps, then 6, in 3, 3 rhythm.

On 16th December she flew to the screen and looked at me for a number, but when I began to tap she joined in and hammered more loudly and quickly than I did, without making any break until I shouted, 'Star, stop tapping.' She stopped and looked at me. She then gave a correct response to 7.

From 17th until 22nd December very mild weather brought territorial matters to the minds of many birds. Star was not interested in lessons and wanted to be outdoors all day.

On 23rd December she flew to the screen and looked at me intently. I gave her 7, which she did correctly, in 4, 3 rhythm, accenting it decisively.

The next day I had correct responses to 5, then to 8, which she did in 4, 4 rhythm. The following day I again gave 8 beats, doing it in 4, 4 rhythm myself. Star tapped 2, then made a very slight break before tapping 6 in 2, 2, 2 rhythm; she then flew to me for her nut. At the time I thought it unlikely that she was giving 8 in four twos, but the following year she showed that she was capable of realising that 2 plus 6 makes 8.

26th December. Star flew to the screen and began to tap. Two other female Great Tits flew at her and she at once left the room. Presently she returned by herself and began to tap a long string of numbers very fast. I called out, 'Listen to me, Star. Stop tapping.' She stopped but did not look at me. I gave her 7 beats. She swung round on her perch and with her back to me tapped 7, in 4, 3 rhythm then flew to me for her nut.

27th December. Star gave gimlet digs into the screen when I gave her a number. Monocle was near the screen and Star would not tap until she left the room. Later she gave correct responses to 5 and to 8, in 4, 4 rhythm.

28th December. I tried to give Star 9 beats but she started to tap before I had finished. Directly she stopped I gave 5 beats, she tapped six but knew this was wrong for, instead of coming for her nut, she bent her head low, her beak touching the screen, then threw a hasty glance at me and carefully, with slow, precise taps gave 5, glanced at me again and tapped 5, glanced a third time and repeated 5, then she came for her nut. All this was done deliberately, without a moment's hesitation, and it was evident that the repetitions of the correct number were to show that she knew the first response was wrong.

Further lessons were prevented until 19th January, when I gave Star 6 beats. She had always before given 6 in 2, 2, 2 or 3, 3 rhythms, but this time she tapped it in 4, 2, rather faintly, then looked up at me, as if to see what I thought of it. I praised her and gave her a nut. Later I gave her 6 in 3, 3 rhythm and she responded loudly and promptly with the same accent.

On 20th January Star gave correct responses to 7 and 6. Later in the day I again tried 9, but she began to tap just before I had finished. The difficulty was to tap fast enough when giving her a number over 8, for a bird's mind works far more quickly than the human's and even my fastest tapping probably seemed slow to her; she was keen to do it herself and waiting for me to finish nine beats proved too much for her patience.

The next day she gave correct responses to 4 and to 6. She accented 6 in 4, 2 of her own accord. I then gave her 8 beats but the number was blurred through an effort to tap much more quickly than before, hoping that I might get results from bigger numbers by faster paces. Star tapped 7 in response, weakly and tailing off to very faint taps at the end, then she looked at me inquiringly instead of coming for her nut. She evidently expected me to give the number again, which I did, clearly and loudly. She at once rapped this firmly then came for her reward.

On 24th January she flew to the screen but when I tapped she gave a call-note and flew away to her nest-box. Territorial disputes had begun; during February and until mid-March this took all her attention. She had become possessive of all the orchard and the cottage front and when I put a nest-box in West Orchard she and Peetur spent much time keeping other Tits from this as well. She was rarely indoors and it was 17th March before she seemed in a quieter mood. That day, when I gave her a number she ducked her head and flew to my coat, which hung on a chair, and began plucking the wool from the collar, then she turned round, looked at me, threw down the wool and flew to my hand for a nut. She had become interested in a petrol tin fixed to the medlar tree, her mind was upon nesting, not mathematics.

The four following days she ducked her head when I tapped but on the 22nd March she gave a feeble though correct response to 4 and to 5, flying to her territory directly afterwards instead of coming for her

STAR'S TALENT IS DEVELOPED

reward. The following week I tried to get her to listen to bigger numbers but she ducked her head and left the room before I had finished tapping.

On 2nd April she tapped 4 in response to 6 then began to scream, her high-pitched, wailing note an unusual sound for a Great Tit. She then flew to her old nest-box which was surrounded by squawking Sparrows. An hour later she flew to the screen and I gave her 6. She restlessly hopped from one part of the screen to the other, then looked at me. I repeated 6 and this time she tapped loudly the correct number, then hurriedly flew to her territory without coming for her nut. Our mathematics now had to wait until after the nesting season.

CHAPTER 3

Star's Further Amazing Achievements

1. PROGRESS CONTINUES

On 13th April (1952) Star began to build her nest in the petrol tin. She and Peetur, who had been carefully guarding their old nest-box as well as the tin and several other boxes in the orchard, now made no objection to their old nest-box being taken by a couple of Great Tit strangers – the female began to build on 17th April. This couple then tried to keep Star and Peetur from entering through the west windows of the cottage. Peetur, seeing their display, gave in to them and went round the other side of the cottage (he was always easy-going and good-natured) but Star, with her usual determination, refused to let these newcomers dictate to her over rights of entry into the cottage. She ignored their protesting displays done on the outside window ledges, and quickly flew into the room. They could do nothing, for they were afraid to enter the rooms themselves. They left the garden directly their young were fledged.

On 19th May, when Star's nestlings were a week old, Peetur disappeared. Star kept flying to a tree-top, giving her special double-noted call which had always brought Peetur to her side, but she now called in vain; he never returned and must have been killed by a neighbour's cat that was continually in my garden hunting the birds; nothing that I did would keep it away.

Four days later, another Great Tit male, a stranger, came to the orchard. Star displayed to him with quivering wings – a nesting display – when he first went near her nest but he ignored her nesting affairs and took possession of her territory. He chased away all other male Great Tits, and uttered squeaky sounds as he went from tree to tree in the orchard. Every evening before roost hour he sang a few 'tee-chu' notes from above Star's nest but she ignored him; he never took food to her young. Occasionally he flew behind her when she was carrying food to the nestlings, and remained outside until she reappeared from her nest. Star acted as if unaware of his presence. When he tried to gain her attention by imitating her special double-noted call she not only failed to respond but gave up using this call and she never again uttered it. Star might lose her valued territory, but I then guessed she would never keep it at the expense of taking this Tit for her mate. Subsequent events proved that I was right. Nesting territory is not the only attraction when a female chooses a mate, the individual possessing it must be to her liking.

This stranger male was a nuisance, he spent all the day feeding on Star's land without contributing to the upkeep of her family and she was finding it very hard to find enough food for them. I helped her as far as possible but she never gave them much artificial food. Monocle, on the contrary, gave her fledglings a lot of cheese, it was easy to get this from me and she always spared herself trouble. She had this year mated Tinky, whose territory, as before, included a small strip of my orchard and the north hedge, this giving access to me for food. As I was often near Star's nest, the timid Monocle had to risk trespassing on her ground and fly to me there. Star chased her away if she saw her flying to my hand, but Monocle had always been good at hiding from her rivals and often when she saw Star approaching she flew to my shoulder and slipped under cover of my hair at the back of my neck. Star, even if she saw Monocle in her strange hiding place, was too busy feeding her young to chase her out of it, so I was spared the hair-pulling which such a chase would have inflicted.

On 30th May four of Star's fledglings left the nest, the following day three more scrambled through the entrance hole, but were too small to fly. They spent the day in long grass under the medlar tree, Star having tried unsuccessfully to coax them upwards to a branch. They fell to the grass again when I placed them on the tree. Star fiercely chased away all birds that perched on the medlar tree and when an impudent Sparrow kept getting in her way while she was taking food to her young she flew at him so angrily that he squealed loudly from panic and went away. I was pleased to see the Sparrow, for once, getting his deserts, for most birds seem afraid of troublesome House Sparrows even when they are stealing their nests.

The stranger male kept away from Star's fledglings, making himself scarce until they left the orchard, then he took complete possession of Star's territory but never came near the cottage. I did not encourage him; it was obvious that Star did not like him, though, having no mate, she could not prevent his taking her territory.

The three weaklings did not survive more than two days; Star then took her four remaining fledglings over the road, where there was suitable cover. She flew back to me several times a day to get food for them and soon they accompanied her on these visits, but she was a careful mother, and never let them leave the cover of trees so I could not get to know them while they were small. Even a month after they had flown she flew to them with scold-notes if they were perched in an exposed position. By that time only two had survived. She occasionally fed them until 30th June, after this they began coming to me. (See Chapter 6, page 101.)

Star now went into moult and it was the end of July before she regained her charming appearance, with her white star shining in the sleek new plumage of her crown.

My intimacy with her had strengthened since she lost Peetur. Having had no mate to help rear her fledglings, she had become more dependent upon me and our quarrel of last year was quite forgotten. Because of her increased friendliness I was puzzled when, in the second week of August, she suddenly developed peculiar mannerisms with me, as if she was self-conscious, and she seemed unsatisfied. On entering through the window, she did not, as before, fly straight to me but paused on the sill and posed stiffly, her back towards me, her tail half-spread and showing the white marginal under-feathers; keeping this pose, her head was first raised very slowly, then gradually lowered. Afterwards she flew to my hand but before taking her nut she often posed facing me and slowly raised her head feathers so that her crown became enlarged, her white star consequently expanding gradually, much beyond its normal size. Sometimes she did not take her nut but hurriedly left the room after these displays. For ten days she continued to behave in this manner, displaying before me whenever she entered the room. In previous years we had not begun our mathematics before September so it did not occur to me that her odd behaviour – as if she was showing off in front of me – was connected with our lessons, until one morning when she was on the window-ledge, posing back to me with her head stiffly raised, I called out, 'Tap, tap.' Slowly she bowed her head and remained a moment motionless, then she flew to the screen and again bent her head so that it was touching the wood. She looked as if trying to recall something. I tapped two beats on the table. After a short pause she slowly raised her head a little, then gave two very soft and careful taps. This done, she threw me a quick look and flew to my hand for her nut. On her next appearance that day she flew straight to the screen without any preliminary poses and looked at me for a number. When I gave 3 taps she at once responded, tapping loudly and confidently. Her manner with me had returned to normal.

The next day, 25th August, she entered the room while I was on the phone and reeled off several very loud taps to attract my attention. I gave her 4 beats and she enthusiastically repeated the number, as if she enjoyed doing it. Now we had begun these lessons she did not again adopt odd poses on entering the room.

It seemed that these were done to attract especial attention and bring the tapping response from me, though she may not have had more than a vague memory of something that we used to do together that she now wanted to continue. As I had before been the one to start the tapping after the nesting and moulting season it would be expected that she would again need to be given the lead this year. On 26th August Star again responded to four taps after flying to the screen and looking at me for instructions, but the 27th being a very warm day she kept out of doors and was not interested in occupations indoors.

In the cool of the evening on the 28th, I was standing near the screen when Star flew to the window-ledge. She turned her back to me, then bent low, her beak touching the ledge. I said, 'Come and tap.' She flew to the screen, I tapped 3. She did an incoherent jumble of quick taps without any rhythm. I said, 'No! Listen to me,' and tapped 3 again. She looked at me, then softly but deliberately gave 3 rhythmic taps, afterwards coming to take her nut from my hand.

Three days later, still in beautiful weather, Star flew to the screen at 9 a.m. and I tapped 4. She turned her head upwards – the sign that she was not interested. I repeated 4, she flew to the top of the piano in the west room and again looked upward at the ceiling. She took no notice when I called to her, so I went towards her, holding up a nut. She took this and flew away. She was not in the mood for mathematics; all the other birds were out of doors on this lovely morning, and autumn territorial displays had just begun; there was restlessness among the young birds and some of them were being driven away by the adults, as always happens in early autumn.

Although on 1st September she gave a correct response to 4 after a little persuasion and repetition of the number, on 2nd and 3rd September she would not tap at all; she restlessly flitted from perch to perch then left the room. Star never gave wrong numbers in response but she was not always in the mood to tap.

On 4th September I tapped 4 when she flew to the screen. She bowed her head then looked at me. I repeated the number. She again bent her head to the frame and silently remained with it bowed until I said, 'What is it, Star? Why not tap?' She looked at me with a queer expression, gave one feeble peck at the screen then flew to the wardrobe, her back turned to me. 'What's the matter? Why not tap?' I repeated. She swung round, and facing me, shouted 'He-hoey.' This was a call she used for drawing attention to possession of territory. She had answered my questions for I now understood that her mind was upon trying to keep her territory by my cottage. The stranger male, called The Intruder, with autumn zest had begun advertising his ownership of the orchard territory, which had been hers. He had no mate and, like her, was always alone, but even to keep the nest-site she had always possessed she made no attempt to woo him. This gave a deeper significance to her patient wooing of Baldhead, although at the time I had wondered if his territory was her main reason for wanting him. It seems clear that the individual male must have special attraction for the wooer. It is often the female Great Tit that woos the male, but there is no set pattern of behaviour, it is individual.

I did not again bother Star with tapping until she asked for it in the language that I had learnt to understand. For the next few days she seemed strung up and only paid hurried visits to the cottage. Sometimes she rapped the screen loudly and inconsequently, flying away immediately afterwards. A youngster Great Tit (offspring of Presto, see Chapters 4 and 6) now started rappings on the screen in imitation of Star, but she would not respond to my taps. The youngster usually did this hammering when I was at the other end of the west room and flew away directly I went towards her, intending to give a number. As soon as I walked away she returned to the screen and began hammering it, turning her head every few moments to watch for me to come towards her again; if I did, she flew out of the east window. It seemed a game she was playing, so I named her Joker.

On the 10th September, while I was sitting by the french window,

Star perched on the arm of my chair, then posed before me with bowed head. This meant that she wanted a lesson. I went into the east room, she followed me and, perched on the screen, looked at me. When I tapped 4 she turned her back to me and very gently repeated the number. The next two days she again responded correctly to 6 and 7 after having bowed her head low to show that she wanted a number. On the 17th September, before she had time to tap in response to my number, the female Great Tit, Dado, rushed to the screen and did a chin-up display, perched beside Star, who flew to the wardrobe with a complaining note. Dado then asked me for food, but I called to Star holding out my hand; she flew to me and got her nut. Dado looked very cross. She had interfered with Star because they were rivals; both had possessive ideas over the trees on the west side of the cottage. Dado, having a mate (Presto) took precedence over Star because she was without a mate. In bird law Star now had to give way to Dado or other mated birds when they displayed on the screen.

In half an hour Star returned and wanted a number; she tapped correctly in response to me but kept twitching her tail while doing it, a slight form of display aimed at other Tits in the west room, whom she thought might disturb her. Dado never again interrupted our lessons. She was a sensitive bird and knew how to take my hints. I was always careful to give prompt attention to her demands when Star was not having a lesson.

The next day Star did not come indoors; when she flew to me while I was sitting in the garden I tried to get a response to tapping, done on my chair. She ducked her head, as if alarmed, and flew away. Hammering out of doors is usually done by Tits in annoyance displays – it was even done by me on Dusty's nest-box – and she thought I was annoyed with her. Later I rapped 5 on the french window-frame when she was in the west room. She at once flew to the screen in the east room to tap the number. This was the first time I had given her a number in the other room, away from her tapping perch.

On 23rd, September, when I gave her 7, accenting it 4, 3 (the natural rhythm) she gave the correct number but carefully accented it 5, 2 and instead of flying to me for her nut, looked at me inquiringly, evidently wanting to know if I approved. She had never before given this variation of accent to 7, and from the marked manner in which she made the accent, with a very slight break between the 5 and 2 it was obvious that the altered accent was intentional – this also being proved by further developments. I held out her reward, and spoke words of praise – she understood the meaning of my words by the tone of voice. She had before given 6 in 3, 3; 2, 2, 2 and 4, 2 rhythms.

2. RIVALS ON THE SCREEN

For the next day or two other Tits were on her mind and she kept looking towards the windows to see who entered, she could not concentrate upon lessons and I did not force her. On the 26th she flew to the chair beside me in the west room, gave one tap to draw attention to her presence, then turned her head upwards to show she did not want to tap. To test this, I rapped 5, she flew off but quickly returned, uttering soft notes, then a short scold-note because I had not yet given her a nut. She had explained that she did not want to do tapping so I gave her a nut.

Smoke had recently returned after a long absence, and this, I think, disturbed Star, for they had been rivals and Smoke was very intimate with me. She liked to perch on my shoulder to eat her nuts. She was the only one among the forty or more Great Tits entering my cottage daily that slightly resembled Star in appearance – it is no exaggeration to say that the resemblance was slight, for Star was so individual. One day, when Star entered the room, being busy, I did not look at her properly and thinking it was Smoke I held a nut to my shoulder, then saw that it was Star, who now looked at me with a piercing stare, flew to a chair back and gave one gentle tap to show me who she was. This became her identity signal on the four occasions when I made this slip of momentarily thinking she was Smoke when my mind was occupied with other things. Star never flew to my shoulder like some of the other Tits did, she liked to perch on my hand or arm or lap and sometimes she clung to my skirt if other birds were on my hand. After giving her identity signal she put her head upwards, to show me that she did not want to tap. If wanting a lesson she sometimes tapped to tell me so, but then she never gave a single tap but bigger numbers, or else bowed her head to the screen in silence then looked at me with her intent expression. The intricacies of bird language are fascinating, each bird invents its own signs for communicating with me over individual matters. This also applies among themselves but close intercourse is necessary for the human to understand their ways of communication.

On 27th September, when Star entered, I tapped 8. She flew to the window, looked out, then returned to the screen, looked at me then bowed her head low. I repeated 8, she responded correctly in 4, 4, rhythm, then hurriedly left the room.

On 30th September after two fine days when Star did not want to be indoors tapping, the weather turned cold and wet, and she was keen to work at mathematics. I gave her 7 even beats which she did first in 4, 3 rhythm, then repeated it of her own accord in 5, 2 rhythm, afterwards flying to me for her nut with an air of confidence. The following day she responded correctly to 5, beating it evenly and she repeated it several times after I had held out her nut. I then gave her 8 in 4, 4 rhythm. She tapped 4, 1, bowed her head close to the wood a moment then looked up at me inquiringly. I repeated 8 in 4, 4 accent. She at once tapped 4, 1, 3. This was done very carefully, the 4, 1 tapped with her normal strength of tone, but the final 3 tapped very loudly after a slight break – not long enough to call a pause. It seemed she remembered that she had got as far as 4, 1 the first time and now she was adding the missing three. She was not tapping for a reward, she had forgotten about her nut in the interest of working at her sums.

Later in the day she gave a correct response to 6, tapping it in 3, 3 and 2, 2, 2 rhythm, seeming to get pleasure in giving the two versions. She also responded to 5, but gave this evenly, as usual. When giving her these numbers I had made no accents. After this she flew to the top of the piano and had some fun tearing and hammering at the strong brown paper covering it. Many other Tits had also entered the west room and were pounding at their roost-boxes, the furniture and other things in the room. A Great Tit outside unceasingly rapped on an empty gourd hung to the cottage wall. All seemed enjoying themselves immensely, and Star could no longer concentrate on sums.

The next day, when Star was being given a number, Monocle entered through the fanlight; seeing Star, she perched timidly on the sill, and looked at me, hoping I would hand her a nut. Star gave several digs into the screen then tapped a wrong number in response, again digging the wood in annoyance at being distracted by Monocle. I gave the latter a nut, getting her to eat it outside; Star understood and watched her fly away then bowed her head to the screen for a number. She was now so interested in mathematics that the continuation of her lesson seemed to mean more to her than my having given Monocle a nut before she had one herself, which used to make her angry. (See page 9.) I gave her 7, without any accent, and she gave a fluent performance of her two rhythms, 4, 3 and 5, 2. Afterwards I gave her 5, to see if she would get muddled and tap 2 at the end of 5, but she rapped out 5 correctly then came for a nut.

Several days of fine weather now followed in which the demolition squad worked hard, chiefly inside the cottage, but some hammered at the trellis work on the outside wall, and at the putty on the window-frames. It was hardly worth while clearing up their litter each day, for the rooms were strewn with it again directly afterwards; it was like having human workmen in the house and being obliged to put up with their noise and mess! Star often joined in this work, choosing, as usual, the piano coverings and perseveringly making a large hole through thick brown paper then tearing the cloth covering underneath, so that I had to put even stronger reinforcements under her hole. When not occupied over this work, Star stayed out of doors, so we did no mathematics for a week.

One day, when Star and the others were not indoors, one of the youngster Great Tits made an important discovery — so it seemed when watching her. In the west room there hangs a large plastic lamp shade, shrouded in dark chiffon to protect the indoor roosters from the glare, which disturbs them. The Tit flew to this shade, inspected it carefully, then bored a small hole through the chiffon and tapped on the broad rim underneath. Discovering the noise this made, she excitedly pulled and tore at the chiffon, to get a larger surface bared for hammering. This done she rained blows on the taut plastic band with the vigour of a Nuthatch, putting her back into it and at times nearly losing her grip of the slippery foothold, but she went on rapping, louder and louder, making such resounding bangs that it brought several Tits hurrying through the fanlight to see what she was doing, one of them so scared by the sound that she quickly retreated again. The others stared a moment, then a male (adult) flew to the shade and chased her off, afterwards perching there himself to make an examination before flying away. The discoverer then returned to continue her drum music. Drummer, as I named her, now began experimenting on different parts of the shade, tearing many small holes in the chiffon then testing the sounds with sharp raps on various parts of the shade. Except on the broad rim (or band) the sound was feeble and low-toned, for only the rim was tightly stretched. She went back to it in between testing other parts, evidently to compare the sounds. She did this with quick, excited movements, obviously thrilled by her discovery. The broad rim was then tested on the other side of the shade, the noise there being the same; she then made hammering tests on one or two other things in the room which produced little noise, but she stayed several moments on the screen, hammering for all she was worth. The noise it made was nothing compared to the shade, so she returned to this for another ten minutes of drum music before she flew away. Drummer often repeated a short performance (always on the rim) during the autumn, but in these later performances the excitement of discovery was missing.

Drummer, Joker and one other female now took to occasional hammerings on the screen while Star was out of doors. They always flew away when I tried to give them a number to copy, except Drummer who one day stayed and looked at me while I tapped, as if interested. It seemed she might be a possible pupil to join Star's classes when she was ready to resume them.

On 12th October Star flew to the screen and began tapping then looked at me attentively for a number, but before I had time to give one, Drummer and Joker flew to her side and Drummer at once began hammering loudly and inconsequently. Star angrily left her perch and clung with her feet to the screen in front of Drummer, with her wings and tail spread and twitching while she uttered protesting notes. With her beak she tried to pluck at the part of the screen which Drummer had been hammering, then the two youngsters flew into the next room. Star immediately took Drummer's place on top of the screen and attentively looked at me for a number.

I tapped 3, also pronouncing very distinctly the words 'Tap 3,' for I wanted to try and train her to respond to words only. She tapped 3, looked towards Drummer and Joker, who were in the other room, then began rapping loudly and incoherently, breaking off suddenly to dash at the youngsters and display at them for a moment before making a hasty exit through the fanlight. They also flew away. In a few

Star protesting to Drummer and Joker

moments Star returned in a calm mood, deliberately tapped 3, then flew to me for the nut, which in her hurry she had forgotten.

Later that day I gave Star 4 beats, also saying 'Tap 4.' She responded correctly, then tapped larger numbers at random, of her own accord. The following day she tapped 7 and 8 of her own accord before she looked at me to give her a number. I said, 'Tap 4,' also giving it in taps. She did this correctly and came for her nut. Five hours later, she came for a lesson, and after a short preliminary of random taps, looked at me for instructions. I said 'Tap 4,' this time without beating it or making any movement to indicate the number. She continued to look at me without tapping. I repeated the words only, saying the four very sharply. She bent her head and then carefully tapped 4. I was astonished that she had so quickly learnt this, for I had never given the figures in words before that day. I thought this might be chance. The next day however I gave her 3, in words only. She looked at me, bent her head to the screen, hesitated, and looked up at me again. I said 'Tap thrreee,' making it very distinct. She at once rapped out three beats. It was two days since I had given her this figure in words, and then I had only said it once. I was very careful to make no indication by outward movements, and later experiments proved that she knew and took my figures from the sound. Later that day she again gave 3 correctly to my spoken word alone. This time she got the figure at once, without my having to repeat the words.

On 15th October she made a mistake, and hesitatingly tapped 3 when I said 'Tap 4.' She did not come for her nut after this, but looked at me with an uncertain air. I repeated the words very sharply, accenting the four. She bent to the screen, carefully hammered 3 beats and added 1, making a very slight break between the 3 and the 1, as she did when giving 7 in different divisions. Later that day she got 4 straight off, to my spoken word only. She had, as on some previous days, rattled off a long string of tappings of her own accord before looking at me for a number. I found it best not to interrupt these hammerings, for when she had let off steam in this way she was ready to concentrate on the serious work, done with me.

On the morning of the 16th Star did no tapping, either of her own accord or for me. The reason was that when she came indoors Drummer had been doing some hammering on the screen and I had tried to give her a lesson, but when I tapped 4 beats on the table, she only looked at me with interest, then went on doing random taps; afterwards she flew to me for a nut. I gave it to her, for she was a little nervous of my taking part in her hammering game, and unlike Star she evidently did not understand about numbers. She was very dominant with other Great Tits, and many of the youngsters were now getting afraid of her, for she often chased them from the room.

That afternoon Star came to me while I was reading by the window in the west room. Perched on my knee, she looked up into my face, wanting my attention. I said, 'Tap 4' (without beating it). Star at once flew into the other room and perched on the screen. I repeated the words only. After giving one quick dig into the wood where Drummer had been hammering so hard that there was a slight hole, Star rapped out four resonant beats then flew back to me for her nut. It completely astonished me to hear her getting the spoken numbers.

The next morning, at 9.30, after going through some random hammering, Star bowed her head to the screen-top, then looked to me for a number. At that moment, a male Great Tit flew to the screen in possessive display, spreading his wings and doing a chin-up at Star. She raised her head feathers so that her crown looked very high, this kind of display being ingratiating and meaning that she had no aggressive intentions when she tapped. She then flew to my hand, still with her crown raised. The male flew away. Star's feet firmly gripped my finger while she watched the interfering Tit leave the room, then she hopped along my arm and looked into my face. I said 'Tap *three*.' She eagerly flew to the screen, gave 3 taps then came for her nut. I had now changed from 4 to 3 several times and always got correct responses, except the one mistake over 4, recorded on a previous page.

Two hours later, at 11.30, Star asked for a number. I said 'Tap 4.' She tapped 4 in 3, 1, rhythm, making a very slight break and giving a quick glance at me before adding the one. I gave her a nut and praised her warmly. She had been astonishingly clever. Before that day, since giving her spoken numbers only, I had kept to the same number throughout the day but this time I had altered to 4 after having given 3 two hours previously. Star ate her nut, then flew back to the screen and, of her own accord, faced me, then rapped out 4 without any break. This, I think, was because she realised she had split 4 into 3, 1, when giving it previously, and she liked to give it without the break as well, showing that she understood.

At 1.30 on the same day I gave her 5, saying the number and beating it for her, since this was a new spoken figure. After giving a correct response, she flew to me for her nut; fifteen minutes later she returned to her tapping perch. I said 'Tap 5' without beating it. She tapped 5 and was given a nut.

On the following morning (18th October), she looked puzzled when I said 'Tap 5.' I had to beat the number to get any response. She did not make the mistake of tapping 3 or 4, but waited for me to help her further over 5. Owing to its being fine, she was not indoors again that morning, but while I was gardening I tried to hammer 5 on my fork, while saying the words. Star perched above me, bowed her head to the branch as if going to tap, then she looked up, gave a loud call-note and flew to my hand. Lessons out of doors were not possible. There were too many distractions and she was nervous of being watched by other birds when she tapped.

On 19th October at 8.30 I gave her 'Tap 4,' in words only. She responded vigorously, with an air of enjoying her accomplishment. At 9 o'clock she gave a correct response to 3 (given in words only). The day was wet and cold, she was keen to get on with her sums, and at 9.30 wanted another lesson. I gave her 5, in words only. She again was puzzled and, after staring at me a moment, went through a series of larger numbers, 7, 8, 6, pausing in between with her head bowed to the screen. After giving 6 she looked up at me; I tapped five, again repeating the words. She did it correctly. I did not then realise that 'five' might be a difficult word for a bird, for it is much less defined than 'thrree' or 4. In fact, to say five sharply is difficult. ('Fife' is therefore used by the telephone exchange.) At 11 o'clock I again gave her five in words only. She tapped 6 in a hesitating manner then gave a dig into the screen. I repeated the words, trying to make five clear by dwelling on it. She then tapped it correctly, but gave 6 afterwards. I did not feel convinced that she really had got the five clear in her mind. At 2.30 I said 'Tap five,' again dwelling on the number. She gave 6. I said 'No. Tap 5,' repeating it sharply as 'fife.' She looked alert at once and without hesitation rapped out 5, nor did she again get confused over 'fife,' as following records showed.

The next morning I gave her 3 and 4 in words (wishing to give her time to forget her muddles over the vague word 'five'). She tapped these correctly and vigorously. I was just giving her 6, when the possessive male Tit flew up, and did a chin-up at Star before she could respond to my number. Star's head feathers were raised in reply to the Tit's display and she edged away from him to another part of the screen, turning her back towards him while she tapped 6 to my given words and beats. I then tapped 3 several times for the male Tit, who took no notice of this and continued to display with spread wings, hopping around on the screen in a possessive manner. To get rid of him, I then held out a nut, he flew to my hand, and I discovered that he was Inkey, who had been absent for two years and four months. He had disappeared in June, 1950, after having lost his nest-box and territory through Star's efforts to help Baldhead regain them. Inkey's frontal markings were exceptionally black and had a special shape, also his manners and poses made his indentity unmistakable.

Star showed annoyance because I had taken notice of Inkey and fed him when he was displaying aggressively to her; she tapped loudly and inconsequently and when I tried to give her a number she flew to a chair and tore paper and a bath towel spread over it.

At 9 a.m. the next day Star was very hungry and tried to get her nut without a lesson. I said 'Tap three' – in words only – she quickly rapped out the number correctly and took her nut. At 10.30 she took 4 correctly from my spoken word, also, of her own accord, she repeated it in 3, 1 division, having the first time tapped it without any accent. At 1.15 she tapped 5, 6 and 7 without having been given a number. Drummer flew to the screen after Star had gone into the west room; she gave a few gentle taps, then looked at me. I hammered 4. Drummer tapped 3 and flew away.

Ten minutes later Star wanted a number, showing me this by perching on the screen and looking at me with her intent expression. I said 'Tap fife.' She did it correctly without hesitation. At 4.30 she again wanted a number. I repeated 'Tap fife'; she did it vigorously.

Star, this autumn, took no notice of the males around her, she was more friendly with me than ever before and her interest in these lessons was much greater than in previous years. Her mind was concentrated upon getting the right number when she had asked me for one. Food as a reward had nothing to do with it, she frequently forgot her nut.

The next morning at 8.30 she tapped 3 in response to my spoken word and fifteen minutes later, when she again wanted a number, I said 4, which she did without accents. At 10 o'clock, I was busy and paid no attention to her when she asked for a number. She then rapped loudly on the screen and inserted digs into the wood, annoyed because I had not taken any notice. I went up to her, she gave two feeble digs into the screen then looked up at me with her intent expression. I said 'Tap fife.' She tapped 5, dividing it into 3 by 2, with only a very slight fraction of a pause between the figures. It was decisively tapped, and she looked up at me afterwards with a confident air of success, then came for her nut. I praised her – she knew by my tone at once when words of praise were spoken. Probably, in Star's case, she learnt to understand many words that I spoke, in the same way as she learnt the numbers.

At 10.15, when she flew to the screen for a lesson Inkey made a dash at her. She raised her head feathers, muttered something in an undertone, then flew to the piano. I told Inkey to go away and coaxed her back, but he perched on the window-sill, still giving a slight chin-up display and Star could not concentrate.

When Star had flown out of the window, Joker took her place on the screen and looked at me. I tapped three beats and repeated this several times. Joker bent her head as if she was going to tap, but hesitated. I said 'Tap 3,' and again beat the number, repeating it 4 times. She then gave three resounding raps and flew away. Later she returned to the screen, but when I gave three beats she at once flew into the other room.

The following day (23rd October) Star gave correct responses to spoken words of 4 and 3 (at 8 o'clock and 8.30 respectively). At 9.30 she came in and rapped 5 of her own accord, following it up by several other numbers. I called out 'Star.' She stopped and looked up. 'Tap five,' I said (pronouncing it normally). She gave two digs into the wood. 'Tap fife,' I said. She at once tapped 5. At 12 o'clock I gave her 6 in words only. To my surprise she got it at once. It was several days since I had given her this number, then beating it as well as saying the figure.

At 1.15 I was sitting in the west room when Drummer went to the screen and rapped 5 and 3 of her own accord. I did not give her any number for Star at once flew to me, her head feathers flattened and a look of great displeasure on her face. The flattened head feathers, used in displays of anger, corresponds to the animal putting its ears back when annoyed, and I always call this the 'ears back' expression. Before I could console Star by giving her a nut, Drummer again hammered the screen inconsequently. Star left my lap and flew at her fiercely, chasing her out of the window, then she returned, and, perched on the screen, looked at me intently. I said 'Tap 5.' She looked at the window; Drummer was entering, Star left the screen to chase her out again then she returned alone and I gave her a nut; Drummer was outside on the window-ledge ready to enter if Star began tapping. Concentration was impossible while disputing for the right to tap! I then gave

Inkey in chin-up display on the screen

Drummer a nut. Neither bird showed any jealousy over food, it was the screen tapping that was their bone of contention.

At 2.30 Star wanted a number but, before I could give one, Drummer flew to the screen and gave a few loud raps, then Inkey suddenly appeared, and with a consequential air chased Drummer and Star from the screen, returning to it himself and hammering loudly for a moment to advertise his possession. I tried to make him take a number but he did not listen to me, he was swaggering about on top of the screen, his chin held up and his wings slightly spread. Star and Drummer, with several other Great Tits, were watching him from the other room and he knew it. I held out a nut, hoping this would distract his attention. He took it, flew back to the screen and began hammering with the nut held in his beak, then he flew around, his head held stiffly upwards, the nut still prominently in his uplifted beak, while chasing all the other Tits from the rooms. There was general confusion and much dodging from room to room and fluttering of wings as the Tits tried to avoid the tyrant Inkey, but he succeeded in getting rid of them all, then perched on the screen, chucked away the nut and flew to a roost-box in the west room. After a moment he, too, flew out of the fanlight. Inkey was always a dominant bird, if he took it into his head to possess the rooms I feared there was trouble ahead for us all!

3 PERSEVERANCE DESPITE INTERRUPTIONS

The next morning at daybreak Star hurried indoors, seemingly keen for a lesson before the tyrant appeared. She first tapped 6 of her own accord then looked at me intently. I gave her 3 in words only. She at once tapped it.

At 9 o'clock she came again without tapping of her own accord. I said 'Tap 6' (words only). She gave 6 in 4, 2 rhythm, making the very slight break and accent customary when she was doing these sums. I said 'Tap 6' again. She bowed her head to the screen for a moment as if in thought, then rapped out six clearly divided into 3, 3. Afterwards she looked up at me to see if I approved. I gave her a nut and praised her. She seemed very pleased and ate her nut on my hand.

From 12 noon until 2 p.m. Inkey took possession of the screen and would not let the other Tits perch on it. Star, Drummer and Joker all tried to get a chance to tap; forgetting their rivalry, they all came together on two occasions, giving Inkey much trouble to hold the screen to himself. When he at last chased them all away, including others who kept entering every few minutes, he went round the west room, examined all the roost-boxes on the picture rails and stayed inside each one a few moments before going to another. He favoured two, returned to them and stayed longer in them. The other Tits kept away, it seemed he had scared them. I was getting annoyed with Inkey for making this disturbance but held out a nut, hoping he would then leave the room. He flew to my hand, looked with a comical air at the nut, gave my finger a poke with his beak, then flew away without it. He seemed a disgruntled bird, always he held his head feathers flattened (the ears-back look) which is an aggressive sign. When the other birds were near him they all raised their head feathers, the appeasement sign with which they tried to hold their ground.

At 2.15 Star slipped into the room and perched on the screen while Inkey was not in sight. I said 'Tap 6.' She gave a clear 6 in 4, 2 accent. Before she had time to come for her nut Inkey flew at her. My anger rose. I chased him out of one east room window, he straightway entered through another just as Star had again perched on the screen. I chased Inkey to the window, then standing in front of the screen I gave Star 7, both saying and beating it, as she had not before been given this number in words only. Just as Star had completed 7 taps, doing it clearly in a new treble division of 4, 2, 1 Inkey flew over my head and pounced at Star. I drove him away and Star held her ground, with her head raised very high. A general turmoil followed; I pranced round the room after Inkey who beat me every time; when I managed to drive him out of one window he entered through another. We went backwards and forwards from room to room while Star watched from the screen. She had not even had a chance to get her rewarding nut for her clever division of 7 into 4, 2, 1 – eventually she flew away without it. Inkey was impossible to banish; for ten minutes he tried to get to the screen and often managed it, though I soon got him off again. I believe he enjoyed defying me. Once he flew to a roost-box, and with his ears-back look, lowered his head at me like a bull going to charge. I took a step towards him, he flew out of one window, and entered quickly by another, then perched conspicuously opposite me with that same look. I did not want to stop his roosting indoors, so I held out a nut. He flew to my hand at once and hopped around on it in a restless manner, sometimes looking at the nut but never picking it up. In despair I gave up the battle with Inkey and went out, leaving him in possession of my rooms.

An hour later I returned. Star, who had apparently been on the watch for me, entered immediately. Inkey was not there so I gave her 7, in words and in taps, for she had not yet learnt this number. I realised that seven might be difficult, having two soft syllables and being indefinite in sound – to a bird's ear. Sharp sounding words were much easier for her to recognise. Eight would, I expected, be easier. Directly I had given her seven, she looked at the window and gave a faint squeak-note, in fear of Inkey's return. She then tried to get a nut from me without tapping, but I withheld it, for I did not want fear of Inkey to stop her tapping. I gave her the number again, she did it in 4, 3 rhythm, then got her nut.

Soon afterwards Inkey rushed through the fanlight, displayed at several Tits who were feeding from my hand and seized a nut himself. This he held in an upturned beak, making it conspicuous, and chased one or two Great Tits from the room. A youngster Blue Tit, called Opal (because of his iridescent plumage) always roosted in a box on the picture rail above my bed; he paid several visits to his roost every day. While Inkey was again perched on the screen, the nut still held high, Opal entered the room, flew into his roost-box but quickly came out again and rushed at Inkey, who only moved to another part of the screen. Opal flew to the electric light flex above Inkey and, clinging to it head downwards, spread his wings in display. Inkey had always ignored Opal – it was the Great Tits that he harried, especially Star, Monocle and others who were territory owners and mates of his former rivals. After a dash into the other room and back to the screen, with the nut still held high, he flitted outside to eat it and I was able to feed the remaining birds in peace. Drummer and Joker that day had not dared to go near the screen because of the tyrant, Inkey.

The next day (25th October) at 8 a.m. Star entered, flew to her tapping perch, gave 3 raps then looked at me. I said 'Tap 4.' She gave it correctly. At 9 o'clock when she entered I said, 'Tap fife,' she at once got it correctly and came for her nut. At 10 o'clock Drummer flew to the screen when Star was absent and tapped 3 of her own accord. I rapped out 7 beats and also gave it in words. Drummer tapped 7, copying my rhythm of 4, 3. This may have been chance, as it was her only correct response although I tried her many times afterwards with other numbers.

Inkey came for half an hour at 10.30, chased all the birds from the room and afterwards waited outside the fanlight for several minutes, to prevent them re-entering. At 11 o'clock he took a nut from me and disappeared. Star at once entered. I said 'Tap 6' which she did in 3, 3 rhythm. She was hungry and after eating her nut on the screen flew to my hand for another. I said 'Tap 7.' She gave a long medley of numbers, then made several digs into the wood of the screen. Other Tits were flying to it and she could not concentrate, but she also did not yet understand seven, in words only.

At 11.30 when I was not in the room, Drummer began hammering the screen. Before entering I called to her from outside the door 'Nuts,' to prevent her and other Tits from flying away when I opened the door. I often did this and it was understood. I said 'Tap 3' to Drummer, who had not left the screen. She tapped 7, which was the number she had previously been given. She did not understand numbers by words so I rapped 3; she did it correctly and went on hammering for several minutes after eating her nut. I tried to get her to respond to 4 but had no success.

At 11.40 Inkey blustered into the room, disturbing all the Tits at their occupations of paper tearing, roost-box inspection, etc. (They examine their roosts several times during each day.) He tried to chase them outside but some dodged him and remained staring at him protestingly while he flew to my hand, took a nut, and as before, flew to the top of the screen with it held high in an upturned beak. After swaggering in this manner, with possessive display, he began to eat it on the window-curtain rails, then chucked it down half-eaten and restlessly flitted from one roost-box to another, still in display poses of chin-up and half-spread wings. He also peered inside the crack of the sliding door roost, where the Blue Tit called Bluey used to sleep when Inkey first was a territory owner here. After a few minutes of this behaviour, Inkey flew away; he left an empty room, for the other birds had been afraid to remain. That night Inkey occupied a roost-box indoors which belonged to one of them.

The following day Inkey was even more of a nuisance. He chased Star away from the screen several times and she had no chance for a lesson. Drummer perched there once and I seized the opportunity to give her 5 beats. She tapped 4 and even when I repeated five taps she did not get it correctly. She had not at any time shown definitely that she knew the numbers she tapped and I think her few correct responses were imitations, given without realising the numbers she tapped. There had been more wrong numbers tapped by her than correct responses, but Inkey was perhaps hindering her concentration on this occasion. He soon appeared and Drummer left the room. Next time she entered she dared not go to the screen.

At 5 p.m. that day, Inkey, having first got rid of all other Great Tits, perched on the same stolen roost-box he had taken on the previous night. Feeling that his possessive behaviour must be checked, I chased him outside but he entered again immediately. I made several more attempts to get rid of him but finally he flew over my head to the roost and settled down. I left him there, for it might give me a bad name with the other Tits if I interfered with a bird when roosting in a box. Meanwhile the Blue Tit, Opal, had been waiting outside the east room window, ready to fly to his roost above my bed when Inkey was settled for the night. Even Opal had now begun to fear him, although so far Inkey had left the Blue Tits alone.

Inkey was a real problem, and my annoyance at his behaviour was not diminished when the next morning I heard that Dr W. H. Thorpe would be coming to see my birds in a few days. I was also expecting James Fisher, who was to bring the American bird artist and ornithologist, Roger Tory Peterson, who wanted to see Bird Cottage and its inhabitants as he had kindly consented to write an Introduction to the American Edition of *Birds as Individuals*. What would these three ornithologists think if there was only one bird, Inkey, to be seen?

For the next two days Inkey continued to create such a nervous atmosphere that few Great Tits dared stay in the rooms; when they entered they snatched food from me and hurried away from the tyrant. Star often flew to the screen, then craned her neck forward to see if Inkey was coming through the fanlight; he generally came, straightway chasing her from the room. At 7.30 a.m. on 28th October I got her alone. She was so nervous of attracting Inkey that she gave her response to my spoken number (four) in very faint taps that were only just audible. She would not stay to take any more numbers and was obviously nervous of remaining on the screen.

The next day at the same hour (7.30) she again responded in very soft taps to 'Fife,' given her in words only. At noon she seized another opportunity to fly to the screen when Inkey was not in sight. I gave her 6 in words and she had just completed her whispered taps correctly when the tyrant appeared and chased her round the room before she had time to get her nut. She gave whimpering cries of distress as Inkey drove her through the fanlight. A minute later she reappeared and flew to my hand for her nut while Inkey was charging round the room, sweeping other Great Tits away. After he had got them all outside he perched on the window-catch to watch for their return; when he saw them coming he dashed out at them before they could reach the fanlight. There were only a few quiet intervals during the day while he disappeared for about ten minutes; then all the others flocked indoors to feed. Most of his time was spent interfering with other Tits and he was always especially vehement in objecting to any bird tapping or perching on the screen. He acted mock possession of Bluey's sliding door roost, although it was never occupied now Bluey was dead. The crevice is too narrow for a Great Tit to squeeze through, but he displayed over it, hanging upside down from the runner and spreading out his wings in a possessive display, although no Blue Tits at that time wanted this roost. He even began chasing Opal when he visited his roost-box above my bed. I removed the roost-box Inkey had been occupying, hoping this might subdue him. He flew to the picture rail and took note of the missing roost, then went inside the cardboard roll-roost nearby, where he slept that night.

Yet, for all his sins, I could not help liking Inkey. For one thing, he was extremely amusing to watch and he had kept his trust in me, despite my attempts to subdue his possessiveness. The previous morning, at 6.20, when he had flown from his bed to the usual fanlight exit he found the velvet curtains blown across the window so that they completely blocked it. He could not get out, and I heard him several times fluttering around the dark room, then there was complete silence. On going to see what had happened, I found him crouched on a curtain fold that lay across the sill. When I drew back the curtains, he flew to another closed window, then tried to get out of one that had always been open when formerly he was a territory owner here but it now was shut. The dawn light was insufficient for him to see which window was open so he flew to my hand and looked up at me, asking for my help. With my other hand I made an upward movement in the direction of the open fanlight and he at once flew out of it.

That day Inkey was less annoying to the other birds. Star came at 7.30 a.m., but would not tap for fear of attracting his attention, so I gave her a nut and did not press her to have a lesson. At 8 o'clock she returned; finding Inkey was not in sight she tapped 6 softly to my spoken word. Three hours later I coaxed her to the screen with difficulty, for Inkey was outside, and she kept craning her neck to watch for his entry when we began a lesson. Inkey was on my mind as well as

Star's, and instead of giving her a number in words I quickly tapped 8 in 4, 4, rhythm. She tapped 4, then rapidly craned her head forward to see whether the Tit entering the west window was Inkey. It was not. Star exchanged a look with me, then bent her head and finished her number, tapping the remaining four beats very softly and carefully. The interval between the two fours was only a fraction of a second, for birds' movements are so rapid.

Until noon all the birds were happily free from Inkey's interference, then he flew to the screen in a possessive pose. I chased him off it. He went to the other room and began a tour of all the roost-boxes; each one he examined with an exaggerated show of extreme interest every time other birds entered the room. They glanced nervously at him before flying to me, but he made no objection and soon flew away. When he returned he rushed with a consequential air to the screen and gave some sharp raps; I looked at him severely and he flew away. His raps were done for possessive reasons and to announce his presence on the coveted screen-perch. Drummer and Joker had been too scared of him to attempt perching on it for several days, and the previous evening Opal had been frightened to enter, so had slept elsewhere. Inkey should have been satisfied, for he had both rooms now empty of birds at night; none dared enter after 4 p.m.

At dusk that evening he came in to roost and tried every box, making a great noise and sounding very busy over it. Sometimes he uttered pretty call-notes, apparently to me, as no bird was within earshot and he had no mate. (Smoke had not appeared for some time and I never saw her again.) Finally, he settled down in a large carton over the west room mantelpiece.

That day I had received a wire from James Fisher, saying he was bringing Roger Peterson in the afternoon of the next day. I wired back 'Come in the morning if possible. Inkey takes possession afternoon. Others dare not enter.' I had some difficulty in getting this wire taken down over the phone but James Fisher understood it!

The morning after their visit, Star came at 8 a.m., tapped 3 and then 4, both without hesitation, to words only, but before she could get her reward, Inkey butted in and chased her out of the fanlight. She entered through another window, seized her nut while being pursued, then flew away.

Dr W. H. Thorpe came at 10.30 that day. I had warned him that

Inkey was hindering the counting lessons which I wanted him to hear. Before he left, Drummer, taking advantage of Inkey's nervousness of the stranger, had flown to the screen and when I gave her a number, she bowed her head preparatory to tapping but Inkey, proving the truth of my words, at once rushed up and took Drummer's place on the screen. Star was always more nervous of human strangers than Drummer, so, together with her fear of Inkey, she did not dare to appear.

The next day, 2nd November, all the birds were nervous, they kept looking round the room before entering, as if expecting human strangers to be there. They naturally dislike visitors, and having had them for long visits on two consecutive days the birds were temporarily upset and many did not appear; even Inkey was timid in behaviour that day and entered very little. Opal took advantage of this and went to his roost-box above my bed during the morning. He slept there that night.

On 3rd November Star entered the room early and gave a correct response to 3 (in words only) tapping very softly, but when I said in quiet tones 'Tap 6' she gave 5. We were having to be very quiet over our lesson for fear of bringing Inkey indoors, this together with her fear of his entering, probably caused her to make this slip. I then tapped 6 for her, she did it correctly at once but instead of coming for her nut, repeated the 6 carefully four times, in a painstaking manner, as if doing it to make up for her mistake. She had done this on other occasions after making a slip, but her mistakes were very few; all are recorded here as well as her correct responses.

4 FINAL ACHIEVEMENTS

For the next two days, Inkey was too troublesome for lessons to be possible. On 6th November Star came at dawn and tapped 6 to my spoken word, doing it in 4, 2 division. Later she loudly tapped many numbers of her own accord, pausing between them to watch for Inkey to appear. He soon darted at her but she dodged his charges and returned to her tapping perch in a defiant pose. Inkey retired to the top of the piano, his head feathers raised in a conciliatory display while he watched Star bow her head to the screen to give 2 taps and one dig

STAR'S FURTHER AMAZING ACHIEVEMENTS

into the wood. I said 'Tap 6,' but she was not listening. Her mind was upon Inkey, and I wondered what had caused her sudden defiance of the tyrant. The previous day I had seen Inkey come to grips with The Intruder, who now came indoors. They had rolled together on the floor, feet interlocked, then both had flown outside. Perhaps Star knew of this, and was encouraged to make a stand herself against the tyrant. Later in the day she went to the screen but could not concentrate until I shouted a number several times, then she gave me 6 correctly to words only. When she had left the room Drummer flew to the screen and gave 3 taps of her own accord. I beat 6 for her, then Inkey flew up and Drummer fled without tapping.

Two days later Joker braved the screen-perch and when I hammered 3 she gave a correct response. I could not get her to respond to any other figure. Joker was always limited to the number 3. Star entered later and hammered furiously of her own accord with an eye on Inkey, who was in the other room. He flew to the screen, she dodged him and got the better of him, but she could not concentrate upon taking my number until he left the room. Then she gave 6, in 4, 2, to words only.

The next day she did 4 and 7 correctly to my words, yet seven had not been given her for many days. She repeated 7 three times in different divisions before coming for her nut, making it 4,2,1, 4, 3 and 4, 1, 2. Later Drummer flew to the screen. At the same moment Star entered at the fanlight, raised her head feathers and flew away. Drummer chased her, then returned and was chased out by Inkey. Star then returned and tapped 8, to words only, without hesitation.

On the 11th November Star tapped 4 to words only, but did not get 7 until I tapped it and said 'Tap sept,' which being sharper I thought might be easier for her to learn. She tapped it in two rhythms, 4, 3, then 4, 2, 1, looking up at me after doing the second one, as if to see what I thought of it. I praised her but before she could take her nut Drummer flew up and chased her outdoors. Inkey, as usual, appeared and Drummer hurried away.

The next day Star came at 8 a.m., and did a brilliant exhibition of 8, to words only, first tapping it in 4, 4, then giving me a hasty glance and doing it in 2, 2, 2, 2, which was entirely her own invention. Two had not been given to her as a number since the first day of the experiment in autumn, but she used it for these division sums although she now rarely tapped it when doing quick successions of numbers by herself; she then liked tapping at the fastest possible speed and big numbers gave her more scope for this. Later in the day I said 'Tap sept.' She looked at me, with her intent expression. I repeated it very sharply and she got it correctly in 4, 3.

The following two days she could not get any chance to tap. On several occasions other females chased her from the room when she perched on the screen, also human visitors made the birds nervous again. On the 15th November she came at dawn, tapped 3 to words only, then 8, giving it in 4, 4 and 2, 2, 2, 2, with a look of satisfaction after accomplishing this. Later I said 'Tap 6.' She did this in 3, 3 and in 4, 2, with an air of competence. It was always astonishing to see and hear this mathematician at her work. Inkey had not disturbed her since she stood up to him, nor did he chivvy others from the rooms. He had now secured his roost in the cardboard roll and seemed content. Opal, the Blue Tit, and another Great Tit (Pippa) now slept above my bed again, in adjoining boxes.

On 17th November Star, as usual, came at 8 a.m., and gave correct responses to '3' and 'fife.' An hour later she was given 8 and did it 4, 4. At 3 p.m. she tapped endlessly of her own accord at a terrific speed. Another female flew to the screen and displayed, trying to stop her, but Star would not stop, she edged away and went on tapping. I called out 'Tap 8.' She would not listen and carried on with her lightning speed, non-stop tapping. Suddenly she broke off and flew out of the window.

The following two days the cold weather made her so hungry that she would not tap before having her nut. I gave her the food at once, and after she had eaten it she flew to the screen and did 3 and 4 correctly to words. Also 'fife' and 'sept' were taken confidently. She did so much random tapping on following days that I gave her a rest from lessons until the end of the month. This proved successful. She got tired of hammering by herself, and on the 30th November she looked at me for a number. I said 'Tap 3,' this she did, then looked at me for another number. I said 'Tap 8.' She gave 8 in 2, 4, 2, a new division of her own invention. She repeated it twice, as if enjoying it, and was praised when she came for a nut. Later in the day she took 6 doing it 3, 3 then in 2, 2, 2. She had precision in her manner of tapping and never hesitated after being given the words only. In all the tests I took care not to make the slightest movement. It would, in fact, be impossible to make 6 or 8 movements rapidly without doing it consciously and with muscular effort, for when giving a bird these numbers in taps, the pace has to be fast and even.

On the next day Star tapped 4 quietly in response to my words, then did a few rapid taps of her own accord. I called out 'Stop, listen to me.' She looked up and I again gave 'Tap 4.' She moved quickly to the very edge of the screen as near to me as possible, and rapped out 4 slowly and extremely loudly. I could not help laughing, for it suggested a rebuke for having had dull ears! She had already done that number correctly but quietly.

The following day I gave her 6 in words only, which she did in 3, 3 rhythm, then of her own accord repeated it in 2, 2, 2. I next said 'Tap 3.' She responded correctly. Later I gave 'sept,' which she tapped in 4, 2, 1, giving a repeat of her own accord in 4, 3. Other Tits had now taken to flying up directly Star began her lesson, mainly because they were hungry and wanted nuts. I fed them to keep them away; Star seemed to understand, she was keener on her lesson than the food, only if very hungry she tried to get the nut before the others could take it; sometimes I let her have it, but usually I withheld it and gave it to the interrupting Tit. Star then flew back to the screen and bowed her head to the wood, waiting for me to give a number.

On 3rd December she gave 7 to words only in a new accented division, 2, 3, 2. The Intruder then flew to the screen and hammered a few beats very rapidly, afterwards flying away. This was done to make himself conspicuous. He was possessor of her old territory, and always liked to demonstrate his ownership, but he did not often come indoors; when he did his visits were hasty. He was an odd, nervous bird.

Drummer and Joker had now lost all interest in tapping and they never again responded if I tapped them a number, even when they were perched on the screen. Although they seemed to have the rudiments of understanding of tapping a number from having watched Star, unlike her, they lacked special talent, perseverance and the desire to improve their counting accomplishments.

On 9th December Star gave correct responses to 4 and 6 in words only, but when I said 'Tap five' – instead of fife – she tapped a medley of numbers then looked at me inquiringly. I said 'Tap fife,' and, as usual, she did it correctly. The next morning at dawn, directly she entered she tapped five of her own accord. Ever since the beginning of the experiment, the few times that she had not understood my spoken number or had made a slip she had repeated the number correctly two or three times of her own accord. One of the many astonishing things about Star's behaviour was that she wanted to learn and to get the numbers right, if in the mood for pursuing this occupation.

Afterwards I gave her 9, beating and saying the figure. As before when I tried nine, she began to tap before I had finished. It was now some weeks since I had tapped 8, for she had been taking the numbers from words only, so I rapped 8 on the table. She again began tapping before I had completed the number, and continued doing it very fast without any break until I shouted, 'Star, tap 8' (without tapping it). She looked at me, then bowed her head, and gave 8 in 4, 4 division.

I now gave her a break for several days as The Intruder was causing a restless atmosphere among the Tits while he disputed with Inkey, who wanted to get his old territory again, which The Intruder had taken from Star when she lost Peetur. Star was not interested in these disputes, nor had she made any attempt to woo either of these males, although her territory would go to whoever won the disputes. This surprised me, for in former years she had been so keen on this territory and spent much time in autumn and winter courting Baldhead. Now the development of her mathematical talent seemed to mean more to her than anything else.

On 22nd December, when Star flew to the screen at dawn I gave 3 in words. She tapped 3, bowed her head to the screen a moment then in a laborious manner gave two slow raps and one single rap, dividing 3 into 2, 1. It was done deliberately, like all the other divisions of numbers, but splitting three into two and one is not so easy to do clearly in tapping as bigger numbers that can be accented rhythmically with a slight comma for the divisions, as I found by trying it myself. This accounted for the unusually laborious way in which she did it. I then said 'Tap 2.' She did not understand and stared at me. I had never given her two in words, nor had she been given it in taps since the autumn. I then tried giving two taps while saying 'Tap two.' But she would not respond, perhaps because she had not been praised or given a nut for her clever division of 3. I gave her the reward and she flew off. When she returned at 11 o'clock she flew to the screen and tapped two of her own accord. I then said 'Tap two' without tapping it and she did it correctly. Next she was given 4 in words. She did it in 2, 2, then in 3, 1. I praised her warmly and gave her a nut. Her rewarding nuts were now important as it was cold weather and she was hungry.

The next day she flew to my hand for a nut on entering the room. I did not give it to her, so she went to the screen and tapped 5 very loudly, then came for it. She was too hungry to wait for me to give her a number.

On the 24th December, to my spoken figures, she again gave 3 in 2, 1, then 4 in 3, 1. Next I said 'Tap 2,' in words only. She got it correctly. Afterwards she hammered some large numbers of her own accord, then flew for her nut. She always seemed to prefer being given larger numbers. When she came later in the day I gave her 7 in words. This she did in 4, 3.

On Christmas Day I could not get her to tap at all. Those who are always on the look out for anthropomorphism will imagine that I think Star would not tap because it was Christmas and a holiday! I therefore will explain that a large feast had been spread indoors and outside for the birds, and as so many of them were flying in and out all day Star could not concentrate on her hobby – or was it now her profession?

On the 27th December at dawn she gave correct responses to 4 and 'fife.' Later she was just going to tap when other Tits flew to the screen in display. Star, with raised head feathers, remained on her perch, but she would not tap in front of the others. The weather had been mild for a few days and a little territorial disputing had begun among these Tits. Many conversational notes were now uttered by them. Star soon left the room; she did not mix with the others.

The next day I gave Star 5 in words. She tapped it in 3, 2 rhythm. Ten minutes later she returned and gave it of her own accord without any accent or comma division. I said 'Tap 6.' She did 5, glanced at me then gave 1. I then tried the experiment of beating 6 in a definite 3, 3 division and accent. She tapped a very definite 2, 2, 2, both in accent and the slight comma in between. After doing it she looked up at me inquiringly, as if to say, 'What do you think of that?' I praised her. Lowering her head to the wood and waiting a second, she then deliberately tapped 4, 2. She again looked at me. I warmly praised her. It was astonishing to see and hear these different divisions.

On 4th January, in response to my words, she tapped 4 in 3, 1, after first doing it without any division. I said 'Tap five.' She did not do it, but gave a hesitant dig into the screen, which meant she was uncertain. I said 'Tap *fife*.' She got it at once, then flew for her nut.

The next day she took 'fife' in 3, 2 division. Other Tits then flew up and displayed at her with spread wings. She would not leave the screen but perched on a lower rung, her head feathers raised. She disliked having her lessons disturbed though she could not display aggressively, for these Tits were territory owners and mated birds so they took precedence, in bird law.

If Drummer entered the room while Star was tapping, then the former angrily chased her outside. Star was now nervous of Drummer because she had begun to woo Inkey.

For several days I tried to get Star to listen while I gave 9 taps; she always interrupted by tapping herself. Now she was used to taking numbers by words, which was much quicker, she found my tapping tediously slow, yet I could not teach her the number nine by words only if she would not listen to the beats. On 20th January I tried tapping 8 instead of saying it. She would not listen and tapped a long while by herself. I said 'Star, tap 8.' She at once did this correctly, in 4, 4. The next day I got her to listen to 6 taps, giving it in 3, 3 division. She at once tapped 6 in 2, 2, 2. As on a previous occasion, she then gave it in 4, 2 – without my tapping or saying the number again – her accents, as always, definite and the divisions made purposely, with a very slight break. In doing these divisions she never made mistakes. Later she took 'fife' from words, first doing it in 3, 2, then without any division or accent.

On 21st January she did not want to tap at all. Her interest now began to wane, for she had begun to take notice of Tinky, Monocle's former mate, who owned the petrol-tin nest-site at the top of the orchard and the territory beyond my north hedge. Her choice of a mate was good, for Tinky was a much nicer bird than Inkey or The Intruder – to the human bird-watcher. He was especially attractive in appearance and was a good parent. His mate, Monocle, had recently disappeared and had probably died of old age.

On 13th February I coaxed Star to the screen to take 'Tap 4.' She did it correctly with no accent, then looked at me. I gave her 'fife,' which she did in 3, 2. I repeated 4, she looked at me a moment then did it in 2, 2. Later she took 'sept' which she tapped in 4, 3. The next day she took 8 (all were taken from words) in 4, 4 and repeated it of her own accord in 4, 2, 2 division.

On 17th February she came in and hurriedly ate her nut; with an air of having important work on hand, she dashed out again. It was useless to bother her with lessons for her mind was upon Tinky and the tin nest-box in their territory. Once or twice during the next four days, when she perched on the screen I gave her a number and she flew to the window, then turned round to look at me. I knew this was to show me she did not want to tap, so I gave her a nut and she flew off to Tinky. After this for several weeks she kept in her territory all day, except for very occasional visits indoors to get a nut. She was nervous of meeting The Intruder and his new mate, or others who were now territory owners around the cottage. Particularly she avoided Drummer, who had paired with Inkey. They had the front garden, and Drummer always chased Star if she saw her trying to enter the cottage. I went to Star's territory several times a day and was interested to find that she never used her former special double-noted call which The Intruder had stolen from her when he took over her territory. He now used the call frequently. Star invented another triple-noted call, gentle in tone, and this always brought Tinky to her side.

At the end of March the weather turned wet after a long drought. Star came indoors, flew to the screen, bowed her head to the wood then looked at me. I said 'Tap 3.' She did it very softly, for louder taps would have been heard by the territory owners outside. I then gave her 4, which she did in 3, 1. The next day (again wet), I gave her 'Tap five.' She looked at me but did not tap. Then I remembered to say 'fife.' She at once did this in 3, 2 and repeated it without any accent. I then tapped 6 in a definitely divided 3, 3 rhythm. She instantly gave me 6, very carefully dividing it into 2, 2, 2, then she looked at me with a satisfied air, as if she had accomplished something, and flew to my hand for her nut. Later I gave her 6 in words only. She did it slowly and carefully in this division, 1, 3, 2.

On 1st April I gave her 'sept.' She tapped 4, 3. Later in the day she was given 6 in words only. She first gave this in 2, 2, 2 division then, after a moment's pause with her head bowed to the screen, she slowly tapped 1, 3, 2. When doing triple divisions her pace was always slower, she seemed thinking beforehand, and taking great care to get the correct number of beats. These numbers were all tapped softly for fear of bringing in the territory owners from outside.

On 4th April she asked for a lesson, I gave her 4 in words, which she tapped in 3, 1, then in 2, 2. Later she did 8 to my spoken word, in 4, 4, then in 4, 3, 1, looking up at me with her pleased expression after accomplishing it. She did not want nuts in reward, for it was too near her nesting season and she preferred natural food at this time.

On 5th April she took 3 from words, doing it in even beats, then she carefully tapped 'fife' (to my word) in 1, 3, 1 division. I had never given her the number 1 at any time, and she only tapped this when making her division sums. It was entirely her own idea to do this. (Her only other use for 1 was the single tap given as her identity signal, to show me she was not Smoke.) When she tapped 'fife' in 1, 3, 1 she threw me a rapid glance before giving the final beat.

It was the last number that this wonderful bird tapped. During the following fortnight she was busy at her nesting-site, always accompanied by Tinky, and they were often in their territory which extended beyond my orchard. I saw little of her during the day but every evening at about 5 o'clock I went up the orchard, calling her name, and she flew towards me with Tinky following her. On the evening of 22nd April, when I called her Tinky came alone; he seemed agitated and restlessly moved from bush to bush near where I stood. He refused his usual nut and flew to a tree-top, calling for Star who did not come; he went on singing and calling from tree-tops for the rest of the evening: even at sunset, after the other Tits had gone to roost, he was still waiting for Star, who never came. At last, in dusk, he sought his roost.

For six days Tinky sang and called continually, then a young first-year bird, who had been reared in my garden, went to him and became his mate. (The history of this bird, called Smiler, is given in Chapters 6 and 7.)

Two days after Star's disappearance on 22nd April, 1953, I saw a neighbour's cat jump from a bough of the tree which held her nesting-tin, this leaving little doubt that she had been killed while going to or from her nest.

Star's most brilliant achievements had been in the last year of her life when she was at least in her ninth year. Her age cannot have been less than this when she died as she had not the appearance of a first-year bird when in the spring of 1946 she first came to my garden as a stranger to build her nest.

Star's unique talent was always astonishing to witness, equally wonderful was the keen interest she took in developing it. She did not work with me for purposes of getting a nut in reward as she was given one whether she was in the mood for a lesson or not, and, as was seen in Chapter 2, she often did not want rewards after she had given exhibitions of her talent. Her interest was in the work for its own sake.

It will have been seen that her achievements could not have been accounted for by any signals or telepathic communications from me as I did not know in advance what divisions of my given numbers she would make; these were her own calculations but she always wanted assurance from me that they were correct. When she had learnt the numbers by name she became impatient of being given them by the slower method of tapping, but if I tapped a number in one division she seemed to derive pleasure from giving it in another.

Some people still have an impression that birds are incapable of counting. For many years scientific experiments have been made with caged birds to test their ability to count, this being done through training them by method of slight punishment for incorrect results. The last published records showed that Pigeons could count up to 5 or 6, Jackdaws 6, Ravens and Parrots 7. Budgerigars learnt to 'act upon two' when the experimenter said 'dyo dyo dyo' and upon three (taking three grains from a heap) when he uttered 'treis treis treis.' A similar result was obtained from a bell indicating two and a buzzer indicating three.

It is astonishing that Star counted up to 8 with no difficulty, and of her own accord discovered that each number could be given with various different divisions, this leaving no doubt, as there was with the caged birds' experiments, that she was consciously thinking each number, in fact she did mental arithmetic, although unable, like humans, to name the numbers. But she learnt to recognise their spoken names almost immediately and evidently was able to hold in her mind the sound of the names. Like the telephone operator, she found 'five' difficult to hear and needed the definite sounding 'fife.'

Star's immediate realisation, in the very beginning, that I wanted her to tap numbers, was extraordinary. Another instance of a remarkable flash of understanding was when the Great Tit called Twist responded at once when I held my face close to hers and said 'Give a kiss.' She instantly touched my nose with her beak – a bird's kiss – and all her life from that time she responded to these words in the same manner. (This was related in her biography in *Birds as Individuals*.) Star's behaviour over the addition of the oak tree territory was also astonishing, for she prepared in advance for a coming food shortage for her nestlings. Other birds did not do this and it seemed she had some intuitive sense or else reckoned the future food supply from the earlier state of the trees.

Birds understand much that I say to them from the tone of voice, but this was not enough to account for Twist's and Star's flashes of insight into my meaning. Star's talent for counting would never have been revealed had she, like the other birds, failed to understand in the first instance that I wanted her to tap in response to my beats. Although Drummer and Joker tried to compete with Star after hearing her lessons it was doubtful whether or not their few correct responses were chance, and they soon lost interest altogether. The following winter after Star had died I tried Drummer with taps but she took no notice and I failed to get any response.

Tests on caged birds may later give additional proofs that some birds have the ability to think numbers and do mental arithmetic such as was achieved by Star. She will, however, be likely to remain unique as a wild bird, who of her own free will pursued the science of numbers with keen interest and astonishing intelligence. The word genius has for long been a subject of dispute, but the word is surely applicable to this bird whose achievements were so far beyond others of her kind.

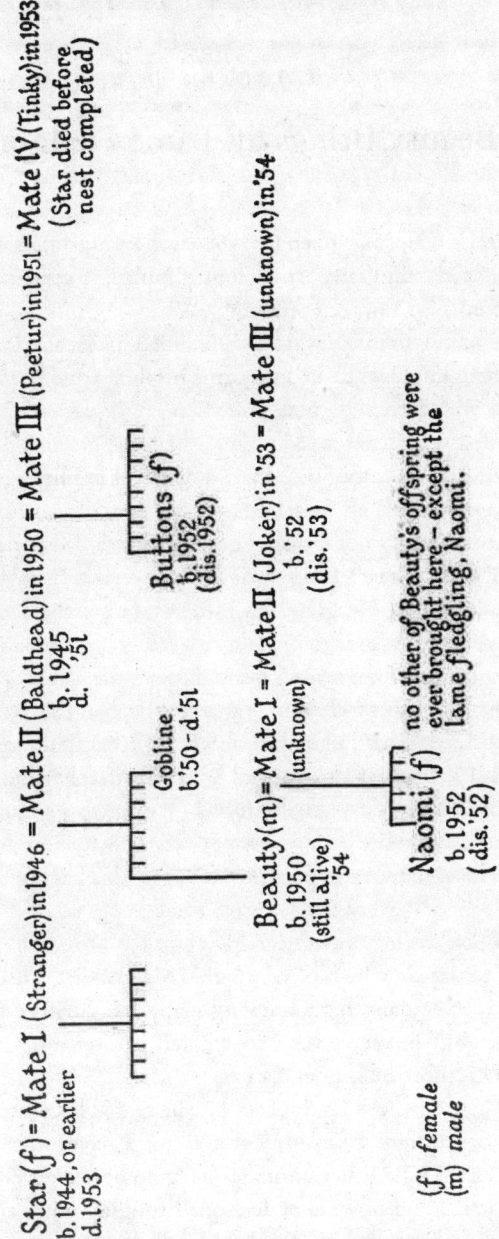

CHAPTER 4

Beauty Brings his Lame Fledgling

One of Star's offspring, born in 1950, was an especially fine looking youngster with unusually irridescent plumage. Everyone seeing my birds singled him out, commenting 'What a beauty,' so he became Beauty by name. In many ways he resembled his father, Baldhead, and from his fledgling days he had the same implicit trust in me. Unfortunately he was driven to nest elsewhere, my garden already being overcrowded with long-standing territory owners and pushful newcomers. Until he was four months old he never left my garden, but on 20th September he, and four others of his age, suddenly disappeared and I feared he might not return. Four weeks later I was writing by the french window when I had the delight of seeing Beauty fly up and perch on my hand. He gazed up into my face for a few moments, examining it all over as if to make sure it really was me, and giving me the feeling that perhaps he was pleased to see me again. While he was eating nuts and cheese, the other three, who had left with him, also flew up to feed. They all stayed about an hour then went roaming again. Beauty returned after three days and from that time until spring he paid visits every day, usually flying straight to my right shoulder and walking round the back of my neck to the left shoulder, where he craned his head forward to peer into my face, this having been his way of asking for food ever since he was a small fledgling. If I handed him the titbit box to let him select his choice of food, he took some moments to decide which piece to take. Many other Tits hastily pick up one piece then another, chucking many away before they make a final choice but Beauty always considered beforehand, and when he had taken his piece he kept and ate it.

In mid-April his visits stopped while he reared his young, probably in a territory distant from my cottage, for I never saw him during these months as I did other intimate Tits who nested nearby. When he returned at the end of June he had one drooping wing and his flight was slightly laboured. This improved a little after his moult but it

1. No, we can't have visitors! (This board is at the gate of Bird Cottage)

2. Great tits on the watch for defaulters. (This board is near the Cottage)

3. Great tit in confidential conversation with the author

4. Star

5. Great tit Peetur on my hand (taken by holding camera under my right armpit)

6. Great tit taking off

7. Great tit Inkey about to alight on my hand

8. Naomi, a lame fledgling, a week after her arrival

9. Presto with food for his nestlings (1953)

10. Presto's fledgling, just before flight

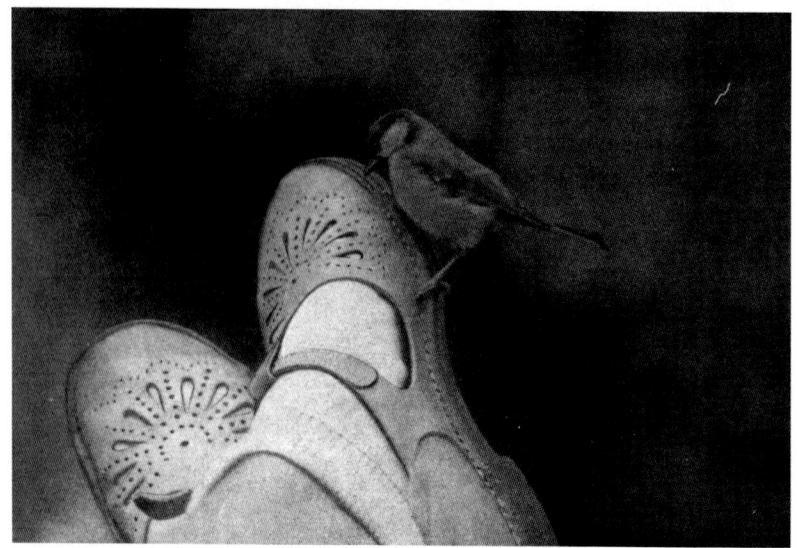

11. Cobbler finds a job

12. Cobbler at work on my sandals

13. Drummer's fledgling, Charmer, content to stay with me (1954)

14. Charmer's sister, impatient for my attention

15. Drummer. Final victory over the toy elephant

16. The Hedgehog drinks from the Tits' jar

17. Blue tit with caterpillar for its nestling

18. Nod, the Coal tit

19. Blue tit

20. Lesser Whitethroat

21. Stalky the robin enters, in typical pose

22. Bouncer in characteristic pose

23. Nuthatch plastering clay nesting box to the tree

24. Pair of swallows nesting in a coil of wire

25. Wren carrying a beam for its domed nest

26. The Song Thrush who sings for his supper

27. Nesting pair of house martins

28. Mistle-Thrush

29. Darkette, alert for Stubbs to appear

30. Stubbs enjoying the sunshine

31. Busby

32. Song Thrush bathing

never got quite right. He now stayed for much of every day in my garden, or indoors when the territory owners were not too possessive, as sometimes they were in autumn if the weather was fine. When it rained, Beauty kept under cover more than most birds because his injured wing, if wet, drooped more and hampered his flight. Sometimes, when he was perched peacefully indoors his expression suddenly changed and became tense, the next moment he uttered a squeak-note, resembling Baldhead's special high-pitched note used when under stress, then Beauty hurriedly left the room and directly afterwards one of the territory owners came in. Beauty seemed to know in advance that this bird was coming although he could not have seen him and there was no sound from outside. This advance knowledge of the territory owner's arrival saved him from being chased, which he disliked as he was rather slow on the wing. His mate never appeared. Perhaps she remained on their territory.

When nesting season approached, his visits again ceased for a few weeks. This time he arrived back on 18th June, bringing with him an injured offspring about ten days from the nest, who was unable to stand. She had the same kind of leg trouble as her grandfather, Baldhead, one leg seeming to be badly strained in the upper joint, and for several days she could not use either leg.

Beauty at once handed her over to me and she accepted the human stranger from the first moment of her arrival as if knowing why she had been brought here. While she lay on my hand Beauty fed her with cheese; then she looked up at my face, staring interestedly for several minutes as Tits do when examining anything new to them. Although strong on the wing she showed no wish to go with Beauty when half an hour later he flew away, presumably to look after the rest of his family. He was away about an hour. The fledgling rested for a time on the arm of my chair by the open french window, then she flew to a tree near the cottage and lay on a branch, looking up at the leaves and crying from hunger for the natural food she needed. Probably she had been lame for a few days, her plumage was dull and colourless and she seemed undernourished, for she was just old enough normally to have been seeking a little food to supplement what her parents had been giving her. When Beauty returned he put a caterpillar into her beak then brought her to me and again fed her with cheese while she lay on my hand. He flew away after ten minutes. This time, when she began crying from a tree I went up to her and held out my hand, making the palm quite flat so that she could alight on it without using her legs. She quickly accepted the offer and let me feed her. When, an hour later, Beauty returned, she was lying on my lap by the french window. He perched just outside and looked at us for a moment, then he fed his baby and flew off again. I hoped that he felt pleased at the immediate success of his sensible idea in bringing his lame fledgling to me. He came back about six times that day to give her a good feed.

I had to get up at 5 a.m. (Summertime) every morning, for Beauty's baby cried on the window-ledge outside, wanting me to feed her. The day after her arrival the weather turned wet and cold and a strong wind drove the rain indoors, yet I had to keep near the open french window for the lame fledgling had not learnt to use the fanlight or to understand glass, and I was afraid she might add to her troubles by hitting against a window-pane. With a mackintosh over my pyjamas, I breakfasted by the open french window soon after dawn, with Beauty's baby, whom I called Naomi, beside me, the other young Tits flying in and out all the while. Beauty came at 7 a.m. (Summertime) and fed his offspring, who then flew to the trees outside, calling to him for more food. He came indoors, got cheese from me and tried to give this to her, but she would not take it from him; having already had enough of this food from me she now wanted caterpillars. Beauty was intelligent, he understood, but he was not going to let the cheese be wasted, if she did not want it he did! He ate it very hurriedly, then found her the natural food she wanted. As on the first day, he did not remain long with her, but paid six visits during the day. For the next two days he fed her three times daily, after that he left her to me altogether and did not come to my garden. Fortunately her complete confidence made it possible to look after her well and in two or three days her plumage had recovered its natural gloss and colouring. She was a good-looking bird with a sweet face. I noticed that her legs were very hot, it seemed there was inflammation. She frequently took baths, then lay on top of the wires of an open bird-cage that was slung to the bird-table. This resting place allowed the air to get to her legs, which she probably found cooling. Naturally, the other youngsters noticed her immobility, and often they tried to poke her off the bird-cage by gently prodding her, but she hissed at them and usually held her ground. At first, when she left the cage they tried squatting on it to see whether her idea was a good one, but it did not suit them; they were soon standing up again, and finding more active amusements.

On Naomi's second night in my garden, she found a comfortable roost in a big hole in the orchard apple tree, but she could not climb up and down the steep slope inside and was going to sleep with her head showing from outside; this was safe when I fixed wire round the hole, giving her security against cats and other enemies. She seemed pleased with this fortified roost and often used the hole to rest in by day. The other youngsters, seeing her there, wanted to get inside too, but she held her own while they hopped around the hole, peered at her, and clung to the edge with a little display. They never tried to use force or any form of attack. Directly she came out they all took turns to go inside. In the days that followed, this hole was a great centre of attraction for many of the young Great Tits. It provided a game that sometimes lasted an hour or more. Taking it in turn, one went inside, the others, about ten of them, played around outside the wire-netting while the occupier inside made a great show of working very hard, with mock fussiness, at pecking the sides of the hole, sometimes coming outside to hammer at the edges and pausing occasionally to glance at the Tits hopping around the wire-netting while giving little chin-up and wing-spreading displays accompanied by twittering sounds. The owner of the hole was often changed, apparently by mutual agreement, and the game continued as before. If the rightful owner, Naomi, wanted to enter they gave way and let her stay inside longer than those who only played at ownership, but until her legs were better she usually kept away during this game and entered her hole directly the others left it.

As Naomi could not join the others in play she was often alone but she seemed content. After she had been with me a day or two, she invented a lovely flight dance which she enjoyed performing, for she was very agile on the wing. This was delightful to watch; she sang a charming soft song as she glided in graceful curves round, through and over a bough above her hole in the apple tree, then she flew from twig to twig, not alighting, but just touching each twig with her breast. Occasionally, perhaps forgetting that she could not grip with her feet, she attempted to alight which resulted in dropping from the twig with her wings outspread, but as if it were part of the dance, she rose again in a sweeping curve to continue twisting and turning in unceasing movement over the apple tree bough. Sometimes this aerial dance was performed in the hedge near her tree. The platform had to be carefully chosen as it needed many upstanding twigs and she liked the sunlight for her performance. She spent half an hour most fine afternoons or evenings, dancing by herself in this manner when the other Tits were roaming the hedges beyond my orchard. She never left my garden, being entirely dependent on me for her food. She often sat on my knee or lay contentedly in the palm of my hand.

Naomi's injury soon began to improve; she used one leg a little after four days, and a few days later she began amusing herself by performing a gymnastic exercise; she turned slowly round and round while on a perch, the revolving movement done by using her wings and giving gentle pushes with the one leg she could now use. At the end of a fortnight she was able to use the other leg too, but if on her feet for long at a time she held it up. I noticed that it still felt rather hot at times.

Naomi was such a sweet-natured fledgling, charming in appearance and in all her ways, that it distressed me much when on 2nd July she suddenly developed acute enteritis, which may have been connected with the leg inflammation. She had violent excretions that caused her so much pain that she jumped up and down, uttering a cry. The underpart of her body was burning hot, and in two days all the feathers came off round the hind quarters and the back underparts of her body. She now could not eat, and it appeared she would die unless I could do something to stop the internal inflammation. Remembering that I had once been given kaolin for a similar kind of illness, I got some of this powder, though the chemist wisely warned me that it might be harmful to a bird even if I could get her to take it, which he thought unlikely.

I made a small pellet of the kaolin powder by mixing it with just enough cheese to keep it intact, then I handed it to the invalid. She had not eaten any cheese or other artificial food since her illness but she took the pellet, at first nibbling it cautiously, then finishing it with confidence. Half an hour later I gave her some more, which she took eagerly and finding that she was improving, I gave a very small quantity several times during the day. She was able to eat a little natural food by the evening, and the following day she seemed very hungry. I continued with smaller doses of kaolin during that day, and although she still suffered a little straining after excreting, she was rapidly recovering and now quite lively. Next day I stopped the kaolin, neither would she eat it when she was better. In four days new feathers were beginning to cover her bare parts, and in a week her appearance was almost normal. Her appetite for natural food was terrific but she would not eat anything else except a little squashed cachew nut, made soft by soaking in water. To complete her recovery I continued to spend much time hunting natural food for her. She was slow at finding any for herself; having always been an invalid she had had no chance to learn, also there was little to be found in my garden because the experienced birds took most of it. I had discovered her fondness for spiders and their eggs soon after she came. She used to come with me, lying on my hand, while I went round the garden searching for suitable food for her. One day I saw a small spider walking up a raspberry cane hugging a silken globe of eggs; unlike some spider mothers, when I tried to catch her she dropped her burden and escaped. Naomi ate the globe of eggs with such an air of excitement that I hunted for another. I soon found one swathed in gossamer attached under a folded edge of a leaf. Naomi pulled out the ball of eggs while I held the leaf. From that time I went hunting expeditions every day and soon learnt the best places to find these small spiders and their eggs. In a day or two I had developed a bird's eye for seeing at a glance the leaves that held them, as well as knowing the sort of hedge and parts of it that would give good results, so in a very short time I could fill a paper bag with many spiders and with leaves containing eggs for the invalid. They are such interesting creatures that I enjoyed pursuing them for the sake of learning about their ways. Some species chose the fresh young leaves of dewberry shoots as cradles for their cocoons, other species made different kinds of nurseries with walls of gossamer spun round stems of grass or leaves of plants. I liked best the small white or coloured species that I found in folded leaves, each mother zealously guarding her cocoon. They were interesting because their reactions were different when I touched their leaves, even among the same species; some were self-sacrificing mothers who would not leave their eggs even when I picked the leaf and put it inside a paper bag, others panicked at the least touch of the leaf and deserted at once, falling to cover among the herbage below. There were some that hesitated, seemingly unable to make up their minds whether to stay or to escape; they hovered on the edge of the fold, falling when I picked the leaf and usually landing inside my bag, which I learnt to hold underneath to trap the deserters when they fell. Although sorry that these spiders were going to be eaten, they would, in any case, die in a few days when their young were hatched and had been released by them from the cocoon. Often I found two or three mothers had chosen the same leaf, which surprised me, for they had the choice of so many unoccupied ones – there was no question of housing shortage. From the survival point of view, making more than one fold to a leaf was a disadvantage as it distorted the shape so much that it was instantly conspicuous to the spider hunters. It seemed they had social instincts or felt safer in company with others. The mothers must have been aware of their neighbours, for they would feel the leaf vibrate while the others worked at their cocoons. I frequently found a curled leaf contained a spider which had not yet laid her eggs; all she had done was to fold the leaf by means of a few taut threads. Unwilling to deprive the creature of her fulfilment, I usually left her undisturbed. As each spider-filled leaf on a hedge becomes quickly memorised, I kept watch over these laggards and on following days found most of them still sitting idle, in the empty leaf. Then warmer weather came and quickly they all set to work and filled their cradles.

Some spiders wrapped their eggs in white silk bags, others in green. Naomi always chose the white ones first. She sat on my lap for these spider meals, with a choice of leaves in front of her, and she soon discovered that I sometimes brought folded ones that had held eggs but were now empty, so she took to weighing each leaf in her beak, tossing away the empty ones without uncurling them, the others she opened and extracted the ball of eggs. Some were at the stage of first hatching and could be seen moving underneath their transparent silk covering; Naomi watched them a moment then pulled off the cocoon and swallowed them in mass, but sometimes she was not quick enough and the tiny spiders, directly they were released from their cocoon – done by their mother under normal conditions – escaped and swarmed at an astonishing speed through the threads of my skirt onto my knees then down my bare legs, afterwards they spread out all over the floor. These minute, grey creatures were too small to be worth picking up separately, so the Tits left them alone although they were apparently tasty when eaten in mass. Some remained in my cottage, others waited for suitable weather then floated out through the open french window on small silken threads.

Often I brought back from the fields a spider nursery, full of lively little black infants. These nurseries, where the young hatch out and remain for a while, are made by a small black species and built on grasses or various kinds of plants. The nicest I found were on the silverweed's lovely leaves, the fine silken walls spun round them, the nursery being about three inches long. The mother had left plenty of room for her young, after hatching, to stretch their legs, and run around before facing the outside world. These buildings are difficult to move without breaking the gossamer and letting out the more adventurous infants, for some were more lively than others. So these nurseries I quickly put into a large box with a well-fitting lid. They seemed to fascinate Naomi; when I opened the box she gazed inside, her eyes following the movements of the baby spiders, some of which were finding their way out up the sides of the box. She ate a few, but her main interest seemed to be in watching them. After a while I would close the lid, for too many were escaping into the room, but Naomi soon flew back to sit on top of the box, her eyes constantly watching for the few black infants that managed to escape from under the lid. Sometimes she leant over the edge of the box, and snapped up one of them, but it seemed they provided her with entertainment more than food.

Many spiders of various kinds from my catch turned up weeks later in different parts of my cottage, especially the bathroom, where the birds seldom go because they fear the sucking sounds of the water running away – understandably a noise full of awful possibilities to a bird. I watched some of these at night. There was a small one with rather short legs and a pale cream coloured body that made a large web with strands reaching from top to bottom of the window frame. For many days nothing was caught on it, so one night I threw an earwig into the lower part of the web. Instantly the spider hurried down from its lair at the top of the window, anaesthetised the earwig, hauled it up to the centre and thicker part of the web and secured it there. By degrees the earwig was sucked hollow. I then put another one into the bottom part of the web. At once the spider came down, but after examining it, left it there and went back to its lair. The earwig soon wriggled itself free. Perhaps the spider thought it too old and tough. No other insects were at hand so the next night I tried putting another earwig there. This time the spider appeared at the top of the web for a second but did not even bother to come downstairs to examine the catch, it seemed to know from the distance that I had tried to foist on to it another tough joint.

The following night the little spider was busy mending its web where the earwig had broken it in getting free. On another part of the window, a foot away from the web, another spider sat motionless. This one was about twice as big; its body was a light reddish colour. The next evening this one was working on the web but the small one was nowhere to be seen; doubtless it, too, was on the web but inside the body of the larger one. I had liked the little spider which had sensibly refused tough meat, and decided that if the other one should starve, I would not even offer it an earwig!

The courting of spiders can be fascinating to watch, especially in the species where the male uses a dramatic kind of signalling. One day in early May, when I was lying on the grass in the orchard, I made the following notes while watching a courtship that was taking place in front of me. The scene of action was a half-rotten plank, about a foot long, five inches wide and two inches in depth.

May 18th, 1953; A small black spider appears on top of the front left side of the plank, having darted up from her lair underneath. Soon a male runs up from the back right side, darting quickly to within three inches of the motionless female. In a grandiose manner, he thrusts out his right foreleg as far as it will go, then he raises the left one in a curved position before throwing it outwards. He now looks as if standing with both arms outstretched and he has edged a fraction of an inch nearer to her. His arms now start quivering, then his whole body quivers, he raises himself on tiptoe, then vibrates from head to foot. He is now a shade closer to her, his body stops trembling, he stands, firmly as a soldier, his feet on the ground. Again he shoots out his right arm, the whole sequence of actions being repeated exactly as before. (For convenience of description I call his front legs 'arms,' for they are used like arms and differently from his other legs.) She remains motionless while he repeats this many times and gradually edges closer. Now only an inch separates them and once more his right arm is flung outwards, his left curved, both arms are outstretched, and at last comes the first movement from her; in a lazy manner she raises one arm (correspondingly I call her front legs 'arms'). Her suitor now vibrates both his arms passionately and she suddenly disappears into her lair. He advances uncertainly and looks over the edge of the plank, she darts up the side and puts her arms on top of it; he retreats a few inches and she comes on top again. He then repeats all his courtship tricks, and goes on repeating them without a break, working unceasingly for half an hour until he has edged so close to her it really seems he has succeeded in winning her, but suddenly she flicks out both arms, hastily, as if in annoyance, and he quickly retreats an inch. At this moment a third spider, presumably a male, is seen at the far end of the plank. He does no signalling but goes towards the two others, now an inch apart, she motionless, he with his right arm outstretched. The third spider rushes at him. She disappears over the edge of the plank into her lair while the males, locked together, spin round on the plank in a heated fight lasting two seconds, then they separate, one male leaves the plank on the opposite side to the female, the other goes down on the side of her lair. It seems he is her accepted mate. A moment later he comes up and walks around the plank, keeping watch. In about ten minutes the other male comes cautiously to the top, on his side. He is immediately driven off and does not again show himself on the plank. The watcher remains on top. Presently a Great Tit, Tinky, swoops down but misses the spider who darts underneath the plank. This species of spider is hard to catch, even for Tits, for it is a rapid darter. Tinky perches on a bough of the apple tree which overhangs the plank; his eyes are watchful. Again, and for the last time, the spider comes on top of the plank; Tinky flashes down, then flies off with it to feed his mate Smiler, sitting on her eggs in the petrol tin. This at least saved the spider from the probable fate soon awaiting him of being devoured by one of his own kind!

To return to Naomi, my spider-catching was effective in completing her recovery from the illness, but on 20th July she suddenly disappeared. For three days previously she had ventured a little exploring on her own, away from my garden, but she had always returned after half an hour. One of her legs still was weak and it seemed unlikely that she would want to leave until more used to fending for herself. The probability of her having become the victim of a neighbour's cat was intolerable, for she was a particularly sweet bird and so much time had been given to helping her through the disasters of her fledgling days. I liked to think that she took advantage of the change that day to fine weather and enjoyed roaming far afield, using to the full her powers of flight, for she had always been agile on the wing.

Beauty was again a daily visitor to my cottage until the following nesting season. In early spring he was not, like many others, chivvied from me by the old-established territory owners, their leniency partly due to his drooping wing, for my Great Tits usually show consideration towards any of their species who have physical disability or weakness. (See Chapter 5.) During March when perched indoors he took to uttering his high-pitched squeak-note, which Baldhead had sometimes used in territorial combats. Beauty, I think, used this as a safeguard against possible attackers.

Beauty had inherited much from Baldhead, both in his ways and appearance, this becoming more noticeable as he grew older. He is alive at the time of writing, Baldhead has been dead for eighteen months, yet sometimes when Beauty enters the room, without thinking, I call him Baldhead, the mistake being made subconsciously because the likeness to his father is so striking. Not once have I called any other bird Baldhead by mistake, nor have I ever mistaken Beauty for one of the many other Great Tits that enter the room in a constant stream all day long. I have also found inherited resemblances between Leg-Presto and his father, Legs (see page 93), and many other similar cases.

As Beauty's territory was not near my garden, I had not, in previous years, seen anything of his love affairs; his mate had never accompanied him on his visits to my cottage. Probably she now had died, for on 8th April, when the young female called Joker came to me for a nut, Beauty at once flew up and shivered his wings in front of her. She appeared not to notice him and took her nut to the east hedge to eat. For some moments, Beauty remained with his body held rigidly, taut with concentration upon her; he did not even see the nut I held against his beak. When he took it he perched by her side to eat it. A stranger male, recently arrived, wanted the east side of my cottage for his territory, so he chased Beauty from that hedge but Joker remained there. Beauty soon returned and talked to her in soft notes, repeatedly uttered. She showed no response and seemed absorbed in satisfying her healthy appetite. She came to me for more food, and

Beauty followed, again perching by her side until the stranger male once more gave chase.

The next day, when Joker was eating a nut under cover of an ivy bush, Beauty took his nut from me but hesitated whether to join Joker and eat it under cover or to perch conspicuously on the wires above her bush to warn off the stranger male. Finally, he perched under cover of the large bush. When Joker flew to me again he remained there and did not see that the stranger male had joined Joker by the cottage and that she had accompanied him back to the bottom of the east hedge and perched near him in a bush. Beauty, the next moment, appeared by the cottage, his half-eaten nut held in his beak. When he found that Joker was not with me, he flew hither and thither, calling to her in sweet tones, then he flitted from one tree-top to another, his drooping wing blown by the wind, while from each tall tree he gave various calls that I had never heard before. Getting more agitated he extended his search to West Garden, but still Joker remained concealed in the low bush with the stranger. At last Beauty came to me and finished his nut on my shoulder. He was taking some cheese from my hand when Joker flew from the bush to the far end of West Garden. Beauty instantly dropped the cheese and dashed after her. He was aware that she had come out of hiding although he had been facing the opposite direction to the distant bush while she flew from it. Birds often seem aware of each other's movements without seeing or hearing them.

Joker continued, for a day or two, to tease Beauty in this manner and I wondered if she wanted to mate with this stranger because he was taking a territory by my cottage, the home that she had never yet left. Then her manner changed towards Beauty, she became responsive to his attentions and shunned the other male. When on 18th April the stranger male chased Beauty, they left my garden, Beauty leading the way over my west hedge and beyond, until both disappeared into the distant landscape where lay his territory. He had taken this direction each year when the nesting season began. The courting behaviour of birds varies much within the species, as will be seen from many instances throughout this book.

Joker did not return, no doubt being too occupied with her nesting-hole. Beauty paid me occasional short visits until 27th April, then I did not see him again until the nesting season was finished. He then returned, as usual, to spend the autumn and winter with me.

CHAPTER 5

Illness and Injury

During fourteen years of living with garden birds and studying them closely I have decisive evidence of only one infectious illness which was confined entirely to Blue Tits. The illness occurred on three occasions.

(1) In August, 1948, when four Blue Tits, all youngsters, got it, one being very ill, three having a comparatively slight attack.
(2) In April, 1952, when only two were ill. One nearly died, the other had it lightly.
(3) In March, 1953, when the epidemic was much worse. Six Blue Tits had it, one died of it, another nearly died, the other four had it less severely but all were very ill.

The symptoms in each case were the same, and as the illness appeared to be caused by a virus, I sent the bird that died in 1953 to a Laboratory for analysis. Before giving the report I will describe some details of the 1953 epidemic.

The first outward sign of the illness was that on the morning of 12th March one Blue Tit kept the feathers round his throat puffed out and he had difficulty in eating – a sore throat indicated. The bird rapidly grew worse; by 2 o'clock that day his eyes were half-shut and all his feathers were puffed out – presumably he felt cold or shivery and was feverish. As with all the Tits who had this illness, he kept mostly on the ground or close to it. The Tit now could not eat anything solid. Much saliva ran down the sides of his beak as he tried unsuccessfully to swallow food which stuck in his throat; even the smallest morsel of cheese would not go down. I gave him a small nob of butter, which he seized eagerly and by degrees managed to take this. He drank frequently and perched for ten minutes at a time on the bowl of water, in between drinking, shutting his eyes and looking extremely ill.

ILLNESS AND INJURY

The next day he was even worse, his eyes were swollen and he could hardly see out of the narrow slits when he tried to open them to pick up food. Frequently he seemed to lose consciousness in the middle of trying to eat or drink. He sat in the food dish as if dazed and unaware that many other Blue Tits were wanting to feed from the dish that he was monopolising. They at first hesitated, staring at the ill-looking Tit, who behaved abnormally. There was never any attempt to molest him but when he would not move, one Blue Tit tried gently to push him aside, while another took hold of the tip of his tail and gave a slight pull. The ill Tit at once struck out with his feet and kicked all the others away. They retired, looking puzzled while the ill Tit made more efforts to eat, but he could not swallow even the small crumbs he picked up. I gave him more butter, this was the only food he could take. He flew with it to the ground and again sat motionless, as if half-conscious, with the butter held between his feet, but by degrees he got some of it down and then drank some water. Most of that day he sat on the lawn and chose places where the sun would shine if it came out, which it seldom did that day. The feathers by his beak were dark from saliva running down whenever he tried unsuccessfully to swallow food. His flight was queer; when possible he flew in a straight line and kept within a few inches of the ground, seeming to float along, with his body feathers always fluffed out.

Often during the day the ill bird tried to sleep with his head tucked under his wing, but after a minute his body twitched and he took his head out again, looking dreadfully ill and having difficulty in breathing.

Sometimes he took cheese from me and flew with it to the ground, then sat motionless, holding it between his feet and staring in front of him, so it seemed, but close inspection showed that the bird's swollen eyes were nearly closed and he did not appear to see my hand held in front of him. Occasionally another Blue Tit flew down and tried to take the food he held – perhaps the excuse being 'if he doesn't want it, I do!' Then, surprisingly, the ill Tit at once showed fight and struck out with his feet, a short scrap followed which the ill bird always won, for the thieving Tit had no intention of fighting for this food if the owner really wanted it. Other Blue Tits never attacked him but his unusual appearance and ways attracted their attention at times, especially if he remained conspicuously perched in a dazed manner on a twig by the bird-table. After staring at him a while they would gently try to push him into movement. He edged away from them, then they let him alone. Other species, including the Great Tits, took no notice of him, and never went close to him or took food he had been trying to eat. This was noticeable with all the cases of ill Blue Tits and perhaps this helped them to avoid catching the illness, although probably other species are not susceptible to the germ, for the birds were in the room together and fed and drank from the same bowls, although not at the same time as the ill Blue Tits.

On 14th March the ill Tit was a little better, then, as was normal, he did not stay all day in my garden, for his territory was elsewhere and he was only one of the winter visitors to my cottage.

On 15th March he was much better, though still unwell. That day three more Blue Tits developed the illness, in a milder form but with all the same symptoms. They often lifted up their heads and held their beaks open after eating, for the food stuck in their throats and they were trying to swallow it. These Tits, not having such swollen throats as the first Tit, usually succeeded in eating very small bits of solid food, but I gave them butter frequently, as I found this had helped the first Tit and others in the epidemics of previous years. The legs of these ill birds did not feel hot on my hand, as was the case with Naomi (page 70).

On 17th March a fifth Blue Tit had the illness. They all sat on the ground, in a row but a little apart, facing the sun, a flower border behind them giving shelter from the wind. All had their feathers fluffed out and their eyes half-closed. For two or three weeks after these Tits had recovered, their plumage was in a bad condition and in some cases darkened, particularly round their beaks, where saliva had run down while they tried to eat. I noticed that the two Tits who took the illness less severely had more discoloured breast feathers, possibly because they preened as usual, while those that were very ill could not preen at all. Their saliva not being normal, perhaps preening discoloured their feathers, judging from the dark lines down either side of all these ill Tits' beaks.

On 20th March the sixth Blue Tit, a resident from my orchard, took the illness, this case being the worst. The others were now improving though they still kept their feathers fluffed out, especially round their throats, and squatted mostly on the ground, out of draughts.

On 21st March the sixth case, the orchard Blue Tit, became extremely ill and unable to eat anything except butter, and even this she could scarcely swallow. She followed me about flying low over the floor or ground. Her symptoms were as described in the first case, but she also had much difficulty over excreting, which in the other cases had only been a lesser symptom. I put her in a wool-lined box during the afternoon, for she seemed very feverish, and had been trying to squeeze under brown paper indoors, or plants if she was outside. (My rooms are full of paper protective coverings.) But she would not stay in the warm box, as was suitable to her illness. At roost hour she tried again to get underneath brown paper, choosing a piece on the floor behind the piano, but she soon came out of this and flew underneath my bed, then she tried the corners of the wainscoting, gliding from one place to another in her queer, low flight. Normally a bird avoids roosting on the ground – or flying low. Eventually she flew to the fireplace near my bed and settled down to sleep in a corner by the grate, behind the electric heater, which I turned off lest she burnt herself.

At 9 p.m. she awoke with violent attacks of rectal straining, these spasms coming every few seconds, sometimes making her jump from the ground in reaction. Her eyes were shut and I think she was unconscious. I put her on blankets in the box. The spasms continued on and off for three hours and later in the night she died.

The other invalids were now much better, but they continued to keep their feathers fluffed out for several days although the weather was sunny and warm at the time.

In the epidemics of 1948 and 1952, the symptoms were exactly the same. In 1952 the first bird to get ill was not a resident, I did not know him well and he had never been indoors, but he knew where to come when needing help. On 1st April I found him clinging to the window frame with his eyes almost closed. He could not eat cheese or other solid food but snatched butter from my hand directly I offered it to him. He was very ill for three days and repeatedly returned to the window frame, clinging to it outside and pressing his beak against the glass to attract my attention. On the fourth day, he was much better and began to eat solid food. The second Blue Tit to get it had a milder attack.

With one exception, the older birds had the illness worse than those in their first year. More of the birds would probably have died of starvation if I had not frequently fed them with butter, the only food that some of them could swallow.

There was a bad epidemic of influenza among humans early in 1953. The Blue Tits' illness resembled a severe form of influenza and from my observations of the birds' symptoms I came to the conclusion it was probably an infectious illness caused by a virus. When sending the dead Blue Tit to the Laboratory I made no mention of any symptoms but said I thought that a virus had caused the bird's death. After receiving the report I rang up the Director of the Laboratory and told him a little about the symptoms, which he said were in keeping with the analytical report, given below.

COPY of REPORT from
Public Health Laboratory Service 79436

Name and Address of sender: Miss Len Howard, Bird Cottage, Sussex.
Species of Bird: Blue Tit.
Where found: . . . Sussex.
Date and Time of arrival: Received from Pathological Laboratory, Royal Sussex County Hospital on 9.4.53, in frozen condition from 20°C. refrigerator, in fairly good condition.
Macroscopic lesions at post-mortem: The only pathological lesions noticed were in the thorax: the trachea was reddened and appeared swollen (though I have not seen a normal for comparison) and the lumen was such as just to admit a medium gauge unlooped platinum wire: there was a purulent exudate within the lumen. The lungs were collapsed.
Result of parasitological examination: No parasites found.
Result of bacteriological examination: Culture of tracheal exudate gave no bacterial growth other than of one colony of bact. coli. Culture of heart blood – Bact. coli. Culture of contents of gut – Salmonella group of organisms not recovered.
Remarks: Miss Len Howard states that a considerable number of Blue Tits, and no other species, were similarly affected.
Probable diagnosis: Virus respiratory infection.

In the summer of 1953, three fledgling Great Tits were unwell with gastric trouble which appeared to be a mild form of epidemic illness.

The first bird, called Thistle, began to be unwell on 7th July. She was unable to eat normally for three days, but she nibbled a very little cachew, soaked in hot water until soft. She spent most of the day sleeping on top of the window curtains. Thistle was an undersized fledgling when she came to me with some other youngsters two weeks before she got ill, her plumage was colourless and she looked underfed. Her nature was retiring and it seemed she had not been given a full share of attention. On 9th July, another fledgling, reared in my garden, had the same symptoms and on the following day a third was off its food. Unlike Thistle, these two did not seem to feel unwell as they were lively for most of the day, but they kept their feathers fluffed out, although it was warm weather, and they ate very little. All these birds had a little difficulty over excreting for two or three days and their appetites did not become normal for six days.

Ten days after Thistle began her illness she looked and seemed better than she had ever been, and her plumage had gained colour, probably owing to good feeding with natural food I found for her as well as cachews. I did not give the invalids cheese until they had quite recovered. One of them refused this for three weeks after it had been unwell, although it had eaten some before. Thistle had never liked cheese, so excess of this food cannot have been the cause of the illness. In summer it is never good for birds, especially young ones, to have too much cheese; food put on the bird-table should always have variety, otherwise hunger makes them eat too much of one kind.

Birds occasionally grow abnormal protuberances on their beaks, as in the case of Baldhead's upper mandible, page 4. Drummer also developed this to a slight extent two months before her first nesting season, in 1953. Like Baldhead, she got rid of her protuberance two days before her young were hatched, this giving proof that birds realise that eggs will turn into young and then need feeding. Baldhead's abnormality of upper mandible grew again and both times he worked hard at bill-wiping two days before his young were hatched to rid himself of this impediment to feeding the nestlings. Drummer did not again grow a protuberance.

On two occasions I have had a bird come to my garden suffering from gapes – a Robin and a Thrush. It seems wild birds do not often get this complaint, caused by thread worms in the wind-pipe. Both birds soon disappeared, probably they died from insufficient food, for they had difficulty in picking it up.

Birds frequently collapse from shock after hitting against windows; usually they lie with open beak, feet clenched, their eyes blinking rapidly as they begin to recover. They are dazed and seem unable to see properly for a few minutes, even after they look normal, then suddenly they fly away unharmed. In these faints it is better to leave the bird alone and not worry it by trying to force stimulants down its throat, but it should at once be put by an open window (one that is not in sunlight), so that it does not again hit the glass directly it revives.

Once a youngster Great Tit, who was a stranger to my room, banged into several of the windows in an attempt to get out, then collapsed. I lifted it up, its eyes were blinking, its beak was open and its feet clenched, but this was not all, after a few seconds its tongue began to flick from side to side of its open beak, then its eyes literally jumped in and out of their sockets, a thing I have never seen on any other occasion. It was horrible to watch the eyes protruding and receding in jerky movements. This lasted only a minute or two, then the tongue remained still, the beak closed and the eyes just blinked rapidly. Gradually the bird regained consciousness and after it had excreted, the feet relaxed and soon it flew away quite recovered. It probably was suffering from nervous shock which produced a kind of fit.

Sometimes, especially when very young, birds die of concussion after hitting against windows or wires. I have often had victims of these accidents brought to me. Some have been picked up on the road after they have hit against passing traffic. Their eyes are open but dazed and they fall over when trying to fly or hop. These bad cases have never recovered. Sometimes it is difficult to distinguish between a form of partial paralysis that birds occasionally get in old age, and concussion resulting from an accident, in both cases the gait can be affected in much the same way. Once a male Great Tit suffering from a mild form of paralysis kept falling over while trying to hop along the floor of my room. This attracted the attention of a resident male Great Tit who first looked at the bird with curiosity then began ejaculating odd notes while he excitedly hopped, in a dancing manner, around the stumbling Tit. This excited bird, who owned territory outside my cottage, was the only one among all the Tits indoors at the time that took any notice of the paralysed Tit, whose flight fortunately was unimpaired, for he was soon driven to leave, with the territory owner in pursuit. If the latter had wanted to harm the paralysed bird he could easily have done so; he was agitated at the abnormal condition of the Tit, but it only provoked in him the desire to chase the bird from his territory. Having done this he was satisfied and no harm was done. If there are cases of injured or ill birds being attacked by others of their kind, there is probably, at root, a territorial cause for the attack. In all my experience of ill and injured birds I have never seen anything that gives reason to think that there are such cases, but fights occur such as the one when Stubbs persistently attacked and nearly killed Darkette (page 193). Anyone who had not followed the details of their previous behaviour would have presumed this to be a case of one Blackbird killing another one that was injured.

The behaviour of birds that have had blows on the head varies much, presumably according to what part of the head has been hit. A Thrush, brought me recently, that had been picked up on the road, looked in perfect condition except for a very slight mark on the plumage of the crown, but the bird was fatally injured and until it died a few hours later it kept up a continual walk round my rooms as if it was wound up and could not stop. Often it hopped on and off my feet, going out of its way to do this, but it did not seem to know what it was doing. It had been brought into the cottage through the front door, and every time I went into the passage it followed me and walked to this door then turned round and went back into the room. Sometimes it thrust its beak to the floor as if picking up food, but it did not eat what I put there or even seem to see it.

Birds are frequently injured by traps. I have had many, especially Great Tits, come to me with injured feet; mousetraps are usually the cause. One case was a female Great Tit, who, one day in early autumn, appeared on the doorstep of my french window, which was closed. She was unable to stand but tried to make a prop of her wings as she stretched her head upwards to look through the window at me. I did not at first recognise this bird, but from her manner of gazing into my face it seemed that she knew me. I opened the window and sat down to give her my lap for a perch, for birds with both feet injured cannot easily alight on the hand. At once she flew to my lap and took food I gave her. Examining her frontal markings I found she was a bird who had been here the previous winter. It was nine months since I had seen her, yet she had come straight to me when injured. It was obvious that the accident had only just happened for she was in perfect condition except for her feet. One leg was crushed above the ankle, the other foot had all the front toes severed. After her meal, she lay on top of the window curtains. When other birds went near her, she called softly what sounded like 'tip-pet, tip-pet,' so I named her Tippet.

The next day she used the open fanlight entrance to the room. When the sun shone she lay outside, on the roof of a nest-box, hung to the cottage wall. Presently the owner appeared and chased her off his box, which he used as a roost now the nesting season was over. I fixed a small shelf to the wall, which she at once used and every fine day she spent much time lying on it. Tippet always responded immediately when I arranged anything for her comfort and the other Tits did not interfere with her. As she could not hold food between her toes to eat it in the usual Tit manner, I arranged for her to use a small table in a corner of the room for her meals, where she could eat at leisure. This plan would have failed had not the other Great Tits showed astonishing good will towards her and apparent understanding of the situation, for they never took the food from her though they saw her slowly eating nuts by breaking them against the table. Their own bird-table had no nuts on it, for normally my Tits are only given this favourite food from my hand. One Blue Tit sometimes snatched from Tippet and he always cleared the food from her table, but fortunately he was seldom in the room and only came in very cold weather. If the other Tits had not been so considerate it would have been difficult to feed Tippet sufficiently, for Tits eat frequently and I could not always be there to help her, or encourage her to be too dependent, since she was permanently crippled.

After a fortnight the injury healed and she could stand or hop about, although one leg was a stump and the other had only the hind toe. Except for this defect, Tippet was a good-looking bird with lovely sheen on her plumage. Her worst difficulty was the wind, for she could not grip when perched, so on windy days she kept mostly indoors.

At night Tippet roosted above my bed, in one of the cartons fixed on the picture rails. Human visitors to my cottage are always asked to leave before roost hour, otherwise the indoor roosters are kept from bed. But one afternoon, when the days were at their shortest, Messrs.

Collins' Editor and Director, Mr F. T. Smith, came down to Bird Cottage to choose with me the photos for my last bird book. The table being small, we spread the photograph proofs on my divan in the east room, below Tippet's roost-box. This visitor could not leave before the job was completed, and when roost hour came we had not quite finished.

It began to grow dusk and one or two Great Tits sought their boxes at the far end of the west room, but Tippet, who always before had gone earlier to bed than the others, did not appear. I turned on the electric reading-lamp and Bluey, the Blue Tit, slipped into her accustomed roost above the sliding doors. Tippet then entered the west room and perched on the piano, facing us. She looked first at her roost-box, then at Mr Smith, who was now not looking at the photographs of my birds, for he was too fascinated by watching the originals. At last Tippet flew to the screen, from there to the top of my head – her favourite perch – and then to her roost. But she immediately returned to the screen, again looked at the visitor and hesitated to go to bed. I called to her softly, she flew to my head then into her bed, this time remaining there and going to sleep. Mr Smith left soon afterwards.

Five hours later, at about 10 p.m., Tippet awoke. Putting her head out of the roost-box, she surveyed the room with interest. Until that evening she had never seen it in lamplight for she went to bed before dusk. She must have remembered her bedtime experience directly she awoke, for she had never behaved like this before. After gazing for a while, she flew to my head, then to the floor, where she began examining every sharp-edged shadow thrown by the reading-lamp. This investigation completed, she flew to the table to examine the lamp and look intently at the light. After a moment she started making little leaps from the table to the globe until she had managed to touch it with her beak – no easy performance for this lamed bird. She then examined the shadow thrown on the table by an ink bottle and again went to look closely at the lighted globe, apparently connecting it with the shadows.

When the curiosity of Great Tits is aroused, they will take endless trouble to make investigations, often putting two and two together with remarkable intelligence.

After Tippet had finished her research, she returned to bed and slept until morning. She never again made lamplight explorations.

In February my Great Tits began disputing for territory. Tippet became uneasy, fearing that the residents would drive her away. So she took the initiative and staked her claim for the east room which contained her roost. Directly the males entered this room she flew at them; taken by surprise, they retreated, but the bird called Cross, who owned the east territory outside the room, at once came back and, with protesting notes, did a chin-up display before her. Tippet returned the chin-up and mimicked every note that he had uttered, this being very unusual in the female Great Tit.

The other males now returned; she frantically flew from one to the other, driving them away. Cross then hopped around the east room in a possessive manner, while singing a varied song of his own invention, for the male Great Tit has a faculty for producing original phrases when he wants to be impressive. Tippet, in reply, rushed to the top of the screen and lifting up her head, shouted every note of his performance, then she flew at him. He retreated to his territory outdoors and began singing, facing the window. Tippet perched on the sill and gave a spirited imitation of all his tunes. Her fluency was astonishing. Female Great Tits do not usually sing, although they have a few call-notes, some varying with the individual, and normally her little note 'tip-pet' was the extent of her vocabulary. It is also not usual for a female to tackle males, yet unceasingly, for two days, this spirited cripple bravely battled against a dozen males and their mates, using song and display as well as chasing and quick attacks. Even if the other Tits were not in the room Tippet craned her head out of the window while singing Cross's songs at the top of her voice. At the end of the second day she looked completely exhausted but she had won. With birds it is the spirit that counts, not the physical strength. The other Tits could easily have got rid of Tippet by using physical force, but not one of them attempted to do so, or to use any form of combat that she could not return. I have seen many cases where this has applied. Such is the fairness of the Great Tits' unwritten laws.

Having secured her roost and the east room, Tippet now resumed her normal quiet demeanour and never made any sound except her own note 'tip-pet.' She was often outdoors, then the other Tits freely entered the east room; when she appeared they withdrew to the west room.

In April Tippet began disappearing for much of the day, although she always returned to her roost at bedtime. One morning, when I was walking in a field about half a mile from the cottage, she flew to me from the hedge. I gave her some cheese from the Tit-box, which I always have with me, and after she had stayed with me a while, feeding from my hand, she went into a wood beyond. She returned that afternoon but her absences from the cottage grew longer as spring advanced and in May she disappeared altogether. Perhaps the urge to nest had become too strong for her and possibly in spite of her defect she may have returned to her former territory to nest, although rearing young would have been very difficult for her.

To avoid causing these disasters to birds, much more care should be taken over setting mouse-traps, or any kind of trap. Robins, Tits, etc., go into outhouses and sheds to catch the insects there, and they do good work. If traps are placed in them or outdoors they should always be properly shielded both above and at the sides by boards or other opaque material, so that the trap is in complete darkness. The mouse can see in the dark and is more likely to go to a trap which is well concealed. If any light shines on the bait a bird is sure to try for it and get killed or cruelly injured.

CHAPTER 6

Great Tit Parents and Young

1

Each summer, while the parent birds are resting after their labours of rearing young and because of their moult, I am worked from sunrise until sunset by the many families of young. Some of the Great Tit parents make a point of handing over their fledglings to me, as a kind of finishing school before they become entirely independent! Watching young birds growing up is fascinating, particularly Great Tits, because they show much intelligence and individuality from their earliest days.

Fledglings are gradually trained to independence and are left to fend for themselves from two to four weeks after leaving the nest, according to circumstances and the characters of the parents. Usually the broods remain dependent upon each other's company for many weeks and their behaviour during this period is especially charming to watch. Much of this chapter will be given to describing their ways.

Besides the young reared in my garden, those from territories near by come to me when wandering in search of a living. Often these youngsters are excessively hungry and have a strained look, for experience in finding food takes time to gain and in bad weather they often do not get nearly enough now their natural food supply has been much reduced by all the poisonous pest destroyers. After a few days of good feeding they look well and happy like my garden broods. Many of the young reared here are driven to leave through lack of nesting territory; they have to avoid overcrowding, which causes food shortages for nestlings. In recent years there has not been sufficient in my garden to feed all the families brought off in it so most of the broods are taken away to the woods and hedgerows directly they fly but their parents bring them back a few days before they stop feeding them.

In 1951 they all returned the third week in June, each brood with a slightly different fledgling cry, either of rhythm, timbre, pitch or speed of utterance. Like their parents, I could distinguish between them even at a distance. First Tiptoe, Monocle, Dado and Star brought theirs back, then Legs returned with two fledglings, the only survivors from a brood of seven. This couple were so lively and their eager cries uttered at such a quick speed that I called them the Presto Brothers – presto being the musical term for very fast.

Following their arrival, Tinky brought off a late brood, eight of them fresh from their petrol-tin nest. It was curious that the timbre of their voices was tinny, so there was a double reason for calling them the Tin family. (Tinky's mate was an old bird; she died that year and he mated Monocle in 1952, Star in 1953, as already recorded – Monocle then having died.)

These six families had all returned within three days and, as usual at this season, my garden was lively all day with the midsummer chatter of young Great Tits, their rapid and rhythmical chorus of fledgling notes reminding me of music in Mendelssohn's *A Midsummer Night's Dream*.

The Presto Brothers showed much character from the beginning. As young fledglings they were very alike in appearance but one of them had inherited from his father, called Legs, a peculiarity of showing, when he perched, the upper part of his legs, above the knee joints, so he was given the distinguishing title of Leg-Presto. He was gentler in disposition than his brother, Presto, who was rather dominant in character. They were great friends and seldom apart.

Two or three days after they returned, the fledgling Presto apparently decided to possess territory by the cottage; every evening he stayed late on the roof of the bird-table, displaying by himself in an excited manner and flinging a succession of rattling scold-notes into the silence of dusk. It was amusing to watch him prancing round the roof, doing chin-ups, and flicking his wings and tail while shouting at the top of his voice. No one took the least notice of his challenge, they were all in bed! But perhaps this display was a stimulation to the fledgling and made him feel big. He needed confidence to secure the coveted territory in my front garden, which by autumn was his.

Leg-Presto was not a born warrior like his brother, and while the fledgling Presto, every evening alone in the dusk, was rattling his sword and shield, Leg-Presto was comfortably asleep in the security of an indoor roost, above my bed. He was more dependent upon me than his brother; he liked to stay longer on my hand and wanted all the help I could give him in the early days of independence from his parents. He soon struck up a friendship with the female youngster who roosted in a cardboard postage-roll over the mantelpiece in the west room. The young Rolline, as I called her, then accompanied Leg-Presto and his brother during the day, making one of the trios so often seen in bird life, although the relationships of these trios have various different forms.

In autumn, when the weather became cold, Presto also wanted to sleep indoors and one day he tried to take possession of the roost which Rolline had now occupied for some weeks. She was so determined to keep it that she remained inside it during the morning while Presto did chin-up displays in front of the entrance, hammered on top of the roll, or tore bits of cardboard from another box nearby, chucking the pieces down with a great display of annoyance. He could not enter while she was inside, for the roll was too narrow, and she pecked him when he attempted to squeeze by her. Finally he went to the window curtains within her view and plucked at them with exaggerated movements of energy, did more chin-up displays facing her and left the room. The dispute began again at 3 p.m., when Rolline was inside her roost. She stayed there for half an hour until Presto flew off; she then took food from my hand but hastily returned to the roost before Presto came back. He flew straight to the coveted cardboard roll, peered at her for a moment, then began trying other roost-boxes, making a great deal of fuss and noise over it, for he was displeased at failing to get the one he wanted. He did not again attempt to take it from Rolline for Great Tits are fair in their dealings with each other. Similar disputes often arise over roosts, both indoors and outside, the one who first takes the roost nearly always winning for both Tits know that the first owner has more right to it.

Although Presto had now given up his dusk hour displays he still liked to make himself conspicuous at bedtime, flying to each window of the cottage in a possessive manner after the other Tits were in their roosts. When he entered the room to go to bed, everyone knew it and each Tit made a stamping sound with its feet on the bottom of its cardboard roost, while Presto, with much noise and fussiness examined some empty boxes before settling down in the one of his choice. The stamping by the others was to warn Presto that their boxes were occupied. My indoor roosters also stamp when newcomers enter the room to find a roost, this preventing the Tit from flying to an occupied box and disturbing the owner, which causes agitation to both birds and sometimes a fight. Most of my indoor boxes have no entrance perch, the bird just flies straight inside. The outdoor roost is different, the bird before entering can cling to the entrance hole outside to see if the box or tree-hole is occupied. It is typical of the Great Tit to invent a sensible way of dealing with a new situation.

When spring came, Leg-Presto mated Rolline, and they were absent from the cottage for long periods during the day. After 17th April they did not roost indoors although they continued to pay short daily visits for food until 9th May, when they were driven off by a resident male whose young had just hatched. Presto, who had mated Dado and owned most of the front garden, never objected to Leg-Presto and his mate entering the cottage, although he drove off many others who, like his brother, were not territory owners in my garden.

When Leg-Presto reappeared on 9th August, he flew straight to my hand, perching characteristically, with the upper parts of his legs showing. Rolline never returned, probably she had met with some disaster. Leg-Presto did not stay long that day, but he returned in late August, then encountering his brother for the first time since the nesting season. He was on my hand, about to take food when he saw Presto flying towards me and suddenly he stood still, his body taut, while his crown feathers were slowly erected in an ingratiating display. Presto alighted on the back of my chair and looked at Leg-Presto, whose clasp of my finger tightened while he remained transfixed, uncertain whether Presto would object to his taking food before he had helped himself. Presto amicably waited while Leg-Presto slowly relaxed and took a nut, then Presto flew to my hand and helped himself. After that morning Leg-Presto came many times daily to the cottage and he was not again nervous of his brother.

Leg-Presto was now glaringly handsome in his first complete adult plumage, which with Great Tits is only attained after their first nesting season, the fledgling moult to adult plumage being only partial and the colour usually less bright. Leg-Presto's colouring was now exceptionally brilliant; his feathers shone as sleekly as polished steel, a contrast to his brother, who had the more curly type of plumage with less shine, and his frontal marking looked slightly barred because of the curl, which was, of course, very slight. Some birds appear to have this type of feather, others the finer, sleeker, type.

Presto's eight young had flown on 30th May. He was a good father and attentive to the weakling of the brood, who could not follow the others when Dado straightway led them from my garden. Presto went with her, but returned often and tried to coax the weakling to fly by holding out food from a perch above. The next day it became the prey of a cat, and I saw no more of Presto's fledglings until 16th June, when the parents brought the four survivors back, – the first brood to be handed over to me that year, 1952.

As in the previous year, within two or three days all the families returned and I was, as usual at this season, worked from 5 a.m. (Summertime) until sunset, while the parents rested during their wing-whistling season of moult. Their tail feathers usually are shed quickly, so for a time they have little or no tail, until the new feathers grow, – many people mistake them for young birds. Their wing moult necessarily is gradual and it is conspicuous to the ear as well as the eye for there is a whistling sound in flight, due to gaps in the wings where one or two feathers have been shed. They are then slower and heavier on the wing and keep much under cover. They also sleep longer at night than the youngsters, sometimes in dull weather going to bed at 6 p.m. and waking at the same hour or even 6.30 in the long days of July. The youngsters at this period go to bed about 8 p.m. to 8.45 p.m. and rise around 5.15 a.m. to 5.45 a.m., although there are exceptions.

That summer, 1952, my hands were very full for I had Beauty's lame fledgling (Naomi, Chapter 4), also another interesting addition, which occurred as follows. On the evening of 17th June, while walking in a wood half a mile from my cottage I saw flying towards me a Great Tit with her four fledglings behind her. I held out my hand and after a moment of keen scrutiny she came to me fearlessly although we had not met for eighteen months. She was an offspring of Cross through his first mate, Puggy (whose history was given in *Birds as Individuals*). Pippa, as I called her, was reared in my garden in 1950, and left early in 1951; I had not seen her since. Her frontal markings were distinctive and she was of a small, neat build, size varying in Great Tits; also there were special mannerisms which verified her identity. When she had fed her fledglings with cheese from my Tit-box, I continued to walk through the wood accompanied by Pippa, the four fledglings trooping behind us. We had to part when I crossed a field, for parent birds avoid taking their young into the open, away from hedges or trees. After I had gone a little way, I looked back and saw Pippa, perched conspicuously, watching my departure. I thought then that she might be reminded of Bird Cottage and pay me a visit before long. She came sooner than I anticipated.

At 7 o'clock the next morning, I was standing outside the french window with Presto's fledglings, when Pippa with her babies came flying along my hedge. She perched on my shoulder, her young alighting nearby and staring with interest at these new surroundings. While Pippa took cheese to one of them, I leant forward to offer my hand to Presto's fledglings. At once Pippa perched on my back, quickly hopped all over it, then went backwards and forwards from shoulder to shoulder via my back, keeping up a terrific speed as if she was wound up and could not stop. As a youngster she had done this when excited, or when I was busy and she was impatient for my attention. It had seemed her way of letting off steam. This was an interesting repetition of her former behaviour, and left no doubt as to her identity. She was excited by her return and because she needed cheese for her other three babies, also she wanted my attention distracted from Presto's fledglings. Fifteen months absence had made no difference to her intimacy.

Her fledglings came to my hand the next day. Pippa was never again absent for long. As no father bird had appeared, even in the wood, it seemed she was a widow. She did not return there but kept in or near my garden and roosted indoors during the rest of the summer until Inkey returned in the autumn and for a time took possession of the rooms (as related in Star's biography).

Speculative match-making is inevitable and amusing when living with so many wild birds and it fell in with my ideas when Pippa and the handsome widower, Leg-Presto, became mates the following spring and nested beyond Tinky's territory, north of my orchard. More will be said later about them and their young.

2

To return to Presto's 1952 fledglings, the biggest one was bold and fearless. She came to my hand without hesitation, and ate more than the others, taking everything she was offered. I named her Smiler, for in disposition she seemed so contented, and there was often a suggestion of a smile in her expression. The smallest of the brood was totally different in appearance and temperament. She was nervous of everything and never seemed happy or at ease. Her appetite was small and she was fussy over choice of food, throwing away much that she took from my hand. The great difference in size between these two proved to be mainly due to plumage, which with fledglings varies much in thickness and length, probably according to the amount of food they have eaten and their capacity for digesting it. The bird with a very nervous temperament often is fussier over choice of food; its health is less robust than that of the more easy-going temperament, – probably its nervousness affecting its health.

Smiler had one brother and another sister, called Joker, already introduced in Star's biography and Chapter 4. Joker was a lively fledgling, much more restless than Smiler, who liked amusing herself quietly and was less active than most Tits. When she had been with me about a month her passion for examining things carefully in detail led her to discover that the metal band on top of the bird cage would turn round. (The cage was hung to the bird-table and always open.) To do this she had to raise the band, thus releasing the pressure on the wires that it covered. It was fascinating to watch her at this occupation which she pursued for many days with intense concentration. With careful movements she gripped the edge of the broad band in her beak, lifted it, then moved it round about a tenth of an inch before gently replacing it on the wires and letting go her hold. Sometimes she moved it farther round than others, occasionally the band fell back without her having moved it at all. When this happened she used even greater care the next time, and with slow, firm movements, accomplished her task. She found this pursuit so absorbingly interesting that she kept at it for half an hour at a time, returning to it two or three times in a day. If other birds approached her while she was engaged in this occupation she protested with a chin-up display then chased them away from the bird-cage, at once returning to continue her work. When hungry, she would break off for a moment to take food from my hand, which she ate hurriedly so as to resume the slow turning of the swivel cage-top, the care and precision of her movements suggesting a skilled craftsman at work. Her reward for the continuous concentration she put into this pursuit must have been a sense of achievement in exercising her skill.

Sometimes, after she had left the cage-top, other Tits flew up and examined it for a moment. They found nothing to interest them and never copied her occupation; probably they did not even realise what she was doing as she would not allow them near her when at work. I had to stand over her and watch before I discovered that her object was to make the metal top turn round.

Some of the fledglings, including Smiler, occupied the indoor roosts within a week of their return. In July they went to bed between 8.15 and 9 p.m., varying with the brightness of the evening and with the individual, for some Tits sleep longer than others. Smiler was at that time an exceptionally late riser, sometimes not leaving her roost until 7 o'clock (S.T.) the other youngsters being up about 5.15. Possibly her concentrated efforts at turning the swivel made her more tired, for it was at this period that she overslept.

Smiler often sang as she hopped about the bushes in the sunlight, – one of the charms of fledgling Great Tits, of both sexes, being their musical little song. One evening, 2nd August, at her bedtime she entered the room singing and, perched on a chair-back, continued her song for some minutes before going to her roost. The young Tit's voice gained much from being heard indoors, the tone being pure but soft. The Robin sounds shrill in the room, except in quiet subsong, and when my Blackbirds burst into full song indoors the effect reminds me of the blaze of sound received in the ears when seated near wind instruments in an orchestra! I have seen a Blackbird, on his first indoor performance, give a start and flee from the sound of his own voice within walls.

Before Smiler went to her roost she always perched on the window-sill a moment to call to her fellow fledglings outside and receive answers from them given in the same notes. Youngster Great Tits always call to each other at bedtime, as if to say good night. The same calls are given in the morning, to reunite them.

Among the indoor roosters was the youngster Drummer, already introduced in Star's biography. She was one of Pippa's fledglings. Drummer occupied one of the two biggest cartons, and when another young Great Tit, a newcomer, took the other big carton on the opposite wall, Drummer flew at him and chased him outside, apparently from jealousy at this second large box being occupied. The newcomer waited until Drummer was sleepy or asleep, then he returned to the roost. Every evening for a week Drummer made this protest, finally the other bird took a smaller box, she then made no further protest. None of the others had made any objection to this bird roosting in the big box.

The newcomer later became an ardent paper-tearer and hole-ripper. He was very determined when on a job of this kind, as the following incident will show. He had spent much time tearing holes in a cloth, hung over a small bookcase, and when I saw him spying through the holes at the books I reinforced the cloth covering with a stiff sheet of brown paper, glazed and so thick that I thought it would be bill-proof. The Tit at once returned to examine the paper and skidded over the shiny surface, looking for a weak spot, but could not find one. His struggle then began. First he tried at all angles to get a foothold on the slope, for the hole had to be made in front of the books, but there was nothing to steady him and he kept slipping and scrabbling with his feet on the shiny surface of the paper. He then used his wings to balance himself while he tried to make a hole by gimlet-action twists with his beak, often failing and falling back but sometimes making a faint impression, which he followed up by some raps, done while fluttering and moving his feet up and down at a terrific speed, the downward movement being unintentional, the upward movement necessary to get him in place again. After ten minutes he managed to loosen a shred of the paper's glazed surface and now there seemed hope of a hole being made. It was a tough job and he worked as if his life depended upon it. By now I was as keen as he was to see the hole achieved, for so much effort deserved success. Gradually, with strong sideways movements of his beak, he wrenched off a fragment of paper, then he got his beak right through and chiselled out a small hole, but he did not stop until he had got it large enough to put his head through and reach the cloth where previously he had made holes. Having achieved his purpose, he jauntily flicked his tail and flew to the water bowl for a drink. It had taken him twenty minutes of hard toil.

One day that summer a Jackdaw appeared on the bird-table and stared indoors at the Tits feeding on my hand; the next moment he had perched on the fanlight sill. The Tits uttered alarm cries and I tried to frighten away the Jackdaw by going close to the fanlight and shouting 'Get out,' but he only uttered some cryptic remarks in reply and entered the room by means of perching on my shoulder. At this, all the Tits vanished. I went to the doorway with him still perched on me, then he flew to the ground and began tearing some cake-paper that the Tits had been pecking. He next tried to tear the label off a jam pot on the bird-table for, like the Tits, the Jackdaw is a paper-tearer. By degrees a few Tits returned and looked at me, then at the Jackdaw. I knew they wanted me to get rid of this alarming visitor, an enemy they had learnt to fear.* He took no notice of them but it was a risk to keep him here, so I flicked dusters and shook large cloths near him hoping this would make him take to flight, but he only turned round and looked at me, as if rather interested in my performance. I then tried running towards the gate calling 'Come on Jackie,' and this was an immediate success, he followed me and I ran down the road with him flying alongside until we came to a meadow, when he flew towards some other Jackdaws feeding in it. I hastily ran home, fearing he might again follow me, but I never saw him again.

That year, 1952, Star had kept her young under her care for longer than usual and (as related in her biography) she flew to them with scold-notes if they left the cover of trees. This made them nervous on first venturing to the cottage after she had stopped feeding them. One of them was very small, her plumage shaggy and colourless but she had much charm of manner and in some ways resembled her mother, particularly in her intent expression when she was watching me. Until she had studied me very carefully, her eyes following every movement I made, she would not come to my hand. When satisfied that it was safe she straightway perched on any part of me with equal confidence, apparently having connected me as a whole, which most full-grown youngsters, new to the human form, do not at first understand. Very small fledglings, new from the nest, often perched anywhere on humans without fear; when a little older they have learnt more caution. Star's little offspring, called Buttons (from her fondness for pulling at buttons on my clothes) behaved in the same way over coming indoors. For two days she would not venture inside but stood on the doorstep, craning her head forwards with her intent expression to watch what was going

---

* Jackdaws devour fledgling Tits.

on in the room. Then she suddenly flew in with perfect confidence and used the fanlight as an exit as if she was an old hand at entering the room. Fledglings usually find the fanlight difficult as an exit at first, unless they have followed their parents through it.

By the second week in August, Buttons' shaggy plumage was replaced by new feathers. With fascination I had watched her grow prettier every day until, in addition to her charm of manner and quick mind, she became the prettiest youngster I have ever had. She followed me about, perching on my head or shoulders the moment I stood still. When she wanted something she placed herself in front of me and looked into my eyes with her intent expression, which always reminded me of Star, her mother. (*See Plate 4*.) From the first day that Buttons entered the rooms she slept above my bed. One morning she awoke at 6 a.m. but would not get up, although I had put food on the indoor bird-table and the others were feeding. For half an hour she stayed in bed, preening and tapping her roost-box, then she slept until 6.45, when she flew from her roost and had a late breakfast. It was a great loss when on 16th August this charming youngster disappeared, probably the prey of a cat. The previous month I had lost Naomi, grandchild of Star. It is so often the birds of special charm or interest that come to grief, which makes much sadness in my life of close intercourse with wild birds.

The cold weather that autumn, 1952, came exceptionally early, and my birds, as often happens, pre-sensed the coming cold spell two days in advance. On 5th and 6th September it was still warm and sunny but on those days my Tits ate ravenously, four times their normal amount. On the 6th, two human strangers came to see the birds, which usually makes them cautious over entering the room, but that day they did not even pause to look at the visitors so great was their haste to take all the food they could get from me. On 7th September the weather suddenly changed; it was like winter and reported as the coldest day ever recorded for September.

This cold spell brought many stranger Great Tits to Bird Cottage, one of them a youngster, who at once took possession of an arm-chair at the far end of the west room. On entering, she always perched there, and made signs for a nut to be thrown, looking keenly at me then searchingly at the floor below her, where she wanted the nut to fall. If I did not respond quickly she rapidly tore at the covering of the chair, knowing that this made me take notice of her. Two days after her appearance I was seated in her chair when she entered the fanlight. I had always before occupied one by the french window in her presence. She paused on the window-sill and looked towards her chair but instead of coming to it, flew to the one I usually occupied, then facing me, she uttered excited volleys of scold-notes, making me feel I had no right to be sitting in her arm-chair! Nor did she calm down until I had vacated it.

This youngster was bossy in her ways with the other Tits as well as with me, perhaps feeling this necessary to gain rights in this crowded Bird Cottage. She at once took one of the roost-boxes, and spent part of every day tearing to pieces a few others that the Tits considered were badly sprung beds; besides being insecurely hung, these were shoddily made and had never been occupied.

After two days, this youngster began taking food from my hand, held on the floor, which she approached slowly the first time, as if nervous, so to make it easier for her I put some peanuts near the tips of my fingers, and concealed a piece of cachew-nut underneath my thumb, which I curved over my palm, the cachew being held tightly and I thought invisible. Although the youngster approached slowly, she ignored the peanuts, stepped confidently on to my palm and bending her head low, looked to see what I was concealing underneath my thumb. Her discovery made, she tried with all her might to lift up my thumb so as to release the cachew. I held it down tightly, for Beauty especially liked these nuts – I had only a few left – and he was waiting, perched on my shoulder, to be given one. But the youngster's efforts were soon rewarded for although she failed to lift up my thumb she managed to wrench out the cachew by a sharp twisting movement. Like most of my Tits, she knew what she wanted and how to get it!

Humans who are over-conceited about the cleverness of mankind should live with Great Tits so as to see things in proper proportion!

CHAPTER 7

Youngsters (continued)

1

Pippa and Leg-Presto were a delightful couple, especially when they became parents. Their nest was in a neighbouring garden where I could not go, but they came to me many times daily, flying through Tinky and Smiler's territory regardless of their protests. My Tits often show interest in each other's nests and Pippa sometimes stared inside all the occupied boxes in my garden, choosing moments when the owners were absent. She never went inside the boxes but put her head through the entrance holes to take a good look. The following are two extracts from my notes, made after her young were hatched:

(1) Leg-Presto would make a good cook. Before taking cheese to his nestlings he always rubs it into the biscuit-crumbs kept in a dish on the table. He does it thoroughly, so that the surface is well coated, like fish for frying. This makes the cheese more palatable, holds it together and being less oily, no doubt it is better for the babies. He is the only bird to have done this. He does not do it to cheese for his own consumption.

(2) Pippa wakens me soon after sunrise every morning, flying into the darkened room over the top of the drawn curtains and hopping on my pillow. She urgently demands food for her nestlings, doing her quick-speed trick of going round the back of my head and peering into my face on alternate sides, until the food is given her. One morning she found the fanlight entrance closed when she came, for I wanted more sleep, but her distressed cries made me leap up, and peering through a chink of the curtains I saw her struggling to open the fanlight. Had she been strong enough she would have succeeded, for she was trying to lift it upwards from the bottom, the correct way. My need for more sleep was

disregarded and she was never again shut out of the room. She looked very cross if offered food unsuitable for nestlings but her expression became eager at sight of a cachew, soaked until soft, – a favourite choice for nestlings. Her flight across the room to the window on spread wings is noiseless as with all Great Tits when carrying food to their nestlings. When outside they continue gliding silently and softly to the nest if it is a short distance away. The touch of their feet on my hand at this season is also very gentle, perhaps from the need to tread lightly when they enter their nest.

When on 29th May, Pippa did not come at her usual early hour, I guessed that her young had flown. That evening while walking along a field-path above a sand pit, north of my cottage, Pippa flew to me, followed by Leg-Presto. Their eight babies were below, in the bushes. After a day or two they were brought for visits to my orchard, the territory owners being too busy feeding their nestlings to object. (Pippa's brood was the earliest that year.)

On the afternoon of 7th June, while I was in the orchard, Pippa called all her fledglings to the apple tree under which I sat, then she and Leg-Presto disappeared for half an hour, leaving them with me. It was their first lesson in independence from their parents, and judging from their cries they did not like it. Smiler was now feeding her brood in the petrol-tin and each time she came to me for food, Pippa's babies fluttered their wings before her, while crying lustily. Smiler took no notice and flew to her nesting-tin. Fledglings will beg from any adult they see, or even from another youngster, though they know their own parents at once. One fledgling followed Smiler and, perched on the tin, cried and fluttered its wings. Suddenly it stopped and craned its head over the edge of the tin to try and see inside the entrance hole, nearly falling over in its efforts; it then flew to a twig by the hole and peered inside, its hunger forgotten in this new interest. Smiler soon reappeared, uttering scold-notes and chasing the inquisitive fledgling from her nest. It perched on a bough farther off and began tearing a leaf in frustration. Leg-Presto then returned, Pippa soon afterwards.

The following afternoon, by chance, I discovered Pippa's retreat after she had again brought her young to the trees near me and disappeared, this time for a little longer, as the training of independence is gradual, the time they are left increasing slightly every day. Twenty minutes after she had disappeared I went to the back of the east hedge and was crouching in the ditch, watching a bird, when I saw Pippa, in a concealed position, resting on a low branch in the overhung ditch. I offered her a soft cachew from the box I always carried with me, – this being food that she liked for her young. Instead of taking it she swung round sharply on her perch, deliberately turning her back towards me. I understood her meaning, she did not just then want to feed her young. In a moment she swung round again, flew to my hand, took a peanut from the Tit-box and went back to her perch to eat it, afterwards remaining there with her back towards me, her head slightly raised and held stiffly, her tail flared. This display meant 'not interested.' Pippa had never behaved like this to me before but I knew she wanted me to leave her because my presence would give away her hiding place to her fledglings, who were starting their training in independence from her. They had learnt that food often came from me to their parents and then on to them, so I was an object of interest and frequently followed, though it had not yet occurred to them to feed from my hand.

Leg-Presto fed the fledglings as often as Pippa and he was usually the first to appear after they had left the young. Sometimes he and Pippa alighted on my hand at the same moment and made open-beaked grimaces at each other while flattening their crowns, – an annoyance display. They both wanted to be first to take food for their fledglings but Pippa always got her own way, Leg-Presto waiting with gentlemanly politeness for his wife to be first served, though his looks showed displeasure. They worked together well and took turns over an occasional short rest and bath during the mornings, only leaving the fledglings alone in the slacker feeding time of the afternoon.

There was often a Tawny Owl or a Jay behind the orchard hedge. Great Tit parents were unconcerned if the Owl appeared and they continued to feed their young while all other species shouted alarm cries and mobbed it. When the Jay approached, the Tits were the first to give an alarm and send their young to cover. On 9th June, the Jay appeared in the afternoon while Pippa's fledglings were alone. They took no notice, not having yet learnt to fear this enemy. The next moment both their parents, wet from a bath, hurried to them with alarm cries. Tits are so alert for danger to their young that it spoke well for the Tawny Owl that they and all other Tits in the garden disregarded his presence.

Mention must now be made of the mating of Tinky with Smiler. From her fledgling days Smiler had shown a calm temperament and more self-sufficiency than the others, this perhaps accounting for her still being unattached when Tinky lost Star on 22nd April. For most of that month Smiler had been absent from my garden, for the territory owners chased her away. After losing Star, Tinky sang continuously for six days, inventing many songs and calls, some soft, others strident, all uttered with an intense fervour which compelled attention. The other male Great Tits in my garden sometimes flew up to perch near Tinky and look at him while he sang, but he seemed not to notice them for he was engrossed in his song. Then Smiler came to him and his excitement was great. That day he would not take his usual 5 o'clock nut when I held it close to him for his eyes were on Smiler. When she flew to me he made baby-cry notes to attract her attention, then he began quickly hopping in and out of the nesting-tin and wooden box beside it. Each time he entered the tin he stretched his head and neck out of the entrance hole, called loudly to Smiler, then slowly withdrew into the tin, many times repeating this lure. Smiler was eating nuts, perched on my hand; she appeared not to notice Tinky and followed me towards the cottage through other Tits' territory. This made him even more agitated; he flew after her with excited cries and fetched her back to the nesting-tin. At 6 o'clock she disappeared for a few minutes and returned carrying a beakful of moss. Tinky flew to her in an excited manner then followed her into the tin. He sang that evening before going to roost, but little song came from him after Smiler appeared.

The next morning, she was building in earnest, then Tinky, like other male Great Tits, was not allowed by his mate to enter the nest but he followed her wherever she flew. He was even more attentive to this young mate than to his former ones, perhaps because of her youth and from fear that he might lose her too.

When Smiler began sitting, Tinky often perched opposite her nest and called to her, she answered by making baby-cries then went to him with vibrating wings, to take food he offered her. I went up the orchard several times daily, calling her name. This always brought her to me and when she had flown to my hand she gave a call to Tinky, either 'tea-chur' twice repeated or a special call of her own, 'tink, tink, turrr,' this always uttered while swaying her body from side to side. If this did not bring him at once, she gave one scold-note then continued to eat her nut on my hand, if he came with an answering note, she perched close to him while eating.

Smiler's nestlings hatched on 19th May and the eight well-developed fledglings flew three weeks later. The Intruder and his mate, who owned most of the orchard, had by then taken their young away, this suiting Smiler very well for she could use their territory and get easy access to the cottage.

The Intruder, whom Star had refused as a mate, had nine young; eight had flown very early one morning and been taken away from my garden by him and his mate, but one did not fly until three hours later. At 9.30 a.m. it appeared at the entrance hole, looked around and remained there for half an hour, its legs gripping the bottom of the entrance hole, its head upturned and its beak resting against the upper edge of the hole. At last it braved a short flight to the medlar tree opposite the nest, and called for its absent parents. After a while it dozed and only cried in feeble tones when other Tits flew near. When Smiler came she stared at it with a who-are-you expression then passed on. The fledgling gave a completely different cry, uproarious and hysterically eager, when at last its parents arrived and took it away to join the others. This was an emphatic example of a fledgling's recognition of its parents and of their voices. They may try begging from other adults, but they always know their own parents. The same applies to the parents' recognition of their fledglings, though occasionally a fledgling may get separated from its brood and become attached to another.

The Intruder's young were not brought back to my garden although he or his mate made occasional short appearances, always giving sharp protesting notes to Tinky and Smiler, Leg-Presto and Pippa, who were making free with his territory.

By 11th June Smiler and Pippa were both bringing their young to the front garden every day. Inkey and Drummer, who that year possessed most of the front territory, were by then usually absent, their newly flown young had been taken away and they seldom returned until they stopped feeding their fledglings.

Interesting behaviour concerning Presto must now be related.

Inkey's possessiveness on his return the previous autumn was referred to in Star's biography (Chapter 3). This had resulted in Presto and Dado being turned out of their territory by Inkey and Drummer, who nested in Dado's box by the gate. In April Presto always sang from a tree by the stream, west of my garden, over the road. When I walked by on the way to the village, he called to me then flew to my hand for a nut, Dado following him. I concluded that they were nesting there. They still paid occasional visits to the cottage for food and on 18th April I made the following notes:

Presto comes with Dado, who eats three nuts – taking a long time – on the east room curtain rods. Presto eats one nut on the fanlight window-ledge, his eye cocked all the while for Inkey to appear, his second he holds in his beak and flying to the tree outside, displays it with upturned head while Dado continues calmly to eat hers indoors. Impatient to be gone, Presto flies to the window-ledge and looks up at her hoping that she is ready to come away but she has just begun her third nut, so he flits outside again to display and protect her from Inkey and Drummer. Again he goes indoors to look at her, but she is still eating stolidly and takes no notice of him. He flies to the tree once more. This time Inkey appears and chases Presto, who flies into the west room, holding up his nut and displaying at Inkey who again pursues him. Presto can hold out no longer and flying swiftly to Dado in the east room, he touches her wing and jerks his head up before her. She takes her nut from between her toes and with it in her beak rushes out of the fanlight, Presto at her side, guarding and escorting her back to their territory by the stream, Inkey in pursuit. The calmness of Dado and the excitability of Presto and his desire to be gone, was very striking. I later knew the reason for this.

The last time they entered was on 30th April, when Dado, as usual, ate her nut on the window curtain-rod, but Presto was nervous of being seen and after escorting her indoors, hastily took his nut and flew to cover of thick bushes outside. When she flew away, he escorted her back to their territory. After this, entrance to my garden became impossible for him. Besides Inkey and Drummer, another couple were protesting at his presence. These were strangers, untidy looking, shy birds whom I named the Gipsies, Gips for short. Their nest-box was on my west apple-tree, their territory being in West Garden except for a small strip by my tree; on the boundary of this strip was Star's old nest-box, which appeared unoccupied, beyond this was the Intruder's territory. But in mid-May I saw a Great Tit quickly leave this box and disappear through the hedge behind it. I thought her another shy stranger, building secretively, though it puzzled me because I saw no mate and the box had no territory. The illusive female never showed herself close to me nor did I see her face, as she always flitted from the box and through the hedge at lightning speed.

On 25th May, after she had disappeared, my curiosity over this phantom female without a mate made me look inside her box; to do this, it had to be taken from the tree but it was unhooked in a second. While I was looking at her six eggs she flew quickly and silently round her tree where the box should have been, then she disappeared through the hedge. I hastily replaced the box, astonished that she had not uttered a scold-note or any sound of reproof or fright, as usual in such cases of interference with a nest-box. All that day I watched for her mate to feed her on the nest, but he never came. When she needed food she glided silently from the box and through the hedge, the other side of which was Gips' territory. I began to suspect him of bigamy and desertion of this female; he was attentive to his mate in the box on the west apple tree.

Four days later the phantom female's eggs hatched, then another male was to be seen, secretively flitting through the hedge to the nest and back again without a sound. I only got fleeting glimpses of him until one morning, a week after the young had hatched, I was near the bird-table when, to my astonishment, Presto glided swiftly from the box towards me and alighted on my hand; giving me a queer sideways look he took some cheese, flew back to the box, then disappeared through the hedge. Soon Dado did the same thing and from that time they frequently came to me, for Inkey's young had now been taken from my garden and they no longer needed to avoid being seen with me. The Gips were now too busy finding food for their nestlings to interfere with Presto and Dado.

I had been right in thinking that Presto's territory was by the stream; he and Dado got their food from beyond Gips' territory, not using my garden except for the nest-box. Presto had not been able to feed Dado on the nest for fear of rousing Inkey's anger. In *Birds as Individuals* Dado and her former mate were called the 'Silent Strangers.' She had, in 1949, used the same box under identical conditions so she must have initiated Presto into this original scheme for getting the nest-box and taught him the necessary secretive ways. He had always before been a conspicuous, noisy bird, so this change cannot have been easy for him; it showed how adaptive to circumstances a Great Tit can be. Dado's calmness and Presto's nervous excitability, mentioned in my April notes, was now explained; she was used to this cunning arrangement and knew what to do, he was having to learn.

When on 11th June, Pippa and Smiler brought their young to the front garden, some of them perched by Dado's nest-box. Presto ignored this noisy crowd of fledglings and entered to feed the nestlings but when Dado arrived, the interest of Pippa's young had been aroused, they were clustered on the roof of her box, one was leaning over, trying to see inside, while another was clinging to the entrance hole with its head inside the box, staring at Dado's nestlings. She fussily hovered over the box for a moment then good-humouredly pushed them aside and entered. They again clustered round the hole, pushing each other away in their eagerness to look at the nestlings. Then Dado came out, this time giving them severe and prolonged looks which sent them away. The earlier broods of fledglings must often find out a lot about nesting affairs, for they take interest in nest-boxes and holes and are quick in putting two and two together.

The same morning Gips' young flew, providing another entertainment for the inquisitive fledglings, who watched with interest until all had flown in an orderly manner and been taken into West Garden. That excitement over, one of Pippa's young, for the first time, flew to the cottage and perched outside the open fanlight. Pippa (like Jane in *Birds as Individuals*) rushed to the window with cheese and held it out to the youngster with the glass intervening so that he pecked the pane, she then showed him the food without the glass barrier, so teaching the fledgling to understand window-panes. The youngster at once began examining the pane with much interest, then he entered through the fanlight, flew quickly round the room and out again without banging into the windows and with the necessary dip under the fanlight. He now made an exploratory flight to the bird-bath, not visited before as Pippa had previously kept her young in the trees. The fledgling tried to alight on the water but finding his feet sank into it, he quickly flew up and perched on the edge of the bath to investigate the water like the glass, by pecking at it with a closed beak, after each peck shaking off the droplets with a sideways toss of his head. After this he cautiously paddled in the shallows, wetting no more than his toes. He had no instinctive knowledge of glass, or, it seemed, of water, yet so quickly do young Tits learn, it had taken him only a minute to realise that glass was hard, windows must be avoided in flight, water – though like glass in appearance – was quite different but needed a careful approach to avoid falling into it. Perhaps the feel of the water aroused in him the instinctive desire to bathe, for the adventurer, after perching above the bath for a second, returned to it and this time slowly and cautiously waded deeper and had his first bath.

I have watched many young fledglings have their first bathe; some make the normal wing-splashing and head-dipping movements at once, others walk through the water and seem uncertain what to do to get their backs wet, then choosing the deepest part without fear, they make experimental flicks with one wing, which nearly overbalances them. Gradually both wings are brought into action and by degrees the normal bathing movements are made.

The adventurer had been watched by others of his brood and soon two of them joined him in the bath. They needed no preliminary investigations, having learnt from seeing and copying him. Fledglings may find things out through their own initiative or by watching others and seeing what happens. Much is also taught them by their parents, especially by the mother bird.

Until all Pippa's young were familiar with glass she would not enter through the half-open french window nor take food from me when I was close to it. At first this sudden whim, as I thought it, puzzled me; she had always before fed from my hand when I was sitting by this window. I soon realised her wisdom; she wanted all her fledglings to use the fanlight, which is always open, the french window was sometimes closed and they would bang into it until quite familiar with glass. Because of Pippa's care none of her fledglings got into difficulties, for they always used the fanlight as an entrance and exit. But when Smiler's young started to enter the room there was trouble. She was easy-going in temperament and did not worry about her young like Pippa did, so they were allowed to fly about freely, and five days after leaving the nest they began following her through the french window; the next day wet weather came, and they fluttered against the glass when it was closed. Young fledglings die easily from hitting their heads, so to avoid catastrophies I kept it open despite the heavy rains of that week which blew into the room, making pools of water on the floor. In the early mornings cold mists drove through the open doorway while I breakfasted in a mackintosh with all the fledglings around me.

This is an extract from my notes : *19th June*. A dreadful day of wind and rain. The birds waken me at 5.30 and I get up to feed them; the rain and the feeding lasts all day. The parent birds look draggled and tired, they give up attempting to search for food outside, but after a time, with gestures of discontent, they begin to chuck the nuts and cheese about, knowing that their young need the natural food which the heavy rain has washed from the trees. There was at times a little snappiness among the mother Tits when they met near me, all wanting food for their babies. Pippa's excitable temperament was roused if Smiler got in her way when she wanted cheese for her clamouring fledglings. Smiler never hit back, she was not impatient like Pippa, who exerted herself far more in the rearing of her young.

Smiler's enthusiasm for her babies waned sooner than Pippa's and she gave up feeding them eleven days after they flew. Tinky carried on alone, attending to them every hour for another three days then giving them morning and evening feeds for a further day or two.

2

After a week, all Smiler's fledglings were using the fanlight except one which had bumped its head through not making the necessary dip in flight when flying through it. When the others had left the room, this one remained fluttering against the lower part of the window for a moment, then she came to fetch my help, flying up to me then going to the window and back again to me. I followed her to the window then held out my hand, she perched on it and I slowly raised my arm; she looked at me until my hand was level with the fanlight then she flew out. Three times she came to me to be helped in this way, afterwards she learnt to climb up the curtain until she reached the level of the fanlight, this resembling the way I had helped her out.

One day, when this fledgling was on my hand she took hold of my forefinger with her beak and carefully bent it into a curved position. I straightened my finger again and the fledgling tried to bend it backwards. Finding it would not curve that way she looked up at me inquiringly then resumed the same experiments with the thumb, again looking at me when the outward bend was a failure. The other fingers were then bent inwards but no more attempts made to pull them outwards. Watching this baby so engrossed in bending my fingers reminded me of her mother, Smiler, turning the swivel. Perhaps it was an inherited interest for this type of occupation.

Smiler's brood were very united. Four out of eight had survived and when their parents stopped feeding them they kept close together, calling to each other in sweet tones, as if wanting to keep in touch all the while. If one of them stayed indoors feeding a few minutes longer than the others, a distant call from the trees would be heard, the fledgling indoors answered it and hurriedly flew off with urgent sounding cries, fearful of losing touch with the others who greeted it with soft notes as it joined them.

Some of Pippa's six fledglings were more independent. One of them had a passion for displaying. Even when first fledged, he was always doing chin-ups, an amusing sight in a young fledgling. This display he developed, making it more impressive by a long drawn-out neck-stretching and slow waving to and fro of his upturned head. He kept this up for a minute or two after the bird it was aimed at had flown away; it seemed he liked doing it. (The female Great Tit has a snake-like neck-waving display, accompanied by a spitting sound, which she uses on her nest if disturbed.) Possibly this continual neck-stretching while he was growing accounted for a peculiarity in the shape of his neck, – or his carriage. Even at a distance he was distinguishable by his long, sloping neck, which reminded me of a champagne bottle, and he had an unusually clear yellow breast, so I called him Champagne. He was a high-spirited fledgling, full of life, and he liked chasing others of his own age.

When Champagne began feeding from my hand he used his display if fledglings of another brood flew near me, which meant that he was constantly displaying for many were coming to me. One day (25th June) when Tinky came to the bird-table, Champagne, perched on a twig nearby, aired his display on this adult male, who went on feeding unconcerned until suddenly Champagne charged at him and rolled him over. Tinky quickly got to his feet, eyed the fledgling with an odd expression of surprise, then, raising his head high, looked haughtily down his beak at the youngster, as if daring him to do that again. This was Champagne's biggest success. Afterwards he tried the same thing on other adult Great Tits but none of them fell over, they merely stepped aside, making way for him. Perhaps this pleased him but really they only did it because he was so young, – consideration for fledglings being their rule. He was not rebuffed for his childish display or attacks until one day, in late July, he began airing his neck-waving chin-up at the female, Gips, who wanted food from the dish on which he stood. She charged at him in return and pushed him out of her way as if he were of no consequence. For the first time his display had been a complete failure, he looked humiliated and hid under foliage below the bird-table, keeping quiet for many minutes, which was unusual for him. I never again saw him display to an adult and he used less of it in his dealings with those of his own age until gradually he ceased using it altogether.

Another of Pippa's fledglings had an original idea about sunbathing. He always liked to do it hanging upside down from a twig, his wings and tail fully spread, his head turned to one side and his beak half-open in the normal sunbathing gape. He had to find a suitable, thin, horizontal twig for this suspended sunbath, with space below and no leaves above, then he swung himself into the pose, his golden breast feathers fluffed out, the undersides of his wide-spread wings and tail shining pale silver in the sunlight, – an upside-down picture in silver and gold. Relaxation was impossible in this position, his head seemed uncomfortable, he kept moving it a little and he fidgeted with his feet, but he got better at balancing after a few repetitions. I have never seen any other bird sunbath in this suspended manner, which was sensible if not comfortable, for they cannot lie on their backs with both wings outspread so the sun does not get to their underparts in the usual sunbathing poses. Although the other Tits watched this original sunbather none of them copied him, not even his favourite brother who was his chief playmate.

These two fledglings had several games they frequently played together, one being to touch beaks in a quick, flying chase, – a Swallow and Martin game. Another was for one fledgling to perch high on an upstanding twig while the other, with twittering notes, slowly sidled up to him from below, swinging his body from left to right in a curious swaying movement as he advanced. When he reached his playmate he touched his wing-tip and they flew round in a whirling chase, then alighted again to repeat the game, taking turns to be the top bird. On fine days their playful moods sometimes interrupted their meals, they both suddenly dropped their food, having an impulse to play at the same moment. After a short game they returned together to finish their meal from my hand.

Much patience was needed in feeding the young Tits to their satisfaction. If I handed one youngster a soft cachew, he tossed it away with an air of offence, suggesting 'Fancy giving me pap food as if I were still a nestling!' He liked something to hammer and dig into with his beak and his choice was peanuts. Another, the same age, preferred soft food and if I offered her a peanut she ignored it and looked me full in the face with a surprised expression, which meant 'Why give me nuts? You know I can't eat those hard things!' If I did not quickly produce a soft cachew she began to pluck gently at my fingers, then looked at me again; the cachew was given her as the charm of her manner was irresistible. They had ways of showing me who they were if I did not for the moment recognise the individual.

One fledgling did not like any artificial food, I had to get spiders and their eggs for him, but he enjoyed the following trick. I always halved the peanuts between my fingers and thumb before handing them on my palm to the Tits and I held the box of whole peanuts (kept half-open) in my other hand. This fledgling flew to my palm like the others but picked up and tossed away the cheese and halved nuts, then turned his back on me as if going to fly away; the next moment he had made a circular flight round me and pounced on the box from behind to seize and fly off with a whole nut in its brown skin, his squeak of excitement showing he knew that whole nuts were forbidden. It was all done so quickly that I had no time to close the box. He did not eat the nut, after two or three pecks he let it fall, but he did this trick frequently and obviously enjoyed it.

The fledglings seemed to like teasing me. One day, when I had been taking some snaps of them, I went indoors to change the film in a dark corner of the room. While at the crucial part of fixing the roll, a dozen baby Tits flew in, some perched on my arm and back, three began tugging at the roots of my hair at the nape and on top of my head, while they all chattered in baby-cry notes, demanding attention. I had no food by me and wanted to get the film fixed but they tugged so hard at my hair and made such a fuss, getting in the way and hopping on the film, that in despair I gave it up and walked across the room to fetch the Tit-box, with two fledglings on each shoulder, one on my arm, another on my hand, all craning their necks forward to look expectantly into my face. A Robin and seven young Blackbirds were also demanding food and I was thankful that no Blackbird had perched on my head to pull my hair.

Evidently one of the hair tuggers had found it an amusing game for, from that day, he repeatedly did it, at unexpected moments making a sudden dash at my head and frantically pulling at the roots of my hair. This fledgling, one of Smiler's, was called Cobbler because he also had a passion for shoes, especially he liked perching on my feet to examine my sandals and hammer at them in various places. (*See plate section.*)

One day when a Sussex bird watcher, Mr A. W. Stokes, was at Bird Cottage, Cobbler flew in and interrupted our conversation by showing off his hair tugging operation. While I writhed under the torment, Mr Stokes sat shaking with quiet laughter. Cobbler did not even notice the laugh, he was so engrossed in his game.

Among themselves the fledglings had beautiful manners. They never pushed in front of one another at feeding time and the various families came in turn to take food from my hand. If very hungry they queued up on a perch beside me and politely waited for their turn, Pippa's and Smiler's broods, according to which arrived first, having priority over the others. Sometimes they alighted almost together and hesitated, each one doing a polite 'after you,' so afraid were they of being out of turn. While all this politeness was going on, I was waiting for them with hand outstretched, and often I shouted 'Hurry up! Pass along, please!' like a bus conductor trying to hurry his passengers! They seemed to understand I was growing impatient and stopped hesitating.

It was often difficult for the fledgling Tits to feed on my hand because parent Chaffinches and Robins kept pouncing in front of them, pushing them away and taking food, but some of them developed masterly hisses which effectively scared the pouncers. Also the Chaffinches became adept in seizing food which the fledglings were eating tucked between their toes, but it was the young Robins that the fledgling Tits feared, for they sometimes flew at them fiercely, making their feathers fly. This species can be very spiteful if annoyed and the young ones seemed jealous of the Tits. When I sat with my toes pointing upwards a fledgling Tit often perched on one foot, a young Robin then flew to the other, at once they turned sideways to look at each other across the gap between my feet, and remained with their beaks wide open in a gaping display of annoyance, the Tit sometimes adding an expressive hiss.

When Gips' young returned they were shy at first and very hungry. One of them watched a parent Robin stuff a big chunk of bread down the beak of its offspring, who remained gaping, trying to swallow it. Suddenly the fledgling Tit stepped close and with the precision of a dentist neatly extracted the bread from deep down inside the baby Robin's beak and flew off with it. When later this Tit came on my hand it began tugging at one of my fingers, using its wings and putting all its strength into efforts to extract the finger, which it seemed to think was food worth having. At last it gave up and took some cheese from my hand.

The Tits often enjoyed indoor games while I sat on the lawn. On 7th August I wrote in my notes: Sounds of hammering and tearing come from indoors; probably some books left on the table are being torn to shreds. Something has just fallen to the floor with a subdued rattle, – my fountain pen? Next I see the toy Blue Tit being lugged to the doorstep and pommelled. I go indoors to see what they are doing and find my suppositions were right. Some of them fly out as I enter, for they know I object when they tear books or play with my fountain pen, – too often they steal the caps of pens which I later find on top of the window curtains or outdoors. One little tailless youngster continues his game of tearing brown paper from the back of a picture-frame leaning against the wall on the mantelpiece. He squeezes his body between the picture and the wall, pulls off some paper, comes out and chucks it down. He repeats the performance but slowly comes out backwards, tugging a half-severed strip of paper. He continues trying to wrench this free, nearly pulling the picture-frame over while doing it. Shaking himself after his efforts, he flies to the curtains and pulls the folds apart, then he makes a dart at me, playfully flying to my arm and running all along it. The others again enter and indoor sports continue, the books having been covered with three layers of brown paper. Their toy elephant now is attacked and receives a final beating (*see Plate 15*). For some years the Tits have played at tearing its coat and pulling out the stuffing. (The same elephant appears in *Birds as Individuals*.)

3

The different broods had by August begun to intermingle for much of the day and some friendships were formed between the different sexes. They spent much time in outdoor games; one which I called 'My bush, my leaf?' was fascinating to watch. The game was played in a bush which caught the sunlight in the cool of the morning, around 9 o'clock S.T. At first one youngster began displaying at others who perched on the bush; while they flew to different parts of it he strutted from bough to bough with his chin held up, making twittering noises. He then plucked a leaf and made a fussy pretence of eating it between his toes. Another youngster went close and pretended to want the leaf, both then did chin-ups facing each other while uttering odd notes. The one with the leaf then hopped around, holding it high and a dozen youngsters joined in hopping behind him, all displaying mildly, with half-spread, drooping wings, lifting up their chins a little. They all made sounds of a display order, small muttered squeaks and high-pitched ventriloqual notes, this being continued for some time. As usual in these games the Tits took turns in being the possessor of the bush and leaf, the holder being the central figure of the game, and the make-believe bush owner. Suddenly they would stop and fly to me for food.

Often, as they had done in earlier fledgling days, they played at flying to my head and chasing each other off it, sometimes two or three together stepping about on it and perhaps displaying for although I could not see what they were doing, it was obvious that my head was the object of possession for this game.

Sometimes they came to me wearing grey veils on their black crowns; they had been spider hunting and these cobwebs occasionally clung for a whole morning, as the top of a bird's head is difficult for it to preen.

On 20th August, when all the youngsters in my garden had grown new feathers after their fledgling moult, I heard above the sound of wind and rain the hunger cries of a newly weaned fledgling approaching the cottage. She was alone and probably the single survivor of a second brood; her parents were unknown to me. From her frequent baby-cries it was evident that she had not long been left to fend for herself and she was very hungry. That day she made many visits to the bird-table and seized food that I threw to her. The next morning when I sat in the garden she watched the Tits flying to my hand and feeding from my lap, then she perched near me and tilted her head upwards, turning it from side to side while she watched a youngster fly to me for a nut. Directly he flew away she daintily alighted on my hand and flew off with the food, her air of complete confidence suggesting, 'That's easily done!' Every time she returned she first faced me from a near perch, holding her head very high and giving it little upward tilts which were most attractive. She was a beautiful fledgling, with a canary-like breast and all her movements had airiness and grace; she looked an aristocrat and never had a feather out of place. Her manner of holding her head up gave the impression that she had been tutored in good deportment, for there was a suggestion of self-consciousness in the way she kept uptilting it! Actually this mannerism was probably self-assertive, due to seeing around her so many older youngsters and adults, while she herself was so very young; she felt the need to look as important and confident as she could, which she certainly achieved. But even when she had grown a little older she did not entirely neglect the upward tilts, by then they may have become a habit and a charming one. She tossed her head up sometimes while feeding on my hand, but none of her mannerisms were like a chin-up display, it was an original action.

After two days her extreme hunger was appeased, her cries ceased and she became one of the indoor roosters, having chosen a box hung above the sliding doors, near the head of my divan. Gay, as I called her, had no fear, she watched all that the other youngsters did, then, with airy confidence, made her own attempt. She adopted a musical three-noted call which she used to attract my attention and in association with the other Tits. Her day was spent in feeding, preening, exploring the garden, and inquisitively poking her head inside every nest-box. In sunny corners of the garden she sang softly while playing with leaves and bits of sticks which she picked up from the ground, took to a bough and toyed with for a moment then dropped, always watching them fall with interest. Although Gay amused herself independently, being younger than the other Tits, she soon attached herself to them as well as to me. On 28th August at 6.15 p.m., while she was perched on my hand, having her last meal for the day, the flock of youngster Tits, preparatory to roosting hour, began their roll-call cries from the orchard and West Garden. Gay lifted up her head and uttered in piercing tones her triple-noted call, a real shout, 'Here I am!' then she flew hurriedly through the window to join them.

Then came tragedy. In September Jet planes swooped through my garden, skimming the roof of the cottage and causing panic among the young Tits. Some, in terror, banged into the window-panes and one of my favourites was killed. The next day several of the youngsters were missing; the terrifying roar of the Jets through my garden continued on and off for several days and there were explosions which shook the cottage when they broke the sound barrier. The remaining youngsters were in constant fear, the planes were rarely out of earshot and I lived in terror of another swoop, as did the Tits. Each day more of the youngsters were missing, Cobbler and Gay the last to disappear ten days after the terror began. Only two youngsters remained and they had become so nervously affected that they would not enter the cottage for some weeks, nor did these two ever regain confidence over coming indoors.

The adult Tits were less afraid than the young ones. None of them left; they had the strong ties of territory to keep them here.

On 16th October Presto became possessive of the front garden and did frequent chin-up displays, which he sometimes made more impressive by holding a leaf in his beak while balancing with a swaggering air on the rambler shoots that hung loosely by the bird-table. He looked as if doing a comic turn as he swayed up and down, his legs stretched out jauntily, his beak pointing upwards, the leaf dangling in front of his chin as a symbol of possession. The other Tits were impressed and waited nervously in the background until he dropped the leaf, took a nut from me and flew away, then they came forward in turn to my hand. It seemed Presto was making sure of getting back his lost nesting territory. This proved correct, and in the 1954 nesting season he and Dado brought off their brood in their former nest-box, while Inkey and Drummer took The Intruder's territory. By June my garden was again full of fledgling Great Tits, and all through this especially wet summer they relied upon me more than usual, for food was scarce.

Before leaving the Great Tits a few incidents must be told about the 1954 nesting season. Smiler met with a tragic accident before her young were fledged. Tinky proved a devoted father, with my help he brought off the brood successfully and fed the fledglings attentively for three weeks. Four out of eight survived, as with Smiler's 1953 brood.

This year Inkey and Drummer were the only parents that took their newly flown young away from my garden. They returned a week later without any fledglings, – probably they were victims of the Magpies and Jays in the neighbourhood.

Drummer quickly nested again but Inkey, who had started to moult, took no part in rearing her second brood. While she was sitting he spent much time hammering loudly at things in the west room and he became bossy towards all other Tits. For the second time in his life he was a nuisance in the room as he kept displaying and frightening the young ones from entering the west fanlight, Drummer's nest being outside the window. I had to encourage all the Tits to use the east room until Drummer's young flew, two weeks after hatching, one fledgling flying on the 2nd July, two on the 3rd, the remaining three on the 4th. (One egg was in the nest when I examined it afterwards.) Inkey then kept in the background for much of the day as his hungry fledglings pursued him and cried loudly while begging with fluttering wings whenever he came within their sight. It was interesting to find that they always recognised him as a parent although he had never fed them or even entered their nest. When they fluttered their wings before him he lifted up his head and drew away from them but they were persistent and he had to escape into hiding.

Drummer, this time, kept her brood in my front garden, where Magpies and Jays seldom come. She had difficulty in feeding them during the continual rain of the worst summer for half a century. They were so hungry that even on their first day of flight they made pathetic attempts to find food for themselves; one of them, after watching some other species feeding on the ground, flew down and began plucking at the grass, opening its beak and shivering its wings between the plucks. I had previously seen a newly flown fledgling do this when its widowed father (Whiskers) could not feed his brood well because of a slight defect of his beak.

Presto displaying a leaf as a symbol of possession

Drummer's fledglings developed an unusual baby-cry, a reeling, continuous note that glided up and down in pitch and carried farther than the usual fledgling-cry, this helping Drummer to find them instantly she returned with food, often after an hour's search away from the front garden. The three young that survived the first days of flight, through their hunger, became unusually precocious in their ways. A week after they flew (having then only been hatched three weeks) they fed from my hand and called me up at 5.15 by entering the east room fanlight and reeling off their special baby-cries until I drew back the curtains and they flew indoors to perch on me and be fed.

I watched the fledglings learn to use their feet separately, like hands, in the Tit manner. They did not do this instinctively. On first coming indoors one of them picked up some food from the floor, which was too large to swallow outright and too hard to break with its beak alone. After trying unsuccessfully it held the food with its beak lowered to the floor, paused a second, fidgeted with its feet then brought both feet forward in a jump, which ended in a slight skid on the boards. It repeated these jumps several times, always making the preparatory beak to floor pose so as to have the food in position for the feet to reach it, but finding that after each jump its feet were no nearer to the food the fledgling fidgeted once more, then slowly and carefully its right foot was brought forward to hold the food while its left leg remained firmly on the floor. When eating food on the ground, putting the beak to the feet is not easy as it is when perched on a twig and the Tit lost its balance and nearly went head over heels when it tried to do this. It was interesting to watch the fledglings in this way learning to use their feet like hands and their toes like fingers. It is the most intelligent species of birds, Crow tribes, Hawks, etc., that make clever use of their feet. Many species, such as Finches, Thrushes, etc., often find themselves in need of using their feet like hands, but it very rarely occurs to them to do this.

Drummer, looking worn out and beginning to moult, stopped feeding her fledglings ten days after they flew, this being sooner than is usual, but she often perched near me to watch when they were feeding on my hand, then she flew away as if satisfied that they did not need her help. They still begged continually from both their parents every time they saw them and after Drummer stopped feeding them they also gave short begging displays before other adults and even to the older youngsters, who stared at them with curiosity and sometimes pushed them aside. But the fledglings' display was much more persistent before their parents and they continued to keep this up for several weeks longer than is normal, as if they felt they had been neglected and were not going to let their parents forget it! Even eight weeks after fledging they gave very occasional begging displays. One of the fledglings, a few days after it flew, also gave Inkey trouble by making daytime use of his cardboard roll roost, which he had occupied every night for some weeks. When Inkey tried to chase his offspring from the roll he was embarrassed by the fledgling making baby-cries and wing flutterings before him, which made him leave the room at once. The fledgling, named Charmer, then went inside his roost, while he hopped around outside the window. In a few minutes he returned to display before the entrance to his roost, but Charmer would not come out and Inkey could not attack his young offspring, for that would be against bird-law. So the tyrant Inkey was defeated in his possessiveness by his young fledgling. She sometimes sat inside the roost for half an hour, apparently having a nap, while Inkey danced around outside the roll as if he was stepping on hot bricks, then made frustration antics of tearing at other roost-boxes or at the curtains. When tired of this he went outdoors, but he must have watched from outside for directly Charmer left his roost he appeared and began his wing-drooping, chin-up displays in front of the roll or along the picture rail supporting it. The innocent fledgling at once flew to him with a food begging display and so always got the better of her frustrated father, who left the room hurriedly, his tail spread and drooping while he muttered something to himself as he flew away. Every evening he went to bed much earlier than the other Tits, so making sure that Charmer did not occupy his roost at night.

Inkey's behaviour was not a good example of the selfless devotion of parent birds, but he had gone into moult and this had affected his appearance more than usual so he probably felt correspondingly off colour. Neither his former mate, Smoke, or Drummer had previously had second broods so he also was unaccustomed to fathering a second one. They are not very common among Great Tits in Britain but I have had two females (Puggy and Jane in *Birds as Individuals*) who reared two broods successfully each year with the help of their mates to feed the young.

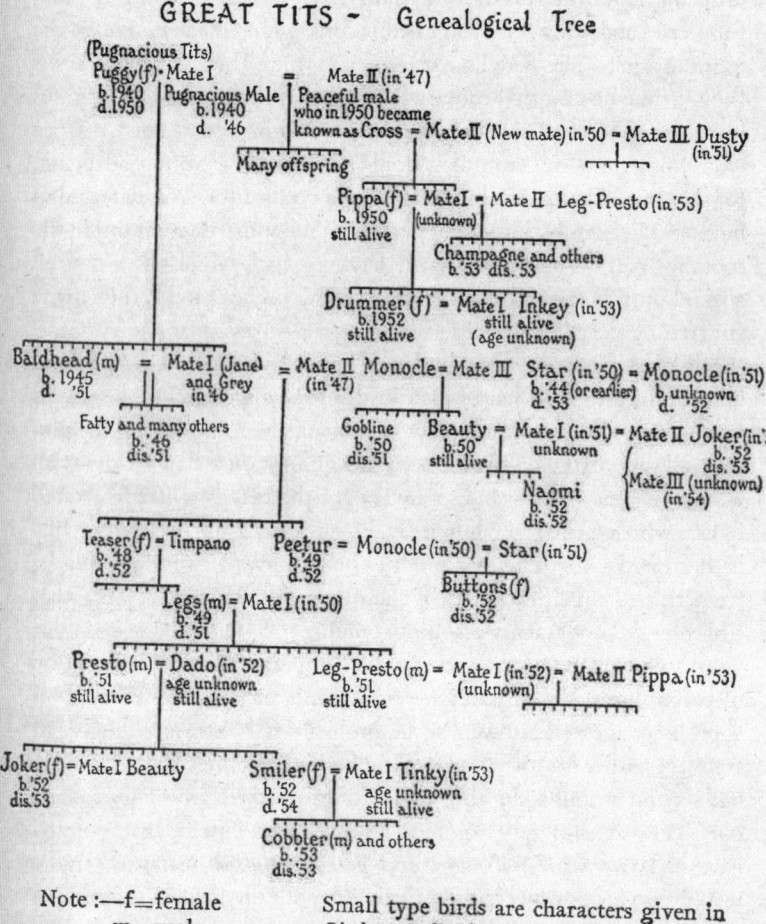

CHAPTER 8

Blue Tits and Coal Tits

Blue tits are more independent by nature than Great Tits and though they readily seek my help in any difficulty or illness they do not become so intimate as the Great Tits. Those that are reared in my garden are taken away by their parents directly they fly and they are not brought back so I do not know if those that come to me later in the summer or autumn have been reared by my resident pairs.

The young Blue Tit called Opal, mentioned in Star's biography, arrived by himself early in August; he became the most intimate of them all. Almost at once he perched on my hand, and soon began coming indoors through the french window. The first time he entered through the fanlight he was unable to find his way out, the other windows were closed including the casement that had always before been open when he was in the room. I offered Opal my hand while he was fluttering against the window-pane; he turned round and stepped on to my palm, then I lifted him level with the fanlight, hoping he would fly out. Instead he flew to my chest and looked into my eyes, perhaps asking to be helped still further and put outside, for the fanlight opening is not at first easy for birds to understand. Opal then flew to the casement window-catch below and turning round, looked up at me as if pleading for this window to be opened. I did not do so because I wanted him to use the fanlight. He then flew to a roost-box and remained there quietly for several minutes before returning to the window, again flying to my chest when I had lifted him level with the fanlight, this being repeated exactly as before, three times, with the same interval of rest taken in the roost-box. Eventually I opened the casement and he flew out.

The following week Opal had learnt to use the fanlight and he now roosted above my bed in a box next to Pippa's. Opal preened night and morning in his roost and he sometimes turned over in his bed during the night when I did, judging from the sounds he made, otherwise he was very quiet. Typing did not disturb him as it did the Great Tits. He went to his roost later than they did and it seemed he saw better in dark corners but on 12th October – with darkness falling more rapidly – he was unable to see his roost-box when he entered, although the room was not dark to the human eye. He tried to perch but landed underneath it, fell over, then flew to the window-sill, and gave me a prolonged look, which meant 'Help me.' While I turned on the reading-lamp he fidgeted on the sill but when the light shone on his roost he flew to his bed. It is surprising that Tits who nest in dark holes have not good vision in bad light. How they manage to see their nestlings is a puzzle. After this, until the winter was over, he expected me to light him to bed every evening, which I did. If I had to be out at his bedtime I switched on the lamp before leaving home. Pippa, sleeping in a roost beside his, disliked going to bed by glaring artificial light, so the lamp had to be veiled as a compromise. Suiting the different tastes and needs of all my birds is as hard as trying to please every member of a large human household. Some people imagine that living with wild birds is restful; they should try it for several years until the population is as large and intimate as mine!

During the winter Opal rose every morning at exactly the same time according to the sun. When I forgot to wind my watch one Saturday night, I set it when Opal left his roost, and later found it right to the minute by the radio time signal. I tested this on many mornings. Other Tits I have found vary their time according to circumstances or weather. One November morning (18th) at 6.50., Pippa flew to the fanlight but did not go out. I heard her fluttering behind the curtains and supposed the window was closed. Getting up, I drew back the curtains; she looked at me, then out of the window, which was not shut. There was thick fog outside. She flew back to her roost and I went back to bed. Twenty minutes later Pippa got up and had another look out of the window. The fog was still thick but there was more light. She flew out but soon returned for breakfast indoors, and another visit to her roost.

In early October Opal was always fetching and carrying for other Blue Tits, although unintentionally. They came to Bird Cottage later than he did and had not yet learnt to come indoors but they saw Opal flying out of the fanlight with nuts or cheese in his beak, so they perched on the outside sill of this window and when Opal had taken his nut from my hand, which he liked to eat on the tree outside, one of the Blue Tits lying in wait seized it from his beak directly he appeared at the fanlight. Opal returned to me for another nut and often the same thing happened several times before he could get to the tree and eat one himself. He was very good-natured over these thefts and never made any sign of objection, as most birds do in similar circumstances, which made it look as if Opal was willingly feeding all the others! After a week of this he began eating his food indoors but by then the other Blue Tits had learnt to enter the room, so Opal continued to supply them with nuts taken from my hand!

The following spring Opal reared his family down a pipe on a shed in West Garden and constantly flew to my hand for cheese which he took to his nestlings. If this was not offered him immediately he appeared, he climbed all over me at a terrific speed, this apparently being an outlet for his impatience to get the food for his young. He came on to my bed at sunrise, hopped all over my pillow and head, despite the curtains being partially drawn, though he sometimes fell over, unable to see where he was alighting. He would not leave until he had cheese to take back to his nestlings. Out of nesting season Opal had perfect manners; when he wanted food he perched on my knee or anywhere opposite me where he could look into my eyes, then he waited for me to open the Tit-box and when I held out the food he stepped on to my hand neatly and deliberately, without haste; after picking up the food he gave me another look before flying off, or sometimes he ate it on my hand. He had more charm of manner than the other Blue Tits I had that year though several of the thirty that came during the autumn and winter months became very tame and most of them perched on my hand.

Although so many come during the winter only two pairs nest in my garden each year, probably the food supply is only sufficient for two families. Great Tits feed their young on most of the same foods as the Blue Tits but there is little rivalry shown during nesting days. One year I saw a Blue Tit mother going backwards and forwards to her nest from a lavender bush. She appeared to be squeezing the juice from the leaves, for she rapidly passed her beak down them without the usual searching glances made when finding insect food among the leaves. Perhaps lavender juice has medicinal value for Blue Tit nestlings. I have not seen this on any other occasion, though Finch tribes eat the lavender flower seeds.

On certain mild days every February I habitually see twenty or more Blue Tits suddenly take to feeding on the lawn; they keep fairly close together and go up and down over it, picking up something too small for me to see. This food seems to be there only for a day or two, after this they do not again look for it. It is an odd sight to watch the flock of Blue Tits working in the manner of gleaners on the lawn. Great Tits never join in this food hunt. When they search for spiders it is round the borders, or under bushes and among the flowers in the beds. Nor do they do it in the same manner, but spasmodically and not in groups. Blue Tits do not seem to eat spiders but I have seen Coal and Marsh Tits eating very small ones.

In winter Blue Tits roost all round the cottage, in crevices under the woodwork outside, and indoors, sometimes in odd places. One December night I had just started to run water from the geyser and was putting the plug into the bath when something flew from the hood of the geyser on to my head. At first I thought it was a leaf, then feeling quick tappings the idea of its being a bat caught in my hair made me put my hand to my head. I then saw a Blue Tit fly to the water-pipe above and look down on me. He was rather excited and fidgeted nervously with his feet. Blue Tits have not on any other occasions tapped on my head and this must have been a result of his excitement. I was sorry to have brushed him away. For his benefit I put out the bathroom light and turned it on in the kitchen, letting the light shine into the passage outside the bathroom; he took my hint and came into the kitchen, which provided better accommodation for the night than the chilly bathroom pipes or scalding geyser. He finally settled down on top of the kitchen cabinet, among some saucepans. The next morning he flew out directly I opened the back door.

A brood of Blue Tits in their nest a few days before they fly is a charming sight if they are fearless of the watcher. They can be very lively at times and, like Great Tits, they practise wing flapping, standing on each other's backs while doing it. They often preen themselves, removing the nestling down which clings to their feathers. I have seen one mother Great Tit, the day before her brood flew, spend half an hour in the evening preening her young and coming from the nest with her beak full of down, which she dropped some distance away before returning to the nest. I think this was an exceptional case and that most mother Tits leave their young to preen themselves; they do it very capably. Unless the parent birds are very tame it is best not to attempt watching any broods of nestlings for it hinders feeding and upsets them. It also attracts cats, etc. if humans have been standing beside a nest, crushing the undergrowth below; for this reason I rarely go very close to birds' nests myself and I wish more people would be as considerate. Much unnecessary meddling is done at the expense of great loss to bird life.

Sometimes one or two Coal Tits spend much of the autumn and winter in my garden but this species (like the Marsh Tit) is getting scarce in this area. In October 1952 a charming pair arrived; she came first and when he arrived she chased him from the bone on which she was feeding, but in a few days they fed together and were seldom far apart. She never had fear of me and fed from my hand the day after she came; he was nervous in disposition and had a habit of frequently nodding his head forward with a jerk when he was facing me and catching my eye preparatory to making up his mind to fly to my hand, so I called him Nod. If she perched near him when he was doing this performance, he flew at her with a slight chin-up, and when he saw her alighting on my hand his nods became continuous until she left me. After a fortnight he overcame his hesitation over perching on my hand, but he generally gave a few preliminary nods before he flew to me. He was very handsome, with gleaming plumage, probably a youngster of that year; she was slightly less bright in colouring, but her ways were more lively than his. They used double notes for calling to each other but when she wanted food from me she gave three sharp notes and tried to catch my eye through the window. If I did not quickly offer her a nut she flew to the window and back again to the bird-table tree, repeating this flight incessantly until my hand was held out of the window, with nuts on it. She had extravagant habits of taking a few bites off the nut or cheese pellet given her, throwing away the remainder and coming back for more, repeating this many times. If I withdrew my hand and closed the window she again began the continuous flights back and forth to make me hold out my hand again. Nod later joined her in this, and a two-way motion was then kept up evenly without a break. It had a mesmeric effect on me if I watched for a few moments and eventually it drew my hand out of the window again; as this happened frequently at all hours of the day in cold weather, I needed an automatic hand that could be switched out by pressing a button indoors. Any food that I put outside was devoured in a few minutes by the Sparrows and other birds and the Coal Tits got pushed aside by the Blue Tits if they tried to feed on the containers slung to the window frame, for in winter Blue Tits often become very pushful on the bird-trays and even the Great Tits seem afraid of them at times. Unfortunately the Coal Tits were nervous of coming indoors. Soon after they arrived they perched on the fanlight sill and examined the room, they then flew indoors to my hand for food, afterwards banging into all the closed windows. They were in a panic by the time I had opened one. With high-pitched notes of agitation they flew out and never dared to enter again.

During a cold spell in January a third Coal Tit came to the window-frame food-trays when the Blue Tits were not there. The other Coal Tits flew at him while he was feeding but he was so hungry that he ignored them. Nod uttered high squeak-notes of protest while making the action of pecking him quickly many times on his rump but without touching him. The stranger Coal Tit took no notice and even stood his ground when a Blue Tit and Robin made small dabs at him with beak snappings. He was a faded grey colour and kept his feathers fluffed out. Probably he was old and half-starved owing to the cold spell. He looked completely different from the other two, whose plumage was sleek and glossy. This third Coal Tit stayed only a week or two and although the others continued to make mock pecks at him and the Blue Tits butted at him with lowered heads, as is their manner of showing fight, the grey newcomer showed spirit and snapped back at them, so he held his place on the food-tray and ate all he wanted. The Great Tits never molested him – they are tolerant of their small relations.

In February Nod and his mate were often away but they returned two or three times daily for food. He always went up to her with his head raised high just before she flew to my hand for food; he wanted to come first but gave way to her, nodding his head several times as she flew to me. Sometimes he courted her charmingly, hopping close with his head held up then touching her beak. She did not move until she had received the bird-kiss, then she flew to another twig and Nod repeated the kiss. Occasionally when he flew after her she dodged him and when he called to her she was silent. He then pursued her and they chased round the garden. I hoped that this love-making might mean that they were nesting nearby and that I should not lose sight of them but in March they disappeared and did not return until the autumn.

A Marsh Tit in summer occasionally feeds on honeysuckle berries by my cottage wall, this being one of their favourite foods. I wish this charming species was more plentiful in my neighbourhood. Both Marsh and Long-Tailed Tits have become scarce and an occasional visit from them is all I now get. When I first came here they were comparatively abundant but like many other species they are suffering from lack of food and nesting-sites, owing to modern agricultural poisons, felling of trees, low-cut hedges, and many other things disastrous for bird-life. Even the water in ditches and ponds often gets contaminated, especially where arsenic spraying has been done from them. Many other bird-watchers besides myself, who have lived in Sussex for some years, notice with concern the decline in population of many small species and the position gets worse every year. Bird-watchers have increased so much in recent years that the few rare species of birds passing through England are now seen, whereas formerly they would mostly have escaped notice. This gives many people an impression that there are more birds in our country than there used to be. But in agricultural areas the outlook is very bad and more thought should be given to this by everyone concerned.

CHAPTER 9

A Hedgehog Comes to Call

In late November of 1952, on a day of hard frost, a Hedgehog came to my doorstep. At first he failed to climb the lower step and went all round it, looking for an easier way up before he made another effort and succeeded. He quickly sighted a board leaning against the corner of the next step and used it as a ladder. Raising his snout he sniffed at the room, wanting to enter, but the last step was higher and though he made many comical attempts to climb it, nearly falling over in an effort to hoist up his troublesome back legs, they were too short to reach it.

Several Great Tits, perched in the doorway, stretched up their necks in a haughty manner and cast glances over their shoulders at this strange visitor. While I fed the Hedgehog with buns and bacon-fat which he took from my hand, many Great Tits inquisitively came near, to peer closely at his spines, then they looked askance at him and made grimaces with their beaks held slightly open, as if in disgust at such an animal. I dropped some nuts on to the Hedgehog's back to see what the Tits would do. The nuts disappeared between the spines before they could get them and they remained staring at the Hedgehog's back with their necks stretched right up and queer expressions of disapproval on their faces.

After his meal the Hedgehog hurried off to the flower-beds, his hind legs conspicuously stretched out behind him at each step as he strode along at top speed. When he came to a thick tuft of grass, he paused, sniffed, then began vigorously scratching with his claws at the tuft and boring into it with his strong snout, a good tool for the job of unearthing hidden slugs and small snails. Half an hour later when I was in the kitchen, I found him on the back doorstep. He put his front paws on the ledge and held his snout inside the doorway while he sniffed at my kitchen. I again fed him with bacon-rind and bread, and gave him a bacon bone, which he gnawed vigorously.

At 11 a.m. the next day, he returned to the front doorstep, and climbed into a shallow box-lid to devour the Tits' fat which it contained. The Great Tits gave him a quick look, then darted up close, intending to seize the fat from him but they drew back in fear of his munching snout. The Blue Tits were eating crumbs from a greased cake-paper. The Hedgehog, seeing this, climbed clumsily out of the box-lid, having trouble with his hind legs which seem often to get left in the lurch with this animal. After nearly overturning the lid, he went to the cake-paper and sniffed at it while the Tits stepped aside and retorted with a display of spread wings and chins-up. The Hedgehog soon decided that the cake-paper was edible and ignoring their display he seized it in the centre to begin chewing it; I thought he was going too far, for the Tits love pecking at these greased papers, so I took hold of the edge and shook him off with a quick jerk. He looked up at me with a mild expression and did not seem to mind. I handed him bread and fat while the Blue and Great Tits returned to the cake-paper, between feeding, throwing expressive glances at this monstrosity who was encroaching on their preserves and eating like a glutton.

The exceptionally cold autumn had made the Hedgehog in need of extra food, especially fats, to build him up before the winter hibernation.

I saw him no more until 22nd March, when at 1.30 in the afternoon, he reappeared on my french window doorstep. He was very tame and at once took meat from my fingers; he did not even bristle or draw his head back when I stroked him. He had ticks clinging to the spines near his ears and he frequently scratched his body with his hind claws. The Tits this time were cautious over approaching the Hedgehog closely for they had lost the rashness of early youth. It had been the youngsters that had gone near him before; with the wisdom of maturity, they now perched above to look down on him with outstretched necks and odd expressions of curiosity and disgust. He did not stay long that day, but sought a sheltered sunny spot against the cottage wall and slept until this was in shadow, when he found another sunny place. I waited until he had curled himself into a sleeping posture with his snout invisible, then purposely sat between him and the sun, to see if he would again move from the shadow. In about a minute he got up, walked a few steps and settled down again just beyond my shadow. There he slept until the sun went off him an hour later.

The next day he kept climbing into the birds' food-box on the doorstep – he just fitted into it. He always stayed there longer than they could tolerate, and, losing some of their caution, Great and Blue

Tits, Robin and Chaffinches began perching on the doorstep, though keeping at a discreet distance from him at first. Then some of them in turn ventured closer, trying to get up courage to seize food from a corner of their box, which he nearly filled, but the Hedgehog's munching jaws and the odd clicking sound he sometimes made when chewing so terrified the birds that they drew back in alarm when they got very close. The Robin was the boldest, he occasionally got a crumb from the edge of the box. My Tits even dislike the sound I make when crunching toast; they draw back and look at me with concern if I continue to eat it while they are perched on me. Perhaps it gives them an impression similar to 'I'll grind your bones to make my bread!' Possibly their fear is derived from the crunching sound cats make when devouring their prey.

The Hedgehog drank often from the birds' pool and from a jam jar filled with water – the Great Tits' favourite drinking vessel. His first attempt at getting his snout inside the jar ended in knocking it over, so I quickly fetched another and the camera, then took the snap on Plate 16, although the light was not good at the time.

During the five days of the Hedgehog's daylight visits, usually from noon until 4 p.m., the weather was sunny and dry. Sometimes he ran apace across the lawn to thick tufts of grass along the borders, where he dug out slugs by scratching with his paws and probing with his snout.

Although he slept most on the first day he afterwards took short intervals of sleep in the sun, always moving when the shadows reached him. The Hedgehog, though a creature of the dark, is a sun-lover. On 27th March he resumed the normal habits of night feeding and I heard but never saw him again.

Another nocturnal creature who sought the sunshine was a small Pipistrelle. At 1 o'clock (Summer Time) in mid-August, I saw this bat come from my chimney-pot to lie with outstretched wings on the sunlit tiles of the roof. I watched it for half an hour; during that time it made four return visits to the chimney-pot but always flew out again almost immediately, to resume sunbathing in bird-like poses. It was a blazing hot day and the heat against the tiles must have been terrific. At 1.30 I went indoors for a minute then returned to watch the bat which I found lying dead on the ground below the part of the roof where it had been sunbathing. Probably sunstroke was the cause of its death.

On summer afternoons at 4 p.m. (Summer Time) I have sometimes seen bats hawking flies on the shady side of my orchard hedge but have not on any other occasion seen one sunning itself.

Most creatures love sunshine but fear of man has made many small mammals wary of strong light. For this reason the Rabbit is seldom seen sunbasking in its attractive pose of complete relaxation, it usually has its hind feet on the ground ready to run. The first time I saw this pose was at noon one July, when I was bird-watching beside a pool in a wood. There were Rabbits feeding nearby and one of them came up to the patch of sunlight on the bank where I was sitting. It eyed me for a moment, then flung itself on to its back and lay with its hind legs stretched out to full length, one front paw curved over its right eye (the side next to me) its left eye closed. This attitude was so human and so suited to the noonday heat that I wanted to imitate it, although I was afraid that my movement would make the Rabbit jump to its feet. The only notice it took as I gradually lowered myself was a slight raising of the paw shielding the eye, which it opened for a second each time I moved. We lay side by side on our backs for half an hour, until the drowsy Rabbit rose to its feet and lolloped into the shade of the trees.

At the present time Rabbits all over the country are being slowly tortured to death by myxomatosis, spread deliberately by Man. That humans should have sunk to such depths of depraved inhumanity as to inflict this foul disease upon wild animals makes it seem likely that most of our own race will also be exterminated by some of Man's vile inventions for destruction of life.

I have had many experiences of wild animals – as well as birds – being fearless of me. One day when I was lying by the seashore in a Devon cove, a half-grown Bank-Vole came up to me. The first intimation of its arrival was the feel of its muzzle sniffing my arm; it then snuggled into the palm of my hand and seemed to like being stroked. When I lifted it close to my face it sat looking up at me without a trace of fear. It ate the cheese from my sandwiches with much relish but refused the bread. This Tom Thumb creature, about two and a half inches long with a quarter of an inch tail, was completely delightful in appearance and in its ways. Wondering if it could swim, I took it over the sands to a narrow pool about nine feet long. Directly I put it on the brink it shot along the whole length of the pool at lightning speed, keeping most of its body above water; then it landed and without hesitation ran back to me. I was so surprised at its immediate return that I repeated the experiment and it behaved in exactly the same way, except that it paused to shake itself after the swim and chose the other side of the pool for its run back. When I picked it up only its underparts were wet.

The voles and mice in my garden would be tame if I did not have to discourage them; otherwise they come indoors. Sometimes when a bone I have put out for the Tits falls to the ground, a vole seizes its chance and lugs it, bit by bit, into the cover of leafage under the bird-table. The Tits watch from a perch above, fidgeting uneasily. Harvest-mice and Pigmy Shrews also feed on the bones, but only the Harvest-mice can reach those suspended on string. I have watched one run up the bird-table and along the twig to which the string was attached, then loop the tip of its long tail round the twig and hang head downwards to feed. After I had removed the string and bones this Harvest-mouse ran along the twig to get another feed, knotting its tail round the twig as before and hanging where the bones had been. It sniffed and searched the air in a puzzled manner for a minute or two, then hauled itself up and ran back to the bird-table and down to the ground. No sooner had it touched earth than it turned round and ran back to the twig, repeating the plunge into space to search for the bones. It must have been able to see that they were not there but it certainly did not believe its eyes, for it repeated the whole performance three times before it ran away.

One summer a Pigmy-Shrew came into the kitchen and got inside the large cardboard carton in which the grocer had sent my provisions, including bacon bones wrapped in paper. The little creature tore off the wrapping and gnawed the bones but left everything else in the carton untouched. After I had removed all the other provisions I found it again in the box and now that the packages had gone it could not get out; its efforts to climb up the slippery surface of the glazed cardboard were as fruitless as those of a spider trapped in a bath. Unlike the patient spider, the Pigmy panicked, rushing round the box, trying first one place then another and crying out excitedly in a high-pitched voice. The rapid, short sequences of notes were much more musical than the sounds other small animals can produce. The Pigmy showed no fear at being lifted out; we were already familiar for it had often come close to me in the garden. It used to open the Tits' match-boxes, containing cheese and nuts, which I always have by me. Its long, pointed snout seemed an efficient tool for this purpose, but it had difficulty in steadying the box and the performance was amusing to watch, for this Shrew can show a lively impatience when it wants something. It can also be very obstinate, as I know to my cost.

One morning there were two Pigmies in the carton, so I turned them out of the house, shut the bones in a cupboard and kept the kitchen door closed, having decided that Pigmies must no longer be allowed indoors. The next morning I was about to push the carpet-sweeper along a rug in the sitting-room when I heard squeaks of protest. Opening the sweeper, I saw one of the Pigmies sitting in a corner of the dust-collector, staring up at me; and it refused to move. I shook and tapped the sweeper and tried both coaxing and scolding in strong language, for sweeping rugs was impossible with the creature inside. When I tried to lift it out, it dodged behind framework too narrow for my hands, so I took the sweeper up the garden and left it there, thinking that my efforts to expel the Shrew would make it glad to take advantage of my absence to escape. Ten minutes later I returned to find it still sitting in the corner and when I bent close, its eyes flashed at me, as if in defiance. Was this Pigmy, the smallest of all mammals, deliberately being obstinate, perhaps even taking pleasure in frustrating me? I seized the sweeper, turned it upside down and shook it roughly without result. Then I tried poking with a stick, but the Pigmy dodged every poke with consummate skill, jumping from one part of the sweeper to another. In despair I fetched a cup of water, and when I splashed this inside, the Pigmy jumped out and ran into the grass. My triumph was short-lived, however, for on the next day and many later mornings I found it back in the same corner of the sweeper, which I had to take up the garden daily in order to remove the Pigmy by splashing water over it. One day when I had got rid of the creature I found that the sweeper would not work, as it was clogged with rust. I feel that one meaning of the word 'shrew' must have arisen from embittered reactions to defeat in personal encounters with this animal.

There seem to be varying accounts of the eyes of Shrews; one book suggests that they see little except bright light and perhaps not even this, whereas another says that the eyes, though small, are well developed. The movements and actions of my Pigmy showed that it had sight, and from the appearance of its eyes there was no reason to doubt this.

That same summer, drought had hardened the clay soil and the Moles may have been having a lean time, for one came out of a tuft of grass in my orchard and burrowed its head inside a paper bag containing cheese on the ground beside me.

I discourage Longtailed Field-Mice because they do so much harm, but they seem unafraid and sometimes perch on the forks of tall stems of hedge-parsley in my orchard, looking most handsome with their white underparts showing. Sometimes I see them with head stretched forward to reach the young seeds which they seem to like in their fresh green state. Field-Mice can be very playful. I have watched their riotous romping on the corrugated iron roof of a wooden hut where I lived for a year. Rats were there too, and the terrific noise made by their feet in their orgies on the roof used to keep me awake. They ignored my bangs on it from inside and frequently I had to go out in the small hours to chase them away. On moonlight nights the sight of them leaping and rushing around the roof was fantastic. During the day one or two Rats often looked at me through the window but the Field-Mice were more discreet.

Unfortunately young Field-Mice as well as House-Mice show little discretion over entering Bird Cottage at night especially during summer and early autumn. Wild creatures watch each other and they probably see the birds flying in and out of the rooms and coming in to roost at dusk. It is very difficult to deal with this problem and I spend many midnight hours trying to cope with it. One night I heard the persistent gnawing of a mouse coming from the direction of the window. I got up and flashed a torch on to the sill. Outside a young House-Mouse was hectically scrabbling at the window-pane with its front paws and pressing its nose against the glass while it danced along the sill on its hind legs, going backwards and forwards, trying to find a way in. I opened the adjoining window to put some cheese on the sill and went back to bed, hoping this would stop it trying to come indoors. It had gnawed the wooden frame in places, and taken the paint off all along it. Presently the gnawing was resumed; I got up, flashed the torch and the mouse again pawed excitedly at the pane. The cheese had been half-eaten so it cannot have wanted to come indoors to get food, for there was plenty left on the sill. I returned to bed much puzzled. Then I heard a slight sound coming from a closed tin on the inside of the window-ledge and guessed that the outside mouse was trying to join its brother – or sister – in this tin. Needing to get some sleep before the Tits awakened me at dawn, I left the tin in another room until morning. The mouse outside was then quiet.

When I opened this half-size biscuit tin, I found a young mouse was sitting inside a bag of sultanas, kept there for the Blackbirds who always want them thrown to them from the window. Both these mice were completely fearless but how this one had managed to enter the tin, which was tightly shut, was a mystery. It must have got inside when I last opened it to feed the Blackbirds, seizing a minute when my back was turned. The noise it made was so faint that I think it would not have been heard through the window, and the outside mouse must have seen its brother get inside the tin; perhaps it had tried to follow him when I unknowingly interrupted their spree.

Last summer I was awakened by an exceptionally light-footed mouse jumping on the paper covering of an arm-chair. It sounded too small to do much damage, so I did not get up to deal with it – regretting this later. The next morning there was evidence from the droppings that a very small mouse had been in the room but after searching in vain I concluded that it had found its way out again. Two weeks later, when looking for my pencil, I put my hand down the side crevices of the arm-chair seat, where such things sometimes roll into hiding, and instead of a pencil I found a pressed baby Dormouse in its curled-up sleeping posture. Flowers when pressed do not keep their colour, but the young Dormouse had kept the beautiful golden colour of its coat. It was completely flat, dry and odourless; there seemed only its skin left. Evidently on that night, two weeks previously, it had gone to sleep down the crevice of the arm-chair and when the next day the cushioned seat was occupied, pressure on the sleeping Dormouse had resulted. Ten days previously I had noticed a slight smell which I thought came from outside, for the chair was by the french window, which had always been wide open for the young birds to come indoors. I was extremely sorry not to have seen this attractive little creature alive. It was barely half-grown and its tail was quite short. In summer, when my young birds are coming indoors, I always have to make sure no fledglings are on my chair before I sit down, now it seems that I shall also have to search the seat for sleeping Dormice!

CHAPTER 10

Robins and Others

1. ROBINS; DOBS, TURK, STALKY AND CO.

In the early spring of 1950 my six-year-old Robin, named Dobs, whose autumn disputes were recorded in *Birds as Individuals*, became aggressive towards every bird that entered the cottage. He stood inside the room, near the fanlight entrance, and attacked the Tits that flew through it, making their feathers fly. I chased Dobs away when he did this but he persistently returned. The Tits never hit back, they tried to avoid him but they would not submit to being turned out of the room though the plumage of some of them became thin at the back of the neck, where Dobs usually aimed his blows. To protect the Tits, I had to frighten Dobs by chasing him with a folded newspaper, which I noisily slapped against the window after his departure, remaining by it for several minutes to prevent his immediate return. Even this had little effect although he soon flew outside when he saw me hold up the newspaper while shouting at him. He understood that I still was friendly towards him though I objected to the Tits being attacked and he still fed from my hand out of doors as if all was well between us, but he was winning the battle; he now often waited outside the fanlight and attacked the Tits before they flew into the room, sending them away. They made little squeaks of complaint and I had to spend much time battling with Dobs. After two weeks of this aggressive behaviour, the reason for it became clear when one morning his mate, called Sprite, entered the room with a beakful of nesting material which she took to a Tit's roost-box hung on the picture rail over the mantelpiece. Because of the aggressive nature of Robins towards other species I could not let Sprite nest indoors and I chased her out many times but it was impossible to stop her from building; cunningly she chose every opportunity when I was out of the room to come through the fanlight to her box; when I entered she flew off hastily. After two days I took her material out of the box in the morning and closed the window for half a day. Sprite was not put off by this; that evening she entered the room with nest material and again started to build in the same box. Most Robins are not sensitive birds; if I had done this to a Tit or other species in my garden they would have instantly left the nest-box and gone elsewhere.

The next day I was out for five hours. When I returned Sprite's nest was almost complete and the mantelpiece underneath the box was covered with leaves and moss, which she had let fall while building. On seeing me she did not even leave her nest but put her head outside and gave me a quick glance – perhaps meant in defiance. Dobs was still trying to slay every bird that entered the room, so I took Sprite's box out of doors and put it in the lawsonia hedge near the back of the cottage. Beside this cardboard box, which was unsuitable for outdoors, I hung an old china teapot, hoping that she would take the hint and transfer her nesting material to it. The next day she entered the room, looked at the gap where her box had been, then flew to another roost in the corner of the room. I chased her outside. That was her last effort to build indoors. She at once took the teapot and in two days had made a beautiful nest, having lined the whole interior of the pot with moss. How she got it to hold firmly to the top, on the glazed surface, was her secret; it was neatly woven, and she did not put any leaves inside this nest as she had done in the cardboard roost-box. Outside the entrance to the teapot she made an elaborate doorstep of moss; the twigs below also were covered with nesting material, probably dropped unintentionally, as indoors this had fallen on the mantelpiece. I was afraid her mossy doorstep would attract the attention of her enemies but dared not interfere with her a second time. The teapot was not easily accessible to cats but a few days after Sprite began to brood her eggs a tragedy occurred. She was missing and one of her eggs was smashed in the nest, the rest were unbroken. A cat must have pulled her off the clutch during the night. It was terrible, for she had been sensible enough to try every means of securing an indoor nest, where she would have been safe, but all the other birds had been viciously attacked by Dobs, and they had to be spared from injury.

The sequel to this tragedy was interesting.

The previous year two of Dobs's offspring had disputed with him for the right to remain in my garden. They were named after their coloured rings, Lemon and Turk (Turk for turquoise). Disputes raged every day and eventually, at the end of September, Dobs succeeded in driving Lemon away; Turk, however, was determined to keep a right of entry to the cottage and during October he succeeded. Afterwards he stayed mostly over the road by the stream but he was cunning and from tree-tops watched his opportunity to make hurried flights to my hand for food when I was on the french window doorstep or in the garden within his view. Often I went to the gate and called his name, for this brought him to my hand within a minute. When I went on the road he usually was at my side at once; it seemed he spent most of his time watching or listening for these chances. Dobs was unable to prevent his making quick flights to my hand but he flew at his offspring and chased him back across the road directly afterwards. This continued all the winter, but towards early spring when Dobs mated Sprite, Turk no longer ventured into the garden; we then only met across or on the road. He still seemed without any nesting territory or mate and his main interest as before was to watch for chances to return to my garden. Frequently I saw him perched on a tall tree in the front hedge of West Garden. Although I had previously thought he was a male, I now began to wonder if Turk was a backward female, afraid of making advances towards a male – the necessary preliminary to nesting.

While Turk was thus awaiting his chances to return, Sprite's indoor and outdoor nests were built and she began to sit. On 26th March, when her tragedy occurred, Turk's chance came; he immediately appeared and took over Dobs's territory, confidently stepping in front of the cottage as if he owned it. At first it seemed he was a female, come to replace Sprite and mate Dobs – for with Robins, there is no difference in appearance between the sexes, although Turk's manners had always suggested a male and I still talked and wrote of him in my notes as 'He.' Dobs, after losing Sprite, looked dejected, he stopped singing and took no notice of Turk, nor did either of them display when they came into contact with each other on Turk's territory near the cottage, but Dobs usually kept hidden from his sight. The next day it became clear that Turk was a male, he began to sing lustily but he still did not display at Dobs, who continued for a week to remain in the same territory, a sad, spiritless shadow of his former self. His plumage quickly lost its sheen and the glow of his red breast had faded when, after a week, a female came to Turk. Then Dobs left his old home. I never saw him again.

Turk's mate built her nest in a hollow on the ground between the stems of a young willow. Tragedy again occurred; her four nestlings were taken when a few days old, probably by the same neighbour's cat, which haunted my garden and even climbed the wire netting I erected around some nests. Turk and his mate then left my garden to nest elsewhere.

I have received many letters from readers of my former book, suggesting remedies for cats entering the garden but nothing keeps them out. Flinging cold water to make them afraid of me is the best safeguard, but they slink into the garden when I am not there and this cannot be prevented.

In January 1953, three Robins often came indoors. One male, named Bouncer, who owned the orchard territory, came to the east room, the other two from the front territories kept to the west room. Later they became mates but at that time the male frequently flew at the female when she entered and after seizing food she had to leave. This male, called Stalky, was a queer Robin; instead of the usual rotund-looking body (often with fluffed-out feathers in winter) he perpetually adopted stiff, lean poses, showing the entire length of his legs and compressing his body upwards or making it look very thin, and cocking his tail high. (*See Plate 21.*) Stalky also was jerky in his movements, he snatched food, whether taken from my hand or the bird-table. He looked as if walking about on stilts and afraid of losing balance when he stooped to snatch worms from the lawn.

Stalky spent much time indoors, singing a soft subsong aimed at Bouncer, who was perched in a defiant attitude in the other room. Bouncer did not sing but he usually outstayed Stalky, hopping about the table and chairs in a possessive manner until the last moment before going to roost. During the short snow spell in January Stalky ceased singing, then Bouncer ventured into the west room and sometimes the three Robins fed together at the bird-table in this room. Occasionally Stalky flew at Bouncer, who then retired to the screen in the east room and, puffing out his feathers, eyed Stalky sideways. Bouncer was never attacked in the east room. I sometimes threw cheese on the floor under the archway between the two rooms to see which Robin would take it and found that they had a clear-cut boundary line indoors as with outdoor territories. Directly I had thrown the food, Bouncer perched on the screen, turned his head sideways and stared down at it while Stalky flew to a chair-back and eyed it with equal care, both seeming to gauge its position so that no mistake over ownership could be made. Bouncer claimed it if it fell just inside the east room; when it was exactly underneath the archway or west of this line Stalky owned it. Often he was slow to take it, for his room contained a bird-table and he had eaten enough but he always kept a close eye on his preserves lest Bouncer should poach. He never attempted to do so although his keen gaze lasted until the cheese was taken by Stalky or often by a Tit, who airily flew down and seized the food while it was being viewed with so much legal care by the Robins.

Stalky was a first-year bird. The previous summer he had arrived in my garden with his adult plumage not yet attained; his stiff poses and long-legged appearance had always been noticeable and he wasted no time in staking a claim for possession of half my front garden.

First Stalky dealt with the young Robins reared in this territory and flew at them, particularly when they came near me; I often chased him away when he did this but that made no difference to his plans for possession. When his adult plumage was complete he tackled the father of the young Robins and seemed to have little difficulty in getting him to leave his former territory. On 22nd August I wrote this in my notes: A thin, long-legged youngster with a fierce-sounding voice is turning out both my resident Robins although they are now in full new plumage and look large and strong beside the skinny youngster, who is full of nervous actions, afraid even to take food from the doorstep or lawn and frightened to go near any other species of bird except its own. It flies at all Robins, young and old.

It seemed that Stalky's stiff poses and jerky movements awed his rivals and made conquests easy for him.

Bouncer gave up entering the east room when Stalky mated the female who had owned the east half of my front garden during the winter. As already stated, she had been entering the west room (owned by Stalky) in January. When they were mated my whole front garden became their nesting territory.

In spring Stalky often sang loudly indoors as a challenge to Bouncer who wanted to enter the west room to get food for his young. Occasionally he succeeded in flying through the fanlight and in a flustered manner pounced on some food and hurried back to his orchard territory.

Stalky was a skilful kitchen thief. Each day I found bits of my butter ration on the floor, where he ate the chunks stolen from the dish. In March he began trying to intimidate the Tits by perching close to them in his odd postures and gaping at them when they were feeding at the west room food-bowl. They were not impressed and continued to feed. Stalky then flitted around the room, singing loudly from various perches. His mate often appeared at the fanlight but would not enter while the Tits were feeding. Directly they left the bowl Stalky and his mate took possession of it, and while they fed the Tits entering the room would not go near it. An arrangement of taking turns amicably then followed, for Stalky found that his gapes and original long-legged poses had no effect upon the Tits, only his own species could be conquered by such means.

A Dunnock (Hedge Sparrow) had attacked Stalky one day in late February, first displaying at him with excited wing-flicking then giving a quick charge which nearly rolled him over. At the time Stalky was encroaching beyond his winter territory into his future mate's domain, the east side of my cottage, but that was the Robin's business, not the Dunnock's. The Robins were already beginning to share their winter territories which in spring became their joint nesting territory. Stalky was intimidated by the fury of the Dunnock and he retreated with a conciliatory display of raised head feathers while the meddlesome Dunnock hopped around him, alternately making a show of false feeding or displaying with the same jerky wing flicks used before the attack. When the season of courtship begins the Dunnock sheds its unobtrusive ways and becomes fantastically spry.

2. WRENS IN SNOW AND SUNSHINE

The Wren also has unaccountable moments of fury towards other species. Last August I saw one with no tail on the bird-table, this loss perhaps accounting for its bad-tempered attacks, first at a youngster Blue Tit, then a Great Tit, finally a Chaffinch. Each in turn drew away and looked with a surprised stare at this small fiery brown ball, bouncing angrily from one to the other for no apparent cause. The Wren never ate bird-table fare so its behaviour had no connection with the food they were eating.

On another occasion I saw a Wren make six attacks on one of Baldhead's newly flown young. The fledgling was on a bough of the medlar tree when the Wren appeared and, perching above it, repeatedly dived down and prodded with its beak into the middle of the fledgling's back. The baby cried more and more loudly with each stab but the merciless Wren continued prodding it until Baldhead arrived and his fledgling, yelling loudly, conveyed to his father that something was wrong, so Baldhead called the baby to another tree. Jenny Wren, like the Robin, certainly has bad moods!

A Wren has sometimes entered my room through the fanlight and shown complete unconcern when it wanted to get out and found the other windows closed. It calmly went round the room giving one peck at the glass of each window, never trying the same one twice, and this methodical search for an open one eventually led it to the fanlight through which it had entered. It was never flustered, even if I went close, and it did not flutter against the panes as most species do when they fail to find their way out.

Recently three young Wrens trooped in through the east room fanlight at dusk and tried to find roosts in the curtain folds, this suggesting to me that I should supply pockets in my curtains for accommodating Wrens! It was not the first time one has entered at roost hour to try for a bed in these velvet window curtains.

One winter, when snow lay thick on the ground, a party of six Wrens flew past my window to Star's favourite nest-box, then occupied by Baldhead as a roost. Five of them perched on a twig above the box while the sixth clung to the entrance hole and peered inside. To their disappointment Baldhead was already in his roost; they twittered together and did not seem to know where to go, for a few minutes they settled down on the twig, cuddled close together with their feathers fluffed out – a compact ball of Wrens. I opened my window wide, hoping they might come indoors, but they soon flew away over the hedge to seek shelter elsewhere. Probably their usual roost was snowbound.

I had a contrasting summer picture in August last year. I was standing by the bird-table when a Wren flew past me, hurriedly crept up the Japonica on the cottage wall, then hopped to the top of the open french window. Spreading its wings and tail, it lay there to sunbathe, looking so completely different in this pose from the perky Jenny Wren with the cocked tail that we are accustomed to see. The sun lit its plumage to a rich reddish brown, the tail was held flat and fully spread like an open fan; a lovely little bird when it shows the wide span of its feathers. Later I saw the Wren family, five of them, sunbathing on a wood-pile. But, like the Tree Creeper, the busy Wren seldom seems to spare time for relaxations.

3. HOUSE SPARROWS; GRIMES AND NOGOOD

There are always far too many Sparrows in my garden and as they frequently molest other species and, in spring, drive away the migrants that might stay to nest, I never encourage them and do not allow them long on the bird-table. I have only to show the crook of my walking-stick and shout 'Sparrows' for them all to fly away. The other species remain, knowing that this is not meant for them any more than my hand-clapping and shouting on the approach of Magpies, cats, etc. It is the crook of my stick that the Sparrows fear. This dates back eleven years to the time when a young Sparrow refused to come out from under my bed and I pulled it out on the crook of my stick and put it outside. Ever since that day, all the Sparrows of all the flocks that come to my garden have feared the sight of the crook in my hand.

Every year I have battles with the Sparrows to prevent them from building under the dormer window tiles. One pair, called Grimes and Nogood, at last learnt that this was forbidden. Last year I saw Grimes, the male, perched on this window with a straw in his beak. I shouted, 'No. Not there!' He looked down at me, dropped the straw, gave a squawk and flew to the hedge. But when my back was turned he brought more straws until I effectively blocked up the crevice.

Last March Grimes began displaying in front of a Tit's nest-box for the benefit of Nogood, who took no interest in the box. I temporarily removed it, thinking Grimes would then fly away, but he remained on the twigs that had surrounded the box and continued displaying in front of the vacant space, as before, with lowered head and tail, his back humped and the feathers on it raised. Every few moments he stretched his head up to the level where previously he had been able to look through the entrance hole of the box, but now there was no hole to look at and he gave quick gapes, this opening and shutting of his beak meaning that he wanted the missing box. I find this particular type of gape usually means that the bird wants or misses something. Nogood was perched just above with her back turned towards him. He interrupted his display to give her tail a sharp pull, she immediately swung round and pecked him. He continued displaying as before and she roughly tugged at his tail, but he took no notice and appeared engrossed in moving his head up and down, gaping each time his head was level with the missing entrance hole. She turned her back on him, he began squawking then flew to another Tit's nest-box. The owner flew at him with scold-notes then entered the box and remained inside until Grimes and Nogood flew away.

The love affairs of Sparrows are not beautiful. I have sometimes seen the female grasp her mate by the beak, swing him off his perch and dangle him in the air. He kicks out with his feet and tries to regain his perch but is at the mercy of his ruthless mate who apparently gets satisfaction from torturing him, so she will not let go her hold for a minute or more. It is typical of this species to torment other birds and they do the same to their mates, or when courting.

A year or two ago, for purposes of identification, I rouged the cheeks of one Sparrow and the underparts of another, using some of Peter Scott's special dye, harmless to birds, which he uses on his Geese for the same purpose. To the human eye, the pink cheeks and breast greatly improved the appearance of the Sparrows but when I released them and they joined their flock there was a terrific babble lasting half an hour; the painted Sparrows were the cause, they were being mobbed and that evening they had to leave my garden and never returned. A few weeks later I read reports of a rare, brightly coloured, foreign Sparrow having been seen in a town six miles south of my cottage. When in the early winter of 1953 a Great Tit with reddish pink flanks came to my cottage I was in no hurry to report a rare species! He stayed all the winter, none of the other Tits objected to his unusual colouring and when he left in March, to nest elsewhere, there were yellow bars across the pink flanks, which meant that the natural colouring would soon return.

One September a Budgerigar was flying around my garden for two weeks, calling loudly in the morning and evening. He often perched on the wires near my windows but the Sparrows plagued him and pulled his tail. He retorted with an angry medley of notes which intimidated the tormentors a little though they never left him alone and were always pecking him from behind or pulling his feathers. At the end of the fortnight he had little tail left and what remained was ragged and torn. The Tits took no notice of him except for one close inspection to satisfy their curiosity. One day, directly he flew from the wire by my cottage, a Nuthatch alighted on the identical spot where he had been perched. The quick change from one blue bird to another was fascinating – they were both so beautifully coloured but so very different, as was their flight. The Budgerigar in flight often reminded me of a Hawk in miniature, as he swept across the garden or over the hedge to the fields to feed. Sparrows always followed after him in a straggling mob; he could never get rid of them. The call of the Budgerigar resembled the Sparrow's in rhythm but it was higher pitched, sounded more dominant and carried much farther. One of my young Sparrows learnt a good imitation of the Budgerigar note but the compliment was not returned. Escaped Budgerigars often join with a flock of Sparrows, perhaps because of the slight similarity of call-note and the same choice of food.

4. NUTHATCHES, IN GARDEN AND WOOD

There are not many Nuthatches in my immediate neighbourhood but in early autumn one sometimes pays a short visit to the hazel-nut tree in my orchard. He was there in September a year or two ago, whistling in his clear, musical voice, 'Chwit-chwit,' many times repeated from a conspicuous perch. Between the loud calls he flicked his wings and looked around, then flew over the garden singing 'Pee-pee-pee-pee-pee,' rapped out in a rhythm as sharp as the quick notes of percussion he strikes with his strong bill when hammering at bark or nuts. He was then quiet for a while but when a hazel nut fell with a rattle on an iron roof by the tree, he uttered a loud ejaculation and flew away. The nuts were mostly rotten that year.

A Starling, singing near the hazel tree, at once copied the Nuthatch's notes and added them to his chattering song. It was a welcome addition, for this Starling's last imitation was the clicking sound of my mop, made when it was shaken to free it from dust. He vigorously shook his head backwards and forwards when singing the mop-tune, as if imitating the movement as well as the sound; it was perfect mimicry but it had been overdone and grown stale. The mop-tune was now discarded, and all the autumn this echo of the Nuthatch's call was constantly repeated. A month later my Song Thrush produced a fine imitation of the Nuthatch notes which perfectly suited his clear voice. Some species, including the Thrush, usually let a few weeks elapse before bringing out their imitations, but Starlings, with the forwardness of their race, instantly brandish a new crib!

The Nuthatch did not appear again until the following April. His call came from a tree nearby while I was feeding my birds at the french window. The next moment he darted down, seized a piece of bread and flew back to the tree-trunk, where he inserted it into a crack of the bark, then hammered with his beak as if it were a nut. Having spilled more than he ate, he quickly returned for more, this time taking three crusty bits and wedging them into the crack but restraining his blows. After eating several more pieces in this manner, he tried a small lump of margarine. This stuck to the roof of his bill and I saw him open his beak wide to lick it off with his tongue. A chunk of suet on the bird-table was surrounded by Blue Tits and when he tried to get near this they pressed closer to the fat with a slight display of spread wings and protesting twitters. So the Nuthatch in a determined manner, speedily rolled each Blue Tit over by energetically pushing it from underneath with his bill. He then hammered loudly at the suet and took a piece to his crevice, ate it and returned to the bird-table, where he picked up a small fragment of fat, and with this held in his beak, darted from one side of the bird-table to the other as if uncertain what to do with it. Finally he poked it inside a hollow stick which jutted from the bird-table. This stick afterwards became his usual depository for food taken up after his appetite had worn off. A Blue Tit discovered this larder and made a habit of looking inside and helping himself to the contents.

The Nuthatch this time stayed in my garden for a fortnight. He sang and preened close to my window and drank from the bird-bath without fear when I was standing beside it. If there was no bread on the bird-table when he was hungry he uttered a soft, flute-like whistle then perched upside down on the edge of the table with his head turned towards the ground, watching for me to throw some to him. He always liked three pieces at a time to insert into his crevice. Once he dug out a hazel nut shell from the turf; it was empty and I had only one left of this kind to offer him, so I tried giving him peanuts. Surprisingly these were not to his liking, he flung them away and wanted bread or suet, which seemed his favourite food. This does not apply to all Nuthatches; birds have individual tastes within the species.

One morning, at the end of a fortnight, I watched the Nuthatch flitting from branch to branch of a tall tree, whistling an imperative-toned single note, in rhythm like the morse code. In between these notes he sometimes inserted the fledgling call, gently uttered while the rest of the song was loud and penetrating. Occasionally he gave two little taps at a branch, then lifted his head and continued singing. Presently he flew to a topmost twig of the tree and from this conspicuous perch repeatedly sang his lovely bubbling note. This song I only heard from him in spring. Suddenly, like an arrow, he shot down from the tree-top to drive away two Blue Tits who were chasing each other lower down in the tree. He then returned to his high perch and continued his song, while often looking in every direction as if expecting a mate to arrive but no female appeared. This Nuthatch seemed intolerant of Blue Tits. He never chased or took notice of Great Tits or other small birds but if there were any Blue Tits on the bird-table when he wanted food, he always swept them away before beginning his meal.

The next day the Nuthatch left my garden. I lost sight of him for a few days, then discovered he was nesting on the verge of a wood half a mile from my garden. When I arrived, his mate was carrying leaves to a nest-box hung to a great oak-tree. They plastered the rather large entrance hole with mud until there was only just room for them to enter the box. While she worked at her nest inside the box, he fetched mud and, perched at the entrance hole, stretched up his neck inside the box to plaster the interior of the roof. Later this plastered ceiling fell on the nestlings; they were not hurt by the disaster and human hands removed the plaster which was covering them.

The Nuthatch was very attentive to his mate; he fed her when she was sitting on the nest or sometimes coaxed her off it by calling 'Chwit-it-it,' from a bough above the nest-box. She fluttered her wings to him, making baby-cries which he also uttered while she swallowed the food he gave her. He continued to do a little plastering even after she had begun brooding her eggs, but whatever his occupation, he left it instantly if a Blue Tit appeared within view, returning to his work when he had chased it away.

One day, after the Nuthatches' nest was completed, two Mistle-Thrushes flew to a high fork in the same oak tree. The female carried a small twig or root in her beak, the male churred loudly and chased off any bird that went near the fork. While she built her nest he often perched in an alert pose on a lower branch of the oak and each time a Nuthatch alighted on this branch, which was their route to the nest-box, the Mistle-Thrush churred excitedly, flicked his wings and rushed at the Nuthatch who then ran along underneath or at the side of the bough and darted down and round the trunk to the nesting-box. The Nuthatches were never intimidated; with their natural agility they were more than a match for the excitable big Thrush.

The Mistle-Thrush, churring loudly, also dived from above at a Blackbird, hunting for food under the oak. The Blackbird, with alarm notes, left hurriedly. When a Magpie flew close to the fork a thundering battle took place with much wing flapping and a din of hysterical churring and shrill chattering. The Magpie was driven off and pursued by the Mistle-Thrush far across the field beyond the wood.

After several days the 'Stormcock' became quieter and stopped chasing small birds, except for an occasional dive from the tree-top to churr at the imperturbable Nuthatches. The name Stormcock was given to the Mistle-Thrush because he sings through rough weather, but this title equally fits his tempestuous territorial behaviour.

When the Nuthatch nestlings were first hatched the male passed all food for them to his mate who received it through the entrance hole. After a few days she was often away seeking food for the young herself when he arrived at the nest-box, he then seemed uncertain whether to enter the nest or await her return and kept poking his head inside the entrance hole, then withdrawing to look around for her. If she came within a minute or two he gave her the food after she had entered the nest but if she was long in returning he finally fed the nestlings himself. After they were a week old he always entered without hesitation to feed them and did not give her the food even if she was on the nest when he arrived.

On 10th June I visited the Nuthatches at 5.30 p.m. and found one of the young was leaning out of the entrance hole with its head craned upwards, intently gazing at the leafy world above its nest. It remained in this pose for many minutes, then slowly moved its head from side to side as it examined all within its view. When the father-bird arrived it was pushed back into the nest, for parent birds do not encourage fledglings to flight from the nest so late in the day. Directly the father had flown off, the fledgling heaved half its body out of the entrance hole then stretched its neck into the quaintest poses while resuming its inspection of the outside world. The delicate colouring of the fledgling Nuthatch – paler than in the adult – is very lovely. Soon the mother-bird arrived and pushed the youngster right inside the nest, where she stayed for a while, apparently to keep the fledglings from flight that evening.

The next morning, when I entered the wood at 9.30, a high-pitched churring note came from the high fork of the oak tree. A fledgling Mistle-Thrush was uttering this call, perched all alone on the rim of its empty nest. A moment later it flew towards the rest of the brood. The cheerful whistle of the Nuthatch came from deeper in the wood. His brood too, had flown that morning.

The following spring I saw another Nuthatch fly with noisy notes at a Blue Tit who had just been inspecting a nest hole in an oak tree. The Nuthatch had no interest in the hole, for he and his mate were nesting in a wood over the road, but it seems that some Nuthatches cannot resist teasing Blue Tits. In this case the Tit's anger rose, both birds struck out at each other with their feet and an excited air battle ensued. The Nuthatch soon gave way and flew to another tree, leaving the Blue Tit with its head feathers standing on end through excitement while uttering loud scold-notes as he returned to his hole in the oak tree. The Nuthatch, being a stronger and bigger bird, could easily have won if he had tried but in bird-law the Blue Tit had right on his side so the Nuthatch let him win.

Last autumn another male, from his appearance a first-year bird, often sang from the tree-tops in my orchard. Soon a young female appeared and in December she began coming to my window-ledge for food; a day later he came but at first was nervous of perching on the glass food container and tried to take bread from it while hovering on the wing. As the other birds got in his way he eventually perched, after watching her do it several times. At the time of writing they have been regular visitors to the window-sill for a month. They often stretch up their necks to look indoors when the Tits are flying in and out of the rooms and feeding on my hand near the window; I am expecting them to enter one day and am hoping this pair will remain to nest in my garden. They both like cheese, bread and sunflower seeds better than peanuts. They pick up these seeds and test them by holding in their beaks with upturned heads, as if weighing them; those of poor quality are tossed away, the others taken to eat in their usual manner, by wedging in a crack of a tree branch and hammering at them. The cheese pellets and bread crumbs they eat as if they were swallowing pills, with their heads uptilted while gulping them down. Their conversational notes on the window-ledge are softly spoken and often I hear a whispered trill uttered by both birds when they meet by the window. These two Nuthatches are friendly to all the Blue Tits and other species that feed with them on the sill.

CHAPTER II

Taming and Attracting the Birds

Many people have written asking me how to get birds hand-tame and as it was impossible to answer all of the letters a few words here may be useful, although it seems to depend upon the individuals, the bird and the person, how this comes about. One or two bird lovers have told me their difficulty is that birds do not like to see their eyes, they have to shut them or turn their heads away before the bird will come near. With me it is the reverse, the birds usually perch opposite and want to catch my eye before they make their first flight to me and nearly always they look up at my eyes when on my hand, this exchange of looks between us one of the most important factors in our intercourse, even from the beginning.

Some birds are more timid than others; these nervous ones usually prefer to take food from the hand without perching on it until they are used to the look of flesh at close quarters. When trying to tame a wild bird never make a move towards it, let it come to you. The hand should be held quite still, with the fingers flat and small pieces of cheese on them – a food which tempts most birds. If they are accustomed to people standing near the bird-table while they feed, the hand can be held against the edge of the table. Birds are encouraged by being talked to in a friendly tone; the call 'come on' or any simple words should be used, keeping to the same call so that it is connected with the offer of food.

The peculiar lip-squeakings many people make when trying to tame birds often frightens them; if visitors do it to mine they fly away in fear and they do not like my doing it. Caged birds probably get much of this so they become accustomed to it – like human babies to the baby-talk used by some mothers. But it must be remembered that birds are intelligent creatures and they should be treated as such to get the best from them. Imitations of their calls are unsatisfactory and unnecessary for intimate intercourse with birds; for one thing a perfect imitation is not possible and would not sound like the real notes to the birds (it never does to the human, and birds have much sharper ears for their own language). Although they would respond to any sound made by the person who offers them food, much more is gained by using the human language, for the bird understands something of what is said by the tone of voice and even learns to know the sound of some simple words, whereas if lip-squeaking or imitations of their notes are used it not only sounds silly but is treating the bird as a creature incapable of learning or understanding anything; this attitude is not the right one for getting intelligent responses or for making the bird feel at ease. People do not make barking noises to dogs and birds have more sensitive ears than a dog for learning to know different sounds. Birds notice all noises and from curiosity they will often investigate the source of any sound whether it is caterwauling, whistling, playing a musical instrument or imitating bird-calls. But to gain the confidence of a bird it is best to talk to it in a friendly way. In my case, using human speech has brought astonishing results of understanding. They have got the meaning of some words from the tone of voice and because bird's are extra-sensitive the tones come through to them with more intensity than to the human; also a bird's mind works quickly, registering impressions at photographic speed and the most intelligent individuals put two and two together equally rapidly.

Most of my birds are sensitive to being laughed at by me although they do not mind a cough. They seem to know the laugh is connected with something they have done but the other sound is not. Once I offered my hand, held close to the ground, to a newcomer fledgling Great Tit. It stepped up cautiously then gave quick tugs at each of my fingers in turn, using its wings with each effort of tugging. Without thinking I laughed, regretting it immediately, for the fledgling retired in confusion and hid under foliage, nor would it again come close to me for two days. Living with birds I have to be constantly alert to their sensitive feelings, and when taming them it must always be remembered that they have extra-sensitive natures.

Naturally the first step towards attracting birds to the garden is to keep a well-stocked bird-table. Throwing food on the ground is not advisable as cats are likely to spring on them while they are engrossed in feeding. The table should be on a pole at least five feet high and there should be room on it for several birds to feed at the same time, one and a half to two feet square being a good size, and an edging about an inch high, all round, is necessary to keep the food from falling off it, also the birds like to perch on this rim. They appreciate some twigs fixed to the table to use as perches and on these, fat and bones for the Tits can be suspended. The table should not be nearer to the windows than eight feet. When some of the birds have become tame they will take food from the window-sills and various kinds of feeding appliances can be fixed high up on the window frames. These can be got from The Greenrigg Works, Woodford Green, Essex.

Some people imagine that birds can eat fermented and bad food, unfit for human consumption. Carrion Crows, Seagulls and some other species thrive on it but it is harmful to garden birds, in summer and in the nesting season it is likely to make young birds ill or even cause them to die. Except in very bad weather or during a drought it is not good to feed birds much in the nesting season as natural food is better for their young, but if the soil is hardened by a drought the Thrush species suffer much and dried currants, sultanas, scraps of meat and bread should be given them. Tits do not usually give their nestlings artificial foods but in wet or cold weather they much appreciate cheese and crushed nuts to help feed their fledglings. Fat is bad for very young birds and should not be put on the bird-table in summer, but later in the year bacon-bones, rinds and other fat attracts birds to the bird-table, as most people know. Birds also like cheese rind, with plenty of cheese left on it, cake and sweet biscuits, nuts and crusts of bread with margarine spread on them. Variety in diet is good for birds; when the only food given to Tits is a coconut they eat too much of it at a time through hunger, then they get indigestion. Together with other food I have not found coconut is harmful, as some people suppose. Processed cheese should not be given to Tits, it can make them ill, especially if it is not quite fresh. Tits and Finch tribes like hemp and sunflower seeds, the latter also attracts Nuthatches. I grow many teazels round my cottage windows for the Goldfinches. When they have stripped the teazel heads of their natural seeds I replenish them daily with French teazel seeds bought from seed merchants. My Goldfinches watch me doing this from trees nearby then they at once fly to the teazels to feed.

A bird-bath is essential if there is no brook or pond near the garden. Any large vessel will do if a stone bird-bath is not obtainable. I have many different kinds of baths for my birds, and find that an old dustbin lid on the ground is the most popular with some of them, while others prefer the raised stone bath.

Tits like drinking out of tall vessels, such as jam jars, and one should be kept full of water on the bird-table or hung to a tree-branch.

When I have primroses, violets or cowslips in flower vases the Great Tits pick out the flowers, tossing them on the table, then they drink the water from the vase, even if they have their own jar close beside it. It seems they think these flowers give the water a pleasant flavour. They occasionally do the same with some other small flowers but not as consistently as with the primroses and violets. Before cutting my lawn in spring, if I have time, I first pick some of the daisies, for I have much love of flowers, as of all else in nature, and it is a real pain to mangle all the daisies by the mower. I have often seen the Tits examining these little bowls of daisies on my table, but they never pluck them from the vases so I conclude they know that daisy-water has not an attractive taste. The ox-eye daisy quickly turns water brown and gives it a rank smell, so probably this applies to a slight degree with the lawn daisy. But how the birds know remains uncertain as they do not remove these flowers to sip the water and test the taste.

There are some people who say they 'love' birds so much that they cannot resist picking up small fledglings and taking them home with them. These 'baby-snatchers' do not really love birds or they would not thoughtlessly take them from their parents to suffer a slow death in captivity. They are also committing a punishable offence under the new Bird Protection Act, which imposes a fine of £5, to £25 for rare species, for taking eggs or birds to keep in captivity. Each spring I have frequently had newly flown fledglings of various species brought me by people who think they are helping the birds. This interference is meant well but is harmful and the same fine would apply for having taken the fledgling away from its natural surroundings. It has no chance of survival unless given constant attention from dawn until dusk and few people have time to do this or the patience to teach the fledgling to find its own food as it grows up, which is necessary before it can be let free. When eventually it is left to its own resources, after human rearing, it has not learnt anything about its natural enemies, which knowledge is gained through its parents teaching it to take cover and from watching other birds. The human cannot teach this, so it quickly meets with disaster when freed after hand rearing. If a fledgling is found on a road it should be placed in a bush or in the hedge and left for its parents to feed. There is far too much interference with birds these days, and everyone should see that people who are ignorant of the Bird Protection laws are told about them.

It is not fair to encourage birds to tameness if a cat is kept in the house; sooner or later it ends in disaster to the birds. Some people have no scruples over this and say that it is 'Nature' for cats to kill birds. I have even known a woman say to her child, who had rescued a Thrush from the jaws of a cat, 'Give the bird back to Pussy, it is interfering with Nature to take it away.' It never occurs to these people that the human is responsible for all the thousands of domestic cats that are housed and fed and so enabled to breed. If it had been 'left to Nature' there would not be any domestic cats in Britain; it is not a native animal but brought here and bred through man's interference. Therefore people should do everything possible to prevent these domestic animals killing our wild birds and no attempt should be made to tame them where cats are kept. They take a terrible toll of the young birds every year.

Anyone who has succeeded in getting a bird hand-tame should warn children on whose hands it might perch never to catch hold of it. A boy once got one of my tame Tits to come on his hand then caught hold of it by the feet. The Tit quickly wrenched itself free of the boy's grasp but in doing so its feet were badly twisted and the bird never recovered.

There are many disadvantages in having birds as intimate as mine. They can be very tyrannical and after sunrise there is often no chance to sleep, for they demand attention; if they fail to rouse me from bed they keep hammering on the iron window-catches or pluck at the curtains. Some Great Tits are even expert at unhooking the curtains from the runners and they do it more quickly than I can. One time when I was ill in bed and unable to attend to them, four Great Tits began alighting on me with the same kick-push leg movement that they employ to push their young off a perch too exposed for safety. They do it to make their young move and I could only conclude that they wanted me to move and feed them. When it did not work they tried something else.

Living with so many birds involves a terrible task of cleaning, and I have learnt much about bird parasites. The wooden screen – Star's tapping perch – was formerly covered with material. One day, when brushing it, I discovered that quantities of bird-parasites had collected between the material and the frame. This accounted for my having had occasional bites from these bird-pests which always left intense irritation for two days afterwards. I removed the material, and the frame makes an excellent bird perch.

After this experience I studied the ways of these parasites and found that if a roost-box is lined, pests accumulate underneath the lining, whereas a bird can keep an unlined box free of pests. I have seen Tits removing cardboard linings which I had put to strengthen the floors of some roosts, the fleas underneath were the reason, for the birds were troubled with them at night. The same applies to outdoor boxes; if nest material is left inside, the birds cannot keep the roost free from parasites and insects. I clean out their indoor roosts every day or two and spread fresh newspaper daily underneath their principal preening perches. Last year two of the Tits that sleep near my bed used to keep me awake by sharply pecking their roosts during the night; they were catching troublesome fleas. I lined both their boxes with velvet, spreading Pestroy underneath the stuff. This was successful both in killing the pests and stopping the Tits (Pippa one of them) from pecking the roosts. Preparations containing D.D.T. should never be used as it is harmful to birds, but Pestroy is not.

When Pippa first entered her velvet-lined roost she came out again quickly and gave me a prolonged look of disapproval. I pretended not to notice her and she flew out of the window, very displeased. She wanted me to remove the lining. Presently she returned, peered inside her roost then stared piercingly at me. Finding that I would not obey her wishes she entered the box and made frantic efforts to pull out the velvet herself but it was pinned to the cardboard. Eventually she settled down to sleep although she fidgeted much during the night and I heard the dull thuds of sharp pecks on her velvety couch. The next morning she spent much time again trying to haul out the lining, between her efforts she gave me many cross looks and uttered protesting notes because I would not remove it for her. However, that night Pippa slept without stirring and I had no more displeased looks for my interference with her roost. As the lining had to be constantly cleaned and sprinkled underneath with Pestroy before replacing and pinning to the floor of the roost I agree with the Tits that unlined boxes are best, – except for the ones above my bed!

I put a good selection of nest-boxes in my garden and the Great Tits make their choice with great care. Once they have started to build they never change to another box. Cases of desertion can, however, easily occur if they are disturbed in any way while building; even movement caused by strong wind to an insecurely fixed nest-box might cause desertion, so care should be taken to see that all boxes are firmly fixed to a solid support such as a tree-trunk or wall. The entrance hole of a Tit's box should be the size of half a crown and it should be eight to nine inches from the floor of the box. This gives the young a better chance of survival, for if the hole is too easy for them to reach they leave the nest before they are sufficiently strong on the wing to cope with the dangers that beset them once they have flown. Nuthatches seem to enjoy plastering the entrances to their nest-boxes so for them the holes can be a little larger.

CHAPTER 12

Migrants in the Garden

1. BLACKCAPS

When the migrant Warblers return, several of these species spend some days in my garden even if they do not stay to nest. Usually in late April a pair of Blackcaps have come and remained for two or three weeks. One year they started to nest. The work of building was shared between them but the female was more practical; when she had gathered her material she took it straight to the nest. Her mate, after picking up some bents, would begin to sing from a bush, the grasses still held in his beak. Often the neighbours' cats pestered them and the singer bravely challenged the enemy; perched just above it, he shouted alarm cries as he danced up and down in agitation; with head feathers erected and wings flapping, he looked a little fiend of fury. When I ran to him with loud hand-clapping he was unafraid and remained on his perch to watch the cat slink away through the bushes. But it returned so persistently that the Blackcaps were driven elsewhere to nest. The way the Blackcap challenges cats is most wonderful to see, and it is typical of the spirited temperament of these little Warblers.

When several get together their behaviour is even more exciting to watch, as I found when five came to my garden one year. The first to arrive, on 24th April, was, I think, the same bird that had come for two weeks the previous spring, for he sang similar imitative Throstle notes, sounding like a bugle call, as a prelude to his song. For two days, Bugle, as I called him, sang continually; then he perched conspicuously, high on a tall tree and for a while sang very loudly, often turning his head searchingly in every direction, as if looking for another bird to appear. Afterwards he flew away, across a field. It seemed he was looking for his mate, as the previous year she had appeared soon after he did. When he returned two days later a female was with him. She remained inactive on her perch, with feathers fluffed out to exclude the cold, for there was a bitter north-east wind with occasional snow showers. Bugle sang more quietly than before and other birds in my garden were almost silenced by the weather, which has much influence on bird-song.

The next day two more male Blackcaps arrived, and the following morning a fifth bird appeared. At first he kept to my front garden but by noon he had joined the others in the orchard. They all fed frequently and amicably on the berries of a huge ivy bush that smothered a tall pear tree in the overgrown hedge. These ivy berries seemed to be the only food they could find, as the prolonged bad weather, with exceptionally late leafing of trees, had caused a food shortage for Tits and Warblers. My garden was still quite bare of leaf – an advantage for watching Blackcaps, which often are hidden by foliage that is usually well advanced when they arrive. When not feeding, the males warbled quietly in sheltered corners of the orchard; only occasionally did they break into full song.

While the weather remained cold, Bugle made no objection to the other three males feeding close beside him on the berries, but when, on 3rd May, it turned milder he became possessive of the pear tree ivy. Directly the other males flew to it he faced them with raised crown feathers, wings lowered and held stiffly, tail alternately outspread and closed, while he uttered sharp notes. At first the others answered Bugle's display by drooping their wings and warbling softly; then they burst into loud song phrases and, with forms distorted in display, began to retreat by degrees from the pear tree. Bugle followed, shouting loud phrases, short and declamatory, excitedly raising and lowering his black crown feathers and performing acrobatic twists of his body. Suddenly his three opponents turned tail and flitted silently into West Orchard. Bugle remained on his perch, his head held up in a defiant attitude while he watched them out of sight. As a parting thrust he shouted some sharp notes, then he returned to the pear tree ivy.

Bugle had won the first round, but the others soon came back to battle for the berries. The Blackcaps' method of warfare was a delightful exhibition of fantastic poses and wing-spreading, in which Bugle always excelled. Frequently they bowed their heads to their feet, showing off their black crowns. In turn Bugle's three opponents took time off to snatch berries from the ivy; when all had fed they dispersed to different corners of the orchard, where they warbled softly and continuously. Bugle remained near the pear tree with the female, who had taken no part in the disputes. Every few minutes the others broke into loud song, then flitted to the ivy. Sometimes they did not rouse Bugle from his quiet singing, at others there was disputing as before.

The Blackcaps were not afraid of my presence, perhaps because they were reassured by watching the resident birds perching on me. Often Bugle and his opponents flew close above my head and alighted within reach of an outstretched hand. How lovely they looked, with their silvery-white breasts, jet-black crowns and mantles of dove grey!

A Garden Warbler also had come to the orchard. He kept apart and generally fed on the berries while the Blackcaps were engrossed in disputes. The pear tree ivy was alive with birds all day long, for many species ate its berries; two Jays, two Wood-pigeons, two Mistle-Thrushes, eight Blackbirds and four Song Thrushes. Always the Mistle-Thrushes charged at the Blackbirds if they fed near, the Blackbirds went for the Throstles, the Throstles flew at the Blackcaps and Garden Warbler, and the Blackcaps sometimes chased off the Garden Warbler.

On 4th May it rained heavily until evening and all the Blackcaps were quieter. When the sun shone the following morning Bugle paid attention to courting and chased the silent female round the pear tree several times. Afterwards she preened and basked in the sunshine on an adjoining tree, while the four males sang superbly from different parts of the orchard. Bugle was the best musician, his song having many original tunes and also imitations of Blackbird and Throstle. When the battles were resumed he produced the new weapon of a high grating note, uttered while displaying with his wings. The others did not use this.

After 5th May the three males usually approached the ivy separately; if they met near it, each bird displayed mildly at the other. Bugle and his mate always kept on the pear tree or the hedge below and I hoped that his excited displaying and possessive disputes meant that the pair were going to nest in my orchard, but food, not nesting territory, must have attracted them, for on 10th May all the berries were finished and the next day the five Blackcaps had gone.

From what I have seen, Blackcaps do not always mate on their nesting territory. One year, after a pair had stayed for two weeks in my garden, I saw the male in pre-mating display on a tree beside my window. He was perched three feet above her, his wings held widespread and motionless, tail flared and head bent forward to look down at her. She remained with wings slightly raised above her back. Both birds kept quite still for several moments, – a beautiful sight. Then he flew down and mating took place. Directly afterwards they left my garden to nest elsewhere – I think in a spinney about ten minutes' walk away – but every few days the Blackcap male paid me a short visit in the evening and gave me the joy of hearing his lovely song.

As with Chiff-Chaffs and other Warblers, far fewer Blackcaps have come to this district the last two or three years. The single bird that passed through my garden this year gave me the thrill of entering the window and perching on the inside ledge where he remained for a minute, staring into the room and at me with crown feathers raised, apparently at me for there were no other birds indoors at that moment. He only stayed two days, which I greatly regretted for there is no bird I love more than the Blackcap, with his fine song and fascinating ways.

Nightingales have increased in this neighbourhood. At the time of writing a pair have been in my orchard for two weeks and each night I have had the joy of his song, coming from outside my East window.

2. GARDEN WARBLERS AND LESSER WHITETHROATS

On 26th May last year two Garden Warblers were preening on the medlar tree behind the cottage while I was standing by it. They watched with interest when Tinky flew up and took a peanut from my hand and one of them inquisitively perched close beside him to see what he was eating held between his toes, alternately leaning over to examine the Tit's nut and looking at me as if wondering whether I had food for Warblers as well. Unfortunately I had not, so missed a chance of enticing the Garden Warbler to my hand. He looked so attractive with his crown feathers raised while in close proximity to the Tit.

These Garden Warblers did not stay to nest in my garden but it was probably the same couple that brought their young in July for a few weeks. They frequently fed on the small sweet fruit of a tall plum tree in my hedge. These half-wild little plums attracted many birds, particularly a pair of Lesser Whitethroats who had reared a late brood in my garden hedge. They were possessive of the tree and spent much time on it, sunbasking and feeding their fledglings on the fruit. When the Garden Warblers flew to the plum tree there was much exchange of the 'tac, tac' notes then the Lesser Whitethroats flew away but returned directly the Garden Warbler family had finished feeding. There was rivalry between these species because both had young to feed. The Lesser Whitethroats did not leave the tree when the other species fed on the plums. Willow-Warblers, Robins, Blackbirds, Thrushes, Starlings and Greater Whitethroats all liked the fruit but their manner of eating it differed; the Blackbirds made rough stabs at a plum, clumsily knocked it to the ground, then tried another, several falling before they succeeded in picking one and carrying it off to consume on the lawn. The Starlings were even more clumsy – I chased them away for they stripped the boughs greedily. The Thrushes were gentle and gave neat pecks like the Warblers; the latter often clung to the fruit upside down like Tits. I have also seen Blackcaps eating fruit in this manner.

One of the young Lesser Whitethroats became quite tame. It perched on the bird-table or on my window-ledges to look inside the rooms; often it came close to me and stared into my face with interest but it would not eat artificial food so I could not entice it to my hand. Such a charming fledgling it was, the texture of its plumage so soft and the pearly white underparts lovely in contrast to the grey mantle and darker grey head. It held up its head more than other birds, showing its white chin to the full. Often the two fledglings basked on a bare branch in the sunlight with their beaks pointing to the sky, as if bleaching their white throats. Once I saw the mother bird resting on a sunlit branch, her two fledglings perched close on either side with their heads upturned and tilted sideways to lean against her.

The fledglings did not, like most other young birds, vibrate their wings when food begging, but they uttered an insistent baby-cry sounding something like 'gweet, gweet,' this repeated on an accelerando while being fed. By 16th August the mother bird only fed them in the early morning and evening but she liked to have them near her and kept a close watch on their movements. When the tame one was with me by the cottage she often called from the plum tree. It flew to her with the clear-cut 'tac, tac' notes, which seem to serve many purposes. The father bird I now rarely saw, he had lost interest in the young. Very occasionally he sang his rattling phrase in a soft tone.

When their young were fully independent the rivalry of the Garden Warblers and Lesser Whitethroats vanished and they fed side by side on the few remaining plums.

On 16th August the Garden Warbler sang a beautiful and varied subsong, except for this the call-note was all that he uttered during that month.

Often I watched the fledgling Lesser Whitethroats going from branch to branch of the plum tree with persecuting House Sparrows at their heels. If the fledglings paused a moment the Sparrows roughly pecked and squawked at them, so that they cried and moved on and, unless I intervened, the Sparrows frequently molested them so much that they flew away. House Sparrows are very objectionable in their behaviour towards other species, which makes me dislike them.

3. WILLOW WARBLERS AND SPOTTED FLYCATCHERS

A pair of Willow Warblers always nest in my garden and last August, 1953, the young ones often watched the Tits feeding from my hand. As they like chasing Tits it sometimes happened that one alighted on my foot or knee behind the Tit it was chasing. One day, as I stood by the open french window, a Willow Warbler flew towards me from the trees at the bottom of my garden, a long flight, swift and straight. It brushed past my shoulder, flew round me and alighted on the inside of the window frame. After looking through the glass a moment it again flew past me then round the room and out at the fanlight. It appeared to be exploring the cottage and seemed to have learnt the fanlight exit from watching the Tits. Although Willow Warblers are each year continually around the cottage, many of them only passing migrants, they have never hit against the glass or tried to fly out of closed windows, so I conclude their eyesight is especially good.

In mid-September last year, while sitting on the lawn, I watched a Willow Warbler several times repeat a flight into the cottage through the open french window and out through the fanlight after pausing a moment on the sill. It then chased the Great Tit, Presto, who was flying towards me with the intention of perching to take food, but he had to fly round me four times with the Willow Warbler at his heels, their speed so fast I felt in the centre of a whirlpool with the noise of fast-beating wings loudly vibrating in my ears. Presto increased his pace, hoping to outdo his pursuer, but the Willow Warbler has a swift flight in chasing games and it skimmed through the air as if it were no effort. The Great Tit made more fuss over his quick speed and his fast-flapping wings fanned me and blew out my hair. On the fifth round Presto snatched food from my hand without perching and it was the Willow Warbler behind him that alighted for a moment, looked up at my face then flew off for more fun, – chasing Spotted Flycatchers.

Three days previously two Spotted Flycatchers had arrived in my garden and taken territories on the front of the cottage roof, one claiming the left the other the right side. There are phone wires on the right and electricity wires on the left of the roof and they glided from these wires down to the eaves and up to the ridge of the roof then back again, keeping this up continuously from 3.30 until 6 p.m. Occasionally the phone-wire Flycatcher encroached a little on the electric-wire side of the roof but when he did this the electric Flycatcher turned round and spat at him, so it sounded, which sent the intruder back to his own side. I see many cases of territory ownership occurring over food supplies especially among these passage migrants (as with the Blackcaps and the pear tree ivy). There were more flies on the electric Flycatcher's side because his territory had the warmth of the sun while the other side was shaded by trees. A Willow Warbler watched these Flycatchers a moment then decided to have some fun. While the phone Flycatcher went down and up the roof after flies, the Willow Warbler persistently flew after him, his beak within an inch of the Flycatcher's tail. The latter took no notice except for occasionally turning to look at the Willow Warbler as he alighted behind him.

Two days later there were three Spotted Flycatchers on the roof. The third bird upset the territorial arrangements of the first two and they all started snapping at each other with clicking beaks and making hissing sounds, as well as uttering their call-notes 'tzee-tzucc.' Sometimes, too, I heard a softer note several times repeated, this being one of their rarer songs and seldom heard in September.

Sparrows often crept up the back of the roof to the ridge and tried to peck the Flycatchers when they perched there but they snapped back so loudly that the Sparrows usually retired and for once were unsuccessful in their persecutions. On 22nd September the Flycatchers left to continue their journey southwards.

This year a pair began to build in a coconut shell loosely suspended on string from my window-frame. It was like a hooded cradle in shape, partially open in front, and it swung to and fro at the slightest touch or breeze. For two days they kept entering it and made spitting sounds at any other bird that went near. The third day the female began bringing moss, her mate accompanied her and sang his warbling song while clinging to the coconut and looking at her. Suddenly he seized the lower rounded edge of the opening in his beak and tugged the coconut with him as far as the string permitted, fluttering his wings rapidly as if making a great effort to pull it away with him. He repeated this many times during the day. No doubt he was trying to flatten out the curved edge of the coconut so that they could see each other from the nest. I have noticed that the Spotted Flycatcher likes keeping an eye on his mate from perches opposite while she sits and she watches all his movements while brooding her eggs. The deep bowl of the coconut would not allow this. Probably for that reason they usually choose flat sites with an open view in front, and only occasionally nest in holes.

The fourth day one of the Flycatchers flew into the room through the fanlight above their nest. From the other room I heard the flutter of wings against a closed window but thought it was the Chaffinch, whom I had helped out several times that day, so decided that it was time he found his own way through the fanlight. When a few minutes later I entered the room, a newspaper on the sill had blown against the window pane and the Flycatcher was fluttering in a panic, caught between the glass and the paper. Directly I removed the newspaper the Flycatcher stood still and turned his head to look up at me, all fear now over. It seemed he knew I would help him for he stepped on my hand of his own accord and let me raise him level with the fanlight, then he flew out. Much to my grief the charming Flycatchers deserted the coconut the next day, perhaps because of this frightening incident, but more probably because they disliked the shape of this rocking cradle, which the male, with all his efforts, had been unable to alter.

The Warblers and Flycatchers in my garden make frequent use of the bird-bath. One day three Willow Warblers went in together and seemed to enjoy themselves immensely; while splashing they turned their heads to look at each other, and often they came out for a second to give their feathers a quick shake then returned to the water for more splashing. As usual the nagging Sparrows put an end to their fun by perching on the rim of the bath and leaning forwards to peck them when they came within reach, so they all flew away.

Watching birds bathing can be very amusing. One September I saw two Blue Tits splashing in a cattle trough. The water only reached the brim where three inches of the outward bent rim was broken off, and here the Blue Tits clung with their feet, dipping their hind parts while fluttering their wings to splash water over them – although only the wing-tips reached the water – then turning round to dip their heads and the front of their bodies. They continued doing this for many minutes. Meanwhile a Blackcap saw them from a bush nearby and flew down to try bathing in the same manner, but when he leant forward he could not reach the water for the rim was only broken where the Tits were perched. The Blackcap kept looking at the Blue Tits then trying to copy them but it was impossible. He stood on the broad rim, looking very puzzled, then flew back to his branch but quickly returned to the trough and after another unsuccessful effort to copy the Blue Tits he flew into the middle of the trough, stretched down his legs and rapidly dipped them while giving his wings a quick flutter on the surface of the water. He flew back to the rim for a second before repeating this dip several times, getting his legs thoroughly wet and a few drops of water on his underparts. The Blue Tits continued splashing heads and tails alternately until all their feathers looked wet.

A Blackbird, last winter, tried to solve the same bathing problem as the Blackcap. The deep tub, usually full of water, which he had been accustomed to use in the same way as the Blue Tits used the trough, was only half-full; bending low he made many efforts to reach the water but, like the Blackcap, he failed. He stared into the tub for a moment then jumped to the water and floated with outstretched wings on the surface while rapidly dipping his forehead several times. Laboriously he flew out, wet underneath but his upper parts dry, except for his forehead. He did not repeat this; if his wings and body had got too wet he would have been unable to fly from the water. When birds stay a long while in the bird-bath they have difficulty in flying directly afterwards, probably for this reason many small species, particularly Warblers, have a habit of leaving the bath every few seconds to shake their feathers before having another splash. This would prevent their plumage getting too sodden.

In late August this year a Garden Warbler took a fancy for bathing several times daily in a flower-pot saucer by the french window, – this being a bird-bath favoured by Tit fledglings. He was afraid to step into the saucer but clung to the rim and used the Blue Tits' head and tail method of splashing water over him. Although he got only a few drops on his plumage he kept leaving the saucer to shake his wings on a twig near by. Because of the constant wing shakings the bath took a long time and he looked quite dry at the finish! However he seemed satisfied and ignored the big bird-bath. He never minded my standing on the doorstep, looking down on him. The Garden Warbler's last bath was on 2nd September, the next day he was gone.

4. TURTLE DOVES

Each spring a pair of Turtle Doves come to my garden; I think they must be the same couple, for they behave with familiarity and never move away when I approach them closely, even when they are nesting. They sometimes have perched near me apparently to watch the Tits feeding from my hand.

On 1st May, 1952, they returned together; he at once began crooning from their previous year's nesting-site, the orchard macrocarpus, where two young had been reared in a nest high in the tree. But that spring a Tawny Owl was a constant visitor to the orchard and the incessant alarm cries of many birds when the Owl appeared made the Turtle Doves choose the front garden for a nest-site.

On 7th May, seven days after their arrival, they began building in the east hedge, close to the road. They worked continuously from 10.30 until 11.30 that morning. Every few minutes he brought her thin sticks and long roots that dangled from his bill as he flew in a ceremonial flight towards the nest, to present the material to his mate with a bow. This flight was fascinating to watch; his neck was stretched upwards, his body drooped, his tail flared and pointed downwards; his pose looked nearly perpendicular while he flew, slowly, as if carrying a weighty burden. Often he remained a few moments bowing before her after presenting the material. Their building was done in silence during that hour, when they worked without a break. She left the nest at 11.30 while he was away getting material; he returned to find her absent and stayed on the nest, crooning a downward-curved single note. She soon came back and he remained beside her while she arranged the material he had brought.

For the rest of the day she rarely left the nest. By the afternoon he had stopped bringing material but often rested beside her on the nest, which I think had been completed. Sometimes they flew up together if startled by exceptionally noisy traffic on the road. When the Owl, mobbed by the birds nesting nearby, flew to the oak tree by the cottage, the male Turtle Dove perched above his nest and looked with outstretched neck towards the oak; he never joined in the mobbings, which were usually confined to two Mistle-Thrushes, Blackbirds and Chaffinches. The Owl often hooted during the day, as he has done in the succeeding years, especially at midday, 2 p.m. and 4 p.m. At dusk he sometimes perched on the wires outside my window and hooted while turning his head in every direction to search the ground for prey. Mice were plentiful around the cottage but his hoots did not aid his hunting.

All the following day (8th May) the Turtle Doves were on or close to their nest and the single down-turned notes were often heard for short periods. This single-noted, soft crooning is different from the song which gave them their name (the Handbook's 'rroorrrr'). The latter song was heard continuously each day before nest-building began and it seemed that this fuller and louder song was for territorial purposes, the crooning down-turned note for love-making and communication between the mates.

On 9th May a neighbour kept a bonfire burning all day, very close to my hedge, just below the Turtle Doves' nest so that thick smoke prevented the birds going near it. I pleaded the Turtle Doves' cause with my neighbour in vain, but everyone is not interested in birds. The result was that the next day the Turtle Doves looked for another nest-site away from my garden, which greatly distressed me, for every year they had nested with me, – it was one of the great joys of summer. Afterwards they sometimes paid me short visits but they have not again nested in my garden. The following year they chose West Garden for their nest-site and spent most of their off-time resting on the wires by my cottage, often perched close together, their bodies touching.

They were devoted mates; one year their nest was lower down than usual and built in a thorn tree close to the cottage in the back hedge, where I had a good view of them on the nest. While she brooded the eggs, he sometimes sat for an hour or more close beside her on the edge of their flat nest.

A pair of Wood Pigeons frequent my orchard every year and one July the male did much fighting with the Turtle Dove male in the oak tree by the cottage. I presume it was the males that fought; their mates kept aloof. There was much clatter of wings and the birds made odd sounds in the heat of the fray but neither suffered any harm. The Turtle Doves never remain with me after the second week in July, and a few days after the fighting began they left my garden. The Wood Pigeons often roost in the ivy bushes on my pear and oak trees, and the possessive behaviour over the oak may have been connected with this. Lorenz, in his book, *King Solomon's Ring*, mentions Doves killing each other when two different species were put together in a cage. This would not happen in natural circumstances; it is not fair to the Doves to give them a brutal character because of abnormal reactions in captivity. The human species sometimes develops similar traits under the strain of imprisonment. Many false impressions can come from watching thwarted birds in cages.

5. SWALLOWS AND HOUSE MARTINS

Alongside the brook, over the road, stand six Lombardy Poplars, seen from my window they are silhouetted against the sky in groups of three, their tall, straight forms adding beauty to the distant view of curving downland hills. These poplars also act as weather-vanes; from the swaying of their slender branches I can tell the strength and direction of the wind. I have always loved these trees, even more since one day last September when soon after sunrise, I, as usual, looked towards these poplars and found them massed with Swallows and House Martins; the trees looked almost black, so thickly were the branches laden with this migration flock.

I went closer to watch the House Martins playing their visiting game, much like they do at their nests when building in a colony. First they all settled in one tree, nearly pushing each other over as they tried to alight on branches that were already overcrowded. Soon many of them rose and after wheeling once round the trees, returned to hover before those that had remained perched in small groups and often they touched them on their beaks with much excited twittering. Then they wheeled high above, quickly coming back to pay more calls with much warbling and fluttering of wings. The game lasted for half the morning and was delightful to watch.

The Swallows flew farther afield but often perched on the wires near the poplars. Large congregations of these species are now rare in this district although when I first came to live here it was usual to see them.

A few days earlier a family of baby Swallows had perched on the electricity wire close by my window, where they were being fed by their parents. Almost immediately a Sparrow flew to the second wire below the young Swallows and, jumping up, pecked one of the babies and roughly pulled its tail. It squealed and they all flew off, never to return. Sparrows everlastingly torment other species and they prevent many from nesting in my garden, especially migratory birds that I most want to encourage.

Sometimes Swallows perch on tree-branches in my garden, especially the young ones if there is a strong wind. One August, during a gale, when they were blown backwards on the wing and borne hither and thither by the force of the wind, some families of young ones spent the afternoon on a tree in my garden, while their parents brought them food. These youngsters had difficulty in alighting because of the wind and even when perched their long wings and tails, blown by gusts, nearly overbalanced them. Sometimes two or three of them rose as if tossed into the air, and whirled round at a great pace, calling to each other in excited tones all the while. During the lulls in the gale they played 'touch me if you can' on the boughs of the tree, this being much like the young Great Tits' game. (*See* page 115.) Young Swallows and Martins often play this on the wing but it was interesting and unusual to see them clambering up the tree-branches after each other to touch beaks when this sport in flight had become difficult.

When planes were overhead the parent birds gave loud shrieks of alarm while circling above the tree but their young still clung to their perches, afraid of launching into the gale. Normally Swallows and Martins take to swift flight in sweeping circles when alarm notes are given. Perhaps they maze the enemy by their convolutions, which are hard to follow when many are on the wing, but a single bird of the Swallow species behaves in the same manner and does not seek cover or remain 'freezed' at an alarm, as do most other small birds. Hawks and other large predators may find it difficult to strike at a small bird swiftly flying in circles.

The return of the Swallows in spring and hearing their lovely song as they fly overhead is perhaps the greatest pleasure that summer brings, but there are now far too few of them in Sussex and many southern districts. Old barns for nesting have become very scarce in this overbuilt country. If all owners of old outhouses and garages, especially those that are converted farm buildings, would leave a small window open night and day during spring and summer we should perhaps get back our big Swallow population. At present they mostly go farther north, as do the House Martins.

I have kept a close watch for many years over the nesting of House Martins in this area and have found that the majority have been turned out of their nests each year by House Sparrows. Even when the Martin has had newly hatched young, Sparrows have been seen pecking both the parents and the nestlings, which they afterwards threw out of the nest. The Martins, thus persecuted, are forced to leave and the Sparrows grab the nest, while the owners build again elsewhere and often meet with the same treatment by Sparrows directly the new nest is completed. Other species also suffer these thefts, for Sparrows will do anything to grab a nest that they think suitable. They are lazy parasites and like to live at the expense of others – though they are capable of building strong dome-structured nests of their own. Their behaviour is serious in the case of the House Martin, a species rapidly declining in many parts of England.

Their nests rarely fall in this area, as there is much suitable clay soil, but last year one fell with young in it, from the eaves of a cottage in this village. The nestlings were put in a wooden box which was left on the window-ledge. The parents hovered in agitation but would not feed the young in this position, which they would consider dangerous, since cats are often seen on window sills, so the kind occupiers of the cottage fixed the box to the eaves where the nest had been. The parent Martins were delighted and quickly plastered the box to the wall in a masterly fashion, with the neatness of an expert builder. I inspected their work and found no cracks were left between the box and the wall; they also plastered the entrance hole suitably. The young flew ten days later and until they left the village, continued to use their nest-box for roosting and daytime rests, also for their usual visiting game.

In districts where their nests often fall, a small board should be placed at the base of the nest. This is done in some villages in East Anglia with the result that the bird-loving residents have the pleasure of House Martins returning year after year to build where they have the support of the boards.

CHAPTER 13

Blackbird Behaviour

1

The spring of 1950 was the fifth nesting season of my Blackbird called Darky. His mate Darkette had been with him for four years and they had kept together all the year round, as I find usual with Blackbirds. Their territory was on the east side and behind my cottage. That year the eggs of their first brood had been taken by a Magpie and a cat had got all the nestlings of a second brood. Darkette built her third nest on a tall tree-stump smothered by a thorny rambler, which looked cat-proof. Her four young were well feathered but not quite ready for flight when on 29th May I heard terrific alarm cries, better described as shrieks, coming from Darky and his mate. I rushed out and my east neighbour's cat fled from the tree-stump, where he had been on the verge of robbing the nest in which the young were crouched motionless. A few moments later, while I was putting wire round their nest, the young left it, although unable to fly properly. Their parents continued yelling hysterically from above until suddenly Darky flew to the lawn and rushed round in circles at lightning speed while continually snapping his beak in an odd way. His behaviour suggested that of a mad dog. Having let off steam in this unusual manner he suddenly stood still, panting heavily, his beak held wide open, then he ran to the bird-pool and took a long drink. Darkette was still 'tchinking' hysterically in a bush near the nest. Darky, now calmer, glanced up at her, then pulled a worm from the lawn and flew to a high perch opposite her on a wire, where he called to her in a gentle 'shreee' note. She stopped yelling and perched beside him, quivering her wings and opening her beak wide in the manner of a fledgling while he leant forward and fed her with the worm. They exchanged a few soft notes and burbling sounds, unusual to Blackbirds, then they resumed less forceful alarm cries which lasted for half an hour. The whole episode was intensely dramatic; their behaviour had been altogether unusual. The male Blackbird does not normally feed his mate nor does she make food begging displays before him. Perhaps because of their previous losses this threat to their third brood made the lasting impression on Darky which subsequent behaviour showed.

The two smallest fledglings perished, as they sought ground cover at night and would not be enticed to roost in a bush. The other two survived and as they were different in size and appearance I was able to note that Darky fed one, Darkette the other and they all seemed happy for a week. Then she began cocking her tail at him as she wanted another brood; his response was to fly to a high perch near their old nest-site, give several loud shriek-notes then fly away from her. She persisted for a week but always his response was to utter a high shrieking note or persistent 'tchinking.' He was very restless and one day in late June he kept flying from tree to tree, repeatedly shouting his loud shriek-note. It seemed that he was suffering from some form of hysteria. The next day he did not appear and I never saw him again.

Possibly Darky's unrest may have been aggravated by a tragedy that had happened the previous month to his old friend Oakleaf, a Blackbird whose earlier history was related in *Birds as Individuals*. These two males were of the same age, their territories had adjoined and each year they had spent much time in friendly games and mock warfare which both birds had seemed to enjoy. Oakleaf's mate this year, instead of building in my front garden as before, chose the tall hedge the other side of the road, probably to avoid the cat that had taken Darky's first broods, – it was a terrible bird killer. Oakleaf's mate was sensible in choosing the hedge, which was thick and the leaves were all out, but when her eggs were nearly hatched the County Council sent along several men to cut it down. The tragedy for bird life was great for it was a long, tall hedge, full of nests of many species. Several people, as well as myself, phoned the County Council, appealing for delay until the young birds had flown, but our protests were in vain. I even offered, at my own expense, to have Oakleaf's part of the hedge removed directly his young had flown, explaining that this bird was a great favourite; this also was refused, and the ruthless hedge-cutting, at the height of nesting season, was continued. Oakleaf and his mate, in terrible consternation, watched their nesting bush being hacked down. The sight and sound all down the road of parent birds crying from their losses was unbearable. Hedge-cutting in spring should be forbidden by law, for it causes unnecessary destruction of many species that are already becoming scarce through lack of cover in which to nest.

The shock was too much for Oakleaf, and the next day he disappeared. His mate remained in their territory and another male came to her. This time she brought off her brood.

That winter there were four females keeping their territories in my garden and West Garden. All the males left soon after Darky disappeared. In former years the males as well as their mates had remained in their territories all the autumn and winter. These females became very possessive of their territories, especially Darkette, who never allowed the others to overstep her boundary on the east front of my cottage.

Like most Blackbirds Darkette had a liking for sultanas and raisins. When wanting one she perched on the birch tree beside my east window and called me in a gentle but persistent 'chook' note. At first the Sparrows, with their pushful impertinence, had roughly seized each sultana I threw, while Darkette stood aside, waiting until they had all grabbed one. But sultanas were scarce, I had none to waste and Sparrows really prefer bread, so instead of throwing one after another until Darkette got one, I threw a single one then closed the window, leaving her to continue her 'chook' unheeded when the first four times Sparrows pounced on the sultana. But Darkette got more and more determined and the fifth time, when she saw I was about to throw one she flew to the edge of the flower-bed underneath the window and pounced with such haste that the Sparrows were taken aback. She flew off with a loud chuckle note to eat the sultana in private, for they would otherwise have seized it from her beak, as is their impertinent habit. After this she almost always succeeded in getting the one sultana I threw and if sometimes she forgot to come close to the window, I pointed to the edge of the flower-bed and called her, she then came, her head craning upwards ready for the catch, which sometimes went straight into her beak if not at her feet. Always Sparrows were there, trying to grab from between her feet, but they rarely succeeded. The other Blackbirds also wanted sultanas but they had not yet learnt the instantaneous and determined pounce by which Darkette had outdone the Sparrows.

Early in January a new male came to Darkette's territory and courted her. She accepted him and the weather being mild and fine she built her nest early in February. But the weather changed and heavy rains flooded the nest. She deserted and began building another at the beginning of March. Her new mate seldom appeared with her on the lawn under the window and he kept away from her new nesting-site, a large ivy bush covering a tall tree-stump, near my window. Darkette worked quietly at her nest from fear of the neighbour's cat and when wanting sultanas, instead of calling me, she tried to catch my eye, turning her head from side to side when I went near the window; she even restrained her chuckle-note as she flew off with the sultana. But her nest progressed slowly for she spent much of her day in chasing another female Blackbird, who was stubborn and insisted upon trespassing on her territory. Stubbs, as I called her, was no beauty, her plumage had no sheen and she lacked the deep colouring which the handsome Darkette possessed. Sometimes the obstinate Stubbs had appeared to be flirting with Darkette's mate and she cocked her tail when she pecked at the apples I threw on the lawn. Darkette frequently flew at her.

Then came the climax. On 19th March I saw Stubbs carrying nesting material to a tree in the east hedge just behind the cottage, this being in Darkette's territory and not far from her ivy bush nest-site. At 5 o'clock that evening Darkette's mate was perched in a sitting position on a bare branch of a crab-apple tree the west side of the cottage, and while singing a continuous subsong he went through an elaborate and unique form of display, aimed at Stubbs who was perched on a bough below him. He was performing in mime all the movements of nest-building. Slowly, with much swan-like neck movement, he lifted up the imaginary material then lowered his head as if weaving it round and giving pokes to tuck in the ends. Afterwards he turned round to do the other side of the imaginary nest. While he made the upward movement, slowly stretching his neck as far as possible, his song glided upwards on a note sounding like 'whi'; with the gradual descent of his neck, the note glided downwards on the sound 'ou,' this long-drawn-out 'whi-ou' sung on an unbroken curve suiting his movements. Besides this weaving-tune, that he always used exclusively for the nest-weaving imitations, which were caricatured to perfection, his subsong contained many of the tunes of his full song, each one fitted to his movements. The staccato notes of one tune he used while giving the pokes with his beak to tuck in the ends of imaginary material, either over the rim of the supposed nest or underneath him. When Weaver, as I now called him, got up to turn round, his song broke into a rippling phrase, like a suppressed chuckle-note, when he sat down to begin weaving the other side of the nest his song glided into the 'whi-ou' weaving-tune, begun low and gliding upwards to the octave above, then gliding down in keeping with the movement of his head and neck. Stubbs remained motionless all the while.

After five minutes of this mime another bird gave a cat alarm-note. Weaver stopped his display and stayed quite still, his song changed to a softly rendered sigh-note, a form of alarm-cry, – uttered with half-opened beak. Stubbs flew to cover in the nearby hedge.

The alarm was soon over, then Weaver flew a few yards to a lawsonia in the hedge and continued his astonishing performance, which is hard to describe. First he made an ostentatious inspection of all the forks on the tree, carefully choosing the most suitable one for a nest, a broad fork near the top, about nine feet from the ground. Having chosen his mock nest-site, he flew down to pick up a fragment of dead herbage and with this held conspicuously in his beak, went back to his fork where he continued to imitate in caricature every action of nest building, always fitting his song accompaniment in exactly the same way as before. The appropriate choice of his tunes for the different movements showed there was similarity between the Blackbird's and the human's idea of music and movement.

Stubbs, who had remained under cover since the cat alarm-note, now flew to the ground several yards from Weaver's tree, and stood still, then Weaver's movements became more and more exaggerated and his song rose and fell dramatically with crescendos and diminuendos and a peculiarly enticing, soft, yodelling phrase, repeated between the medley of other dramatic notes, in quality more like those of a Thrush than a Blackbird. As if mesmerised, Stubbs slowly drew nearer and nearer to him, finally perching on a bough directly underneath his fork. There she remained perfectly still in a curious pose, her head and tail hanging downwards on either side of the bough, her back humped with the feathers raised. On two occasions, when Weaver was curving his head, with a swan-like movement, to weave his imagined nest, he suddenly craned his head downwards for a quick glance at her, resuming his mime immediately afterwards. She remained motionless. This display lasted fifteen minutes, until Stubbs flew to an apple on the ground under my north window, Weaver following close on her heels, then suddenly, like a fury, Darkette appeared, rushed at Stubbs and chased her into West Garden, returning quickly to her ivy-bush nest. Weaver flew to a high perch on the filbert tree adjoining the bush where Stubbs had that morning taken nest material. A few moments later Stubbs returned to perch beside Weaver on the filbert tree and in turn they kept up a display of wing and tail shivering, as if shaking water off their feathers, although it was a dry day and they were not wet. Their shivering duet was repeated many times, in a rhythmical manner, always in turns of about four seconds, each bird instantly taking up when the other ceased. After this display, Weaver flew to the oak tree between his two mates' nesting bushes and sang.

Darkette waited for the freshness of a new day before tackling Stubbs about this scandalous behaviour. Soon after dawn the next morning she began stalking her and did not even pause to come for her usual breakfast sultana. Without break until 9.30 a.m. the two rivals stalked in and out of the flower-beds in the front garden, each leading the other on in the usual Blackbird manner, and occasionally flying up beak to beak. Then Stubbs snatched some grasses and dead leaves and held them in her beak while strutting across the lawn. Darkette rushed at her, then turned round, Stubbs dropped her material and chased after Darkette, afterwards they continued endlessly stalking. Weaver kept out of sight most of the time but he occasionally pretended to feed under my window, while cocking his eye at them. At 9.30 a.m. he flew past them, almost brushing them with his wings; soon afterwards he reappeared and began feeding on the lawn near them. Stubbs at once rushed to the strand of grass she had previously thrown down, and posed on a mound, holding up the material with outstretched neck, and eyes fixed on Weaver. Darkette heatedly rushed at her and the next moment they were rolling together on the lawn with feet interlocked. Darkette at last got her beak on to Stubbs's rump, pommelled her hard, and plucked her feathers until she screamed. I intervened, and Darkette, 'tchinking' furiously, chased the dishevelled sinner across the lawn, until she took to her wings, flying as if with difficulty, some of her tail feathers hanging down, her rump half-plucked. Darkette flew after her, still 'tchinking' excitedly as if roused beyond control. They passed over the next door hedge and out of sight. Soon Darkette returned alone and perched on the ridge of the cottage roof, where for half an hour she kept up a perpetual 'tchinking,' at the top of her voice. Then she flew round the garden, alternating chuckle-notes with 'tchinks' and for the rest of the morning not once was she quiet for more than two minutes at a time. Stubbs was not to be seen, Weaver also hid from sight and did not sing as usual. In the afternoon he uttered some chuckle-notes and conspicuously flew from tree-top to tree-top in looping flight, looking for Stubbs. Darkette still uttered frequent 'tchinks' and chuckles, especially when she went near her nest. She did not eat and when I threw her the sultanas always before demanded at every meal, she did not even take them.

The following day, 21st March, turned very cold, with a biting east wind. All the birds were hungry and among them, feeding on the lawn, was the irrepressible Stubbs, her plumage though scantier than before was now trim as far as it went. Her two remaining tail feathers stood out straight and she showed no signs of any discomfort. Darkette silently chased her from the lawn to the back of the cottage; she went without trouble but soon returned to the front lawn to feed and was again chased, calmly, without fuss, this happening many times. Probably the cold spell was influencing the situation, for when birds are really hungry during exceptionally bad weather, they relax their territorial disputes. Darkette still uttered many 'tchinks' and chuckle-notes every time she went near her own nest or Stubbs's nesting-bush at the back. The latter kept to the front lawn unless chased. Weaver took no notice of either of them, but he sang a little during the evening, although the cold weather had damped bird-song.

The next day, 22nd March, a third female Blackbird, of slender build, appeared on the lawn, apparently to help Darkette, for she spent all the morning chasing and stalking Stubbs while Darkette watched from a flower-bed, sitting hunched with her back towards them but looking over her shoulder all the time. She seemed exhausted after her recent battles and she looked depressed. This third female, whom I called Slim, was, I think, a first-year bird and she had not been in my garden before. At noon the new owner of Oakleaf's old territory by my front hedge chased the two stalkers into West Garden, but Stubbs returned, Slim at her heels, and they continued to stalk as before. This new male, whom I called Bottom, – he owned the bottom territory – watched from the hedge but did not again interfere that day. Weaver had washed his hands of the whole affair and was not to be seen.

Again on the following day, Darkette rested while the obliging Slim took on the work of chasing Weaver's mistress and stalking her on the front lawn. Weaver still kept aloof and hid among the bushes at the back of the cottage. At 4.30 p.m. Stubbs stood on a high bare branch of the macrocarpus tree, near Weaver's imaginary nest, and cocked the two remaining feathers of her tail at him while he watched from a distance. Darkette quickly flew to another branch of the tree, on a level with Stubbs, and sat hunched with half-closed eyes, her back towards her rival, looking utterly bored. Stubbs squatted motionless on her branch and there they remained for half an hour. Then Stubbs hopped to a higher perch, Darkette followed suit and perched a little higher, still keeping her back towards Stubbs. For another half-hour they stayed without moving until Slim flew up and chased away the disreputable female. Darkette flew leisurely to the ground and watched her out of sight. Weaver now appeared and flew with Darkette to her nesting-bush, afterwards he sang for a short time. It was still very cold, with a north-east wind, which probably accounted for the short duration of his song.

The next morning Darkette had recovered from her exhaustion and resumed her battle with Stubbs. From 7 until 9 a.m. they stalked each other and chased round the lawn, while Slim, keeping a little apart, walked backwards and forwards by herself, making all the movements of the stalkers. When they closed, beak to beak, Slim ran to Darkette's side, ready to help if needed, but the rivals separated and resumed their stalking, so Slim retired and paced backwards and forwards again by herself. A few minutes later Darkette attacked Stubbs, this time getting her under and immediately Slim rushed forward to help in the pommelling. Fearing the two attackers might injure Stubbs I interfered for the second time, perhaps unfairly, considering the trouble Darkette had with this obstinate female, who, after all, was still unhurt except for losing some feathers. The stalking then continued, with Darkette and Slim taking turns at the work. Once when Slim was running round the lawn after Stubbs, Bottom appeared and rushing past Slim tried to take the lead in chasing Weaver's mistress, but Slim quickly pulled his tail, meaning 'Don't interfere, leave this to me.' Bottom retired and Slim, her head held up and well forward, resumed her chase with a confident air. He seemed willingly to leave these females to settle the matter but he liked watching them and followed their movements closely from the pergola in his territory. His mate – formerly Oakleaf's – was now sitting, so he had time to spare and the weather was still too cold for much singing. When Bottom's mate came to the lawn by the pergola she took no notice of Darkette's battles, which were not her concern. Weaver and Bottom had seldom disputed for boundaries, though Darkette had often flown to the edge of her territory by the flower-beds if Bottom or his mate made small encroachments, but this quiet couple had given her no trouble.

During the afternoon Darkette was lively in her attacks on Stubbs and several times rolled her over and plucked her feathers but never hurt her. Stubbs's two remaining tail feathers were now hanging down half-broken and her rump was almost bare. Once when the chasing was in progress I threw Darkette a raisin, for she had scarcely paused to feed all day; even when Slim had chased Stubbs for her, she had watched from the flower-beds without moving. Darkette picked up the raisin then chased with it held in her beak, her head tilted upwards. Later she threw it down; Stubbs pounced on it and tried to swallow it but it was large and stuck in her throat; Darkette was at her heels, she had to keep moving and, nearly choking, she ran onwards. Every time she stopped to tilt her head upwards in an effort to gulp down the raisin, Darkette, with a swift rush and poke, prodded her back which sent her forward again. At last she found a chance to stop, but while stooping to rub the raisin on the grass Darkette charged into her from behind and knocked her over. Quickly scrambling to her feet, she seized the raisin then ran many times round the lawn with it in her beak, Darkette always close on her heels. Half an hour later Stubbs still had not been given a chance to swallow it, and the chase was continuing as before. Slim watched with keen interest but took no part during the afternoon. Weaver kept out of sight all that day.

The next day, 25th March, it seemed that Darkette had won. Stubbs had not gone near her nesting-bush behind the cottage for six days nor had Weaver been with her again. The bedraggled Stubbs, now without any tail, appeared on the lawn occasionally but was quickly chased from the garden by Darkette, who now had other work to do. She began laying her eggs in the ivy bush nest and Weaver started to display a little with Bottom in the east hedge. During the next few days Stubbs sometimes walked across the lawn with her eye fixed on Darkette's nesting-bush. Darkette usually flew down and rapidly dismissed Stubbs. Once Weaver chased her, but Darkette, with an imperious gesture, pushed in front of him, perhaps fearing that his chase would be provocative to the irrepressible Stubbs!

For the next ten days, Weaver, to all appearances, was a model mate, giving Darkette his sole attention and keeping constant watch over her ivy bush nest-site. If, during this time, he paid any attention to Stubbs it had been done without outward signs. But Stubbs had a new idea in mind when she was gazing at their nesting-bush and on 5th April she came hurrying across the lawn towards Darkette's ivy bush, a load of nesting material dangling from her beak. Quickly she flew into the bush with it, then went for more material. Darkette, who had been absent, now returned to her nest and when Stubbs flew up with her second load she rushed at her and chased her from the garden, soon returning alone to her nest. Stubbs waited a while, still clinging to a huge beakload of material, then she ran to the foot of the ivy bush and for half an hour tried to dodge the protesting Darkette, who angrily defended her nesting-site. At last Stubbs got into the bush with her material, for Darkette could no longer leave her eggs.

After Stubbs had deposited her load, she flew to the lawn and cocked her ragged stump where a tail should have been at Weaver, who had been watching her from above. He was soon on the lawn beside her, and for the next few days he followed her about and stood close to her while she fed on the lawn. Darkette was perpetually leaving her nest to prevent Stubbs from entering the bush and she spent much of every day chasing her round the lawn, Stubbs always carrying her beakload. Even if she was feeding near the bush Darkette flew down and chased her away.

Darkette's nest was too high up for me to look inside it without steps, which would have crushed the protective undergrowth of the bush and have led cats to it, as usually happens when humans interfere with birds' nests. I can therefore only surmise that Darkette's eggs, when nearly due to hatch, were left uncovered too long while she chased Stubbs, so they failed to hatch. If they had been taken by a Jackdaw or other thief, she would not have continued, as she did later, to use that same nest-site.

Darkette now, for several days, gave full attention to dealing with Weaver's mistress and preventing her from sitting on the nest which she had managed to build by degrees. Often Stubbs stood on the lawn looking up at it while making clucking noises and broody movements, and every time Darkette pounced on her and chased her away. On the few occasions when she got to her nest, there was a frightful row, for Darkette fought her in the bush and forced her to leave. By 14th April Stubbs had given up the attempt and Darkette was laying another clutch in her nest, to which she had added a little material. Weaver was now giving her full attention and avoiding his mistress now she had left her nest. Stubbs looked utterly grotesque, with few feathers on her head or body and even some from her wings had been plucked, so that her flight was weak. She had been well punished for her obstinacy in trying to steal Darkette's mate and territory, yet she made one more attempt. On 22nd April she started to collect nest material which she tried to take to a tree-stump near the same ivy bush. Darkette, who now was sitting, had to spend time chasing her round the cottage and when Stubbs ran towards the tree-stump Darkette got there in front of her and furiously flew at her, driving her from the site. I feared that the obstinate Stubbs would ruin Darkette's nesting season as well as her own, but fortunately this attempt was short-lived. On 24th April she at last gave up the idea of nesting in Darkette's territory and took her material to the front hedge of West Garden, but if she completed the nest, she never used it, for she had no mate. No other male would take interest in such a battered oddity as she now looked!

Darkette's young hatched out at the end of April and flew on 11th May. Before then Stubbs had given up all efforts to nest and was concentrating entirely upon food, which she stole from Darkette's territory. The latter only occasionally gave a mild chase, – she now had nothing to fear from her. Stubbs looked so miserable that I often gave her sultanas, afterwards regretting it, for her behaviour even over food was difficult, because of her greed. She not only took what I gave her but snatched all food from the young fledgling Blackbirds and Thrushes, pecking them roughly if they got in her way. Some birds who have failed to rear young of their own will feed other fledglings and almost all adult birds will let very young ones feed unmolested. But Stubbs was always a bad character and perhaps frustration had made her ill-tempered. Her rough treatment of the young and her attempts to drive them from the bird-table so that she could have all the food to herself made me tackle her sternly. I gave her a good feed then said, 'Now go,' accenting the 'go,' then chasing her to the bottom of the garden. In two days I could give her food, then say sternly 'Now go,' and immediately she turned round and ran away, leaving the fledglings and other birds to feed in peace.

The last notable event in connection with Stubbs that nesting season occurred one day in midsummer. I was indoors when a strange kind of screaming note came from the macrocarpus tree outside the window. The screams continued and I hurriedly went out, to find that the tailless Stubbs was dangling in mid-air beyond reach of my outstretched arm, her legs kicking, her feather-plucked wings feebly flapping, her beak slightly opened while she shrieked; yet in her beak was held the thin twine from which she dangled, the other end being attached to a dead branch high up in the tree. It was not man-made twine; I think it was a long stem of dead bindweed, which can be tough to break. High up on the adjacent crab-apple tree Weaver was watching her intently. Even if this was an attempt at suicide by the frustrated Stubbs, her screams indicated that she might have changed her mind! So I fetched a rake and could just reach the twine above her with the prongs but could not release her until I gave a sharp jerk to the rake, then she fluttered to the ground and ran across the lawn, flapping her wings as she went but not able to fly. Weaver broke into a chuckle-note as she was released and he craned forward on his perch to watch her disappear across the lawn. He had remained absorbedly watching, without moving, while I thrust up the rake, this being surprising, for the prongs went very close to his perch when I jerked the twine. How this queer hanging incident occurred remains a puzzle, for the twine was not entangled round her beak, although possibly it had got caught round her tongue. I noticed that her weight, for a Blackbird, was astonishingly light, – she had so few feathers left and now moulting had added to her previous losses. A normal Blackbird would probably have pulled itself free through the weight of its body and the bird would have used its wings to fly to a perch above. Only Stubbs could have got into this suicidal situation, a fitting finish to her frustrated nesting season.

2

During the autumn and early winter the males left my garden as in the previous year, while the females held their territories. Stubbs, renewed and strong after her moult, took possession of the top part of Bottom's territory, which adjoined Darkette's front boundary, while Bottom's mate kept to the bottom part of the garden. When the males returned in early January, Bottom took all his old territory and Stubbs became his mate after she had thrust out his former one (who was once Oakleaf's mate). Weaver paid no attention to Stubbs that year, 1952, so Darkette had no quarrels with her. Stubbs appeared content with Bottom. He was a handsomer bird than Weaver and he sang a better full song but he did not possess the alluring love-song and unique weaving display which Stubbs alone had inspired Weaver to perform.

While Stubbs was building her nest the weather was dry and she needed damp soil and material, so she collected dead leaves from under the trees and ran across the lawn with them to the bird-pool where she dipped them in the water several times until each leaf was soaked, then she took them to her nest. She repeated this too many times for it to have left any doubt that she did it deliberately. Often my Blackbirds soak dry bread or dried currants in the bird-bath before taking the food to their nestlings.

When the young birds were around the bird-table at feeding time, Stubbs, as in the previous year, treated them roughly, she even snatched peanuts from fledgling Tits, pecking them while they were eating the nuts held between their toes, so that they dropped them with a cry. She stopped feeding her young sooner than most mother Blackbirds and chased them from her fiercely when they begged food from her. I have never seen other female Blackbirds behave in this ruthless manner to such young fledglings, – only half-grown.

In 1953 Darkette again had some anxiety over Weaver and Stubbs. That year both Bottom and Weaver had stayed in their territories all the autumn and winter except for occasional visits to feed in a field near by. On the first of April Stubbs's young had hatched and Bottom still flew across to this field sometimes to get worms for them. On 3rd April he flew off on this errand while Stubbs went to the bird-pool, – a sunken sink in the middle of the lawn. Directly she began bathing Weaver appeared on the lawn, first he glanced round Bottom's territory to make sure he was not watching, then he advanced slowly towards Stubbs, halting every few moments to jerk his tail upwards and pose in curious attitudes. Stubbs continued to splash in her bath, apparently unconcerned, while Weaver gradually drew nearer, continually jerking up his tail and distorting his body in display. Soon he was standing on the edge of the bath with his beak and tail pointing upwards, a comical sight to the human eye. The next moment Darkette flashed round the cottage with a chuckle-note, rushed towards Weaver and fiercely charged into him from behind. He turned round and both flew back to their territory. Stubbs calmly continued bathing as if she had not seen either of them. A few minutes later Bottom returned with food for her young, no doubt unaware of Weaver's advances to his mate.

A day or two later, while Darkette was sitting, Weaver again tried flirting with Stubbs. Perched in the same lawsonia tree as two years before, he was displaying to her in his original manner, by nest-weaving movements accompanied by his love song, sung under his breath but dramatically, some notes being uttered loudly, others in a forced whisper. This time Bottom flashed from his territory towards Weaver, uttering excited chuckle-notes as he flew, while Weaver continued his love song, but interspersed some return chuckle-notes. A skirmish ensued between the males, while Stubbs quickly retired to her own territory. Bottom then chased Weaver to the back of his orchard territory, where from cover he continued to sing broken phrases of excited love song alternating with his full song, which he gradually dropped and flying to the oak tree near Darkette, continued to sing his full song. Bottom, after settling the affair with Weaver, had returned to Stubbs and their young in the front garden.

After this, Darkette was always running to the front garden, her expression as sharp as an Eagle's, while she watched what Stubbs was doing and made sure that she was in her own territory. (*See plate section.*) One day she found her sunbathing on their boundary line, near the cottage. Darkette tried to make her move by strutting up and down close to her, with her head erect, her expression haughty. Stubbs ignored her and continued sunbathing with wings and tail outspread, her head feathers raised and her beak half-open in sunbathing pose.

Darkette then assumed an attitude of display, with cocked tail and body distorted while continuing to strut backwards and forwards with the regularity of a policeman on his beat. When I went close to them they stalked each other for a minute then returned to their nests, Darkette's being at the back of the cottage, Stubbs's down the bottom of the front garden. In three minutes both left their nests at the same moment, Darkette, with her eagle-like expression, running to meet Stubbs, who chased her to the back of the cottage. Then both returned to their nests. After this they were too busy rearing families to take much notice of each other and Weaver confined his attentions to Darkette and her young.

During the spring, a male Blackbird from West Orchard had frequently come to me when I was in the garden. He was a beautiful bird with extra thick plumage and his fine crop of head feathers was usually erected, making him look as if wearing a busby. This display of raised crown feathers is sometimes used by trespassing birds to show that they have no aggressive intentions. Busby, as I called him, became very tame, he fed from my hand and followed me about, especially when his young were hatched. He frequently came to the front garden and into the cottage for food and he often sat beside me indoors or on the lawn when I was sitting there. Neither Weaver or Bottom took any notice when Busby trespassed on their territories. It was the females that objected, particularly Stubbs, who chased him in all her spare moments. Occasionally Darkette and two other females, Slim and Sepia, from neighbouring territories, joined in trying to send Busby back to his own domain but he would not be driven away until he had food from me for his young. It was amusing to watch this imposing-looking bird with his high-raised crown, marching at a steady pace along the lawn, with the four females, Stubbs, Darkette, the obliging Slim and Sepia, in single file behind him. This dignified procession paraded several times round my chair, up the french window steps and down again, then round the lawn until Busby suddenly made a quick dart towards me, seized some food from my hand and flew away. The females then dispersed; they had work to do and had no time to pursue Busby when he returned soon afterwards. Perhaps the slackness of the males over territorial rights made the females occasionally join forces in this manner to keep up a show of ownership of my garden, but it seemed that they also enjoyed parading after the splendid and immaculate-looking Busby! The obliging Slim, always ready to help, was nesting in East Garden, Sepia in West Garden.

Later all their young were continually with me and going indoors, as will be recorded in the next chapter.

I had hoped that the case of Darkette and Stubbs would end amicably but the day after I wrote the last paragraphs (December, 1953) I happened to open the back door just in time to prevent murder being committed down the kitchen drain. This was being done so silently that it would have escaped my notice had not the movement up and down of a fern, which lay across the drain, attracted my attention. I removed it and found that the drain held two Blackbirds, Darkette at the bottom, half-submerged in water (as some leaves were blocking it), with Stubbs standing over her and ripping her head open. At my interference Stubbs hastily disappeared into a bush near by while Darkette, dazed by the bad gash on her crown, slowly crawled out of the drain. One of her wings hung down and she walked with difficulty. She was injured, wet and draggled yet, unbroken in spirit, she tried to follow Stubbs instead of hiding from her savage opponent. I chased Stubbs away and attended to Darkette. After she was dry and had eaten a good meal she was able to fly, though laboriously. Her head wound was bad and her eyes were half-closed but she now found her tongue, and from tree to tree on her territory she gave angry 'tchinks' aimed at Stubbs. Weaver had all the while remained perched on a tree, craning his head forwards to watch the females; he had not tried to help Darkette, or to protect their territory from the intrusion of Stubbs.

A few days before this incident Stubbs had often encroached on Darkette's territory both in front and at the east side of the cottage. Bottom, an amicable fellow, who seldom entered into disputes, had sometimes come behind her, yet Weaver had not put up any defence. It had been left to Darkette to cope with them unaided.

In all her former attacks on Stubbs, Darkette had only plucked feathers. Birds rarely inflict flesh wounds on each other even when they come to grips but Stubbs was an exceptionally rough-natured bird and a confirmed law-breaker, as was shown in her treatment of young fledglings. She appeared conscious of my displeasure at her behaviour to Darkette for she kept away from me and from the front of the cottage for two days; afterwards when she came for sultanas I threw an empty match-box at her. For the rest of the winter I had only to show one to her when she came near Darkette's boundary and she flew to the bottom of her territory. Darkette continued for a week to 'tchink' loudly at sight of Stubbs; in spite of her injuries, which healed slowly, she was not broken in spirit. Until February, whenever Stubbs appeared on their boundary, under the east window, Darkette uttered a squeal warning note which attracted my attention, the match-box was held up in a threatening manner and it never failed to send Stubbs away.

One day in late January, 1954, Stubbs flew to a tree in Darkette's territory when Weaver was perched on it. He reprimanded her by loudly snapping his beak. She cocked her tail at him in reply. He showed anger and pecked her, then she flew away. This was the only time Weaver had snubbed her. He was now on Darkette's side.

Bottom made occasional plunges to the window-sill for food but I saw little of him or Weaver and they never had territorial disputes. During a cold spell in early February many Blackbirds came under my window and all day they uttered the 'chook' call which Darkette had used for getting sultanas from me. I could not supply them all with this food and Darkette found her call went unnoticed so she took to using her piercing alarm squeal – an effective way of attracting my attention to her presence.

A Mistle-Thrush became very tame during this cold spell. He used to perch on the oak tree outside the east window and watch my movements. Directly I began cutting up apples and bread to throw outside, doing this on the window-sill before opening the window, the Mistle-Thrush flew down, chased away other birds, and was ready to pounce on the apple directly it was thrown outside; until he had finished feeding the Song Thrushes and others – even the Blackbirds – kept at a distance. A Pied Wagtail became very knowing over how to avoid the pestering Sparrows, who, if the Mistle-Thrush was not there, always pecked him and prevented his feeding on bread crumbs, his favourite food. From a perch in the plum tree the Wagtail watched for the Mistle-Thrush to fly down from the oak tree to chase away the other birds from under my window, then while the Mistle-Thrush was eating the apple the Wagtail came and picked up the bread crumbs. He was not chased by the Mistle-Thrush who found his quick darts too elusive.

When milder weather came Stubbs again attacked Darkette, this time wounding her on the rump as well as the head and plucking all her tail feathers. For a week Darkette hid in bushes at the back of the cottage. She was now unfitted for taking part in nesting and Weaver after a few days mated with another female who built in a bush just beyond my east hedge opposite the back door. Until she began brooding her eggs she and the wounded Darkette seemed friendly, though they spent part of each day in mild, slow stalking, backwards and forwards, outside the kitchen door. Darkette wanted to keep a right of entry to the kitchen now Stubbs prevented her from going to the front windows. Weaver, from a perch above, watched his new mate gently stalking with Darkette but he never interfered and they formed an amicable trio. After Weaver's young were hatched Darkette made herself scarce and on 16th May she left my garden for a time. Just before she went Stubbs had her rump plucked, but not, I think, by Darkette as she was afraid to go near her while unfitted for combat.

At the end of June Stubbs began brooding a third clutch in my front hedge. Two days later she disappeared, probably having been killed by passing traffic, as she often flew over the road to feed in a field. Darkette at once returned. Moult had now added to the skimpiness of her plumage and her head was bare where it had been wounded but she held her stump-tail pertly cocked which gave her the appearance of a giant-sized Wren. Busby was often with me, as in the previous year, but this season he had reared no young and lost his mate while she sat on her second clutch.

One of Stubbs's full-grown young now became the problem bird. He had his mother's rough nature and all other Blackbirds and Thrushes, young and old, were afraid of him, so he had the lawn to himself after he had attacked them all many times. He even pecked some fledgling Tits while they were in the bird-bath; crying loudly they had to leave the water. I had to intervene and gave him the same match-box treatment as Stubbs but he was more difficult to dismiss. He flew away for a moment but kept watch for Darkette and Busby to appear on the doorstep then he flew down, pushed in front of them to get food, and attacked them both. If I threw a match-box at him, Darkette and Busby were more frightened than he was. When I tried to chase him away he ran round the lawn in circles and I got tired of this circular chasing, which the youngster probably enjoyed; he was always on the doorstep when the chase ended! So I stopped putting food outside and after a fortnight he left my garden. Darkette and Busby then returned; they seemed friendly and always came together. Bottom also sometimes appeared and looked over his shoulder at Darkette, who was gradually regaining her plumage and handsome appearance. Weaver and his new mate seldom came to the front garden nor did Darkette now enter their territory, she preferred the company of the two widowed males. When the time comes to make a decision will she choose Bottom or Busby for her mate?

CHAPTER 14
Young Blackbirds in Drought, Wind and Rain

In the summer of 1952 there was a long drought, the clay soil was hardened and the Blackbirds were hungry and very troublesome. All day they badgered me for food and when twelve at a time came indoors it was overpowering. The parent birds chased each other round the room and flew up beak to beak, with noisily flapping wings, disputing at each other's presence; the turmoil was terrific for in the heat of the fray they used no discretion over where they alighted and knocked over flower vases and other things on the tables. Their flying chases also were unsuited to the interior of a small cottage! The young Blackbirds had squabbles on a smaller scale, with beak-snapping thrusts at each other and occasional running chases. All this confusion upset the Tits, whose behaviour, in comparison, is so elegant. I tried to drive out the Blackbirds by waving towels or throwing crumpled paper at them, but they only stepped aside or flew a few feet away then came running up directly all was quiet. They knew I meant them no harm and probably mistook these actions for the house-cleaning activities which the birds dislike as much as I do! They stepped aside in the same manner when I shook out dusters or other cloths when cleaning the rooms.

Sometimes the youngsters became very possessive, as is the nature of this species. On one occasion, when four of them were feeding from a dish on the doorstep, a mother Blackbird, Sepia, from West Garden, wanted food for her fledglings but the youngsters prevented her from getting near the dish by flying at her, snapping their beaks angrily. For a few moments Sepia looked confused and uncertain how to act; she walked away hesitantly, often looking back, then suddenly she came forward in a determined manner and approached the youngsters in an imitation pose of a fledgling begging food from its parents, with quivering wings and opened beak. The youngsters stared at her a moment then stood aside to let her take food from the dish. When she returned a few minutes later they were still on the doorstep but made no protest although this time she did not adopt the fledgling-beg pose, nor did she need to use it again. Parent birds do not normally assume this begging pose before youngsters, so instinct did not account for their amicable response to it, but birds are rarely at a loss over communicating with each other – or with the human whom they trust – when necessity demands, and they use various means, according to circumstances. Some adult Great and Blue Tits use the same fledgling-beg before me when wanting food in winter or for their young in nesting season, others communicate their need in different ways.

When Sepia's babies first flew they kept in their territory next door but sometimes perched on a branch overhanging my gate. Without my having had any close intercourse with them, they distinguished me from other people and never left the gateway when I went in or out; anyone else entering or leaving made them fly away in alarm. From the distance, they had watched their mother coming to me for food and immediately learnt to recognise me personally as a friend, although other humans were instinctively feared.

During the drought Sepia had a late brood to feed and was incorrigible over coming indoors to steal food, even from the kitchen if she could get to it. Darkette would not allow her to enter by the back door and frequently, when I was going from the kitchen to the sitting-room, I encountered Sepia running along the passage, and if I let her she passed me, entered the kitchen and helped herself to the best she could find, often making much clatter while doing it. After the drought I disputed with her, for I thought her fledglings needed natural food. The ground was now softened and it was easy to get but Sepia had grown lazy over seeking it, as sometimes happens with Blackbirds who have food given them during their nesting season. Her young, now half-grown, came on the lawn with her, but she never gave them worms or anything except food supplied by me or stolen against my wishes. So I kept all the doors closed and stopped putting food outside. She then took to walking around the doorstep all day; many times I drove her away but she immediately returned and gaped at me, opening her beak wide then shutting it, repeating this while looking into my eyes. I understood that she was asking me for food but pretended not to notice her. Her babies got hungry and cried while she waited by the doorway hoping I would serve her! I remained firm, except for giving her a little bread and cheese three times a day. In two days she overcame her laziness and began to hunt natural food like the other Blackbirds were now doing.

During droughts my Song Thrushes also frequently come indoors and, as with Sepia, that year I often encountered a parent Thrush hurrying along the passage to the kitchen to get food for its fledglings. Later one of the youngsters became attached to me and was always at my side. Dapple, as I called this little Thrush, was smaller than the normal size even when full grown; it was neat and slick in all its movements and an especial beauty because of its exquisitely marked plumage. When several Blackbirds, Sparrows and other species were standing around, waiting for me to give them food, I enjoyed throwing one piece only, so as to watch the lightning speed of this agile Thrush, who always won the race for the food – an astonishing sight in a species usually slow and retiring compared to the others. Dapple seemed to gain the Blackbirds' respect for they never chased it away, as they did the other Thrushes.

Dapple often came indoors and perched on top of a tall corner cupboard to take a rest, remaining there quite still for ten minutes or more, giving the impression of being a fine statue of a Song Thrush. But when the summer was over this attractive youngster had to leave, for the parent birds chase away their offspring when the autumn territories are taken up.

Dapple's father, although not as quick a sprinter after the food I threw, gradually learnt to outwit the pouncing Sparrows and possessive Blackbirds by standing close to a leafy plant when wanting food thrown and looking up at me then down at the plant, hinting that I should make it fall there, which I did, he then picked it out from among the leaves. He was sharper than other species at doing this, for the Thrush is used to spying out the hidden small snails and slugs which feed on plants and are secreted among the leaves. The Blackbirds were second best and the Sparrows rarely attempted to look for the food I threw if it was hidden under leaves. This Thrush also attracted my attention to his needs by perching underneath the window and singing loudly, his head turned upwards towards the room. He went on singing until I responded, the tone of his voice being more imperative and his phrases taken at a quicker speed than when singing from a tree, so that even if I was in the kitchen – at the side of the cottage – and he was under the front window, I recognised that the Thrush was singing for me to throw him food. Blackbirds and Robins sometimes do the same, although not so persistently as this Thrush.

Another method of gaining my attention used by some of my Thrushes and Blackbirds is to fly up from the french window doorstep and hit the glass. At first I thought they did it accidentally but have discovered that it is intentional knocking, done to bring me and a sultana!

My Song Thrushes are as tame as the Blackbirds but the possessive nature of the latter species intimidates them, and they often submit to being chased away. In nesting season, especially during droughts, the Thrushes are determined to get food from me for their young, then they show spirit and retort with their aggressive display of a lowered body and rapidly snapping beak. This defiant attitude is usually effective against the Blackbirds if carried out with sufficient spirit, for a bird's determination, not its size or strength, is the main factor in disputes.

When on 2nd August the long drought of 1953 was broken by a heavy rainstorm, the young Blackbirds, perched in bushes near the cottage, sang a chorus of high-pitched chuckle-notes, as if laughing long and loudly at the rain. Some perched on the exposed twigs surrounding the bird-table and kept shaking their feathers, enjoying a rain-bath. Four days later there was a sudden downpour with large drops, which made them even more excited; many broke into loud subsong with exuberant sounding chuckle-notes interspersed, while one youngster flew to the lawn and rapidly danced around in curves, wing-flicking and at intervals leaping upwards with a loudly snapping beak to catch the raindrops. It was a whirling dance and the bird gave high-pitched chuckle-notes every few seconds. A wind had sprung up with the storm and this may have heightened the youngster's excitement. I have on other occasions seen youngster Blackbirds perform dances on a windy day; possibly the waving leaves and movement in the trees affects them. (I described one of these dances in *Birds as Individuals*.)

Some young Blackbirds also play puppy-like games. I wrote the following notes while watching a male youngster, Busby's son, a beautiful bird with expressive brown eyes, whom I named Tarn.

31st July, 1953. Tarn is having a game. With a leap, he pounces on an old walnut shell near a flower-bed, throws it a foot away, does a rapid wing-flicking leap into the air and down again to the shell which he picks up, and still flicking his wings high above his back, he springs upwards and throws the shell over a lavender bush at the corner of the flower-bed. He then does a twirling flight round the lavender, keeping low over the bush, afterwards picking up the shell, which he tosses towards a Starling engrossed in probing the lawn for food. Tarn leaps after the shell, but before picking it up, darts at the unperturbed Starling and touches the base of its beak, then quickly springs away, snatches the shell and carries it to the other side of the flower-bed, again making a wing-flicking flight around the lavender bush and other tall flowers in the bed, then he circles the lawn in a leaping, dancing run which ends in a sudden stand-still, with head bowed low to the ground for a few moments, afterwards turning his head from side to side as if looking for the shell which is not in sight. He then twirls round in a figure of eight, pounces on a dead, giant cornflower with a long stalk, lying on the grass; with this trailing from his beak he runs round in a circle, then again darts up to the Starling, drops the flower near him, rushes away to the flower-bed, and quickly darts back to the Starling, who goes on probing for food and seems unconscious of the playful youngster, although I think an invitation to join in the game is intended. Suddenly sobered, Tarn picks up the flower and in a slow, strutting walk, returns to the flower-bed and carefully places the cornflower underneath a rosebush. His game is finished. He walks up the lawn towards me and asks for a raisin. The day is breezy and there has been some rain. Later Tarn sang a quiet subsong lasting half an hour.

Tarn invented another game which he played when the spirit moved him. Bordering my pathway there is a string-and-stick fence, about one and a half feet high, – put there to prevent callers from walking across the lawn to the french window entrance, the front door being at the side of the cottage. Tarn's game was to rush towards the fence and, jumping up, give tugs at the string with his beak. This set it swaying, for the string was loosely set. Tarn watched its movement a second then jumped again and tried to snap it with his bill but often failed to catch it while it swayed. He made many quick successive leaps until this airy tug was achieved; sometimes he even tried using his wings while pulling at it, as if he meant to haul it down. This game was frequently continued for ten minutes. The other youngsters often glanced at him but this sport had no attraction for them. They had not Tarn's wild moods; they amused themselves more lazily.

One of Stubbs's first brood regarded a bowl of overblown daffodils on the doorstep as her plaything. She often spent ten minutes or more pulling and shaking at each leaf in turn; when tired of the game she sat down beside the bowl and snapped at any other youngster that went near it. Another fledgling, offspring of Darkette, tried to tear the paper label off a jam jar lying on the ground. He found it difficult because the jar rolled towards him every time he tugged at the loosened paper, so he sprang on top of the jam pot, fell off the slippery surface and jumped on it again, this time balancing himself carefully and, with the slight aid of his wings to steady him, he pulled at the label and got off several bits. After that day he often played at jumping on and off the jam jar without tearing at the label, apparently enjoying the trick of balancing for a few seconds on the slippery pot.

Tarn and another young male Blackbird of a different brood were lazy over seeking food for themselves; both had a passion for raisins and frequently stood by me for half an hour or more, staring up at me, waiting for some to be thrown. I called them The Waits. They seemed to have formed a friendly partnership over this waiting business and never disputed with each other for the raisins I threw or handed to each bird in turn, but if any other young Blackbird came near they protested angrily and drove them farther from me. The Waits only allowed them to come when they had been given their fill. One day in July, when Mr Simpson had been indoors photographing the Tits for about an hour, he remarked, 'Those two Blackbirds outside don't seem to do very much. They have been standing there all the while I have been here.' The birds he had noticed were, of course, The Waits, who had patiently stood close together outside the french window, their heads tilted up at me, their eyes fixed on my face, trying to catch my eye while I was getting the Tits to pose before the camera. As The Waits were then moulting their fledgling plumage, we did not ask them to pose for their portraits.

When Tarn had recovered from his moult he was the most beautiful Blackbird I have seen. I had never been able to resist for long the look in Tarn's eyes, so he had much more than his share of raisins – perhaps this helped to produce his thick, luscious plumage. His sudden playful moods, between the passive waiting, were also fascinating. He had inherited much from his attractive father, Busby, but even surpassed him in charm.

Tarn's partner in the waiting business was not exceptionally good looking. He was slightly timid in nature when a fledgling, but he overcame this by degrees, – I think Tarn's confidence helped him. One day I watched him catch a Cabbage White butterfly. He held it by the body and tried to swallow it but the butterfly's wings fluttered from either side of his beak. After holding it a few seconds he put his head upwards and tried again to gulp it down without success. He then decided that it must be put on the ground, probably to be dragged, this being the Blackbird's method of preparing food for consumption. But the butterfly never reached earth, for as the bird stooped his head and released his hold the white wings fluttered and the butterfly rose unharmed. Although I sat some feet away it flew over my shoulder as if it knew I was interested in its escape! Meanwhile the Blackbird, in a puzzled manner, looked on the ground, to the right and left, then he made a noise in his throat, a slight cough, 'Ahem!' and turning round, came towards me for consolation in the form of food without wings!

There is a peculiar cough-like sound made by some young Blackbirds when wanting food. They develop it just before their fledgling moult but lose it after a few weeks, the period varying with individuals. Only a few youngsters make this sound. Neither Tarn nor his friend developed this 'cough'; the noise made when the butterfly vanished was, I think, an expression of astonishment, or defeat.

Near the end of September, Tarn and his friend were absent for a few days; they returned together on 1st October, hungry for raisins, which they now asked for separately. They stayed two days and again disappeared, these short absences and reappearances being continued until 16th October, when Tarn returned alone. I never saw his friend again. Tarn stayed only one day, then was away for many weeks, his next and last visit of a few hours being on 3rd December. On arriving he eyed me keenly as if taking in all the landmarks of my face after his long absence and until this inspection was over he did not eat the raisin I had thrown him. He afterwards consumed several with an air of relish, then made curious false-feeding movements and bowed his head to the ground, remaining a few seconds in that pose; he also cocked his tail while looking towards the east hedge, although I did not see any Blackbird there. Probably Tarn wanted a territory in my garden but the old residents would not allow it, especially the aggressive Stubbs, who always chased Busby, his father, when he came for food. Tarn's luminous brown eyes were now beginning to show the yellow rims of maturity and his beak was pale gold almost to the tip; this gold would soon deepen, for his first nesting season was drawing near. He was no longer free to wander from his distant territory to the home where he was born, but perhaps when a territory falls vacant in my garden he will return, as this sometimes happens when birds have fared well in the home of their youth.

CHAPTER 15

Codes of Behaviour and General Conclusions

Throughout these biographies the behaviour of the birds has shown that they are not confined to any set rules of conduct, even in such things as territorial and mating affairs. Although birds have evolved certain codes of behaviour which help to regulate their actions, any generalisations are impossible, for these codes are kept only if it suits the circumstances and will of the individual bird. The Great Tit, Star, broke the law that in territorial disputes between one mated couple and another the males dispute with males and the females with females. She tackled Inkey as well as his mate, Smoke, when the need arose; on the other hand Monocle, under the same circumstances in a previous year, had behaved completely differently from Star. It is the character of the bird that counts.

Star also broke the law that once a territorial boundary is settled and nesting has begun, the pair owning a territory do not start demanding a large increase or even any increase to their land. After building her nest, Star insisted upon a big addition to her territory because a coming food shortage would mean starvation for her nestlings without more land. These were big deviations from the supposed definite codes of behaviour. If every bird acted like Star there would be pandemonium in their nesting affairs, but she was justified in her conduct because in both cases she was breaking a code of behaviour to fit extremely difficult circumstances.

The conduct of the Blackbird, Stubbs, showed that she had no inclination for keeping laws! Darkette, the female against whom she transgressed, was aided by another female, Slim, but in spite of all opposition Stubbs pursued her own line of behaviour. Her treatment of very young fledglings was another infringement. Usually all young birds are well treated or left undisturbed by adults. If all parent birds began behaving towards the young of others in the way Stubbs did they would have no peace, this would hinder their healthy development and lessen their chances of survival, for the small fledgling who has been molested in any way usually becomes timid and so is handicapped when starting to make its way in the world. The behaviour of adult birds to young ones of other parents varies from exceptional cases such as Stubbs's rough treatment and the Wren attacking Baldhead's fledgling (pages 187 and 147), to instances of actual protective behaviour as in the following incident.

The Blackbird, Bottom, gave warning notes on seeing a cat in my hedge, then he showed concern on seeing that a young fledgling Blackbird was on the lawn, not far from the hedge where the cat had been concealed. As his brood was full grown and almost independent of him, he could not have mistaken this young Blackbird for one of his own fledglings, yet he went to its rescue. First he flew several times backwards and forwards from a tree branch to the fledgling but it would not follow him, so he perched for a second on the branch and stared down at it, then deliberately flew to the lawn, quickly pulled out a worm, showed it to the fledgling and flew back to the branch, where he perched, leaning over so that the worm, dangling from his beak, could be seen. The fledgling at once fluttered up to the branch with hunger cries and food begging display, but Bottom would not feed it. Having got it to a safe perch he instantly turned tail, dropped the worm and flew away. The fledgling remained about ten minutes on the branch, uttering hunger cries. Bottom, perched on a tree nearby, took no further notice of it and it later returned to its own territory in West Orchard. It was an offspring of Busby who probably had not gone to feed it in the front garden because Bottom had given a cat alarm-note.

One of the most important codes of behaviour is that a bird on seeing an enemy gives a warning note. This is not an advantage to the bird who utters the note for it attracts attention to his or her presence, but the warning benefits all the other birds near by and this system must mean that every bird, especially in a cat-haunted garden, saves dozens of lives. Each species has a different alarm-note, but young birds soon learn to understand the alarm-cry of their own species and that of all others in the area. Even the Robin, who has no social instincts, enters into this general life-saving scheme which has developed through the ages, in some species to the extent of different alarm-notes being given to specify the type of danger. Some individuals give more agitated alarm cries than others.

My birds sometimes have shown a conscious wish to help others of their kind, and injured birds have received especial consideration, as was seen in the case of Tippet (page 88). My resident Great and Blue Tits have helped strangers of their own species to find their way out through the fanlight. (Cases were given in *Birds as Individuals*.) Sometimes my Great Tits watch uneasily when a Blue Tit is fluttering against the glass in an effort to get through a closed window and on one occasion a male Great Tit actually assisted a Blue Tit and led it through the open fanlight. He had first watched the agitated flutterer for several moments, then he flew six times backwards and forwards from the fanlight to the Blue Tit before it responded to his offer of help and turned round to follow him out of this window.

With the exception of birds of prey who have to kill for food, there is a bird law that a larger species must not hurt a smaller species of bird even if it is being exceedingly tiresome. Small disputes and chases may arise but the larger bird never, under natural free conditions, takes advantages of its superior strength. The small bird, in fact, often wins the dispute because of this law, which is essential for the preservation of all the species, the bigger birds would otherwise get almost all the available supply while the smaller birds starved when food is short in winter or in droughts, for although the different species have different tastes in food there is much overlapping, and many kinds of grubs, caterpillars, insects, etc., are suitable food for various species and for their young. Yet Blackbirds, Thrushes, Robins, Great and Blue Tits, Chaffinches and Sparrows, etc., all share the same territory without fighting each other, even when food is very scarce. I particularly noted this in the spring of 1952 when many birds were finding it very hard to get enough for their nestlings and certain foods were much in demand. Each species behaved as if respecting the right of the other to live and breed. This probably is the reason why small birds are not hurt by Hawks when they share the same nest-site.

Watching the behaviour of my Great Tits I am often struck by their fairness towards each other. They even seem to adopt methods of avoiding strife in new situations which arise from their intimacy with me and their use of the cottage. For instance, the youngsters queue up to come to me for food and they stamp on their roosts to prevent others entering (pages 117 and 94). It is customary with mated Tits that keep together all the year round for the female to be subordinate to the male during autumn and winter and at this period she stands aside for him to have first choice of food from my hand. Towards their nesting season this is reversed and usually there is a short period when both birds hesitate, each politely waiting for the other to be first. It is noticeable that this indecision does not take the form of both birds grabbing at the same time. The change-over is made much sooner with some pairs than with others for it depends upon their characters. As might be expected, Inkey, who is always over-enthusiastic about his own importance, sometimes forgets to be gallant and pushes in front of his mate even in their nesting season!

As my records show, there is much intelligence and infinite variety in the behaviour of birds even over courting, mating and territorial affairs. The theory, still believed by many people, that the male bird has first to take a territory then attract a female through his song does not apply in most cases. More often than not the bird singing in his newly taken territory has chosen his mate long ago, or she has chosen him. Either sex does the wooing, Star persistently wooed Baldhead, Beauty ardently courted the capricious Joker, their behaviour being according to their characters. It is quite usual for pairing to take place among youngsters of a few weeks old, as in the case of Leg-Presto and Rolline and other young couples I have had. Sometimes a male takes a female with her territory, without any outward show of courting her, as was the case when young Presto took Dado's territory and her with it. But they have to like each other; Star gave up her much coveted nest-box and territory sooner than be mated to The Intruder. Most birds are faithful to their mates for life, so in many cases they only have to warm up their feelings towards each other, usually by various displays when their nesting season approaches.

Bigamy is not common among garden species but the Blackbird, Weaver, apparently found Stubbs so irresistible that he was inspired to invent an original nest-weaving display, used for her only, this being set to music that perfectly fitted his movements. His astonishing display was a masterpiece of miming, fascinating to watch and perfect from an artistic point of view, but it was also interesting as evidence that birds and humans are alike in the way they hear sounds. If this is not so, how did it come about that Weaver composed music that in each phrase exactly suited every movement to the human ear? I see little foundation for the theory that birds hear sounds differently from us. They have keener hearing, probably due to training, for their safety depends upon continually keeping their ears alert, even for discrimination of the smallest sounds. The average human does not develop any subtlety of hearing unless this is needed for a particular purpose. Human hearing varies much with the individual and probably also this applies to birds (I notice that their sight varies individually). Their ears are perhaps capable of hearing higher-pitched sounds than man but I have not myself any evidence that they utter notes of a higher pitch than can be heard by a trained and sensitive human ear.

Another interesting point about Weaver's display is that the male Blackbird does not take part in nest-building, yet he acted, in an exaggerated manner, all the movements made by a female while doing it.

Although it is much more usual for the males to settle affairs of territory, sometimes this is done entirely by their mates, as was seen in the case of Darkette, who kept her mate Darky's territory after he disappeared. When her new mate, Weaver, came to her there, she continued to do all the work of holding their territory and disputing for boundaries. The same applied to Stubbs when she became Bottom's mate. When he lost her and Darkette was no longer Weaver's mate these two males took on the territory disputes, while their new mates kept in the background. It seems to depend upon which have the most forceful characters and usually this applies to the males. Weaver excelled in artistic and romantic affairs but he was not adept in practical matters! Darkette was! For instance he liked sultanas but when I threw one to the birds he always made a sudden dash to within a foot of it then let another bird push in front of him to get it. Bottom also behaved in much the same manner. But their new mates being even more retiring in disposition, the males had to take territorial action.

Here again Weaver used originality in display and posed before Bottom with his wings outstretched, like an aggressive Swan. He gained considerable ground by stalking him in this pose. One of the important factors in display seems to be the invention of something new to outwit the opponent. Baldhead succeeded by his original methods of display and high-speed action, Oakleaf by various inventions (related in my former book), the Robin, Stalky, by unusual contortions of his body, etc.

Another Robin, Turk, took his father Dobs's territory without display from either bird. (*See* page 144.) That episode is material for a dramatic poem. It also sets the mind roaming along channels of speculation. If tragedy had not befallen Dobs's mate, would Turk have continued all the nesting season optimistically waiting for a chance to return to the land of his birth? Or was that tragedy the link in the pattern of Turk's life for which he subconsciously was waiting. It was in any case surprising that Dobs accepted without dispute or display the loss of the territory where all his life until then he had successfully reared his broods, and that Turk took it from him without any show of possessive display which Robins usually use at sight of any other Robin on the territory they are taking or have taken. The crestfallen appearance of Dobs doubtless was a restraining factor but Robins do not usually consider this. Display is said to be automatic because some Robins have been aroused to display before a stuffed bird or even the red breast feathers alone, placed on their territory. Turk disproved any cut and dried theory that the sight of red feathers automatically brings display for even encountering the the red breast of Dobs on his territory did not make him display.

Taken as a whole, bird display is a form of language by which they can communicate with each other when they have need and it is often used together with vocal utterances or song. Each species has evolved its particular type of display but how and when the bird uses it is under control of its mind, and can vary according to circumstances and special needs. Watching individual characters as closely as I do, the interesting part is not only how they make use of the inborn display, but how they enlarge upon this and invent fresh ones; even they use displays of various kinds as a means of communication with their human friend. This helps me to understand their needs as was seen in many instances throughout Star's biography, and Pippa, in her hiding place turning her back in display at me (page 106), etc. These are not automatic reactions but done consciously, their poses and actions in the displays very expressive to one who understands birds. So that display develops into an ingenious form of communication through acting, though in casual observation of birds it may appear only an exchange of stereotyped poses, such as those of aggression and conciliation.

Generalisations about bird behaviour, even within the species, are therefore impossible; their actions are largely dependent upon the differing qualities of mind and spirit which constitute the personalities of the individuals. Those who ignore the fact that these individual qualities exist in birds and talk of their behaviour merely in terms of automatic actions and responses through releasers are avoiding the full truth.

Star's achievements prove that special talent even exists among birds, together with the intelligence and will to develop it, the results being so astounding and far above others of her kind that she can truly be referred to as a genius. Many other wild birds may possess similar talent but no comparable result could be achieved without Star's other qualities, her keen interest in the subject and her desire to develop this talent, her faculties for intent concentration and perseverance, and the enterprising spirit which she showed in many ways throughout her life.

THE END

Photo Credits

The estate of Len Howard and publisher gratefully acknowledge the permission granted to re-produce the copyright material in this book. Every effort has been made to trace copyright holders and to obtain their permission. The publisher apologises for any errors or omissions and, if notified of any corrections, will make suitable acknowledgment in future reprints or editions of this book.

First Plate Section

Photographs taken by Eric Hosking at Bird Cottage.

Second Plate Section

1. © Estate of Stanley Bayliss Smith
2. © Estate of Stanley Bayliss Smith
3. © J. M. Simpson
4. © Len Howard
5. © Len Howard
6. © Owen Martin
7. © Estate of Stanley Bayliss Smith
8. © Estate of Stanley Bayliss Smith
9. © Len Howard
10. © Len Howard
11. © Len Howard
12. © Len Howard
13. © Estate of Stanley Bayliss Smith
14. © Estate of Stanley Bayliss Smith
15. © Estate of Stanley Bayliss Smith
16. *Unknown*
17. © Cecil W. Teager
18. © Owen Martin
19. © Owen Martin
20. © Cecil W. Teager
21. © Estate of Stanley Bayliss Smith
22. © Cecil W. Teager
23. © Estate of Stanley Bayliss Smith
24. © John Markham
25. © Cecil W. Teager
26. © Cecil W. Teager
27. © Erik Hosking Trust
28. © Cecil W. Teager
29. © Len Howard
30. © Len Howard
31. © Leonard Hugh Newman
32. © Leonard Hugh Newman